Language Variation
in North American English

Language Variation in North American English
Research and Teaching

⌒∽⌒

Edited by A. Wayne Glowka and Donald M. Lance

The Modern Language Association of America
New York   1993

This book is a publication in the Centennial Series of the American Dialect Society in celebration of the beginning of its second century of research and teaching about language variation in North America.

Library of Congress Cataloging-in-Publication Data

Language variation in North American English : research and teaching /
    edited by A. Wayne Glowka and Donald M. Lance.
        p.   cm.
    Includes index.
    ISBN 0-87352-389-X (cloth) — ISBN 0-87352-390-3 (paper)
    1. English language—Study and teaching—North America.
    2. English language—North America—Variation.   3. North America—
    Languages.   4. Americanisms.   5. Canadianisms.   I. Glowka, Arthur
    Wayne.   II. Lance, Donald M.
    PE1068.N55L36   1993
    428'.00707—dc20   93-9451

Pages 86–88, 90, 93: Maps and figures from Timothy C. Frazer, *Midland Illinois Dialect Patterns*, Publication of the American Dialect Society 73 (University: University of Alabama Press, 1987). By permission.

Page 89: Photograph of the Lincoln Home. Courtesy of the United States Department of the Interior, National Park Service.

Page 106: Figure from Hans Kurath, *A Word Geography of the Eastern United States* (Ann Arbor: University of Michigan Press, 1949). By permission.

Pages 107–09: Figures from Peter Orleans, "Differential Cognition of Urban Residents: Effects of Social Scale on Mapping," *Science, Engineering, and the City*, publication 1498 (Washington: National Academy of Sciences, 1967) 103–17. By permission.

Page 115: Figure from Wilbur Zelinsky, "North America's Vernacular Regions," *Annals of the Association of American Geographers* 70 (1980): 1–16. By permission.

Second printing 1995

Printed on recycled paper

Published by The Modern Language Association of America
10 Astor Place, New York, New York 10003-6981

Contents

Preface

❧

PERHAPS the greatest miracle of language is that we can actually understand each other when we use it. If we had to be as constrained as a computer when we communicated, we would find it difficult indeed to send or receive the kinds of information that human beings normally exchange by means of language. The successes we have in communication, however small or large, result from our ability to abstract the essential from the nonessential, to perceive discrete units when iterations of the "same" units differ from speaker to speaker and from one time to the next in the same speaker's language use.

Interest in the study of the welter of variation in language use led a group of scholars to form the American Dialect Society (ADS). In the century since the founding of ADS, in 1889, dialectologists have advanced the study of variation beyond the geographical focus that had characterized dialect research in the first half of the twentieth century, and in 1982 the ADS Executive Board appointed a Committee on Teaching to gather information on instructional programs on language variation in the United States and Canada. The committee consisted of Donald M. Lance (Chair), University of Missouri, Columbia; Lynn Beeme, University of New Mexico; Lawrence M. Davis, University of Haifa (now at Wichita State University); Crawford Feagin, University of Virginia, Falls Church Regional Center; A. Wayne Glowka, Georgia College; Virginia Glenn McDavid, Chicago State University; Rose Nash, Inter-American University, Hato Rey, Puerto Rico; and John Tinkler, University of Tennessee, Chattanooga.

In 1983 the committee distributed a questionnaire through the *Newsletter of the American Dialect Society* (*NADS*) to determine where courses in language variation were being taught. Fifty-seven professors responded from fifty-three colleges and universities in North America and Europe. The chair of the committee tabulated the results in a seven-page report distributed in December 1983 at the annual convention of the Modern Language Association of America, in New York City. The report summarized data on forty-four courses exclusively or primarily in dialectology or sociolinguistics and thirty-six courses that included units on language variation. The respondents reported a wide variety of subject matter, course requirements, and academic levels; sixty different books were listed as required texts for the courses.

At the 1983 meeting, the committee agreed that the next project should be a collection of articles on teaching about dialect (i.e., the many kinds of language variation). We (Glowka and Lance) agreed to serve as editors of the volume. Glowka sent a preliminary inquiry to the MLA in January 1984 and received an encouraging reply; then came the longer process of soliciting and editing manuscripts. We placed notices in several issues of *NADS*, beginning with the September 1984 issue. Within about three years we had received thirty-five essays and proposals, but there were still some gaps in the coverage. By the summer of 1989, we finally had essays in all areas that we had wanted to include. As the collection grew, it became clear that we had a book not only on teaching but also on research.

Thus, in response to the interests expressed by the ADS Committee on Teaching and the ADS Executive Board, we offer this collection of thirty-nine essays. They cover a wide variety of topics and offer treatments of the various subjects for many classroom situations—from middle school to graduate school and professional research. Within the diversity of topics, the contributors offer a recurrent theme: language variation is an intriguing subject worthy of attention in and of itself and essential to any understanding of human communication. Some sources of language variation receive only brief mention (e.g., register), but most of the topics of interest to ADS members are represented here, though in varying degrees of thoroughness. While many of the essays focus on activities for specific academic levels, an enterprising teacher or researcher can use them at other levels. In July 1992 the ADS Executive Council approved the designation of this volume as a Centennial Publication of the American Dialect Society. An analogous volume assembled for the second centennial of the ADS will no doubt still discuss regional, social, and situational variation, but who can guess what new approaches lie ahead in the next several generations as the world grows smaller?

We wish to express our appreciation to the contributors for being so patient with delays as we squeezed the work on this book in between the teaching, research, and service duties that professors face daily, and we especially thank them for their courteous responses to our requests for revisions.

We hope most of all that the readers of this volume will find the essays as interesting, informative, and useful as we have.

AWG
DML

Acknowledgments

WE RECEIVED assistance from several sources. Our home departments and institutions covered the expenses of telephone calls, paper, postage, and other necessities. The reviewers of the manuscript and the MLA Editorial Board helped us monitor the quality of the book's contents. Joseph Gibaldi (Director of Acquisitions and Development, Division of Publications, MLA) and the Executive Board of the American Dialect Society encouraged us to continue with the book since the editing and delivery of a collection of thirty-nine articles took more time than we had anticipated. Our particular thanks are expressed to Patricia Harn Harris, University of Missouri, Columbia, for examining the manuscript for typos, oversights, and occasional stylistic lapses and making sure that we had included in the Works Cited all the references cited by the contributors. By no means, however, do we intend to shift blame for shortcomings onto any of those who have been so generous in helping us put together this diverse collection.

Guide to Phonetic Transcription

❧

Vowels

i ɪ e ɛ æ	front vowels in *beet* [bit], *bit* [bɪt], *bait* [bet], *bet* [bɛt], *bat* [bæt]
u ʊ o	back rounded vowels in *boot* [but], *put* [pʊt], *boat* [bot]
ɔ	back rounded vowel, mid-position in some dialects, low in others, as in *caught* [kɔt]
ɑ	low vowel, with neutral lip position, central in some dialects, back in others, as in *cot* [kɑt] and *father* [fɑðɚ] (most dialects of American English)
a	low central or low front vowel, articulatorily between [ɑ] and [æ]; used in the diphthongs [aɪ] and [aʊ]
ʌ	mid-central stressed vowel in *son, sun* [sʌn]
ə	mid-central unstressed vowel in the first syllable of *above* [əbʌv] and the last syllable of *sofa* [sofə]
ɚ	*r*-colored mid-central vowel in syllabic position, as in both syllables of *murder* [mɚdɚ]. (Note: The postvocalic *r*-colored off-glide, as in *ear, car*, is transcribed in this volume with [r], as in [ɪr], [kɑr].)

Diphthongs

aɪ aʊ	vowel combinations in *high* [haɪ], *how* [haʊ]
ɔɪ yu	vowel combinations in *boy* [bɔɪ], *cute* [kyut]

Consonants

p b t d k g f v s z h m n ŋ l r	stops, fricatives, nasals, and liquids: *pet* [pɛt], *bet* [bɛt], *tad* [tæd], *dad* [dæd], *cot* [kɑt], *got* [gɑt]; *fat* [fæt], *vat* [væt], *sip* [sɪp], *zip* [zɪp], *hit* [hɪt]; *mit*, [mɪt], *nit* [nɪt], *sing* [sɪŋ]; *lot* [lɑt], *rot* [rɑt]
θ ð	voiceless and voiced interdental fricatives in *thigh* [θaɪ], *thy* [ðaɪ]
š ž	voiceless and voiced alveopalatal fricatives in *Confucian* [kənfyušən], *confusion* [kənfyužən]
č ǰ	voiceless and voiced alveopalatal affricates in *chin* [čɪn], *gin* [ǰɪn]
w y	bilabial and palatal glides in *we* [wi], *ye* [yi]

Phonemic Status

/ /   Slashes are used when the author is commenting directly or
             indirectly on the phonemic status of a sound.

[ ]   Square brackets are used to indicate specific pronunciations.

[Ø]   Lack of an expected phoneme: e.g., lack of [r] in Eastern New
             England pronunciation

Diacritics

˜   Nasalized vowel: e.g., *him* [hĩm]

ː   Phonetically long vowel: e.g., *maze* [meːz]

ˈ   Phonetically half-long vowel: e.g., *mess* [mɛˈs]

˘   Phonetically short vowel: e.g., *ate* [ĕt]

(For details on these and other phonetic symbols in common use, see
Geoffrey K. Pullum and William A. Ladusaw, *A Phonetic Symbol Guide*, U
of Chicago P, 1986.)

General

American English Enters Academe

Harold B. Allen, University of Minnesota, Minneapolis

AS Allen Walker Read has so thoroughly documented in numerous articles, awareness of innovations and variations in the English of the New World attracted attention early in the colonial period and increased in the first half of the nineteenth century. Collecting examples had reached such proportions by 1848 that John R. Bartlett was able to fill 412 pages with them in the first edition of his *Dictionary of Americanisms* and then 814 pages in the fourth edition, in 1877. But not until 1872 did M. Schele de Vere provide the first comprehensive description in his 685-page *Americanisms: The English of the New World*.

A steady flow of articles on American English appeared during the next several decades, some by such distinguished writers as George P. Marsh when he was United States ambassador to Turkey, Thomas Lounsbury of Yale University, Brander Matthews of Columbia, C. H. Grandgent of Harvard, Louise Pound of the University of Nebraska, and George Hempl and Fred N. Scott of the University of Michigan. The academic world was paying attention to American English in minor publications, but there were no textbooks, no special courses, although it may be conjectured that at least casual comment about it must have appeared in professorial lectures in courses in the English language. Indeed, when, in 1919, the second comprehensive book, *The American Language*, appeared, it turned out to be by a newspaper reporter, H. L. Mencken, who delighted in ridiculing various aspects of the academic world. In its subsequent, greatly revised editions, Mencken's work became probably the most influential book in the field, but it was not a textbook. Nor did it need to be, for as yet there were no courses likely to use one. Even George Philip Krapp's scholarly and important two-volume work, *The English Language in America*, published in 1925, was not a textbook, although, like Mencken's book, it may have been so used by a resourceful teacher. In fact, not until 1952 was there published a book prepared for classroom use, Thomas Pyles's *Words and Ways of American English*, followed six years later by Albert H. Marckwardt's *American English*.

The continuing expansion of dialect research and the lack of any subsequent single-author textbooks on American English and its varieties led, then, to the 1971 publication of two anthologies derived from the already rich store of available articles in professional journals. Gary N. Underwood and I collected and edited *Readings in American Dialectology*, and Juanita V.

Williamson and Virginia M. Burke did the same for *A Various Language*. Although certainly some courses must have used other text materials, the fact that there were no competing textbooks at the time makes reasonable the assumption that the total sales of these anthologies before they went out of print, about six thousand copies, provide a minimal estimate of the extent of courses in American English during the 1970s.

But a specific course in American English was not to wait for the publication of a course-aimed textbook, and I am reasonably sure as to where that particular course was first offered. In a survey funded in 1935 by the National Council of Teachers of English for the purpose of ascertaining the nature of English-language study in colleges and universities, I had included an item inquiring whether courses were given in Old English, Middle English, Modern English grammar, the history of the language, and American English (see Allen, "Teacher-Training"). No institutions offered American English. Several replies indicated bewilderment over the inclusion of this designation; the head of the department in Gonzaga University volunteered the perhaps sarcastic comment that naturally his staff taught only in American English, so why should there be a course in it? The situation was like that of American literature three decades earlier, interesting but surely not to be dignified by a place in the English department curriculum.

Here an incident is relevant. While teaching Old English in the Linguistic Institute at the University of Michigan in the summer of 1940, I was asked by Thomas A. Knott to take over his class in American English for the last two weeks of the eight-week session so that he could leave early on a planned trip to England. At the time, he casually remarked that, as far as he knew, he had taught the first course ever offered with that title. Aware that he had taught at the University of Iowa before going to the G. & C. Merriam Company in 1926 as general editor of the second edition of *Webster's New International Dictionary*, I tacitly assumed that he was alluding to his teaching there; indeed, in rather unscholarly behavior, I so told my students over the years. I now know better, having learned that the English-language course Knott taught at Iowa was labeled Modern English. In it, he dealt with the sounds, vocabulary, and syntax of English as a whole since the time of Caxton, and the catalog description contains no hint of concern with distinctive American English.[1] Since Knott did not teach again until he went to the University of Michigan in 1934 to head the Dictionary of Early Modern English, the title of a research project and a publication, apparently he was correct in believing that the first course to be designated American English was the one he taught in the English department there in 1934–35.

It is a reasonable assumption that Knott's eight years as a dictionary editor concerned daily with the English language from an American point of view added a component to his interest in teaching the language. It is likewise a reasonable assumption that he was familiar with the work of his pronunciation editor on the Merriam staff, John S. Kenyon. Kenyon was a phonetician who, in the 1920s, began teaching courses in phonetics and the English language at Hiram College. Kenyon's book *American Pronunciation* had appeared in 1924, and Knott used its fifth edition as a textbook in his seminal course that in the 1934–35 University of Michigan catalog was listed in the English department offerings simply as "109. American English. TuTh, 2.2215 A [ngell] H[all]. Knott. Three hours credit. Second semester."[2] In the 1935–36 catalog, the course was similarly listed but with the notation that it would not be offered that year. It should be observed that the association with Kenyon led Knott to join him in preparing *A Pronouncing Dictionary of American English* (1944), most of the work on which was done by Kenyon.

Regional Variation

Admittedly, attention to American English had for more than a century focused on contrasts with British English, taking little or no systematic interest in regional or horizontal variation. The founding of the American Dialect Society, in 1889, indicated a growing interest in regional varieties, usually in terms of vocabulary items peculiar to a given community, but it remained for George Hempl of the University of Michigan to make, in 1896, the first systematic, albeit inadequate and tentative, attempt to establish a boundary between one dialect region and another, that between the Northern [grisi] and the Midland and Southern [grizi]. Unfortunately, no researcher soon followed his lead, so that neither Mencken nor Krapp had further evidence to enrich their own treatments of major geographical differences in American English. Indeed, it is unlikely that in that "first course" Knott could have included much content defining specific dialect regions, for the data were simply not yet available. It is true that Kenyon had frankly acknowledged basing his descriptions on "the cultivated pronunciation of his own locality— the Western Reserve of Ohio" as "fairly representative of . . . the speech of the North" (iv), but despite sporadic references to pronunciation variants elsewhere in the country, there is no attempt to describe dialect regions as such.

Quite different must have been the content of the course when it was first offered in the Linguistic Institute in Ann Arbor, in the summer of 1936, for it was taught by Hans Kurath, director of the Linguistic Atlas of the United States and Canada. He brought with him unpublished materials from the atlas files at Brown University and hence supplemented his course in

American English with another, The Linguistic Atlas of New England. For the first time, a course in American English could draw on the resources provided by the development of linguistic geography in the United States. Knott again taught the course in the 1937 institute, but almost certainly with a different approach because of the availability of those materials. Subsequently, the course was taught by Albert Marckwardt, whose initial concern for differences between British and American language appears in the first class assignment: "Examine carefully the classified advertisements in the London *Times*, the Manchester *Guardian*, and the advertisements and regular departmental articles in *Country Life*, *Chamber's Magazine*, and *The Strand* for words and expressions which would be used in British English but not in American English. Compile a list of the terms you find—not less than ten and about twenty-five if possible." Only twelve of the twenty-eight class meetings were devoted to regional variation, largely as definable in data from the field research on the Atlantic Coast and in the North Central States.

The presence of Kurath in the institutes of 1936 and 1937, and of his atlas associate Bernard Bloch and his prime fieldworker, Guy Lowman, in the three subsequent institutes laid the granite foundation on which courses in American English and American dialects were to be constructed in future years, as by Marckwardt and then by Norman Eliason, Frederic Cassidy, and Raven McDavid. Sometimes these courses were taught by such teachers as E. Bagby Atwood, Lee Hultzen, Miles Hanley, and Claude M. Wise, whose initiation had been in the form of fieldwork for the Linguistic Atlas of New England under Kurath's direction. But it was essentially the linguistic atlas research of the 1930s that sparked the beginning of formal curricular attention to American regional variation. Scholars with a different background tended to retain emphasis on American English as a whole. In 1947, for instance, Allen Walker Read devoted to dialect geography only the fifth day of his twenty-eight-day course, The English Language in America, which he taught in the graduate faculty of philosophy at Columbia University. But three years later, the course had expanded to two semesters, and he gave four days in the first term.

When the attained doctorate led to my leaving the University of Michigan in 1940 to accept a position at San Diego State College, it was with the understanding that I would develop a course in American English there and that its library would help by adding a number of relevant publications, such as *Linguistic Atlas of New England* (Kurath) and *American Speech*. There was also the hope that eventually I would undertake an atlas project on the Pacific Coast. But that course had a short life, for World War II created an opportune vacancy at the University of Minnesota, where in 1944 I joined the English department and offered its first American English course in the winter quarter of 1945.

It is a safe generalization, I think, that those of us with the linguistic atlas background believed in the value of teaching about, writing about, and lecturing about the varieties of American English. It was important to us to help dispel some of the myths about language variation, such as that about the so-called Southern drawl, to awaken awareness of the fact that Standard English in the United States is not monolithic, and to squash the notion that one variety is the "best" or the "purest" or "correct" and that other varieties are presumably inferior. It was important to me, too, that my students should see themselves and their own speech as part of the content of the course.

American English Assignments

It was because of my belief in the significance of every variety of speech that, during the thirty years of my teaching a course labeled American English, I usually gave this as the first assignment:

A study of American English requires some consideration of the sources of America's population and of the subsequent population movements within the country. It also demands attention to the various linguistic and cultural influences operating to produce a variety of English distinct from British English.

To aid you in seeing yourself as an inheritor of and contributor to the complex known as American English, you are asked to write a paper in which you describe the pertinent facts in your family history and also the influences that, to your own knowledge, have helped to make your speech what it is now.

The following questions are offered not as a specific outline but rather as suggestions as to what might be included in this paper. You are not limited to them.

1. What facts do you know about your family genealogy? (Sometimes a chart showing the family tree will help to make clear the relationships.)

   What racial or ethnic elements does your family background contain?

   Who of your ancestors first came to what is now the United States?

    When did others come? Where did they come from?

    Do you know any causes for their emigration?

    Where did they settle in the New World? What later changes of location occurred?

    Did marriages bring together persons of different origins and background?

2. What is the language background in your own home—that is, what were the geographical or educational or foreign-language environments of your parents or others who were members of your immediate family during your childhood?

    What geographical influences have modified your speech? Where have you lived and how long in each place? Can you trace any of your speech characteristics to any specific changes in residence?

    Can you cite examples of conscious attempts to modify, alter, or correct your speech by members of your immediate family, companions, teachers, and others?

    Do you know of any speech changes that you have made of your own accord?

    What led you to make these changes?

Students had three weeks to complete the assignment, for often nonresident students had to write home for information. I grant that this assignment may be undesirable in some areas and with some students, but I have never had a student object; on the contrary, most students express considerable satisfaction when they have finished their explorations. I often tabulated the returns for the class discussion so that the students could see themselves as a kind of microcosm of American speech variation.

After the initial family background assignment, which was for later use, I generally had half a dozen exercises intended to demonstrate the ways in which American English has developed as a variety distinct from British English. The exercises varied greatly over the years as new source materials became available. Usually the questions called for drawing inferences from the evidence to which students are directed.

Semantic development was the thrust of one exercise, with ten questions such as these: What new semantic development occurred in the United States with respect to *nation*? Consult Evans and Evans's *Dictionary of Contemporary American Usage* and *The Oxford English Dictionary* for the meanings of *saloon*. Is the American use later or earlier than that of the British? Is the difference between the two chiefly in range of meaning or in attitude toward the word? Find out all you can about *flapjack* in both countries, using both dictionaries and also linguistic atlas evidence. Do the same with *guy* and suggest an explanation for the recent semantic development in this country.

A similar exercise focused on morphology with respect to compound words, suffixes, and shortening. Students examined the semantic significance of contrasting stress patterns, as in *blue grass* and *bluegrass, check out* and *checkout*, and *bare foot* and *barefoot*, and then asked themselves what special fields of the American vocabulary are suggested by *bluegrass, garter snake, popover, club car, dark horse*, and *rock band*. They consulted *A Dictionary of American English on Historical Principles* (Craigie and Hulbert), *Dictionary of Americanisms* (Bartlett), and other dictionaries to see how *bakery* is treated and whether the *-ery* ending has been prolific in this country, along with such other endings as *-cade, -ist, -ize,* and *-wise*. They deduced what processes yielded *auto, gas, phone, gym, home ec, Amerindian*, and *travelogue*.

Marckwardt suggested three exercises to me to demonstrate the facility with which American English adopted and adapted words from other languages used in the colonies and then in the United States. One required the students to consult a variety of dictionaries to get information about such Romance words as *gopher, hoosegow, rodeo, depot, crevasse,* and *cafeteria*, along with French and Spanish place names. Another similarly called for study of Dutch and German borrowings, and still another dealt with words from American Indian languages. For these assignments, I provided the class with lists of relevant articles in *American Speech, Quarterly Journal of Speech, German Quarterly Review, Studies in Linguistics*, and others, for students to read and summarize.

But because concern with language varieties can go only so far without at least a minimal familiarity with phonetics, in order to deal with pronunciation, I always used exercises in sound discrimination in terms of the International Phonetic Alphabet as modified for American dialect fieldwork. One exercise required the students to record phonetically various key words in the standard passage used in the disks made by the British Drama League, such as *mates, little, girl, down, house, abide, deaf, tongue, tune, hark*, and *noise*, as a basis for comparison with the vowel variation in American speech. This activity was followed by one calling for the students' attempts to deduce the sounds of early New England speech from the spelling on the copies I provided of "Extracts from the Accounts of John Bate of Sharon, Connecticut (A.D. 1767–84)" (Whitehall). The following list contains samples of the 150 entries:

	£	s	d
By wauen 20 yards of clorth	00	10	?
By your cart to fach 3 lod 1 mild	00	00	?

	£	s	d
By ma 1 par of lather breches	07	06	
By ma 1 plat and brads and md 1 pen and md worshors	01	02	09
By hoopen hoxets and barles	00	06	?
By bel 3 days looken after your crators	00	02	00
By haf a booshel and 4 qorts of whate	0	03	0
By coten out 1 gratcot	00	01	00

About this time in the course it was necessary to have a fact-finding exercise to acquaint the students with linguistic geography through a directed study of the published atlas materials edited by Atwood, Kurath, and McDavid. The objective was to replace any popular misconceptions of dialect as a miscellaneous collection of funny words used by uneducated country people with an awareness of regional variation on all social levels that can be scientifically studied by trained researchers who gather evidence on which valid generalizations must rest. Among the directions were these:

1. What is a linguistic atlas? Put into a single statement the aims and purpose of the linguistic geographer.
2. How many communities in New England does the *Linguistic Atlas of New England* represent (Kurath)? Are they evenly distributed or not? Why? How were they selected?
3. How many informants per community were secured, and in what age and social groups?
4. How did fieldworkers proceed to obtain the necessary information? In which of the following aspects of the language does the *Atlas* seem to be centered: pronunciation, vocabulary, inflection, or syntax? Which in *A Word Geography of the Eastern United States* (Kurath)?
5. In general, how does *A Word Geography* differ from the New England *Atlas*? Consider both the content and the method of presentation as well as the element of editorial selection and interpretation. Answer this also for *A Survey of Verb Forms in the Eastern United States* (Atwood) and *The Pronunciation of English in the Atlantic States* (Kurath and McDavid).

Now, equipped with some knowledge of the American vocabulary, an understanding of the nature of dialect research, and at least minimal skill in phonetic transcription, students were prepared to choose either one of two subject areas in which to produce a term paper.

One choice was an individual and original investigation to be prompted by the readings in a topic area indicated on an organized list of articles in *American Speech*: (1) structural and phonological developments in American English; (2) specialized vocabularies of interest groups: business and commerce, advertising and selling, religion, recreation, politics, foods; (3) slang and argot, military cant, taboos, and euphemisms; (4) regional dialect features (native dialect characteristics, speech features in non-English-speaking communities); (5) proper names (Americanization of foreign proper names, place names); (6) American English features in the works of individual authors. Students could supplement their reading by reference to a distributed collateral list of more than 150 items, and they had access to my personal card file of 20,000 classified items in language and linguistics.

The other choice was to investigate the Upper Midwest occurrence of variants of a specific language item for which data were collected by fieldworkers for the *Linguistic Atlas of the Upper Midwest*. A student electing this choice was given a manuscript containing the phonetically transcribed responses of 208 field informants to a specific item along with side comments by informants and fieldworkers, an outline map of the Upper Midwest (Minnesota, Iowa, North and South Dakota, and Nebraska), item analysis charts for five states, a summary chart, and a list of the field informants with relevant information about each.

To prevent incipient chaos, I provided detailed, step-by-step directions about the recording and tabulating of the significant data, the subsequent computations by state and by the region, the production of a dialect map demonstrating the distribution patterns either by symbols or by bar graphs as well as, if feasible, by isoglosses, and then such interpretation as could be obtained by comparison with the Atlantic Coast situation and that in England, by the facts of settlement history and population movement and by anything at all in the informant's background, and so on. All maps, charts, and tables were to be included with the final paper. Among the items suitable for such treatment were *thunderstorm, blinds, eaves troughs, frying pan, swamp, bull, castrate, pancake, cottage cheese, sweet corn, dragonfly, swam, climbed, woke up,* and *earthworm*.

While students worked on term papers during the last half of the course, class attention focused on items other than lexical variation, primarily phonological but to some extent grammatical. First came an exercise on differences between British Received Standard and usual American features, with supplementary time to be spent in collecting specific examples from the speech of BBC news commentators and of such American figures as Edward R. Murrow, Walter Cronkite, and David Brinkley. Students listened, for instance, for the vowels, as in *shop/top/hot, after/class/path, chance/branch/can't, tune/duke/nucleus, was/wash/swamp*; for the presence or absence of [r] as in *word/Thursday/firm/farm, near/four,* and *law(r) of nations;* for the sound of inter-vocalic /t/, as in *daughter, later, little;* for the pronunciation ([w] or [hw]), as in *whether, wheel, why;* for the presence or absence of secondary stress in such words as *dictionary, secretary, allegory;* and specifically for pronunciations of *schedule, been, either, missile, Asia, clerk.*

Along with lectures and discussion, attention to regional variation in the United States utilized the twenty-four long familiar but now unobtainable "Grip the Rat" records. For several days, students listened to them and recorded in phonetic transcription indicated key words in order to prepare a comprehensive chart showing the variation in several Northern, Midland, and Southern communities from Maine to Illinois and from South Carolina to Texas. If class was not too large, I would then hear each student in conference in order to check the accuracy of the transcription.

Then, before the final lecture and discussion on the educational impli-cations of knowledge about geographical variation, students noted and ana-lyzed speech differences heard as I played tape recordings of the speech of Upper Midwest atlas informants. One particular exercise used a battery of excerpts from the voice records of seven selected informants from the three types. Unlike an earlier exercise in which students were asked to determine the speaker's region, this task called on them to identify the type to which the speaker could be assigned. Each selection was played twice, so that the students had ample time to note and classify everything relevant to type categorization: pronunciation, grammatical forms, and syntax. Not unex-pectedly, grammatical forms were most useful for classifying the speakers by type, but it was syntactic matters that distinguished two informants, one in type 2 and one in type 3, who otherwise could not be differentiated.

Social Variation

In the 1960s such an exercise served as a convenient bridge to my class concern with a rapidly expanding field within the American English disci-pline—that marked by the vertical social parameter rather than the hori-zontal geographical parameter.

For the first time in dialect research, the concept of social variation had been systematically attended by fieldworkers when Hans Kurath insisted that socially distinct types of informants must be sought in the investigations for the *Linguistic Atlas of New England.* Hence types 1, 2, and 3. But implications of these data for other disciplines apparently were not explicitly indicated before Raven I. McDavid's article in *Social Forces* in 1946. Even then attention was desultory until William Labov's published dissertation in 1966 provided a new model for the detailed and scientific investigation of social differences, a model that determined the direction of such research for the next two decades (*Social Stratification*). Although Labov's study was of the speech of white informants, the sometimes violent social and political ferment of the 1960s had already thrust into the forefront of linguistic attention the speech not only of blacks who for socioeconomic reasons had moved in great numbers from the rural South to the urban centers of New York, Boston, Washington, Philadelphia, Cleveland, Akron, Detroit, and Chicago but also, to a lesser extent, that of whites from Appalachia who for similar reasons had also migrated northward. By the mid-1960s the preponderance of the former population had nearly led to the limitation of the term *social dialect* to mean "Black Vernacular English."

Classroom interest in the study of urban social dialects developed slowly. On 27 February 1965, the Center for Applied Linguistics recognized the emerging emphasis by calling together a small group to discuss the matter of urban dialectology. Present were Alva Davis, John Fisher, Robert Hogan, Albert Markwardt, Raven McDavid, William Stewart, and I. The group resolved to continue formally as the Clearinghouse for the Study of Social Dialects, to serve in that capacity as a liaison for the center and the National Council of Teachers of English, and to encourage curricular attention to social dialects. Incidentally, it was this group that subsequently recommended the publishing of Labov's dissertation in book form, an action that indirectly led me to develop a course in social dialectology.

I think it was Roger W. Shuy who later reported that two or three other courses were initiated in the next two years. If so, mine was either the third or fourth in the country when I first taught it during the 1968 summer session at the University of Minnesota. That the time was ripe for such a course is shown by the enrollment. Lacking a textbook in the field, I had prepared thirty copies each of a variety of documents I had collected at various conferences and meetings and of articles that had appeared in various journals. Already the burgeoning stock of secondary source materials was so great that Shuy had been able to compile an excellent annotated list of forty-six articles for the June 1968 issue of the *Linguistic Reporter*. To my surprise, fifty students turned up in my class, and there probably would have been more had I not advised my own graduate students to wait to take it during the regular year.

Exercise materials in this class and the subsequent classes before my last one in 1972 were both general (for the entire class) and specific (designed for the student's personal interest). All students, for example, had to construct a grammar and phonology of inner-city Black English from their study of a set of papers written by black students in the Community College of

Philadelphia.[3] Besides the generally assigned materials, all students had to provide annotations for a set number of articles they chose from a list of 197 readings that I supplied. Then the entire class was divided into five groups, each group having as a term project a jointly prepared report on some aspect of the current situation. Topics used during the years before my retirement included, for example, the phonology of Black English, the morphology of Black English, the controversy over "bidialectalism," pedagogical problems raised by teaching a mixed class containing children speaking only Black Vernacular English and children speaking only Standard Spoken English, attitudes of employers toward applicants speaking Black English, attitudes in the real estate business toward prospective renters or purchasers speaking Black English, the attitudes of black children toward the teaching and the learning of Standard (white) English, and the problems involved in creating attitudinal change.

The preparation of the group papers sometimes called for individual exercises and reports that ultimately were synthesized in a common production. In order to ascertain relative degrees of economic opportunity in the Twin Cities, for example, a student interviewed an employment officer who would listen to a tape containing samples of the speech of nine subjects, some black and some white. The officer would indicate whether the speaker might be hired by the company, might be promoted to a supervisory position, and might eventually be promoted to an executive position in which he or she would officially represent the company.

Another student, a black woman who could switch codes—from her family speech of the Saint Louis ghetto to the meticulously learned dialect of Northern American English—investigated the real estate situation. On the telephone she would use Black Vernacular English in answering an apartment-for-rent advertisement, to ascertain its availability for inspection. Invariably some kind of put-off occurred, either a flat statement that the apartment had been rented or some excuse about its relative unavailability. Then an hour or two later she would call again, this time in crisp Minnesota Standard English. And invariably the apartment was available, and, yes, she could come at any time to inspect it. These conversations were all recorded— I suppose illegally—and, if anything was still needed to convince the class members of the reality of discrimination, those recordings and their transcriptions did the job.

A graduate student who was an elementary teacher bravely worked on a curricular plan for her fall classes, a plan that called for the white children to translate their speech into Black English and for the black children to respond by imitating white speech—that is, to reverse their usual speech roles in class conversation and storytelling. She was counting on children's natural love for play-acting and imitating. Unfortunately, I do not know whether she actually tried this experiment or, if she did, how it succeeded.

I am well aware that some of the student activity described here would be less appropriate today than it was between 1940 and 1970. Today, I think, I would try to put more emphasis on social, economic, and political implications and associations, perhaps with the thought that the course would and should serve as a basic introduction to the interdisciplinary field of American studies. But inappropriate as some of these exercises may now be, I hope that they still may hold a suggestive value for instructors who have the privilege of teaching a course in American English or its varieties.

Notes

[1] Information appreciatively received from John Racburn of the University of Iowa.

[2] Information appreciatively received from Richard W. Bailey of the University of Michigan.

[3] Copies of the papers were helpfully provided by my son-in-law, Alexander G. Russell, who teaches in the Community College of Philadelphia

Teaching the Grammar of Vernacular English

Walt Wolfram, North Carolina State University

STUDENTS new to the study of social dialects often have difficulty understanding one of the most fundamental sociolinguistic premises—that vernacular dialects consist of linguistic patterns just as systematic as the patterns that characterize standard varieties. The popular stereotype holds that vernacular dialects are simply imperfect attempts to speak the standard variety and therefore faulty approximations of a more perfect way. In addition, students tend to think of grammar rules as prescriptive dicta that take on life through their written specification in grammar books.

Given the notions about the status of vernacular dialects that most students have been exposed to, it is a formidable challenge to convince students that patterns in vernacular grammars are highly systematic. Students may not be persuaded simply by the instructor's linguistic pontification, because an understanding of vernacular linguistic structure must also be linked to authentic respect for vernacular dialects as communication systems. Furthermore, specific knowledge of the linguistic rules that produce these patterns is the foundation for many applied considerations as well, such as the effect of dialect on writing, reading, and language assessment. There are few challenges of more significance than instilling these basic concepts in students who enter the study of dialects from varied academic backgrounds with a wide range of stereotypical notions about the structure and origins of vernacular dialects.

A pedagogical program to deal with both the attitudinal perspective and the need for specific knowledge about the systematic nature of vernacular grammar is most effectively broken down into a number of didactic stages involving both inductive and deductive approaches. The goal of such a program is to provide students with a healthy respect for the linguistic patterning, or "rules," of vernacular dialects and a knowledge of how the rules work. In the following sections, different pedagogical stages in such a presentation are outlined, and useful substantive material is included at each stage.

Stage 1: The Cognitive Basis of Linguistic Patterning

The first hurdle in presenting vernacular structures is to get students to understand that all dialects show rigorous linguistic patterning and that such "rules" have their reality in the minds of the speakers. Linguists may be able to capture these rules with varying degrees of adequacy, but variation in linguists' descriptions does not detract from the fact that underlying linguistic patterning exists and can be observed. The key to specific rules is found in the orderly use of items by speakers following their cognitive schemas.

In this initial stage, a simple exercise may convince students that the basis of linguistic patterning is found in the speaker's mind. One inductive exercise that has been used with great success in underscoring this point focuses on the attachment of the *a-* prefix, in items like *He was a-hunting and a-fishing*, a form found in a number of rural vernacular dialects. The *a-* prefix is introduced to students with the observation that this form can occur with *-ing* forms and that there is some question about the kinds of *-ing* forms to which it can be attached. The students are then asked to give their impressions about the kinds of *-ing* forms *a-* might occur with by reacting to some sentence pairs given on a handout. The exercise presents forced-choice sentence pairs; students select the appropriate form for the *a-* prefix attachment in each sentence pair. The idea behind the task is to demonstrate that students can make systematic judgments about the grammatical contexts for *a-* attachment—judgments that correspond to its patterned distribution. The advantage of this particular exercise is that it can be assigned to students who use the *a-* prefix as a normal part of their dialect and with other native English speakers as well, since previous experimentation has shown that both groups will give orderly responses that verify the existence of the grammatical patterning (Wolfram, "Language Knowledge"). This exercise is given below, along with instructions.

The Structure of *A-* Prefixing

Some dialects of English put an *a-* sound before words that end in *-ing*, so that you hear phrases like *a-hunting we will go*. There is some question about how this form is used, and I'd like to get your reactions to it. For each sentence pair given below, you should choose one of the sentences for the attachment of the *a-* form. Choose only one sentence for the *a-*, and if you are not sure, just make your best guess.

1. a. The man likes sailing.
    b. The man went sailing.

2. a. The woman was coming down the stairs.
    b. The movie was shocking.
3. a. He makes money by building houses.
    b. He makes money building houses.
4. a. Sam was following the trail.
    b. Sam was discovering the cave.
5. a. William thinks fishing is silly.
    b. William goes fishing every Sunday.
6. a. The movie was fascinating.
    b. The movie kept jumping up and down.
7. a. Sally got sick cooking chicken.
    b. Sally got sick from cooking chicken.
8. a. The man was hollering at the hunters.
    b. The man was recalling what happened that night.

[The correct answers to the exercise are 1*b*, 2*a*, 3*b*, 4*a*, 5*b*, 6*b*, 7*a*, 8*a*.]

The vast majority of students will identify these responses correctly. What is more important are the structural reasons that account for the correct answers. Although students should be asked why they chose the responses as they did, in most cases they will be unable to articulate precisely why they made the selections. This is an important process for students, as it demonstrates that the ability to use grammatical structures systematically is unrelated to the ability to talk about the linguistic patterning in metalinguistic jargon.

Sentences 1 and 5 illustrate the fact that the *a*- prefix can occur only with verb complements and *not* with -*ing* participles that function nominally; sentences 2 and 6 indicate that the *a*- can attach to verbal -*ing* forms but *not* to -*ing* participles that function adjectivally; as sentences 3 and 7 show, the *a*- can attach to -*ing* forms but *not* when they follow a preposition; and sentences 4 and 8 illustrate that the *a*- can attach to verbs that have a stressed initial syllable (in *follow* and *holler* the first syllable is stressed) but *not* to verbs whose initial syllable is unstressed (in *discover* and *recall* the first syllable is not stressed). This is a fairly intricate set of linguistic constraints on *a*- prefix attachment that involve both grammatical and phonological structure. (For more detail on the structure of *a*- prefixing, see Wolfram, "Toward a Description" and "Language Knowledge.") Few, if any, students will be able to describe the linguistic parameters precisely. The important observation, however, is that students, using the resources of their language intuitions alone, will choose the correct structural responses for this vernacular form.

As students grope for explanations to account for the patterning, I often tell them, "You don't even have to know the definition of a noun or verb to make the correct response—these terms are just labels for an existing organizational principle you've got in your minds." Grammatical patterns do not exist because linguists have thought up fancy labels to describe them; linguists simply try to capture the kinds of principles of organization that already exist in the mind of the speaker. This observation is essential to the next stages of instruction, in which dialect features are presented in explicit detail from a more deductive perspective. It is a point worth making about language in general, but it has particular significance for vernacular dialects.

Stage 2: The Presentation of Dialect Grammar Rules

In this stage, actual dialect grammar rules are presented to students. Along with the presentation, students are assigned reading that profiles vernacular dialects (for general descriptions, sources such as Wolfram, "Language Variation"; Wolfram and Fasold; and Wolfram and Christian are used). The following kinds of linguistic patterns are typically included in the presentation:

The verb phrase
1. Irregular verbs
   a. past form generalized as past participle
      I had *went* down there.
      She has *ran* there before.
   b. past participle form generalized as past
      She *seen* him yesterday.
      He *done* what he could.
   c. bare root as past form
      He *come* down there yesterday.
      They *give* him a lot of trouble last year.
   d. regularized past tense
      Everybody *knowed* he was late.
      He *throwed* a curve ball.
   e. different irregular form
      He *brung* the mail to the post office.
      They *hearn* something in the basement.

2. Verb subclass shifts
    These include (a) verbs with shifts in transitive status, (b) verbs
    derived from other classes, (c) verbs plus co-occurring items.
    a. If we *beat*, we'll be champs.
    b. We *doctored* the sickness ourselves.
    c. We *happened in* on the party.
3. Verb auxiliaries
    a. completive *done*
        He *done* finished the work.
        They *done* ate all the food.
    b. habitual *be*
        Sometimes the children *be* playing in the yard.
        They usually *be* up there at night.
    c. remote *been*
        I *been* had it for about three years.
        I *been* known him for a long time.
    d. *a-* prefixing
        She was *a*-fixing the garden.
        They made money *a*-planting herbs.
    e. double modals
        She *might could* do it.
        She *useta didn't* like it.
    f. special modals, *liketa, poseta,* etc.
        She *liketa* died when she saw the thing.
        You don't *poseta* do it that way.
    g. absence of *be* auxiliary or copula
        She ____ taking the dog out.
        He ____ in the house today.
4. Subject-verb agreement
    a. absence of third-person singular, present-tense forms
        She *go* to the store every day.
        He *don't* like it.
    b. generalized conjugated forms of *be*
        We *was* in the store yesterday.
        Most of them *is* younger than us.
    c. agreement with special kinds of plurals
        Some people like*s* to talk a lot.
        Him and me get*s* in a fight sometimes.

Adverbs and adjectives

1. Comparatives
    a. regularized forms
        That's the *beautifulest* dog.
        The *baddest* people sometimes win.
    b. pleonastic marking
        She's *more nicer* than him.
        It's my *most favorite* song.
2. *-ly* absence
    She answered the question different ____ from me.
    He come original ____ from Virginia.
3. Special adverbs
    a. She stayed a *right smart* little while.
        He was *plumb* tuckered out.
    b. adverbial *but*
        He ain't *but* fourteen years old.
        They didn't take *but* three dollars.
    c. different linear order
        He did *everwhat* he wanted.
        They *all the time want to go out.*

Negation

1. Multiple negatives
    a. negative indefinite or adverb after the verb
        They *don't* do *nothing* about *nobody* else or *nothing* like that.
        She *couldn't hardly* do the work.
    b. negative indefinite before the verb
        Nobody didn't like the mess.
        Nothing couldn't be done.
    c. inversion of a negative verb phrase and an indefinite
        Didn't nobody like the mess.
        Can't nobody live in that place.
2. The auxiliary or copula *ain't*
    a. *have + not*
        He *ain't* missed the show yet.
        She *ain't* taken the test.
    b. *be + not*
        She *ain't* in the class.
        They *ain't* home.

   c. *did* + *not*

       He *ain't* go there yesterday.

       They *ain't* know what to do.

Nominals

1. Plural nouns
   a. plural *-s* absence

      She took forty cent __.

      It's three mile __ down the road.
   b. regularized plurals

      The farm has three ox*es*.

      The deer*s* were in the field.
2. Possessives
   a. possessive *-s* absence

      Carla __ hat fell down.

      The people like the man __ suit.
   b. regularized possessives

      The hat is *mines*.

      Mines is here.
3. Pronouns
   a. regularized reflexive forms

      He cut *hisself* shaving.

      They bought *theyselves* a new car.
   b. second-person plural

      I think *y'all* will like this lesson.

      Youse like these sentences?
   c. extension of object pronouns in coordinate structures

      Him and her will go to class.

      The *farmer and her* got along.
   d. personal dative forms

      I got *me* a new car.
   e. relative pronoun absence with embedded subjects

      The man _____ come down there is nice.

      They brought the lady _____ told them about the accident.
   f. different forms

      The man *what* came yesterday was nice.

This inventory of grammatical structures, which is not exhaustive, may seem somewhat imposing to students at first glance, but the effect is calculated to overcome notions that these varieties do not have their own grammatical systems. To pique the interest of students at this point, tape-recorded samples of vernacular speech may be interspersed with the presentation of structures. In these sample recordings, structures that are being introduced are identified. I have used sample interviews from studies I have conducted over the years for this purpose, but the collection of dialect recordings undertaken by Donna Christian (*American English*) and the documentation by Michael D. Linn and Maarit-Hannele Zuber of available recordings have made more general resources for these illustrative dialect tapes now available. If it is appropriate, students can be encouraged to conduct conversational interviews with vernacular speakers to provide relevant, firsthand data as well.

Stage 3: Reinforcing the Identification of Vernacular Grammar Rules

Because of the extensive inventory of vernacular grammar structures, it is necessary to reinforce knowledge about the patterns that have been studied. Rote memorization of these patterns is tedious and ultimately not conducive to active learning about dialects, yet students often need such information for sociolinguistic application. Therefore, to help students recognize the structures and rules, I prepare illustrative sentences and present them to students, with the simple directions to identify the vernacular structures found in each. Sentences may have single or multiple instances of vernacular structures. Students work together in identifying and reviewing the structures found in the sentences. Following is a sample of this type of exercise:

> The sentences below contain examples of different structures in various vernacular dialects of English. In each sentence, identify the structure(s) and review the major features of the linguistic pattern that governs the form.
>
> 1. The students be going to class every day.
>   [Answer: habitual *be* occurs with habitual activities]
> 2. The man done brought home a nice present.
>   [Answer: completive *done*; used with simple past to indicate "completive" aspect]
> 3. They throwed the man coat away by mistake.
>   [Answer: regularized past tense of irregular verb; possessive *-s* absence]
> 4. She go to school, but he at home.
>   [Answer: third-person present-tense *-s* (or *-es*) absence; copula *be* absence]

5. Ain't nobody mess with him when he come home late before.
   [Answer: multiple negation, inverted negative; *ain't* for *didn't*; bare root form for past tense of *come*]

The instructor can expand this recognition exercise considerably by providing a passage representing connected discourse as well as isolated sentences. More important, the instructor should include a sufficient number of sentences so that students can achieve a comfortable level of success in identifying the structures.

Stage 4: Identifying Violations of Vernacular Rules

One of the most important aspects of understanding linguistic patterns is to know the precise limits in the operation of the patterns. That is, the rules have restrictions on their application that are akin to the kinds of restrictions that characterize patterning in the standard variety. For example, in Standard English, a structure like *Rules the have boundaries* is not a well-formed sentence. It is, technically speaking, "ungrammatical" because it violates the English pattern that specifies that articles must come before nouns in the noun phrase. In the same sense, a violation of the rules of a vernacular dialect will lead to ill-formed, or "ungrammatical," dialect structures. In fact, poor mimicry of vernacular dialects by Standard English speakers often shows violations in the grammatical patterns of the dialect. To reinforce this important dimension of a vernacular dialect rule, I make up sentences in which the structures violate the rules of the dialect. In this exercise, the students are asked to specify what is wrong with the sentence from the standpoint of the vernacular dialect pattern—or, more technically, to explain why the items constitute "ungrammatical vernacular" sentences. Following is a sample of this type of exercise:

> The items below are not well-formed vernacular dialect sentences. That is, they violate some aspect of vernacular dialect patterns. For each sentence, specify what aspect of the rule has been violated.
>
> 1. The students be playing right now.
>   [Answer: *be* is used with habitual, not momentary, activities]
> 2. The man was a-remembering the story.
>   [Answer: *a-* prefixing cannot be used with verbs whose initial syllable is unstressed]
> 3. The man done tells lies all the time.
>   [Answer: completive *done* is used with past, not present, tense]

4. They here last night.
    [Answer: absence of copula *be* occurs in present, not past, tense]
5. A-fishing is fun.
    [Answer: *a-* prefix is used with verbs or adverbs, not *-ing* forms that function as nouns]

This task helps students reinforce the precise patterning that governs the various vernacular forms, with emphasis on the restrictions of the rules. At the same time, it counteracts in a practical way the popular stereotype that "anything goes" in vernacular grammar.

Stage 5: Sorting Out Well-Formed Sentences in Vernacular Grammar

At a subsequent level of presentation, the kinds of exercises presented in stages 3 and 4 may be combined into a single exercise. (I actually prepare one handout with the exercises of stages 3, 4, and 5 sequentially ordered.) Students are once again given a set of sentences, but this time they must decide between well-formed sentences and sentences that are not well formed. This may be considered an optional stage for students, but I have found that this extension gives a more realistic challenge to students' understanding of the precise patterning of the grammar rules. Here is a sample of this kind of exercise:

Some of the following items are well-formed sentences representing vernacular dialects, and others are not. Those that are not well formed violate some aspect of vernacular dialect grammatical rules. For each item, first determine whether it is a well-formed vernacular sentence or not. If it is well formed, write "OK" and identify the rule or structure; if it is *not* well formed, write "No" and specify what violation of the rule makes it an ill-formed vernacular sentence.

1. She run down the road yesterday.
    [Answer: OK; irregular base form uses bare root.]
2. The TV program was a-fascinating.
    [Answer: No; *a-* prefix cannot occur with adjectival *-ing*]
3. She been met her a minute ago.
    [Answer: No; remote *been* is used for distant past]
4. Him and me ain't go to the show.
    [Answer: OK; object pronoun form with coordinate; *ain't* for *didn't*]

5. I nice today.
    [Answer: No; copula *be* absence doesn't occur with first person
    singular form *I*]

Again, such examples may be expanded until students reach a prescribed
success level in identifying the structures and understanding how the vernacular grammar rules account for the structures in a precise way.

Stage 6: Back to the Language Laboratory

In the final stage, students are again asked to listen to tape-recorded samples
of speakers from different dialects. As they listen, students identify various
vernacular structures, as in the samples. At this point, the students should
be able to identify the structures and make appropriate comments about
how the patterns work. They can also check vernacular speakers' natural
language production with the rules they have now learned in order to confirm the rules. On occasion, this exercise has even led to the reexamination
of a rule parameter. Students are constantly asked, "Does the rule work as
presented in the descriptive account?" The kinds of sample tapes used at
this stage depend, of course, on the emphasis in the course of study, but
typical samples include Southern white, Black English, Appalachian English,
and Northern white vernacular varieties.

   The program for the presentation of vernacular grammatical structures described here holds several advantages for students. First of all, it
instantiates the rule-governed, systematic patterning of vernacular dialect
structures. It is virtually impossible to undergo such an experience without
appreciating the complexities and exactness of the grammatical patterns of
a vernacular variety. What is engendered is a respect borne of exposure to
the notion of linguistic grammaticality as applied to any variety of language,
but the lesson is particularly relevant to the study of vernacular dialects. I
have had students walk away from such a pedagogical experience without
sharing my social concerns about vernacular speech, but I have never had a
student leave without gaining a new respect for the intricacies of linguistic
patterns as applied to dialects regardless of social status.
   This discussion focused on grammar, but a similar approach has been
used successfully in the presentation of phonological features as well. The
program format is therefore flexible in terms of the level of language under
study. The general approach may also be used for the study of a specific

vernacular, such as Appalachian or Vernacular Black English, or it may be used to survey a more broadly based overview of vernacular dialects.

If carried out in full, the program can occupy a number of class sessions, particularly when combined with lab sessions in which tape-recorded language samples are played. It can also be used in a more restricted format by limiting the set of grammar structures and the sample of recordings presented to students.

Perhaps most important from a pedagogical standpoint, the stages in the presentation of structures provide an escape from the drudgery of rote memorization. Students learn through repeated exposure to the structures in different formats and by the application of emerging knowledge to progressively more divergent formats and more complex tasks. Students tend to view the various exercises as a relatively painless way of learning how the vernacular grammar patterns work. Retention should therefore be enhanced, as well as the potential for applying this information beyond the particular program of study.

In my teaching over the years, I have not had the good fortune of being guaranteed students who come to the study of vernacular grammar with great enthusiasm about grammar. In fact, students often confront this task by recalling stories of educational abuse inflicted on them in their earlier bouts with Standard English grammar rules. But I must honestly report that some of these same students have expressed to me the sentiment captured in a "Kudzu" comic strip in which a student, sitting at his desk, conjugates the verb *be* in the first two frames—"I be, You be, He be, We be, Y'all be, They be"—and expresses satisfaction in the third: "I LOVE CONJUGATING VERBS IN JIVE!" Many of the students who previously abhorred the study of grammar have found genuine enthusiasm for examining the structures of vernacular dialects. In a real sense, studying the patterns of vernacular dialects has opened up a new life for the study of grammar.

Sociolinguistic Analysis of Dialogues and First-Person Narratives in Fiction

Barbara Hill Hudson, Indiana University of Pennsylvania

∼⌠⌡∼

LANGUAGE arts teachers should consider using first-person narratives and sections of dialogue from selected novels and short stories to help students appreciate the diversity in English dialects past and present. In this essay, I suggest ways in which teachers may use findings from linguistic research to help their students examine how dialogue and first-person narratives serve as social mirrors that in many ways reflect language use in various regions among different social-class, ethnic, and racial groups.

Social-Class Dialects

Peter Trudgill (*Sociolinguistics*) and others have pointed out that different social groups use different linguistic varieties and that people have learned to classify speakers according to the language varieties they use. Since dialects differ in syntax, phonology, lexicon, and other features, teachers may wish to use a chart similar to table 1 to help students become familiar with some of the most common socially diagnostic features. Even though some students may know about many of these elements, it is still a good idea to go over the chart thoroughly before asking them to attempt an analysis of dialogues or first-person narratives. Of course, as they proceed, the students should be encouraged to add to the chart.

As part of this exercise, students should be made aware that the differences, listed as *Standard* and *Nonstandard*, do not represent two discrete social dialects; rather, they should be told, the dialects merge to form a continuum in which there is a higher frequency of use of nonstandard features on the end represented by the speech of members of lower socioeconomic groups and a much lower frequency of use of nonstandard features in middle- to upper-class speech. Social class is reflected in regional, ethnic, racial, and historical dialects.

Students should be challenged to find evidence of social variation not only in the speaker's language but also in nonlinguistic internal evidence in the text, such as indications of employment or wealth. Students may discover

Table 1. Socially Diagnostic Features

Category	Standard	Nonstandard
Phonology		
Pronunciation of -ing	"-ing"	"-in' "
Vowel sounds	No dialectal pronunciation indicated in spelling	Great deal of dialect marking in spelling
Contracted pronunciation of verb form followed by infinitive	Clear distinction between the two verbs, or slight reduction of juncture—e.g., *going to* + verb	Moderate to extreme reduction of juncture—e.g., *gonna*; *I'ngna*; *I'mana*; *I'ma*
Loss of initial unstressed syllable	Retention of first syllable—e.g., *arithmetic, remember, about*	Suppression of first syllable—e.g., *'rithmetic, 'member, 'bout*
Verb Forms		
Past tense of irregular verbs	*swim–swam, know–knew, see–saw, take–took*	*swim–swimmed, know–knowed, see–seen, take–taken* or *taked*
Variation in irregular form of present perfect or past perfect tenses	I've *seen* it; I had *seen* it.	I've *saw* it; I had *saw* it.
A- prefixing of verb	He was *running* and *jumping*.	He was *a-running* (or *a-runnin'*) and *a-jumping* (or *a-jumpin'*).
Ain't	Infrequent occurrence	Frequent use of the form
Nouns and Pronouns		
Plural forms of nouns	*desks, children*	*desses, chirren* or *chirrens*
Relative pronouns	I bought one of Fred's houses, *which everyone knows are built right.*	I bought one of Fred's houses, *which everyone knows he builds them right.*
	This is a word *whose meaning I don't know.*	This is a word *that I don't know what it means.*
	A man *who doesn't* run around is a good catch.	A man *what don't* run around is a good catch.
Demonstrative pronouns	*this thing, those things*	*this here* (or *'ere*) *thing, them things*
Reflexive pronouns	He washed *himself*; they washed *themselves.*	He washed *hisself*; they washed *theirself* (or *theirselves*)
	He gave the tickets to my friend and *me.*	He gave the tickets to my friend and *myself.*
	The girl next door and *I* went to the show.	*Myself* and the girl next door went to the show.
Possessive pronouns	It's *yours, mine, his.*	It's *yourn, mines, hisn.*
Plural of *you*	*you* as plural form	*yiz, y'uns, youens, youse, you-all, y'all*
Syntax		
Multiple negatives	He *never* cries; he doesn't *ever* cry.	He don't *never* cry.
Fronting of negative auxiliaries	Nobody has said anything; nobody knows anything.	*Ain't* nobody said nothing; *don't* nobody know nothing.
Auxiliary inversion in indirect question	I wonder if he finished the job.	I wonder *did* he finish the job.
Other Features		
Forms of address	*Yes, madam; No, madam; Yes, sir; No, sir*	*Yes'm; No'me* or *No'm; Yes, sorr; No, sorr*
Rough talk	Infrequent use	Profanity, obscenity, name calling, use of derogatory terms
Polite terms	*thank you, excuse me*	*thankye', 'scuseme*
	Softened expressions, euphemisms, modal constructions—e.g., *darn, passed away,* Would you shut the door?	Direct terms—e.g., *damn, upped an' died, Shet the door!*

[Many of these features and others have been discussed in Walt Wolfram (*Study*), Peter Trudgill (*Sociolinguistics*), William Labov (*Sociolinguistic*), Fernando Peñalosa (*Introduction*), and Elaine Chaika.]

that they can locate only a few phonological features that represent differences in the way social classes in general use language, but they may find a large number of syntactic or grammatical features. A particular author may mark regional and ethnic differences more frequent in the language of certain characters that in the language of others.

Below are examples of how a teacher may lead students in an analysis of two passages, both of which contain speakers representing different social groups. If we were to ask students to find the socially diagnostic linguistic features, most of them would be able to do the initial analysis simply by drawing on their own ideas about the way language was used in earlier times. In itself this is a useful learning experience, for it points up the little-understood fact that all members of the speech community are linguists to some extent. It will also serve to highlight some of the subtle ways in which language is used in marking social context. The teacher may begin by having students read the passages by Dickens and Parker and asking them to respond to the following questions on the basis of table 1, as well as of their knowledge of language use:

1. How many characters are involved?
2. What are the ages, genders, and social classes of the participants?
3. Describe the status relationships. Who has the higher status? Who has the lower status? Which characters are social peers?
4. In what social setting does the activity take place?
5. In what country or part of the country does it take place?
6. What is the racial or ethnic group membership of each character?
7. What time period does the passage represent? (Broad answers are acceptable—e.g., late twentieth century, the 1940s, during the Civil War.)
8. List any prominent phonological features. What do they tell you about each speaker?
9. List any prominent syntactic features. What do they tell you about each speaker?
10. List any unusual or unfamiliar lexical items. What dialectal or socioeconomic information do you get from these words or phrases?

Sample Exercises

Exercise A: Dickens

Dickens, Charles. *Great Expectations*. New York: Signet Classics, 1963.
Ch. 13, 113–14.

"You are the husband," repeated Miss Havisham, "of the sister 1
of this boy?" 2

It was very aggravating; but, throughout the interview, Joe 3
persisted in addressing me instead of Miss Havisham. 4

"Which I meantersay, Pip," Joe now observed, in a manner 5
that was at once expressive of forcible argumentation, strict confi- 6
dence, and great politeness, "as I hup and married your sister, and 7
I were at the time what you might call (if you was any ways inclined) 8
a single man." 9

"Well!" said Miss Havisham. "And you have reared the boy, 10
with the intention of taking him for your apprentice; is that so, Mr. 11
Gargery?" 12

"You know, Pip," replied Joe, "as you and me were ever 13
friends, and it were looked for'ard to betwixt us, as being calc'lated 14
to lead to larks. Not but what, Pip, if you had ever made objections 15
to the business—such as its being open to black and sut, or such- 16
like—not but what they would have been attended to, don't you 17
see?" 18

"Has the boy," said Miss Havisham, "ever made any objection? 19
Does he like the trade?" 20

"Which it is well beknown to yourself, Pip," returned Joe, 21
strengthening his former mixture of argumentation, confidence, 22
and politeness, "that it were the wish of your own hart." (I saw the 23
idea suddenly break upon him that he would adapt his epitaph to 24
the occasion, before he went on to say.) "And there weren't no 25
objection on your part, and Pip it were the great wish of your hart!" 26

Analysis

It would be surprising if most of the students didn't recognize the social
status of the narrator (Pip), of Miss Havisham, and of Joe. It might be
surprising to some of them to learn, however, that even Miss Havisham is
speaking in dialect, since readers are not generally aware that Standard

English is represented slightly differently in diverse dialects (e.g., American English, British English, Australian English).

Once it is clearly understood that the narrator (Pip), Miss Havisham, and Joe are all speaking in a dialect, it is useful to go over the passage again and have the students pick out socially diagnostic features of all three speakers. One of the things they might discover is that Pip and Miss Havisham, though both are speaking Standard English, differ slightly in their style of speech. Once Joe has been identified as being a speaker of nonstandard English, it is interesting to analyze how his speech stereotypes him. His speech contains a number of stigmatized forms.

Phonology

Line 5: "meantersay" for "mean to say" (eye dialect "er": the British spelling of the reduced vowel of informal speech in the preposition *to*)

Line 7: "hup" for "up" (hypercorrection: adding initial *h*- inappropriately)

Line 14: "for'ard" for "forward" (consonant elision)

Line 14: "calc'lated" for "calculated" (syllable elision)

Line 16: "sut" for "soot" (regional dialect)

Line 23, 26: "hart" for "heart" (either eye dialect or information about difference in pronunciation of these two words)

With the possible exceptions of "hup" and "calc'lated," these items would not firmly place a speaker in the lower class unless they were combined with other lower-class markers. The "er" in "meantersay" is the common eye dialect way of spelling the British unstressed vowel; British "er" is pronounced something like the American "uh" but is higher in the mouth, as in the tongue placement of the vowel in *bird* in dialects in which postvocalic *r* is not pronounced. This particular spelling could be used simply to indicate informal, relaxed style; however, in combination with the other features of Joe's speech, it very likely is intended to mark him as being less well educated than Miss Haversham or Pip. The pronunciation "for'ard" could be produced naturally in rapid speech, but the apostrophe in this word, along with "calc'lated," suggest that Joe leaves out portions of his words and thus is not well schooled. "Sut" is a regional pronunciation in both England and the United States, but Dickens uses it to indicate that Joe speaks a folk dialect that differs from preferred London speech. The spelling of "hart" probably indicates a dialectal pronunciation that differs from London Standard, though some research on British English would be necessary for the class to make a firm decision on why Dickens used this particular spelling. Any of the items below, under "Syntax," could serve as springboards for further research by students on regional and social variation in British English.

Syntax

Line 8: "I were" for "I was"
Line 8: "If you was" for "If you were"
Line 14: "and it were" for "and it was"
Line 21: "well beknown to yourself" for "well known to you"
Line 23: "it were the wish" for "it was the wish"
Line 25: "there weren't no objection" for "there was no objection"

It should be obvious from this list that most nonstandard features contain some form of the verb *be*.

After the students have gone thoroughly over this passage, identifying the smaller features, they can go back one more time to make an assessment of the general social context by looking at the discourse styles of the two speakers (Joe and Miss Havisham) to discover whatever else they can about the social situation. For example, we might ask:

1. Who has the higher social status? Who has the lower?
2. What kinds of linguistic evidence can you point to? (For instance, Miss Havisham is the questioner, and Joe's replies are overly polite.)
3. How does stereotyping of speech contribute to the reader's characterization of an individual as a protagonist (hero), antagonist (villain), or neutral participant?
4. How do developments in the plot match the way in which each character is marked by his or her speech?

Exercise B: Parker

Parker, Dorothy. "The Standard of Living." *Fifty Great Short Stories.* Ed. Milton Crane. New York: Bantam, 1952. 25–26.

Together they went over to the shop window and stood pressed against it. It contained but one object—a double row of great, even pearls clasped by a deep emerald around a little pink velvet throat.
"What do you suppose they cost?" Annabel said.
"Gee, I don't know," Midge said. "Plenty, I guess."
"Like a thousand dollars?" Annabel said.

"Oh, I guess like more," Midge said. "On account of the emerald."

"Well, like ten thousand dollars?" Annabel said.

"Gee, I wouldn't even know," Midge said.

The devil nudged Annabel in the ribs. "Dare you to go in and price them," she said.

"Like fun!" Midge said.

"Dare you," Annabel said. . . .

. . . .

"Is there something–?" the clerk said.

"Oh, we're just looking," Annabel said. It was as if she flung the words down from a dais.

The clerk bowed.

"My friend and myself merely happened to be passing," Midge said, and stopped, seeming to listen to the phrase. "My friend here and myself," she went on, "merely happened to be wondering how much are those pearls you've got in your window."

"Ah, yes," the clerk said. "The double rope. That is two hundred and fifty thousand dollars, Madam."

"I see," Midge said.

The clerk bowed. "An exceptionally beautiful necklace," he said. "Would you care to look at it?"

"No, thank you," Annabel said.

"My friend and myself merely happened to be passing," Midge said.

Analysis

This passage also points out clearly that language use reflects social context. As with the passage from Dickens, we see representatives from two social classes. In this case, the clerk is representative of an upper class, and the young women represent a lower class.

By having the students examine the change in style of speech Midge and Annabel use when they are outside the shop and when they are inside the shop, the teacher can show that language use is one of the behaviors that mark differences in social situations. As part of the overall analysis, students might notice that when the young women speak to each other, they use slang ("Gee"; "Like fun!") and truncated sentences ("Dare you"). They might then observe that when the young women speak to the clerk, they use a very stilted form of language, including the inappropriate use of reflexives ("My friend and myself") and a nonstandard form of indirect question ("wondering how much are those pearls") in attempts to be "correct" in the awesome surroundings of the shop and the presence of the clerk. This phenomenon, called *hypercorrection*, also occurs in the Dickens passage when Joe uses stilted, overly polite, and circuitous language to address Miss Havisham.

The language of the clerk should give the students an opportunity to examine an example of upper-middle-class dialect. Labov (*Sociolinguistic*) has argued that the language of store clerks often reflects that of the clientele. Students should notice the clerk's precise wording ("That is two hundred and fifty thousand dollars"), his polite question ("Would you care to look at it?"), and his use of formal terms of address ("Madam"). As a final exercise, students may be asked to identify paralinguistic features (stance, body movement) that also point out social class or age differences.

This type of analysis can be incorporated in a number of different classes at various levels. Instructors wishing to make use of this model can easily develop lessons planned around both familiar and unfamiliar passages from the standard anthologies available. Listed below are five additional passages that may be used for similar classroom exercises. A resourceful literature teacher should be able to find many other appropriate passages. Students should be encouraged to look for such passages in assigned readings, in the public press, and in their recreational reading.

Other Suggested Passages for Analysis

Kipling, Rudyard. "The Courting of Dinah Shadd." *Fifty Great Short Stories*. Ed. Milton Crane. New York: Bantam, 1952. 69–70 (near the beginning of section 2: conversation between narrator and Mulvaney).

Main features. The language features here represent a regional dialect that differs considerably from the standard literary language of Kipling's time. The students may not be able to place the dialect within England, but they can analyze the spelling as indicative of pronunciation and can find nonstandard word forms and syntactic constructions.

Wolfe, Thomas. "Only the Dead Know Brooklyn." *Fifty Great Short Stories*. Ed. Milton Crane. New York: Bantam, 1952. 109–13 (whole passage is first-person narrative).

Main features. Phonological features represent a regional dialect, specifically New York City. The passage also contains some nonstandard verb forms and local slang.

Gaines, Ernest J. "The Sky Is Grey." *Discoveries: Fifty Stories of the Quest*. Ed. Harold Schechter and Jonna Gormely Semeiks. Indianapolis: Bobbs, 1983.

320 (whole passage is first-person narrative; section 5 contains dialogue between two young people).

Main features. Phonological features, word forms, syntactic features, and lexical items represent ethnic (black) dialect, with some features also found in the speech of Southern whites. In addition, students can be asked to identify those features that indicate that the two people in section 5 are quite young.

Bambara, Toni Cade. "The Lesson." *Discoveries: Fifty Stories of the Quest.* Ed. Harold Schechter and Jonna Gormely Semeiks. Indianapolis: Bobbs, 1983. 296–98 (whole passage is first-person narrative; dialogue between young people begins on second page of story).

Main features. See Gaines entry.

Malamud, Bernard. "The Idiots First." *Discoveries: Fifty Stories of the Quest.* Ed. Harold Schechter and Jonna Gormely Semeiks. Indianapolis: Bobbs, 1983. 232–33 (dialogue between Mendel and Fishbein begins about one third of the way into the story).

Main features. Syntactic features, phonological features, and lexical items represent ethnic (Jewish) dialect and educational level (consequently, social class). Syntactic features reflect Yiddish influence in the speech of less-educated speakers.

Speechprint Spectrography Confirms Idiolect in Dialect Study and Speaker Recognition

Henry M. Truby, Language and Linguistics Research Laboratory, South Miami

SPEECH individuality is the primary aspect of language variation. This has been my premise throughout some forty-six years of acoustic-phonetic—and especially speech-spectrogram—analysis.

Idiosyncrasy of individual human vocalization is evident from birth, in the form of distinctive neonatal visual-crysound patterning, as demonstrated in Stockholm from 1957 with birthsound tape-recordings and correlated cineradiography (X-ray movies) of 155 paranates ("being-born babies") during respiration establishment (initial lung-filling) and immediately postnatal and subsequent neonatal (first week, here) crysound articulation, originally published with approximately three hundred crysound spectrograms plus correlated sound-track (Truby, Lind, and Bosma, 1960). My coinage "cryprinting" regarding this phenomenon of speaker individuality was spontaneously spun during the critique of a 1960 paper read in San Francisco at the sixtieth meeting of the Acoustical Society of America (Truby, "Some Aspects"), and the 58-page "Cry Sounds" article reappeared as a portion of the 1965 NIH-sponsored book treating also the *articulation* of birthcry and neonatal cry and containing some four hundred crysound spectrograms complete with a correlated soundtrack (Truby, Bosma, and Lind).

As this universally consistent vocalization individuality proceeds, crying intermingles with what appears to be prespeech and quasispeech utterance, and as infantile *approximations* (often erroneously called "mispronunciations") and childhood intelligibility progress, this truly phenomenal utterance individuality continues apace, with developmentally increasing idiospecific complexity, throughout the speech lives of normal individuals and analogously in auxiliary language or dialect acquisition (all above references plus Prescott; Prescott was one of my doctorands; a portion of her 1966 thesis was based upon cryprints and subsequent speechprints of five of my six children, all of whom I had tape-recorded during birth and at five minutes, five hours, five days, five weeks, and five months and the first three of whom I had tape-recorded at five years of age as well; there was clear and consistent soundprint individuation throughout). In fact, there is literally no time, from birthcry until ultimate inaudibility, that individual vocalization—and specifically speech—is not producer-specific.

The earliest obvious English-language reference to what is a common-place recognition phenomenon appears in the hand-me-down translation of John 10. 4–5: "and the sheep follow [the shepherd]: for they know his voice: And a stranger will they not follow, but will flee from him: for they know not the voice of strangers" (King James Version). Every reader of these words will agree that relatives, friends, and otherwise familiar personages such as actors and politicians are recognizable from their speech, and pets readily recognize familiar human voices.

I was awakened to the realization that language is an essentially infi-nitely variable, individual manifestation when, as an engineering math in-structor in 1946 at the University of Wisconsin, I began examining speech spectrograms under the mentorial auspices and tutelage, respectively, of phoneticians extraordinary Miles L. Hanley (1939–43) and Martin Joos (1948). Almost immediately I observed that spectrograms of my own speech were demonstrably different phonetically from those of any other speaker, even when "the same word" was uttered. From the outset it was evident to me which speaker correlated with which speech spectrogram. We each cry differently, cough differently, sigh and sneeze differently, shout and sing differently—and we speak differently. In 1947 I had begun espousing a hypothesis that I termed *idiolinguistics*, which places individual speechsound approximations and interpretations at the core of language development for every speaker-listener (user) of whatever language. Language is thus literally a conclamation of mutually intelligible *idiolects*. Each user (NB) of language is, consequently, an independent linguistic microcosm of idiolectal dimen-sion and a contributing factor to the variational flux that characterizes every language.

Students of language should find intellectual comfort in learning that the premise of speaker uniqueness had been postulated in both the early and later publications of such eminent linguists as Edward Wheeler Scripture (*Elements*, 1902; *Researches*, 1906; "Analysis," 1933), Edward Sapir (*Language*, 1921; "Speech," 1927), Otto Jespersen (*English*, 1912; *Language*, 1922), Leo-nard Bloomfield (*Language*, 1933; "Set," 1926), and others directly and indi-rectly. Quite possibly the first scientist of record to recognize speaker uniqueness was Alexander Melville Bell, the father and teacher of Alexander Graham Bell, who demonstrated publicly from 1849, with one or another of his three sons, a phonetic system for depicting speaker individuality (Bell, 1867; for citations, see Truby, "Voice Recognition," 1971; "Voiceprint [Speechprint] Identification," 1985). And in my acoustic-phonetics doctoral thesis (1959), featuring 1,100 speech spectrograms[1] and 318 X-ray cineframe prints, all processed at the Speech Transmission Laboratory of the Royal Institute of Technology and at the Wenner-Gren Research Laboratory, both in Stockholm, I treated this observation as axiomatic, to wit: "it is not pretended ... that there do not exist the inconsistencies from individual to individual and from utterance to utterance which are characteristic of all speech" (Truby, *Speechprint Spectrograms*, sec. 0.2, 1993), even though I had not yet found other linguists' published references to this physical fact when I made my own above declaration in 1959, or for a dozen years thereafter.

In expansion of Sapir's 1927 observation that "the individual has his method of handling ... particular patterns of society, giving them just enough of a twist to make them 'his' and no one else's" ("Speech" 892–94), Paul Garvin and Peter Ladefoged wrote in 1963 that "human beings are indeed capable of recognizing not only individuals but classes of individuals by voices" (193), with "idiosyncratic speech patterns" reflecting "social and/ or regional varieties of speech" (Truby, "Voice Recognition," 1971, 244n12). My personal experience with sonocineradiography (X-ray soundfilming) had confirmed the anatomical-articulatory idiosyncracies among speakers that account for linguistic "facts" visible in spectrogram form (e.g., idiosyncratically distinct aural-visual pattern correlates of particular phonemes) (Truby, "Sonocineradiography," 1972).

The principle of visual "voiceprinting" (better: *speechprinting*) was conceived in the early 1940s at Bell Telephone Laboratories (Gray and Kopp) to specify the spectrogram patterns that enable qualified researchers to recognize speakers by their "voices." In such sense, *voice* is articulated voiced-voiceless airflow, and thus: *speech*—which is to say: *speech* is linguistically programmed *voice*. And *voiceprinting*, as used forensically, is visual demonstration of the *speechsound* product of speaking and consequently distinguishes each speaker's unique pronunciation and enunciation (but not "voice quality").[2] (See Truby, "What the Speechprint Spectrogram Can and Cannot Do for Dialectology," 1990[3])

Newborn infant "cryprint" analysis was initiated by me in 1957 in Stockholm, in association with Karolinska Children's Hospital, primarily for the purpose of developing an acoustigraphic pediatric technology for the diagnosis, at birth, of infantile brain-damage or other serious systemic neuropathy. These novel crysound analyses provided advance "signaling," confirmable by karyotypy (clinical chromosome analysis) or other conventional neurological assessment, not only for diagnosing specific neurological disorders but, serendipitously, for establishing the identity of infants, hale as well as infirm (Truby, "Phoneme Illusion," 1971). In this latter sense, "cryprinting" has served, in a few critical instances, in accurately identifying accidentally "shuffled" infants, and once, in Stockholm, in ascertaining, after the fact, the order of birth of a set of unexpected quadruplets. In analogous analysis applications in Florida, from 1965 on, I began identifying distinguishing danger-signaling features in the earliest neonatal crysound of newborns of birthing mothers addicted to drugs; without appropriate withdrawal medication, such critically endangered infants face almost certain demise. And during 1965 my use of spectrographic analysis was extended to the sound-printing of nonhuman animals, marking the beginning of my twenty-plus years of bioacoustics research with the bottlenose dolphin (*Tursiops truncatus*) and the orca (*Orcinus orca*) (Truby, "Sound-spectrographic," 1965; "Language and Dolphins," 1969; "Voice Recognition," 1971; *World Dolphin*, 1971).

In some four decades of examining thousands of acoustigrams in over a dozen different scientific research laboratories, I have never met two identical speech spectrograms, nor thus utterances, except in instances of artifactuality—for example, instrumentally produced *synthetic speech*; and my professional roles as a scientific speechprint-identification expert, in some two hundred criminal cases since 1971, have, without exception, reinforced my initial, ensuing, and present positive conclusions about speechsound spectrography (Truby, "Voiceprint [Speechprint]," 1985). The inherence of language variation rests with each speaker and every instance of speech, and similarly as regards writing.

Beginning with the 1950s birth and neonatal cryprinting research, complementing thirty years of spectrographic analysis of the speechsound of individuals of all ages—often the same person over many years—I have been convinced that, from birth, the individual's vocalization and, later, speech begin as unique phenomena and develop in further unique ways. The development aspects of speech consistently precede corresponding language characteristics *in* the developing child. Each infant crysound is physically (and thus acoustically) different from every other, as is the case for all other types of human neuromuscular production (Truby, Lind, and Bosma 45, 1960). Maternal speech idiosyncrasy is reflected in the related infant's neonatal crysound-patterning, elicited prenatally by the mother's vocalization-conditioning of her prenate (unborn baby). Thus the potential for the perceptual similarities and physical dissimilarities displayed in spectrograms of each speaker stems from prenatal developmental-hearing conditioning, normally from as early as the twenty-fourth week of pregnancy (see Truby, "Prenatal," 1976). That is, the prenate begins to hear and respond at "minus sixteen" weeks.

Discriminating *voicesound* details are rarely displayed discretely on the speech spectrogram but are highly dependable markers when present. Because each instantiation of speechsound is physically (thus acoustically) unique and verifiably idiosyncratic, the speech output of a given person inevitably varies from utterance to utterance; but, ironically, deliberate attempt at speech/voice disguise is betrayed by detectable dissimilarities in spectral and temporal patterning. Although even the educated human ear must take a backseat to the speech spectrogram in all documenting of pronunciation-enunciation features of speechsound, the "ear" is (so far) unexcelled in interpreting distinctive impressions of voice quality, timbre, tonality, intonation, vowel color, and other esoteric paralinguistic sound-features, especially where the elusive element of interspeaker familiarity is an aspect: "That's *Joe*—I'd know that voice of *his any*where." But, unfortunately, there have been many documented instances in forensic speaker-identification in which a "familiar listener" has been confounded by tape-recorded and, especially, by telephone-transmitted speech. However, every case of valid speaker-identification or -recognition "by ear alone" may be further confirmed with spectrograms. And as a corollary, wherever an auditory assessment has been proven erroneous on other grounds, speechsound spectrogram details will invariably support that the "ear judgment" was indeed erroneous. "Like pronunciations" by different speakers are phonemic illusions and are speechsound *caricatures* of the physical-acoustic facts. That is, the speech spectrogram confirms that speakers cannot reproduce even the simplest or most familiar vocal utterance with physical—and thus phonetic— exactitude, not even their own family names (Truby, "Pleniphonetic," 1964; "Perception," 1967; "Validity," 1969; "Prenatal," 1976; "Voiceprint," 1985). And the attempts of any other speaker to duplicate a given speaker's idiovocal signature—or any manner of vocal utterance— will fail quite evidently.

As noted above, certain earlier language scholars postulated the uniqueness of an individual's speechsound production and suggested the apparent impossibility of someone's reproducing another's speech—or any utterance—with absolute facsimilitude. Perhaps the first so to surmise was the senior Alexander Bell:

> The plasticity of the [articulatory] organs is so great, that shades of vowel quality are endless, arising from infinitesimal differences in the relative positions of the lips and tongue. The number of possible varieties can as little be estimated as the number of possible shades of colour. (*Visible Speech* 27 [1863], 15 [1867])

In 1902, Scripture made very similar observations:

> A speech sound [sic] produced by an individual is the result of a very large number of fine adjustments of the speaking apparatus influenced by an infinitude of past and present experiences in hearing, thinking,

and speaking. The sound [sic] varies from moment to moment and from one occasion to another. With sufficiently accurate methods of measurement no two sounds [sic] would be found alike. . . . (*Elements* 118)

The Danish phonetician-grammarian Jespersen observed a decade later:

It should be borne in mind that no two people in any country speak exactly alike. This naturally applies to English too, which is spoken by so many people in so many parts of the world. (*English Phonetics* 5)

The anthropologist-linguist Sapir wrote in 1921:

Two individuals of the same generation and locality, speaking precisely the same dialect and moving in the same social circles, are never absolutely at one in their speech habits. A minute investigation of the speech of each individual would reveal countless differences of detail . . . in the pronunciation of particular vowels and consonants and of the combinations of vowels and consonants, in all those features, such as speed, stress, and tone, that give life to spoken language. (*Language* 157)

In 1933, in his long-classic book *Language*, Leonard Bloomfield commented at least three times on inter- and intrapersonal variation in language:

If we observed closely enough, we should find that no two persons— or (even) no one person at different times—spoke exactly alike. (45) The difference between speakers is partly a matter of bodily make- up and . . . of purely personal habit. . . . (45) Speech-utterances are infinitely varied. Everyday experience tells us that different persons speak differently, for we recognize people by their voices. The phonetician finds that no two utterances are exactly alike. (*Language* 76)

Daniel Jones wrote in 1938:

If I perform the action which we call "pronouncing the vowel *u*" *once*, I make a concrete sound which is audible to me and to others who may be near. If I perform the action on another occasion, I make another concrete sound; if I perform it 20 times I make 20 concrete sounds. . . . If I utter the vowel *u* 20 times in the same manner, ordinary people will say that I have produced *the same sound* 20 times—that it is *one* sound repeated. . . . ("Concrete" 2)

Speaking analogously of two tennis balls, Jones said:

Two different tennis balls may look exactly like each other, but they are not the same ball. . . . But they are both tennis-balls: the term "tennis-ball" does not as a rule mean one particular ball. So also "the vowel *u*" does not as a rule refer to one particular utterance: it is something common to all utterances—the general conception of "quality" or "timbre" which this vowel has. . . . This is an abstraction. . . : It is the [*phonemic*] quality "*u*-ness" which distinguishes every concrete *u* that I make from every other concrete sound. ("Concrete" 2–3)

All of these scientists had arrived independently at their conclusions long before the advent of the sound spectrograph, in the 1940s, at the Bell Telephone Laboratories (Gray and Kopp, 1944; Potter, Kopp, and Green, 1947). At least three generations of British phoneticians were trained (in the ethereal illusion of some "pronunciation standard") to use the "Cardinal Vowels" uttered by and recorded by Daniel Jones as a tangible "fixed standard" pronunciation frame of reference both for listening and transcribing and for uttering "vowelsounds" in isolation and in discourse. During my nine-year sojourn in Europe (1954 through 1962), I recorded DJ (as he was commonly referred to) and made spectrograms of his "live" iterations and his Gramophone model recording of the famous Cardinal Vowels. My spectrograms disclosed no two acoustically identical "same vowels" in the Jones renditions. Although I ego-sensitively withheld this technical information from him during his lifetime, I now realize, in the light of his 1938 Ghent paper ("Concrete and Abstract Sounds"), partly cited above, that DJ would have indeed relished my instrumentally aided 1950s confirmation of his 1930s observation and tennis ball analogy. I was overly protective of one who needed no protection.

(Jones's tennis ball reference is not haphazard, as he was an incurable tennis buff, and every competent tennis professional, which I was at that time and long afterward, will confirm that, no matter how meticulously fabricated, no two tennis balls are physically identical or perform identically; added to that fact is the philosophically obvious truth that, by definition, they are not the same ball. Analogously, no two speechsound utterances are identical. The abstraction "tennis ball" is to every actual tennis ball as the abstraction "phoneme" is to every phonetically relevant "speech sound," however contextually modified. This last consideration could well be the most fundamental demonstration of language variation.)

In harmony with the above observations, my independent conclusions were elicited solely from examination of speech spectrograms from 1946 on. My definitive impression of language hierarchy has its basis in the variational complexities of speech and of all aspects of language and has led me to view language in terms of the following imbricated hierarchy of concepts: *idiolect,*

familialect, communalect, regionalect, dialect (geographical; social), *language*—
all with primary reference to speech.

An *idiolect* may be defined as the seminal idiosyncratic language microcosm for a given speaker. At whatever stage of developmental or of auxiliary
acquisition, each instance of speech is—and, concomitantly, all interrelated
grammatical and linguistically stylistic idiosyncrasies are—*idiolectal* for any
speaker. A given speaker, however, will have differing idiolects at different
(developmental, variously maturated, or evanescing) stages of "speechhood";
may well have combinations (and/or mixtures) of idiolect under such exceptional circumstances as fluctuations of cultural or even of physical environment, unstable health, "good behavior" (e.g., "platform language"),
excitement, and the like; and, unusually, at least for most—monolingual—
Americans, could have a repertoire of two or more distinctive idiolects at any
stage of life, depending on the speaker's particular language (and related
lectal) versatility. But whatever the extraordinary or extenuating circumstances, each idiolect has a unique phonological description, all physical details considered; and although the idiolects of different speakers may share
even so much as a plurality or even identity of phonemic and other phonological features, the phonetic details—and similarly the sum total of idiolects
for a given speaker—will ensure ultimate speaker individuality. It should
be remembered that pronunciation is not the sole aspect of idiolect, albeit
certainly the most immediately apparent auditorily, and on the speech spectrogram it is demonstrably the most definitive, at least where intelligibility is
concerned. Even the prominent Yale professor of linguistics Bernard Bloch,
longtime meticulous editor and maven intellectual guardian angel of *Language*, the journal of the Linguistic Society of America, identifies both idiolect
and dialect with speech alone. In his forty-four-page definitive opus of 1948,
"A Set of Postulates for Phonemic Analysis" (57 postulates, 48 corollaries, 97
definitions), Bloch mentions *idiolect* twenty-one times, but always with reference only to speech. Accurately, idiolect (as any lect) comprehends all relevant linguistic modes, features, products, and so forth for each speaker and
for all speakers. And just as there are neither physically (physiologically) nor
intellectually identical persons in our earthly universe, so are there no phonetically—or otherwise linguistically—identical speakers (Truby, *Speechprint
Spectrograms*, 1959, 1993; "Language and Dolphins," 1969; "Voice Recognition," 1971; "Validity," 1969; "Century," 1984; "Voiceprint [Speechprint]
Identification," 1985; "What the Speechprint Spectrogram," 1990).

I must emphasize that speechprint identification[3] enterprises and research have confirmed my understanding that each speaker-listener *is* a
distinctively unique language microcosm—of idiolectal dimension; and idiosyncrasies identified with pronunciation are similarly evident for all aspects

of grammar, vocabulary, semantics, and stylistics that implicitly individuate language users. Brave teachers-of-"English," auxiliary-language tutors, and dialectologists of whichever bent and involvement, please copy!

Thus idiolect, it is clear, embraces all idiosyncrasies of language particulars characterizing interpersonal communication; and many of the literate—as well as the not so literate—mechanistic (i.e., written-language) individualities become evident in corresponding individual spoken-language performance, such as the factually erroneous "forTAY" for monosyllabic *forte* (homophone[4] of *fort*), "OFF t'n" for "OFF'n" (*often: t*-less, as *soften, listen, castle, whistle*), "ex cetera" for *et cetera*, "NOO-cue-l'r" for *nuclear*, "lay" for *lie* ("recline"), "REEL-a-tor" for *realtor*, "MOS coe" for Mos*cow*, "media *is*" for "media *are*" (cf. *criterion, phenomenon*, "data *are*," "bacteria *are*," etc.), "PEEanist" for "piANist," and the most pervasive hypercorrection of all: *lingerie* with "-AY" rather than "-EE"!

Add the population-wide contributions of deplorable—and vacuous—obscenity and vulgarity generally, of inevitable slang, in its item-by-item ephemerality and unpredictable life-span, of ubiquitous cants, argots, as well as jargons, specialized and often exclusionary, and language is seen to be a fluxile coalescence of both the appearance of uniformity of pronunciation, vocabulary, and syntax and of essentially innumerable manifestations of diversification of these three basic language constituents.

When the idiolects of familially (or otherwise "household-ly") related speakers share a substantial abundance of phonemic and complementary phonological or other linguistic features (of vocabulary, grammar, style, etc.), said idiolects constitute what I have neologistically termed a *familialect*, the earliest and most persistent dialectal commonality that most speakers naturally encounter and fall in with or are constrained by. As with especially the phonological aspects of idiolect, familialect is, in large part, genetically determined, expressly as regards anatomical-neurophysiological (e.g., voice and articulatory) aspects of speechsound production; and it is empirically confirmable universally that familialects are individuational not only from family to family but from one generation to another in culturally constrained circumstances: "Sure, an' that's a *Murphy* for y', you c'n be *certain* of it." And it is a commonly observed and observable feature of familialect that the voice, speech, and language style of daughters often closely resembles that of their mothers—and of sons, their fathers—with other concomitant language-developmental determinants consistently functioning idiosyncratically (Truby, lecture series 1954–60, 1966–75; cited in Pugh).

A related dialectal commonplace obtains when distinctive speech habits and usage particulars characterize the members of a *community* who reside in a specific locality, are similarly focused as to occupational concerns, and

share features of cultural and historical heritage. For this breed of homoge-
neity I have proposed the concept and term *communalect*, an interrelated
constituent population of familialects—and thus of idiolects. A community
without a common cultural, historical, and thereby linguistic heritage is not
at all likely to evolve its own communalect.

A given *regionalect* comprises those idiolects sharing a commonality of
language features identifiable with a particular geographical *region*; that is,
regionalects are distributed topographically, with communalectal and famili-
alectal overtones (or *undertones*, if you like). Thus, there is an explicit inference of communalectal commonalities for each regionalect, as well as of
variance from some hypothetical norm or "standard" or prime form. Relat-
edly, a particularly sensitive aspect of language variation may be subsumed
under the however nebulous rubric *dialect*. The definitive spectrum of this
term and concept has been very broad indeed, historically; and in the language hierarchy indicated herewith, a dialect remains a variety—on all practical communication levels—of a language, the linguistic characteristics of
which variety do not render its native users more than minimally or occasionally unintelligible to first users of another dialect of the language in question.
For cogent examples, American English and British English are *dialects* of
English, each in turn comprising numerous language *varieties* (or *regionalects*),
just as are, for example, Bahamian English, Canadian English, Jamaican
English, Scottish English, "Strileyun" (Australian) English, and so on. In
fact, every dialect is the sum of its respective regionalects. Typically, the
regionalects of *British* English are more or less mutually intelligible for most
British English speakers but might, in certain cases, be highly unintelligible
for speakers of (certain regionalects of) American English, for example, as
well as of (certain regionalects of) other dialects of English. Differences
between British and American English, and lectal differences within Britain,
will be more clearly understood with the eventual publication of Allen
Walker Read's Dictionary of Briticisms, based on a vast inventory of citation
slips collected since 1938, now numbering over 100,000. Final publication is
scheduled for completion by the dialectologist John Algeo. In 1947, as the
British and American usage editor for the *American College Dictionary*, the
Columbia University professor Read wrote:

> [T]he "standard" form of English developed out of a multiplicity of
> dialects . . . [M]any Englishmen have assumed that their form of En-
> glish is the only one with validity, [but] if the frequency or incidence
> of a word is greater in one region of the English-speaking world than
> in another, it is a fact that deserves to be recorded. (xxx)

Some dialects of a given language are more similar (and less subject to
interdialectal confusion) than others. In my writings and lectures, at least

of the past three decades, I have cited a minimum of some six thousand independent languages presently in use on our planet, as well as an uncountable number of dialects of all of these languages collectively. There are from several to many dialects of most (if not all) of the languages tallied. Thus our "counts" leave much to be desired, for both languages and dialects, however defined.

Think, then, what we might expect from the files of the vast *DARE* (*Dictionary of American Regional English*), whose director and editor, Frederic G. Cassidy, is emeritus professor of English at the University of Wisconsin and in 1946 was my first professor of phonetics, of Anglo-Saxon, and of Middle English. This current prodigious collection from the idiolectal repertoires of 2,777 field informants, answering 1,847 questions focused on regional "nonstandard" American English, has been over twenty-five years in the making and provides us a documented inventory of a vivid cross-section of our—till *DARE*, unsung, but vitally alive—regional language vocabulary. Cassidy, in 1964, was obliged to formally dichotomize "dialect" and "regional" in selecting the ultimate title: *Dictionary of American Regional English* (see Cassidy, *Dictionary* xiin5). His relevant statement of note is, "Actually, the state of dialect in the United States makes the present title [i.e., *Regional*] more appropriate."

A useful rule-of-thumb for treating two or more language varieties as independent languages rather than as dialects specifies the former when there is consistent lack of intelligibility between or among the said varieties. (For a comprehensive discussion of "dialect, etc.," see Martinet, ch. 5, esp. 145–49.)

In regard to dialect and regionalect, I am currently producing speech-print spectrograms of the 1,843 half-hour field recordings of the 592-word *DARE* version of the linguistically classical "Arthur the Rat" phonetic contrivance, first used for dialect study by Henry Sweet (see below) before 1885, later adopted by my mentor-colleague Columbia University professor of phonetics Cabell Greet in the 1940s for a phonograph-record study of United States speech (see Cassidy, *Dictionary* xivn10) and variously incorporated in surveys of twentieth-century dialect. My final "visible speech" product will comprise relevant dialect glosses and 1,843(!) individuated idiolectal sets of voiceprints (more accurately, speechprints—that is, visible speech-sound patterns of pronunciation and enunciation; see pp. 39 and 40 of this essay).

Language, in terms of its oral-aural (and/or written) particulars, is the sum of its dialectal and ultimately idiolectal parts. And there are (and have been) more idiolects than there are speakers living at any instant (or that ever lived); the situation is compounded by the fact that many individuals are fluent in more than one language, and a few in more than one dialect of (a) different language(s). In this vein, Bloch, expanding on Bloomfield ("Set of Postulates" 155, 1926), stated, "An idiolect is not merely what a speaker says at any one time: it is everything that he COULD say in a given language" (7, 1948). Thus, when language variation is contemplated universally, every independent language is found to be ultimately defined by its particular totality of idiolects and, as stated above, not restricted to the spoken mode. *Idiolects* are the basic, individualistic, speech and language constituents of a particular *familialect*, and consequently of a linguistically definable *communalect*, itself identifiable with a subdialectal variant or *regionalect* of a particular *dialect* of a given conventionally specific, distinctive independent *language*.

A paradoxical aspect of the diversity of language is inherent *in* its dialectality—its apparent linguistically homogeneous specificity. Any "dialect," like any "language," is an intellectual caricature of linguistic precision—and a viable interspeaker medium. The speech of a given dialect is living proof of this fact, in that all relevant instances of idiolectal production are, at the least, ostensibly linguistically interpretable by any listener who shares that dialect—which is to say that primary information-exchange is not precluded by idiocratically unsimilar pronunciation, vocabulary, syntax, idioms, or style. In short, a speaker who utters the words *ate, aid,* and *aim* intends that each of these words features "the vowel *A*" (IPA /e/), and if any listener accepts these as the same three vowels intended by the speaker, then certain linguistic criteria have been exchanged. However, "the vowel *A*" (/e/) is phonetically (i.e., physically/acoustically) different for each of the words uttered: the *short* vowel [ĕ] of *ate* (or *eight*) is of noticeably shorter duration than the *long* vowel [eː] of *aid (ade, aide)* and [ẽː] of *aim,* which last *long* vowel is additionally nasalized throughout; yet "the vowel *A*" (/e/) has been linguistically produced and received for each of the three items, [ĕ], [eː], and [ẽː], regardless of the phonetic variations. As identified above, then, each uttered vowel "*A*" is a *caricature* of the abstract vowel (or phoneme) "*A*" (/e/), the essence of which abstraction characterizes every uttered vowel "*A*" regardless of its particular phonetic context, or its physical, acoustic, phonetic makeup, or its lectal identification. The caricature analogy is a complement of the phoneme concept: *phonemes are mental images of speechsound characteristic,* on the basis of which the respective *allophonic sets* (Truby, "Phoneme, Allophoneme" 947, 1972) constitute respective, corresponding, finite allophone inventories; in turn, every contextual allophone uttered (and perceived) is a phonetic caricature of the pertinent hypothetical phoneme imagery and is a unique variant of some hypothetical speechsound correlate. It is for me professionally and otherwise intellectually distressing to still find universally published "speech scientists" continuing to write—and teach—that the vowel /æ/ of *at, ad,* or *am* is "a short *A*," the *A* (/e/) of *ate, aid, aim* being miscalled by them "long," when the physical and semantic facts are that one can sustain a "short *A*" (/æ/) indefinitely and it will never become a "long *A*" (/e/)—or any other kind of *A*—and that the "long vowel" [ĕ] of *ate* (or *eight*) is consistently shorter than the "short vowel" [æː] of *ad(d)* or [æ] of *am*; nor can one ever "shorten" a so-miscalled "long *A*" (/e/) so that it will become a so-miscalled "short *A*" (/æ/). The durationally graduated allophonic set of [æ]-vowels (e.g., *at, ash, add, as, Al, ant, and, am*) represent /æ/ (the phoneme æ); the durationally graduated allophonic set of [e]-vowels (e.g., *ate, ace, ade, ail, ain't, aim*) represent /e/ (the phoneme e = "*A*"). Thus neither "short" nor "long" is appropriate for discussions of English *phonemic* distinction. Similar caricature considerations hold for consonants. Here, for example, the consonants of *at/ate, add/aid*, and *am/aim* may be either exploded (released) or imploded (unreleased, often "swallowed"); either final-position manifestation is a *caricature* of the relevant phoneme abstraction /t/, /d/, or /m/. An interesting corollary to the caricature premise is *intradialectal individuation,* which permits the classification of speakers according to dialect on one linguistic level, while distinguishing idiolectal (or other lectal) independence on another level. For example, there are as many versions of "Black English" as there are black *speakers* of English, and there is no way to enumerate all Black-English *dialects* or calculate respective black-dialect populations or any other lectal populations (see Pugh, below, citing Truby, 1966–75 lecture series).

My observations and conclusions are, then, that as intellectual matters stand, there is presently no unequivocal way to define the term *dialect,* nor to normalize any concept associated with the term, whether the reference is professional or otherwise. In fact, there is no viable professional consensus regarding this aforesaid-nebulous language aspect, which is to say not even among linguisticians. Geographical, political, social, cultural, and linguistic considerations interact and interfere where unambiguous definitions of either *language* or *dialect* or whatever-*lect* are concerned. The criterion of "mutual intelligibility" among all the speakers of each particular language tends to establish a valid, viable, unambiguous inventory of the languages of the world. Were such a complementary criterion imposed that to qualify as independent, given languages must be mutually exclusive, this "common denominator" immediately admits to the classification an uncountable membership of interpersonal oral-aural communication systems presently, historically, or variously traditionally considered dialects, each of which would thus qualify as an independent language. The definition dilemma described above is a secondary indication of the language variation complexity of focal interest to this volume. One has but to consider, additionally, the corpus of terms/concepts/scopes: *patois, creole, sabir, pidgin,* "accent," "foreign accent," *argot, cant, vernacular, lingua franca, jargon, idiom, tongue, brogue,* and other imprecise, ambiguous, specialized, idiomatic, and unintentionally equivocal quasi-categories, such as the ephemeral *jive*, variously, as well as omnifarious *slang*; the ever-productive, unquenchable inventing of *neologisms* (e.g., my *prenate* for "unborn baby"); and *borrowings* (e.g., *glasnost, perestroika*) (sec, e.g., Carver, *History*). What are "related varieties" for some speakers would be mutually unintelligible for speakers in other areas or of other persuasions. Language variation implies both system and user. Nothing, of course, can guarantee absolute, unambiguous information exchange, considerations of which universality are beyond the scope—but not inference—of this essay.

My own demonstrations of interdialectal differences for Sweden and its twenty-four usually dialectally distinctive provinces at one extreme[5] (Uppsala, 1956–62) and, at the other, for the numerous Black English varieties (Stockholm, Berkeley, Miami, 1955–75) materialized in a 1968 paper entitled "Dialectal Variance Interferes with Reading Instruction" (Smith and Truby) and in my 1971 recording produced for Harper & Row, of nine major United States dialect versions of oral test materials accompanying the 1971 Smith-Truby phone discrimination tests. Students using these dialect-keyed materials register statistically higher test scores when the "phone-discrimination" test lists are presented to them in their own dialects. In 1970, Ed Arahill, perennial Greater Miami high school principal father of eight, at the time of his doctoral dissertation, whose thesis fieldwork I supervised in the sixties, also demonstrated that oral tests presented to students by teachers sharing respective student dialects elicited demonstrably higher test scores as contrasted with scores under cross-dialectal conditions. In 1973, Lee Pugh, an indigenous American English speaker and teacher of English, French, and Spanish, presented for his dissertation field-taped recordings for the dialectal assessments of white and black male junior high school students, by twenty-six (13 white, 13 black) male and female, young-to-old, junior high school teachers and found that the teachers universally made stereotyped, bigoted, educationally damaging judgments of students' academic abilities—on the sole basis of language features hypothetically reflecting racial-social characteristics. Pugh knew his topic firsthand and well, and his fieldwork emphasized the grossness of the ambiguous cliché "Black English" all too familiarly—and ignorantly—perpetuated then as now by American school boards, school system administrators, school teachers, and the media countrywide. He proved an exceptionally qualified doctorand, whose particular pluridialectal and polylingual repertory substantiated his especial awareness of the versatilities of language, in both linguistic and social implication.

For an example of stellar "dialect detection," the authentic historical prototype for Professor Henry Higgins of George Bernard Shaw's 1912

Pygmalion (and its 1956 musical successor, *My Fair Lady*), was the nineteenth- and turn-of-the-century British phonetician Professor Henry Sweet, Shaw's close personal friend and a master dialectologist who could identify the precise neighborhood and livelihood of any British speaker on the basis of his or her phonetic performance. Sweet's was a cross-dialectal, dialect-distinguishing linguistic awareness of those speech particulars indicating the speaker's *communalect* (Truby, "American," 1954–78; "Language," 1990). Other dialectologists of exceptional phonetic acuity have demonstrated similar abilities to pinpoint precisely where individual speakers hail from, or, alternatively, the relevant parental influence. (In my Kiel 1954–55, Swedish 1955–62 lecture series, I cited several such "publicly performing phoneticians" of my personal acquaintance, 1946–54, as Henry Lee Smith, Charles K. Thomas, Miles L. Hanley, Allan Hubbell, Marshall Berger, Raven I. McDavid, Jr., and others, whose radio shows or other public demonstrations featured extemporaneous dialect-detection. (See Truby, "Voice Recognition" 241, 1971.)

A final word about the effects of orthography, as of grammar, upon idiolect: it is demonstrable that each speaker is phonetically unique, and complexly unique in other linguistic aspects.[6] It is also evident that each literate individual has a unique interpretation of the special correlation of letter(s) with speechsound, throughout all idiolectal output and perception. Explanation of this fact lies in the premise that for every speaker-listener, letters—like phonemes—are but psychological caricatures merely *representative* of speechsound. That is, read letters elicit individualistic speechsound correlates of the order of phoneme category for each speaker-listener, yet each utterance is a complex product of phonetic context compounded by idiosyncrasy.

And as to that "English look," easily a most distinctive characteristic of the English language is its orthography. Clearly, although there is undeniably a slow and essentially surreptitious spelling alteration process constantly under way, the "curious spellings" some critics accuse our traditional orthographic forms of having are not only of instructive historical significance but of exceptional identificatory-function service. The semantic domains of the forms *right*, *write*, *rite*, *wright*, and *Wright* are instantaneously obvious; were these all respelled *riet* or *ryt* or even *rite*, the "English flavor" would evanesce. Our traditional spelling is as much a part of our language as is our traditional pronunciation "standard" (with all its alternants) or our traditional formal grammar, perhaps more so, but it admittedly contributes colossally to the language variation aspect of our language, as analogously for any other literate language.

But don't feel *bad* (for erroneous *feel badly*) about our English. Its very complexity, diversity, open-endedness is its especial trademark—its colophon. "American English" is a primary cultural attribute of the diversiform and egocentric "American people"—just as idiolect is a primary aspect of human individuality.

A highly significant observation about language and human conduct is that, except for the inclusion of, or in .the case of, memorized passages, no speaker of any language, however competent, knows precisely what he or she is "going to say next" in spontaneous speech—that is, regarding choice of word(s), emphasis schedule, intonation, pronunciation specificity, grammar consistency or acceptability, or even "meaning" as a subjective-objective compromise. The mature vocabulary is of such magnitude, dimension, versatility, ambiguity, redundancy, and freedom—randomness—of access that it allows for and permits incalculable, unpredictable permutations and combinations of linguistic events. This very extemporaneity is by definition the primary catalyst for language variation. In fact, the single, absolute consistency about language—*any* language—is its flux—its continuously changing flow, due almost exclusively to the inherent inconsistencies and dissimilarities of its users. Nor is there an ideal-form of any language, no *Hochsprache*, no absolute standard. For those wondering how many speak "the King's English" (or "the Queen's English")—or "the Kaiser's German," the answer is, Only one king or queen or kaiser at a time . . . and *no*body else.

Notes

[1] The spectrogram is a tangible, measurable, permanent, visual-mode registration of the instrumental conversion of audible speech to a visible-form pattern correlate. Displayed in spectrogram format are the spectral-frequency components of vowels, the spectral rangings and modifications of consonants, phonation (vocal-cord excursions—see note 2), intonation (fundamental-frequency flux), speech-signal relative intensities, hiatuses, and other interrelated phonetic features (e.g., "vowel color," unit emphasis or prominence and deemphasis, pauses and occlusions, and corollary features of voicing, nasality, aspiration, voicelessness, voice onset, voice decay, transitions, and phonetic assimilations and accommodations). The patterns displayed in spectrogram form are the acoustic correlates of the fluxing vocal-tract speechsound resonances, as determined by interfunctional articulatory-anatomical particulars of the tongue, teeth, lips, and so forth that shape the interconnected oral, pharyngeal, and nasal air-chambers.

[2] In technical speech physiology, *voice* (voiced, voicing, etc.) specifies the *quasi-periodic* speechsound source, at the glottis, of *phonation* (itself defined as "rapid, [quasi-] periodic opening and closing of the glottis through separation and apposition of the vocal cords which, accompanied by breath under lung pressure, constitute a

source of vocal sound" (*Random House Dictionary of the English Language*, 1st and 2nd eds., entry written by Truby; the *Webster's Third* definition is inadequate); that is, voice generation per se is the almost-periodic train of lung-air releases that actually constitute the *fundamental frequency* of voicing and is *not* due to "vibration" of the vocal cords (historically, *musculi vocales*; later, *cordae vocales* and thus *vocal cords*, but often, in recent years, speciously "updated" as "vocal bands [or folds or lips]" and other "speech scientist" contrivances and misconstructions), the physical facts of laryngeal mechanism being that the only relevance to voice (phonation) of the physiological function of these membranous muscle *phonators* (by whatever name) is to release an apparently periodic (hence the psychoperceptual illusion of "pitch") vocal sound source. In short, the very pulsations of lung air *are* the voice fundamental (see Truby, *Speechprint Spectrograms*, in extenso, sec. 74—as first published in 1959).

The misidentification of voice with "*vocal cord* vibration" appears in such familiar dictionaries as *Webster's Ninth New Collegiate Dictionary* (1983), *Webster's Third New International Dictionary* (1966 on), *The American Heritage Dictionary* (1969), Funk and Wagnalls *Standard College Dictionary* (1966), *A Dictionary of Linguistics* (1954), *A Grand Dictionary of Phonetics* (1981), and others, any and all of which "authorities" could have consulted such a classical work as the 550-page *The Mechanism of the Larynx* (Negus, 1929) for such gems as "That the laryngeal sounds are not due to vibrations of the vocal ligaments themselves is common knowledge. . . . It is cutting of the air current into rhythmical puffs . . . which is the important factor" (368); "The vocal cord itself is extremely extensible and could not alone be of any use in respiration or phonation" (458); "The vocal cords as a whole are elastic, and if blown apart by increase of air pressure in the trachea they tend to come together again. If the air pressure remain[s] constant, and at a suitable level, the action will recur at rhythmical intervals, and an audible tone will be produced" (459).

[3] An entry for *voiceprint* appears in *The American Heritage Dictionary* of 1969, with especial note of individual speaker characteristics, and in *The Random House Dictionary* of 1987 and *The Random House College Dictionary* of 1968.

My term *speechprint* (Truby 1975, 1989, 1990) is an apt and accurate replacement for *voiceprint*, and I have introduced it into the transcripts of a dozen or more federal speaker-identification trials and elsewhere. This is its initial launching in a publication of this magnitude.

[4] *Homophones* ("same sound") are pronounced alike but spelled differently, as fort/forte; cart/carte; bridal/bridle; you/yew/ewe; *homonyms* ("same name") are both pronounced alike and spelled alike, as *bear* (ursa) / *bear* (carry) / *bear* (endure); *break* (vb.) / *break* (n.); *run* (fast) / *run* (for office) / *run* (operate) / and many more *runs*. Homophones, as described here, are often miscalled *homonyms*, which error renders both terms ambiguous and ineffective.

[5] In contrast to "native speakers" of North American English, native users of the usually "mutually exclusive dialects (?)" of these twenty-four historically independent Swedish provinces also speak regionally specific varieties of "native Swedish," making for a most complicated linguistic assessment and status quo. Similarly complicated linguistic circumstances obtain in many another of our planet's language communities.

[6] 1993 addendum: In proofing the final galley, I have recalled a 1966 mention of *idiolect* by a longtime colleague for whom I spoke on this topic in 1960 at Queens College: "Despite an apparent conformity to group or regional usage, each individual [has] certain speech patterns—subtle variations of pronunciation, vocabulary, and syntax—that are uniquely his [or her] own. The [sum total, for a speaker] of these individual characteristics is [termed] an *idiolect*." So wrote (as slightly edited by me) Arthur Bronstein, Berkeley emeritus professor of speech, in "The Pronunciation of English," his prefatorial article (xxiii–xxiv) for the first edition and the college edition of *The Random House Dictionary of the English Language*, for which I have served since 1964 as phonetics consultant (1st ed., 1966; 2nd ed., 1987; college ed., 1968; etc.). (I may have [unintentionally] overlooked similar statements by others.)

When Students Collect Data: Ethics, Cooperation, Self-Discovery, and Variation in Linguistic and Cultural Behavior

Boyd Davis, University of North Carolina, Charlotte

LANGUAGE variation itself is inherently interesting and relatively easy to notice. What is hard is to progress from noticing variation to describing it systematically, then separating observation from interpretation, and, finally, examining what language is and how its intricacy demands special care in investigations of variation. Because variation is intimately related to the way we identify or classify other speakers, we must, when we collect data on language variation, be sensitive to our responsibilities as we subconsciously link our previous assumptions about the speakers and the data we are studying.

When students first notice variation in spoken language, they seldom consider how that variation reflects regional, social, ethnic, or gender influence. Their initial discussions of variation reveal that each of them has unexamined notions of a norm or standard of usage, about which they have developed quite firm, if previously untested, attitudes. Their surprise comes in discovering not only that they have a set of firm convictions but that these convictions often conflict with those of other class members.

The students' surprise is genuine. Asking students to do research in variation thus promotes their thinking about ethics and their responsibility to other human beings and pushes them to examine their previously untested assumptions. Whether we are teaching linguistics or composition or literature, evoking this sort of critical thinking about language and its speakers leads students to collect their data in a responsible manner. The assignments that follow have this in common: they help students confront their own assumptions and the important ethical issues associated with gathering linguistic data.

Because I teach at a comprehensive university, I offer one or more courses in freshman composition or technical writing each semester as well as upper-division and master's-level linguistics courses. An assignment I devise for introducing a particular methodological or theoretical point to a linguistics class becomes a writing assignment for the technical writing group; the research my freshmen do on usage by taping radio sportscasters becomes

data that my graduate students can analyze in greater detail. The assignments for each class are tailored to include a way for the students to look at
questions about the ethics of collecting the data.

Privacy in a Collaborative Project

The linguist in the field collecting data from human beings operates under
a conventional code of ethics. The privacy of speakers is not to be jeopard-
ized. Their wishes are to be respected. Investigators whose work is funded
by grants or contracts must have their data-collection methods reviewed by
university committees before budgets can be submitted. Their field may be
a village in New Guinea, a neighborhood in New York City, or a classroom
in New Zealand; the linguist can be taping, filming, or taking notes, but the
same principle applies: *Primum, non nocere* (First, don't harm).

Students we work with must observe the same code of ethics. The most
effective way I have discovered to familiarize students with the ethical code
that governs professional researchers is to have them participate in collaborative teams with real, if limited, research. The limits are, of course, the length
of time—part or all of a semester—that we will have together and the depth
or paucity of resources that I can bring to bear on their questions. If they
are to achieve the autonomy of thought and the delight in research I wish
for them, then I must model for them, coach them, respond to them, and,
ultimately, get out of their way.

In devising assignments that enable the students to confront issues
such as the privacy of the speaker, there is a risk, the same risk I face
whenever I elicit data. I cannot allow the students to approach this jeopardy
unknowingly. I am not talking about the hazards of evaluation or grading
here—though that is another ethical dimension in establishing a mode of
collaborative research with students. Nor am I talking about the possible
danger in having my role or authority as a magister diminished, for I have
never found that to be an issue. Rather, the point is that one does not plunge
students into situations involving people and the language they use without
reviewing the ways those people—and the students—could be embarrassed
or harmed.

Because it is not always possible to invite a class of thirty to fifty students
to collaborate directly in an ongoing project or to arrange internships, I use
my own research as an example, asking the students to identify the areas in
which I must ask permission or protect privacy. As they begin to unravel the
ethical dilemmas I face, they prepare themselves to separate observation

from interpretation, description from explanation. We begin to select something we can study together for a short time, based on the mundane features of the school culture we share at our university, and then we move on to projects that include the communities the students come from.

For example, I have been working with speech therapists at our area school for multiply handicapped children. One of our collaborative projects was a weekly conversation circle for nonverbal students, which we videotaped. But first we obtained permission from school administrators and parents, and from the children as well, to make the tapes. Before my students in a recent language acquisition class could view the tapes and begin learning how to make field notes on a particular child, parents were again asked for permission. Each college student signed an agreement protecting the privacy of each child and the privacy of the tapes and field notes.

Signing the agreement made each college student more sensitive to issues of privacy and to children whose communication they would learn to chart. The first tapes introduced variation and code switching. Some of the seven children used American Sign Language in varying degrees, others used synthesizers programmed for words and phrases in Spoken American Voice chip, others spoke regional or social dialects of American English; one used all three languages. One child's first expressive language was Signed English learned in a different part of the country; another's first receptive and expressive language until 1986 was Farsi. The conversation circle was devised to promote greater conversational competencies. As the circles have continued, the participants have increased their abilities in whatever language they prefer and have begun learning some of the others. But that is another story for another time, and the field notes taken by the college students will continue to contribute to that story.

The college students knew that their field notes would be used by the therapists, the teachers, and the parents of the children, whose privacy was zealously protected. The speech therapists and I deliberately included the college students in our collaborative work: What better way to introduce students in a language acquisition class to variation than to expose them to seven courageous conversationalists? And since logistics would not allow the college students on site, the tapes had to be the entry point.

The Campus as Cultural Context

What follows are several exercises that gradually involve students with progressively more difficult fieldwork situations. That is, students must look at how they observe as opposed to how they interpret a situation, and they must also begin to identify ethical dimensions for their own activities as researchers. The exercises can be used in a sequence or can stand alone.

The Walk-About is an exercise that prompts students to examine their degree of comfort with the notion of watching or listening to people. We do this exercise early in the term, as it sets up a number of other assignments. After spending five minutes asking students to identify campus locales where people congregate and talk, I distribute note cards and ask each student to go to one of those places; they must make notes on five cards—openly—of what they see and hear. They must remain in one locale for five minutes, fill up all the note cards I have handed them, and then return to class.

When they return to class, I ask them to remain silent in order to write for five minutes about their experience. They describe the locale and give what they thought was the context for the speaking interactions they observed or heard. They comment on how closely they felt they could approach the speakers, how comfortable they felt while taking notes, and what reactions their note-taking evoked or seemed to evoke.

Next they divide a sheet of paper into two columns, one for recording directly observed or heard data and the other for entering interpretations and questions, and fill in the columns from information on their cards. Only then may they talk. Their questions and their reactions help them identify issues of privacy and confidentiality. They are primed to discuss different methodologies for collecting data and see their notes as texts that can be critiqued just as one might analyze a poem.

The classroom itself can serve as a locale for collecting data. Just as we have "found poetry" in our verbal environment, we have "found variation" in the pieces of paper distributed in class. One semester I seized on an unplanned opportunity and used my class syllabus to show students that variation can be found in written texts. The first occasion for the exercise happened by accident; the second time I set the situation up deliberately. Currently I use this exercise in classes in both linguistics and composition.

Each term I create a syllabus for my linguistics class, carefully listing texts, readings, test and paper dates, goals, and policies. Three years ago, because of a shortfall in supplies in the department, I had to put everything on one page. My class found the result totally incomprehensible and brought syllabi from other courses to the next class meeting to explain to me what they were talking about. They were suddenly faced with ethical questions about data collection when I asked them to go through the syllabi and obliterate any mention of instructor, class, or section before displaying anything or before talking about what they had brought.

In one sense the syllabus is a public document on a campus, operating outside of copyright and functioning as a sort of broadside. Yet it has a quasi-legal status, serving in some instances as a compact. Though issued to students within a class and intended for them, it is clearly the written work of one person. Before discussing how my syllabus might vary from their idea of a norm, they had to establish what that norm might be. What about a syllabus is predictable? What is important or unimportant? What criteria were the students using to interpret syllabi? What typologies were apparent?

Other questions surfaced. How can we detect and describe variation in written texts, and what do we as users of these texts have in common with editors of manuscripts? Are there cues in some syllabi that call up cultural responses for differing disciplines? What do student readers have to decode, reconstruct, and deconstruct in order to use syllabi on a daily basis?

What was "wrong" with my syllabus was the calendar of dates. To save space, I had listed only the days on which tests would be given or papers would be due. The students expected a full, second sheet listing each class meeting—in other words, a semester at a glance. Now each semester I present students with both kinds of calendars; they unanimously prefer the full version even when it lists blank days. In making this choice, they can spot some of their own cultural assumptions about time, space, and document format conventions.

Another classroom-centered activity is a case study using a question log on how directives function in a class they are taking. Cultural constraints surface quickly when students investigate such matters as the time at which my own class is being offered, for this affects how and where they can take notes and underlies a number of assumptions they have about schools and classrooms. My daytime students are usually enrolled in three to five courses; my evening students, however, generally take only one class. They may not have another class in which to observe directives, and frequently they cannot take notes on the job. Their concern about where and how they can take notes often leads to discussions of privacy and confidentiality from the perspective of corporate security. Evening students have to identify class-like situations on their job; they tailor the assignment to fit their working environment, a change in the task that allows us to discuss, with new intensity, the applicability of various elicitation strategies.

Observations of classroom behavior call into question the way we note and interpret what we think we see and hear. Like the others, this exercise is useful only if accompanied by discussion of its implications for the study of language and of ourselves as speakers and researchers. The instructions are minimal and translate well into manager-trainee or supervisor-subordinate situations. Here are the directions for the assignment:

Divide a sheet of paper into three vertical columns and, at the top of the sheet, note the date and time that the log covers. In column 1, note the context in which an instructor asks questions; in column 2, note who else asks questions in what contexts and who answers them. In column 3, note the reactions to the interchange you observe in any particular student or group of students. Use as many three column sheets as you need; participate, observe, and record the class for one week or the equivalent of three hours. On each day that you collect information, write a brief reflection or summary that discusses changes you see in your ability to observe, record, and interpret information. You may wish to reexamine previous summaries or question-log sheets in order to monitor your changes and develop a reflective discussion.

While the instructions may be minimal, their implementation is not. Students must decide on their own if they wish to ask permission of the instructor or the students; generally they find themselves bombarded by the problems surrounding questions and directives and realize that there are syntactic and pragmatic cues in a question-and-answer situation that lie beyond the scope of the original assignment. Writing a three-part case study of a class or of their work helps the students focus on their own questions about language, variation, and methodology. And the case study does something else: it allows the students to identify both their assumptions and their errors as a part of learning about becoming members of the community of researchers. Such a lesson may be even more important than finding out that directives can be very complicated.

Part 1 of the final written report of this case study is a two-page overview of students' preliminary findings, in which students tabulate and chart whatever they have found. In part 2 they analyze the kinds of assumptions, interpretations, and attitudes that the assignment has identified for them. Part 3 is an appendix: their notes, drafts, and log sheets. Completing the week of note-taking for a question log really takes two weeks: classes get canceled; emergencies arise. In a linguistics class, this exercise is an informative warm-up that helps students focus early in the term both on their choice of a more extended research project and on the ways in which quantitative and qualitative analyses are linked. Directives, "teacher talk," and school cultures are also fine topics for composition classes; technical writers can explore the role of writing in the job setting as well.

I often use the question log assignment as a way to build collaborative research communities within the class, regardless of which class it might be. I deliberately set aside some class time during each of the two weeks students are doing the logging for them to meet in groups of four or five to exchange comments, complaints, and drafts. I ask them to exchange names and telephone numbers; I tell them to elect a parliamentarian who will make sure that nobody talks for more than five minutes without polling the group for permission. I ask the parliamentarian to give me the list of questions the group can't solve for itself and wants me to answer. Those questions will tell me what I must emphasize in my next presentation. Creating that list of questions forces the group to focus on its task. If the class meets for an hour on Monday, Wednesday, and Friday, Friday is a good day for this activity, with thirty minutes allocated for the students to work with each other. The instructor should get out of their way so they can ask for help. It is often useful for the students to meet for a third time to review each other's final drafts of the case studies before turning them in. This session allows each group to report to the whole body on the questions they encountered and the answers they decided on.

Another useful group activity that gives practice in devising research questions on variation is to work with the process of writing and evaluating abstracts. Once students have completed a question log, they are painfully aware of all the errors that they have made, particularly after meeting in small groups to discuss their work. They know now what they wished they had known when they started. Ask them to write a one-page abstract that has three parts: part 1 identifies the question about classroom or management directives that the student would like to investigate; part 2 explains how this question should be studied; part 3 presents the rationale for looking at this question. Ask the students to bring the unsigned abstract to class.

For this activity, provide anonymity to student writers by assigning them letters of the alphabet or numbers to use instead of signatures on their abstracts. Depending on the physical layout of the classroom, devise a way for students to pass the abstracts to each other. Provide them with scoring sheets on which they record their reactions to each other's abstracts. Allow, one minute for the reading of each abstract, with the instructor serving as timekeeper to tell students to stop, score, and pass the abstract along. This activity is, of course, a simulation of grant proposal evaluation, so criteria will need to be provided for reading and evaluating the abstracts on a 1–5 scale. Class and instructional priorities may require calculation of means, medians, standard deviations, and other quantitative measures.

Maps, Names, and Cultural Variation

Whether students work in collaborative groups or independently, they find informative a study of urban and suburban street names, beginning with a city map provided by a local realtor. Most such maps are divided into squares or rectangles; students select a section whose street names they will investigate. Here they will interview residents, thereby collecting speech samples that lead the class into discovering other forms of variation rather easily. But before students can venture forth, they must discuss several issues. Should the class first experiment with checklists rather than conversational interviews? How will the investigators introduce themselves and display their sincerity? Must they ask their sources for permission to tape or write down their answers? What if the source calls in friends or relatives? How do the students determine whether their sources are reliable? And once they have acquired some data, how can they defend the ways in which they elicited it?

For example, Shannon Park is a community keyed to a subdivision developed near our university. Irish-sounding street names proliferate (*Shamrock, Tipperary, Dunlavin*), but they are mixed with names from J. M. Barrie's *Peter Pan* (*Tinker Bell*) and a collection of names that may represent both women and flora (*Ruth, Rose*). Was the developer Irish? How many residents have Irish connections? Interviews with local residents have turned up little: the area has high mobility, and "old-timers" who still own businesses they started years ago are few; many have been replaced by Golden Arches, office buildings, parking lots, and so on. Questions to city planning offices have revealed that the area was developed in several stages. The original name was keyed to a family-owned farm that was sold for development, and the floral and women's names are often family names from a predevelopment stage. No class has been able to chart the full history of the development, at least during one short semester. New highway connections have been made since I first used this assignment, and franchise names have become the landmarks. Now students find it interesting to discover that their questions are different from those asked by their predecessors a mere decade earlier.

When students work on these kinds of projects, they find themselves ransacking the library for anything by William Labov, Dell Hymes, Ralph W. Fasold, Walt Wolfram, Donna Christian, Shirley Brice Heath, Courtney Cazden, Lesley Milroy and James Milroy, Crawford Feagin, or Charles A. Ferguson they can get their hands on. They report that James P. Spradley's *Participant Observation* explains to them the practical aspects of doing field research, just as recent studies of conversation or current articles in *Language and Society, American Speech*, or *English Today* expand the context of the projects they have begun. The questions the students ask when considering how best to collect data responsibly are the queries that lead them to examine the methodology used, the findings reported, and the underlying assumptions about language and variation.

Learning from Dictionaries

Frederic G. Cassidy, University of Wisconsin, Madison

EVERYBODY knows what a dictionary is, in a vague way, but not enough users realize what a tremendous lot of information is compacted into the one or more volumes, or what generations of scholarship and practical ingenuity have gone into its preparation. The approach of most dictionary readers is immediate and limited. They want to check on a spelling, a meaning, a grammatical point, or (bless them!) an etymology or historical source. That is what they do with the dictionary, and it is perfectly legal. But they are not really using the dictionary. For that, one has to have more than a momentary interest. The true reader of dictionaries is the person who, having (like everyone else) a question to be answered, gets out the book and starts leafing toward the proper place but does not get to it directly—perhaps not at all. This reader's track is a zigzag, like the flight of a bee, ranging here and there but not methodically. Among so many kinds of flowers the temptation to sample is irresistible. They all furnish nectar and wax—what Matthew Arnold called "sweetness and light"—and the supply is inexhaustible.

So this poor wight (see under *W*), leafing along toward, let's say, *eschew* or *hebetude*, spots a picture of an *oryx* or a *festoon* and pauses to learn about it. Or else the corner of his eye catches the letter combination *spl-*, which runs down from *splash* to *splatter* to *splenetic*, all of which stir his curiosity. Or up comes a cross-reference with the mysterious abbreviation "*cf.* this" or "*cf.* that," which needs to be explained. So the obedient reader looks up the list of abbreviations and finds that *cf.* is short for Latin *confer*, which means *see further*, and such knowledge starts another chase. A "true reader" really enjoys the dictionary, has fun with it, rides it like a pet horse, builds up the Scrabble muscles, gets his or her money's worth out of it.

Dictionaries have to be of different sizes, from pocket size up to the multivolume, according to the user's need. For most people, most of the time, a medium-sized one-volume book, easily portable for quick look-up and for playing word games, will have most of the words they want and a great many more than they would probably ever use. But that's where the "money's worth" begins. Within the limits of its size, a good one-volume dictionary gives an astonishing amount of information. The basics are spelling, pronunciation, grammar (part of speech), etymology (historical source), meaning or meanings, and some indication of the word's status in use.

Familiarity with these elements is, of course, essential if we are really to understand the word and use it appropriately.

The *headword* under which this information is listed is given in the currently accepted "standard" spelling. Readers who want to know how people spelled a word in past times must go to a much larger, historical dictionary with dated entries, such as the big *Oxford*, of which the first edition has twelve volumes plus four supplementary ones. If a portable, medium-sized book does not have the information they need, they can consult the big one. It covers the English language from Anglo-Saxon beginnings to its present worldwide use. There is so much in it that even experienced readers find it difficult going. For most people, the medium-sizer is enough.

How do lexicographers (dictionary makers) decide what words to put in and what to leave out? The language has had, and lost, many thousands of words, formerly common, now no longer used. They have become fossils, historical curiosities. The useful contemporary dictionary will try to include all the words now or recently current that anyone would be likely to look up. How recent? A rule of thumb says, anything used in the past hundred years. But the closer we get to the present moment, the more difficult it becomes to decide. New words are popping up every day; many writers invent or concoct words as a feature of their style; new inventions, methods, discoveries, attitudes, and happenings become facts of contempory life and have to be named. The dictionary cannot possibly put everything in. Further-more, those new words are of uncertain viability; many will disappear in a short time, others in a few years; yet others will have come to stay. The lexicographer has to estimate future trends and omit the probably ephemeral words. For the most recent words and meanings there are *The Third Barnhart Dictionary of New English* (Barnhart) and the Merriam *Twelve Thousand New Words*.

Since some words have more than one accepted spelling—with the variants about equally frequent in use—the spelling of both or all should be recorded. Examples are *forbade–forbad* (an older and a newer form), *scull— skull* (in boating), and (in the big Merriam-Webster's *Third New International*) triple variants, *piggyback*, *pickaback*,, and *pig-a-back*, which represent slight differences of pronunciation associated with different ways of interpreting or understanding the word.

When such variants are given, it must be understood that they are equally acceptable. A second or third spelling would not be given unless it occurred about as often as the first. Word-frequency counts help the lexicographer decide which form to enter first, but when the tallies are roughly the same, the older form is usually given precedence (as in the case of *forbade*) as the more "conservative." Writers using the dictionary may choose between alternative spellings according to their own stylistic taste or purposes.

It is probably most often in regard to pronunciation that people misunderstand and misuse the dictionary. They assume that there is only one "right" way to pronounce words and that the dictionary is a sort of judge, exercising linguistic laws to condemn mispronunciations. For them what the dictionary prints has the force of gospel truth. Such commandments are not what modern scientific dictionaries try to write. It is true that the pronunciation or pronunciations given are intended to represent a kind of standard. But since pronunciations, even those of educated speakers, vary widely throughout the world, the dictionary maker has to choose. For whom is the book intended? Users in England, in America, foreigners learning English? What shall it recognize—British differences, Canadian, Australian? Limitations of space again come into play: the prevailing differences of pronunciation among educated speakers in one nation or another may be given; beyond that, only conspicuous variants. But a modern dictionary's pronunciation is descriptive—it does not tell the reader how he or she *should* pronounce. Nor can it record all the variant ways in which a word *is* pronounced. For example: British *prĭvacy*, American *prīvacy*; British *med's'n*, American *medis'n*; British *coróllary*; American *córollary*. If one wants greater detail, there are pronouncing dictionaries—in Britain, Daniel Jones's, in the United States, John Kenyon and Thomas Knott's. If you are looking for folk speech or regional differences, that's, as they say, a whole nother ball game: consult the *Dictionary of American Regional English*, edited by Cassidy. It does not at present go beyond the letter *H*, but it covers the whole country, and more volumes are in preparation.

In indicating pronunciation, each dictionary has its own scheme, which will be found somewhere in the book, usually in the introduction. More scholarly dictionaries approximate the International Phonetic Alphabet, and the middle-size are moving in that direction. Whatever the scheme favored, it is essential that the user find it and apply it; otherwise the information about pronunciation is sure to be misunderstood.

Dictionaries generally record the part of speech, or grammatical class of each word, as it stands in the present state of the language. But the English language is subject to easy variation, and even the best writers, with a sensitive feel for what is acceptable, may use a word as a part of speech it has never been used as before. This is especially evident in the way English can shift back and forth between verbal and nominal uses and has been doing so ever since it lost a distinctive inflectional system late in Anglo-Saxon times—and the practice is increasing nowadays. *Talk* as a verb came into English in the thirteenth century; in the fifteenth it also became a noun, and both are quite normal today, though the first time the word was used as a noun it must have seemed a bit strange. *Tail*, an old Germanic word, is a noun in the earliest Anglo-Saxon records; it did not come in as a verb till the seventeenth century, but once in, the usage became fully established. Today we are quite accustomed to having detectives or secret service people *tailing* their victims.

The earliest record of *syllable* as an English noun is found in Chaucer's late-fourteenth-century use; it did not become a verb till the early seventeenth, when Milton writes of "airy tongues that syllable men's names." Such shifts or "conversions," now commonplace, may be deliberately used as elements of style. Under sensitive control, functional shifts can be very effective; they can also produce blundersome results. Other converted parts of speech, in effect new words, include adjective to noun: "a serious *dry*"; preposition to noun: "an *in* with the management"; noun to adjective: "a *fun* party"; and so on. Such conversions are easy to make, but the dictionary can record only those that have become accepted in general usage.

There is nothing intrinsically wrong with new words. In a changing, developing world we need them. Many will be attempted: those that prove really useful will survive. A recent example is the word *hopefully* in the sense of "it is to be hoped" or "I hope": "Hopefully I can finish this job today." It had appeared occasionally from the 1930s forward; then suddenly in the 1960s it began to pop up everywhere. Puristic critics, always suspicious of any novelty or vogue, strongly condemned it. One writer in the *New York Times*, which holds up a high standard of usage, enclosed the term in quotation marks as if it smelled bad. Certainly he did not accept it fully. However, *hopefully* in this sense has proved so useful and has been adopted so widely in following years that some former critics have recanted; only the most conservative still object to it, and it has spread from the United States to Britain, Australia, and other parts of the English-speaking world. It may now be considered established in acceptable usage.

Nowadays we are less afraid of neologisms than in former centuries. Foreigners producing pseudo-English expressions are a source of humor to native speakers, and some natives can blunder ludicrously, but those who have a sensitive feel for the language can produce effective and acceptable new words.

An important guide for full understanding of the meaning of a word is its etymology—its historical source, where it came from and how it developed—generally given in middle-sized and larger dictionaries. Some words retain their original meaning closely; very few ever lose all connection with it. Because English began as a Germanic language, the majority of its basic words are of that origin: *head, foot, body, arm; strong, weak, great, small; love, hate, land, sea,* and thousands more. They form the core; not many have been displaced by later acquisitions. The French words brought in with the Norman Conquest and after are the only other body of terms to become deeply planted, especially short words of everyday occurrence, such as *chief, corps, brace, fort, grand, voyage*—in frequency of use, only one step behind the Anglo-Saxon vocabulary.

Latin words began coming into English with Christianity—*deacon, altar, Satan,* and others—and continued down the years also in secular uses into the Renaissance and later. As such words became common, new ones were formed with the addition of Latin prefixes and suffixes. Since Latin was the first language of education, these derived words, competing with the native Germanic words, carry an air of importance and, at their best, dignity that the simpler words may not have. Compare Anglo-Saxon *strength,* French *power,* Latin *potency*—with their decided though subtle differences of implication.

The growing influence of Latin as the language of the church and of law led to sometimes false latinization of earlier words: Anglo-Saxon *igland* became modern *island* under the influence of Latin *insula,* to which it is unrelated historically. Similarly, the word *soldier* came into English in the thirteenth century from Old French *soudier* (a fighting man paid with *sous*), but by the next century, under the influence of Latin *solidus* and *solidarius,* it acquired the *l,* which it has preserved ever since. (Incidentally, the pronunciation without *l* can still be heard and is colloquially spelled *soger.*) To know the origin and development of a word can add greatly to our appreciation and effective use of it.

Many dictionaries include lists of synonyms, or words of closely similar meaning, as in *strength, power,* and *potency* noted above. These have a basic similarity of meaning but at the margins they can differ greatly, and no sensitive user of the language would confuse them. In fact, though many meanings come close, it is safe to say that no two words are ever identical. The careful speaker and writer must be perpetually aware of this. Good definitions show the core of similarity and the shades of difference among words; synonymies come closer by putting the words side by side.

Dictionaries pay attention in another way to the differing colors or weights of words—specifically, the types of speakers who use or avoid them, the occasions on which they are ordinarily used, the kinds of discourse to which they are appropriate. Such indication is usually done with usage labels, which vary according to the editors' purpose. A prescriptive dictionary— common in the latter eighteenth and the nineteenth centuries—sought to warn the reader against usages considered unsuitable to elegant, careful, upper-class, or literary style. Labels often used were *illiterate, vulgar, low, cant, dialectal, provincial.* With the rise of general education, prohibitions of this kind have been greatly moderated. The former literary or written standard has been adjusted toward an educated colloquial standard: usage labels are less threatening. Nevertheless, words cannot be rightly used without respect to context: plain objects such as "shoes and ships and sealing-wax" may need no more than a plain definition, but for a great many others a guiding label of some sort is clearly necessary. Usage labels that appear frequently today are *colloquial* (which many people confuse with *local*), *dialectal* (which is still widely taken as condemnatory even when not intended so), and *slang*, which is the most difficult to define and therefore tends to become a catchall for anything nonstandard. Conservative publications with an ear for style hold to a less colloquial level, but stories and plays that depict speakers of all social levels and types must represent their speech accurately—and the dictionary that does its descriptive duty and aims at a wide body of users must put in all kinds of language and must label entries appropriately. Careful editorial notes are often added when space can be afforded.

Finally, of course, and of prime importance, are the definitions. The writing of definitions is both a discipline and an art. The discipline consists in extracting the senses of a word or phrase by collecting, comparing, and digesting actual examples of its use and working out ways—sometimes formulas—for stating the result. The familiar formula "of or pertaining to" appears as early as 1623, in Henry Cockeram's *English Dictionarie*: "*Locall*. Of, or belonging to a place." This and other established methods of concise statement enable the definer to come neatly to the point.

Defining as an art requires that one find an accurate synonym or a paraphrase that describes the thing referred to, usually in simpler terms, and says neither more nor less than necessary to do so. Dr. Johnson's often derided definition of *network* is an example of Homer nodding: "*Network*. Anything reticulated or decussated at equal distances, with interstices between the intersections." The familiarity of the word and the apparent simplicity of the thing make such a definition seem ludicrously ponderous—like using a sledgehammer to crack a nut. But these lapses on Johnson's part were few. Every so often in the *OED* one finds a definition taken from Johnson's *Dictionary* and repeated verbatim with the simple acknowledgment "Johnson." This is the highest form of praise: James Murray, the editor, is admitting, "I cannot improve on this."

The most often used, apparently most simple, words develop many different senses. A good dictionary normally presents these meanings in a rational sequence that gives due attention to the dates at which each new meaning developed and others died out. The lines of sense development are usually straightforward, the literal meanings coming first and the transferred or metaphorical ones later. But there are some curious exceptions, as in the case of *fast*. This was present in Anglo-Saxon as both adjective and adverb, with the simple meaning of "firm" or "fixed"; the word developed within the period the further sense of "tight," then "vigorous," and ultimately "quick" or "rapid"—the exact opposite of the first sense. Both senses survive today: "Tie it fast" is completely ambiguous out of context.

Some dictionaries list variant meanings not in the order of historical development; but, assuming that the reader is most likely to want the current senses, they give those first and the older meanings later. This "quick lookup" feature may be more convenient for the reader who presumably comes to the desired information sooner, but it does not illustrate as well the chronology of sense development, which shows the life and growth of the word.

Finally, it is safe to say that every user of the language, without exception, can learn from a good dictionary. It is a compendium (see under *C*) of most that is known about the vocabulary or lexicon of a language and usually includes the parts of morphology and syntax reflected in the form of words, the common phrases and collocations into which the words enter, and their stylistic status. We learn our language to a great extent piecemeal, haphazardly, putting it more or less in order as we go. But the structure as a whole does not always emerge clearly: we tend to remain with a jigsaw of partial patterns and missing pieces. The dictionary, intelligently and regularly used, is a great aid to completing the picture, to ordering, enlarging, and refining our command of the language both as speaker and writer. The *maker* of a dictionary, in Dr. Johnson's rueful words, may feel at times like a "harmless drudge," but no *readers* of a dictionary need ever feel that way. Between the two covers of that one book they have, in Christopher Marlowe's phrase, "infinite riches in a little room."

Using Toponymic Onomastics
in a Pedagogical Setting
to Demonstrate Phonological Variation
(An Essay on Names)

Thomas L. Clark, University of Nevada, Las Vegas

NOW, what sort of title is this to put on an article? One would think that the title on an article should be useful to the reader. But this one is like those complex-sounding names on writings designed for specialists. Normal people are not supposed to be able to understand such things, right? If people want to understand what we are talking about, then we have to use words that make sense to the general reader, right?

Actually, I want to make a point with the title of this article: the names that we use (and the title of an article is the *name* of that article) have different functions. Sometimes the function of a name is to identify something, some place, or somebody. At other times, a name is used to hide information or to give information. Let us examine these points more carefully.

First, the function of a name is to identify something. If I want to identify a piece of furniture that has four legs and a seat and a back and is designed for someone to sit on, I use the name *chair*. To identify some place, I may use a common noun like *lake* or a proper noun like *Lake Huron*. And to identify somebody, I may use a common noun like *woman*, a group identifier like *editorial board* or *New Yorker*, or a proper noun like *Connie Chung*.

Second, a name is used to hide or give information—or, more specifically, to give various types and degrees of information. For example, a child in an aboriginal tribe may be given a secret name known only to the shaman and perhaps the child's uncle. In this way no one can ever have power over the bearer of the name. Such a child is then given a public name to be known by the rest of the members of the tribe. Another example of using a name in this fashion is the custom of police departments in large cities to have code names for undercover operations. In the case of either the shaman or the police department, some information is given while other information is withheld.

Now to come back to the name of this article. The title, "Using

Toponymic Onomastics in a Pedagogical Setting to Demonstrate Phonological Variation," is both informative and noninformative. For people who already know the meanings of the phrases "toponymic onomastics," "pedagogical setting," and "phonological variation," the title can be informative (though what we have discussed so far has only a little to do with those phrases). Many readers of this book, however, may not have prior knowledge of these technical terms. For them, a better name, or title, might be something like "Using Place Names in the Classroom to Show Pronunciation Differences." But then I wouldn't have been able to make my point, would I? My point is that the study of names (*onomastics*) can give us insights into the way we use language.

We use different kinds of names for different kinds of functions. We have names for places (toponyms: *gully*, *Deadman's Gulch*), and names for people (*Thomas, Mr. Clark*), names for things generally (*book, cafe*), and names for things specifically (*Moby-Dick, Hard Rock Cafe*). These names help us in our discourse. Depending on how we want to say something, different kinds of naming can help us. If we want to be name-droppers when we discuss fashion, we can use names like *Guess, Bugle Boy, Giorgio, Saks Fifth Avenue, Neiman-Marcus*. Conversely, if we want to transmit another image about fashion, we can mention names like *Penney's, Sears, K-Mart, Mervyn's*.

Discourse refers to the interchange of information that occurs when we talk with or write to other people. But not all the information is transmitted by the words themselves. Very often, the choice of words will help to give information to the listener or reader. On seeing the title I used for this article, the average reader might have thought I was being hoity-toity. I could sniff down my nose at such readers and point out that every term in this title is a perfectly understandable and reasonable word in English. But when I showed you another, simpler way to refer to the same information, then I suggested that the attitude of people who use such titles must arouse suspicions—namely, that those who use complex titles needlessly are perhaps putting on airs. Or in the words of my Irish grandmother, such people are "no better than they should be." This is not to say that the name on an article should never be complex or difficult. In fact, the titles of articles in learned journals are very often complex—and need to be—in order to serve their functions. But the authors of such articles are careful and know specifically who their audiences are.

Another way to look at the phenomenon is to examine the use of your own name. Let me use my name as an example. When I was growing up, most people called me Tommy. I knew at an early age to respond to Aunt Lyda when she called me that. As I became older, I wanted to sound more grown-up, more mature. I responded best to my brothers, who called me

Tom. But when I heard my mother use my complete name in a highfalutin manner, I knew she was doing more than calling me by my name. When she used my full name, I didn't have to suspect I was in trouble: I knew it. She used my name in a way that demonstrated she knew her audience, just as those people who use difficult names on articles know their audiences.

As I matured, I had to decide how best to use my name in formal situations. I tried out different combinations of initials and names, in much the same fashion as most students. Sometimes I longed for additional names and initials so that I could sound slightly mysterious, like K.J.V. Rasmussen, the Danish explorer. At other times I might be tired of my first name and use only the initial and middle name, like T. Boone Pickins, the financier. Many people are satisfied with the names that seem to develop for them, while others experiment with their own names and names of those around them. Hence, one colleague refers to me regularly by my initials because, as she says, they also stand for "tender, loving care." And one young woman I recently interviewed told me that in different parts of the country she is known as Kamy or Velvet because she does not care for her given name, Clara Ann.

The point is that people can manipulate their names and the names of things around them. Sometimes the name has significance, and sometimes it is not significant. *Thomas* is derived from Aramaic (a language spoken by Christ) and means "twin." The fact that I am not a twin illustrates that in our culture the earlier meaning of a name may play no role in the bestowing of personal names. Often, parents use a name because it commemorates a relative. Sometimes they simply like the sound of it, or the popularity of it. This latter point accounts for the cyclic popularity of certain names. In the late 1980s, popular names for children included *Jennifer*, *Tiffany*, and *Caitlin* for girls and *Sean*, *Jason*, and *Zachary* for boys.

The powers of naming and speaking a name are believed by many to be great. In the book of Genesis, we are told of the chore given to Adam to name every creature that crawled, walked, swam, or flew. By doing so, Adam (and presumably by extension all of us) suddenly had dominion over them; in some cultures, the power derived from bestowing names also includes a responsibility to care for those who have been named. Priests, conjurers, magicians, and shamans have long known the importance of using words correctly in prayers, petitions, hexes, and incantations. In fact, the oldest grammar book we know of, Panini's work on Sanskrit, from the fourth century BC, gave rules for the pronunciation of various prayers. Because the vernacular dialects, known as Prakrits, were diverging so much from the language used when Sanskrit served as the standard for scholarly writings, Panini felt obliged to write his grammar to help maintain proper forms in the speech of the educated. Almost two millennia later, Christopher Marlowe has Faustus conjure up Mephistopheles with an incantation using that devil's name. In those Elizabethan days, it was commonly believed that if a devil was called on by his proper name, he had to appear. In Marlowe's play, Mephistopheles tries to downplay this belief by telling Faustus that he was in the neighborhood when Faustus called and decided to drop in. But Marlowe's audience knew better.

From Panini to Marlowe—even today—people have known that appropriate pronunciation of names is important. Thus variation in the way a place name is spoken is often a source of conflict, with local usage generally resolving arguments about correctness. Just as I can determine the appropriate name for myself and give my name the spelling and pronunciation I wish it to have, residents of an area, town, city, or state can determine the appropriate name and pronunciation for the place in which they live. Whenever a group of people must decide on a name and pronunciation, however, there are considerations that an individual does not have to be concerned about when dealing with a personal name. A group of people depend on tradition and often are guided by long-standing use when the word being pronounced is a place name. For example, there are at least two major ways to pronounce the name of my state, Nevada. Westerners generally pronounce the name so that the letter in the second syllable rhymes with *add* (/nɛ 'væ də/), while Easterners often say the name so that the second syllable rhymes with *odd* (/nɛ 'vɑ də/).

People who live in Nevada grew up with the pronunciation they use; in other words, there is a tradition behind it. In addition, the people who use the local pronunciation (which they consider the "correct" one) feel comfortable with others who use this pronunciation—that is, people who pronounce the name of the state the same way they do are regarded as friendlier, more homey and folksy, whereas those who pronounce the name with the middle syllable rhyming with *odd* are regarded as *auslanders*, foreigners. And often people from "out there" are regarded with suspicion, considered city slickers at best, rude and uncaring at worst. Data on attitudes toward the pronunciation of the *a* in *Colorado* parallel what Nevadans feel about the *add* or *odd* pronunciation of this vowel in the name of their state.

Human nature being what it is, most newcomers to both states soon accommodate to the "correct" pronunciation—that is, to the pronunciation used by most westerners. However, some outsiders are understandably proud of their native dialects and are willing to maintain them as best they can regardless of the consequences. Such people either put up with suspicious stares or try to convince the local folk of their sincerity and general harmlessness in other ways. Often they will use humor or self-deprecating comments such as "I'm too old now to be trained" or "Just think of me as an old country boy."

Such suspicion is not restricted to the West. Some people in Missouri feel that down-home folks pronounce the name of their state as "Missour-uh"(/mɪˈzurə/) and that tonier, more up-to-date speakers enforce the pronunciation "Missour-ee", (/mɪˈzuri/) whereas others have the reverse attitude, namely that "Missour-uh"(/mɪˈzɚə/) is the correct pronunciation. Similarly, the pronunciation of Iowa as /ˈaɪ o wey/ is considered rustic or old-fashioned.

Even more often than with states, the names of cities and towns differ in pronunciation according to local usage. And tradition is paramount. Loyal citizens of Spokane, Wooster, Baltimore, Natchitoches, Cairo, La Jolla, Stoughton, and Pend Oreille have their "correct" pronunciations. Some folks are very accommodating. The citizens of New Orleans will accept a variety of pronunciations between /nu ˈor lɪnz/ and /ˈnɑ linz/ but will vociferously reject /nu or ˈlinz/.

The "correct" pronunciation can serve as an attention getter. One insurance firm, for example, spends a great deal of money as it makes a point of advertising nationally that the company name is pronounced in the same fashion as the city it is in: Wausau, Wisconsin.

The consequences of incorrect pronunciation can be great. Nowhere has this fact been more evident than in the Bible, Judges 12.5–6. About thirty-five centuries ago, two groups of people, resembling each other physically and linguistically, were battling near the banks of the Jordan River. The Gileadites had the upper hand and held the fords across the river in that district. Their enemies, the Ephraimites, were fleeing from the victors. Whenever someone came to a ford at the river, the Gileadite soldiers would ask whether the person was an Ephraimite. If the traveler said no, then the soldiers would make the person say the word *shibboleth,* which had two meanings: *shibboleth* "stream" and "head of grain." But Ephraimites pronounced the word in their dialect as *sibboleth* and so were caught. According to the story, forty-two thousand Ephraimites were captured and killed as a result of their response. A high price to pay for mispronunciation! Other accounts in the Bible also reflect the importance of language and pronunciation, from the story of the Tower of Babel, in Genesis 11, to the Galilean accent that gives Peter away, leading him to deny Christ for the third time, in Matthew 26.73.

All the instances of language variation and naming practices and pronunciations have one feature in common: pattern. Sometimes the patterns are very simple, as the addition of -*s* at the end of most nouns to show they are plural in form. But sometimes the patterns are more complex, as children learn if they first try to write an -*s* for plurals of words like *ox* or *man.*

Here are some suggestions for having students look at aspects of names and their pronunciations, along with some suggestions for comparing their answers with those of other people. Any number of questions that might provoke curiosity could be answered by looking at maps or telephone books, asking other people of different age groups, or searching the library. Why, for example, do some cultures use single names to designate people? Why do popular first names for children seem to run in cycles? What are the most common first names in the institution where you teach? How would the students find such information?

In a particular part of the state, which names reflect Indian borrowings, French or Dutch or Basque or other immigration, earlier American settlement, different contemporary language groups? W. Edson Richmond, in an article in 1970, described how the investigation of names leads to a better understanding of the culture itself. Marshall McLuhan advanced the idea of the global village, in which every country has a responsibility for the survival of the world. If the planet is to survive, individuals and nations must understand people from other cultures. Understanding of this sort means more than familiarity with a language or descriptions of political, religious, or economic systems; it entails such notions as what constitutes meaningfulness, and knowledge of the naming processes in a culture can shed light on this concept. What kinds of things are named? How many names are children given? Do names change after important events in life such as marriage, death, rites of passage?

Allen Walker Read ("Challenge") points out that name study is cross-disciplinary and is particularly useful in creating historical awareness. A systematic method for examining patterns in naming is described by Clark ("Environment"). In a series of steps, students interested in naming patterns can move from the familiar territory of personal names to place names and beyond. Since everything from large houseplants to sailboats may be given names, a number of practices can be observed. For example, some forms referring to individuals from specific localities follow simple patterns; others have complex patterns. Describing a person from a city or state that ends in *-on* might seem simple: *Washingtonian, Oregonian, Bostonian*. Notice the shift in stress to the *-on* syllable. And the designation for a person from a place that ends in *-o* might have just *-an* added: *Chicagoan, Ohioan*. But does that pattern hold true for a person from Toronto, Mankato, Waco? It certainly does not for a person from New Mexico: the *-an* is added, but the final *-o* disappears—*New Mexican*.

As noted, changes in form require a shift in pronunciation. For instance, a person from the Bahamas (with /ɑ/ in the stressed syllable) is *Bahamian* (with /e/ in the stressed syllable). In other cases, such as *Moravia* and

Moravian, the vowel in the stressed syllable is pronounced /e/ in both forms. What other endings are used to designate people from particular localities? Which place names take *-ite*? Which ones, like *Illinois*, are hard to predict? Which ones do not readily convert to another form? An easy way to frame a question is to ask students to fill in a blank like this: "If a person from Oregon is an *Oregonian* and a person from Denver is a *Denverite*, then a person from Montpelier is a ＿＿＿."

Localities, like people, have nicknames. Students might be interested in finding out how cities get names like the *Crescent City* (New Orleans, also called the *Big Easy*), the *Big Apple* (New York City), and *Beantown* (Boston). A nickname is like an alias. The word itself comes from the Middle English phrase *an eke name*, improperly divided in late Middle English times. The word *eke* meant "also," so the phrase is "an also name," or an additional name. The typical use to which information about nicknames can be put is described in an article by Clark, "Noms de Felt: Names in Gambling," which deals with sobriquets of people, places, things, conditions, and processes. The journal in which the article appears is called, appropriately enough, *Names*.

Overall, that journal, published by the American Name Society, is the best source of articles on names. The journal covers names from various languages, forms of pronunciation, names in literature, humorous use of names, strange names, names of cars, stars, bars. Every type and use of onomastics is either found in the journal or referenced there; it even occasionally has cumulative listings of research on special topics, such as Pauline A. Sealy and Richard B. Sealock's bibliography of place name research, published in 1972. Useful references on place names in individual states include books by Helen S. Carlson (Nevada), Lilian L. Fitzpatrick (Nebraska), Erwin G. Gudde (California), Stanley W. Paher (Nevada), and Robert L. Ramsay (Missouri). General works on place names in the United States include Kelsie B. Harder's *Illustrated Dictionary of Place Names*, Joseph Nathan Kane and Gerard Alexander's book on nicknames of United States cities, and two books by George R. Stewart on American place names. A very useful collection of essays on onomastics is Harder's *Names and Their Varieties*. Three comprehensive resources on personal names are Elsdon C. Smith's *New Dictionary of American Family Names*, Leonard Ashley's *What's in a Name?* and Edwin D. Lawson's annotated bibliography on personal names and naming.

Studying the English of Rituals

Richard W. Bailey, University of Michigan

THE essay that follows is informed by a conviction and by a prejudice that I have brought to teaching the introductory undergraduate course in English language over the past twenty years. The conviction is this: most of what our students retain after taking our courses involves an aura of attitudes. Do they understand language variation and recognize the legitimacy of the English of those who speak differently from the way they do? Can our teaching raise up a generation of students who will recognize in the young they may eventually parent or teach the inevitability of linguistic change (so they will view the new English of a later generation with the same tolerance that older people bring—or ought to bring—to such entirely standard-oral innovations as *like, blow off,* and *party* in "So she's like, 'Let's blow off class and party on Friday' ")? Will they understand that the study of the English language is a discipline in which discoveries are constantly made and in which the small discoveries lead eventually to large and worthwhile generalizations?

This conviction does not, of course, translate into a semester of sermonizing about tolerance or marveling over the thrill of the new. Those attitudes must emerge through engaged attention to the English language that students see, hear, and read about them. So, for instance, I have often assigned students the task of keeping language diaries for brief intervals throughout the semester (an idea that I owe to Michael Halliday). A language diary records pronunciations, vocabulary, grammatical structures, and contextually dissonant usages—all defined in terms of what students would *not* say or write themselves. These diaries record genuine innovations mixed with more familiar observations (that people from southern Ohio say *warsh* or people from Missouri *quarter till three* or people from southeastern Michigan *pop* instead of *soda, coke,* or *tonic*). When students discover, as they always do, that the usages they regard as "weird" strike their classmates (parents, sorority sisters, cousins, friends from elsewhere) as entirely normal, they have learned a portion of that lesson about attitudes. Language diaries also bring out a kind of linguistic priggishness in students: the professor who says *gonna* in a lecture ought not to; the newscaster who says *foggy* in a way that doesn't rhyme with *doggy* as the spirit of our language, tradition, propriety, and manners all demand. But this priggishness is a stage on the road to understanding the dynamics of English and of the community of those who use it.

That's the conviction. Now for the prejudice. Courses in English language are not courses in linguistics. My prejudice is not against the discipline of linguistics, but rather in favor of illuminating the English language from within the communities of its users. (The discipline of *linguistics*, as I view it, regards English as one instance among many of the possible means of manifesting human psychology or social organization. The discipline of *English language* draws on the principles of linguistics to illuminate particular aspects of the language.) The consequence of this prejudice is reflected in my willingness to teach about differences between "John is easy to please" and "John is eager to please" and my unwillingness to present that difference in the larger context of government and binding.

Perhaps the consequences of my prejudice emerge more clearly through what I ask students to study intently, rather than from my desire to have them pursue general linguistic theorizing elsewhere. Our study of sexist English provides a good example of the sort of inductive pedagogy I aim for.

Despite their reputation for political liberalism, most University of Michigan students are not eager to discover the vanguard of innovation and plunge forward toward new forms of linguistic conduct. Though a few students feel offended by sexist language and are eager to expunge such usages from their own English and that of others, most accept gender-biased usages with equanimity or indifference. (A few embrace them with the conviction that the revealed word of God is couched in sexist language and thus demands reverence; for a contrary view, see Schaffran and Kozak.) Yet whatever their prior beliefs, all can become engaged in defining the problem and offering reasoned solutions.

Most students have not thought much about the issues of sexist language beyond a few examples: *herstory, personhole cover*, or whether good grammar requires that indefinites referring to human beings have singular pronouns associated with them. But this fragmentary knowledge (like much else they know about English) is a beginning toward a larger view of greater generality. Our readings on this issue provide a useful expansion of context. For instance, Alleen Pace Nilsen admonishes that "using sex-fair language requires skill as well as commitment" (51). And Dwight Bolinger challenges us to consider the idea that "the writer or speaker has to choose between perpetuating sexist language and making a mess of the grammar" (96). Through practice with actual English texts, students come to acquire the "skill" that Nilsen mentions (whether or not they wish to use it in their own speaking and writing). What it means to make "a mess of the grammar" requires even more profound understanding of the principles of English structure. Defining *mess*, after all, reaches outward from the local instance to larger issues in the description of English syntax.

For a generation, linguists have emphasized the creative use of linguistic principles and offered as evidence the fact that we have never encountered before most sentences that we read or hear. That idea of making infinite use of finite means reduces behaviorist notions of human learning to a properly small corner of the intellectual universe. Yet if linguistic inquiry fastens only on the idea of novelty, there is a danger of forgetting that there are a good many sentences that we have heard often before and are glad to hear again ("How ya doin'?" and "I love you"). As everyone knows, these are not mere phatic utterances or autonomic responses to predictable stimuli. The familiar is as much a part of our linguistic repertory as the newly made.

Distinguishing *formula* from *free expression* was an important part of Otto Jespersen's grammatical theory. In formulas or formular units, "everything is fixed" and "no one can change anything in them." Free expressions, on the other hand, emerge from the application of principles, and, in Jespersen's words, "the sentence . . . may, or may not, be different in some one or more respects from anything . . . ever heard or uttered before" (*Philosophy of Grammar* 18-24). Our attention as scholars to the creativity of linguistic competence has nearly obscured the idea that English in use is a constant exchange between formulas and free expressions. Examining this exchange from the perspective of a functional grammar—one that takes the context of the utterance into account—teachers and students can gain a fuller appreciation of the range of our language and the deeds we accomplish through it.

To teach this lesson, I have assigned an exploration of "ritual English" as a research topic in the introductory English-language course. By ritual English, I mean those utterances that occur predictably (and satisfyingly) as part of ceremonies in which serious linguistic work is accomplished:

Dearly beloved, we are gathered here in the sight of God and this company. . . .

I pledge allegiance to the flag. . . .

Two, four, six, eight. Who do we appreciate? . . .

By the authority vested in the Regents of the University by the State of Michigan and by them delegated to me, I now confer upon these graduates . . .

Why is this night different from all other nights?

Doug and Debbie sitting in a tree,
K - I - S - S - I - N - G.
First comes love, then comes marriage;
Then comes Debbie with a baby carriage.
How many babies does she have?
One, two, three . . .

Utterances of this sort are almost entirely formular, yet they have linguistic characteristics that need to be puzzled out. What are the consequences of their use? What sorts of participants are involved when they are used in real life (and what is the effect if some participants are absent or not authorized to utter them)? Why do some have an archaic flavor? What would be the effect of changing them (even in small ways) on the occasions on which they are used? What makes verbs like *pledge, vest,* and *confer* different from verbs like *appreciate, is,* and *sit*? Why are words like *here, now,* and *this* important? Students who explore some of the domains in which such ritual English occurs are likely to make discoveries on their own that lead them to delighted insight—not only linguistic discoveries but also contextual ones about the pledge of allegiance, cheerleading, and the Haggadah, or the functions of language and gaming in the socialization of the young.

Interesting as an explication of these ritual formulas may be, however, even more intriguing domains of exploration lie beyond rites in the rituals on the boundary between formula and free expression. Without ever having thought much about analyzing it, some students know a good deal about the English of military cadence calls, auctioneering, square dancing, cheerleading, or carnival sales pitches. (Commercial tapes are available to illustrate the first three of these types.) Even more have lifelong experience in listening to DJs on MTV or rock radio and of play-by-play sports broadcasting. Having selected one of these rituals for analysis, they first determine the formulaic parts (not only in sounds, words, and clauses but in tone, pace, volume, and participant roles). Then they discuss the parts where free expression comes into play.

Students use their own tape recorders (or borrow one from the media center) to collect specimens of the ritual English they have chosen for study. Instructed beforehand in the need to inform participants that they are being recorded, they gather communications from waitstaff to kitchen workers in restaurants (and report that *smother a baby* brings forth a small burrito with salsa topping); examine the language used by sales personnel in stores where *floor* is the selling area; distinguish interruptions from friendly overlaps in looking at male-female language interchanges on the campus bar scene; or describe euchre playing in dormitories (which produces such locutions as *pick that biscuit up* or *dish me the rock*). (Fraternity and sorority rituals provide excellent models, but, sworn to secrecy, students are unwilling to write about them.) Reports of the subjects investigated begin with descriptions of the communication and its function and then proceed to analyses of the structure of monologues or dialogues, discourse structures, and salient examples of linguistic organization at the clause level and below. The best essays show how ritual language is used to form and maintain discourse communities, how language of the ritual reflects attitudes toward innovation, and how the purposes served by rituals connect to other social conventions.

Language elicited in rituals provides opportunities to lead the students into secondary activities that yield insights of surprising value to them. For instance, the use of *floor* to refer to a sales area offers a chance to nudge the students in the direction of their dictionaries, where they will discover that this sense of *floor* is not to be found in collegiate editions they are likely to own: *The American Heritage Dictionary* (2nd college ed.), *Webster's New World Dictionary* (3rd college ed.), and *Webster's Ninth New Collegiate Dictionary*. (*The Random House Webster's College Dictionary* [1992] has, at long last, listed this sense of the word.)

Through this assignment, students employ what they have earlier learned: the phonetic alphabet, categories of change in vocabulary and word meaning, syntactic description, and discourse analysis. They are engaged by these real-life topics, though they are sometimes daunted by the complexity they encounter. Nonetheless, teaching about the complexity of language is just what we ought to be doing in our classes. Schoolbook English-language instruction is doused with fear (and dread about job interviews that will drown applicants in ignominy if they fail to learn the difference between *infer* and *imply*) or is so trivialized that students find themselves helpless if faced with analyzing English beyond that offered in the workbook. By encountering the real challenge of describing English in its context, students gain new respect for themselves and tolerance of other language users. That is not a bad lesson to learn.

Regional Variation

Settlement Patterns and Language Variation: A Model for Research

Timothy C. Frazer, Western Illinois University

FOR teachers and students who want to conduct studies of language variation in their own communities, other essays in this volume as well as other published works offer guidelines and ideas. Here we are concerned with the relationship between language and community history, which in turn ties together language variation and other factors that make each community unique. Other sources will help you discover the varieties of language in your community; this essay will help you discover the social and historical causes for those varieties. It would be a good idea, by the way, to read this essay with a good atlas of the United States on hand.

Anywhere you might live in the United States, most people, of course, speak English. They have been doing so, however, for only a few hundred years on the average—actually, over three hundred years on some parts of the East Coast, a little less than a hundred in some parts of the West. Compared with other parts of the world, then, the United States has been settled relatively recently, and the different ways in which Americans behave in different regions of the country have much to do with settlement— questions of who first came to live in an area and where they came from. These different ways of behavior show up in many forms; I concentrate on traditional house architecture and, to a lesser extent, religion, to show how closely these patterns of behavior relate to our special concern, language. And I also suggest some ways in which you can investigate the relation between the settlement history and linguistic makeup of your own community.

A good illustration to start out with is my home state of Illinois. In fact, I began studying regional dialectology because of the different varieties of English I had heard spoken around the state as I grew up. People had different words for different items, and this was true among members of my own family in Sterling. For example, what we now call *cottage cheese* was called *Dutch cheese* by an aunt on my mother's side, but *smearcase* by my paternal grandfather. I noticed an even greater difference when I traveled to the southern part of the state; there it seemed to me that people spoke with what sounded like a Southern accent. To understand the source of this accent, we need only look at the settlement history of Illinois, an examination from which, in turn, I hope you will get some ideas for use in your own state or community.

At the close of the Revolutionary War, Americans of European origin were concentrated on the East Coast. The first real movement west came from the Upland South (that is, the more hilly or mountainous parts of the South), as settlers from central and western Virginia and from the uplands of the Carolinas poured through the Cumberland Gap into Kentucky. By 1790, the woods and fields of "Kaintuck" (as Daniel Boone called it) boasted a population numbering in the thousands. In 1800, most Americans living west of the Appalachians were in Kentucky and Tennessee. This area was what people meant by the "West" at that time.

North of the Ohio River, the Midwest was still sparsely populated except for the indigenous Indian groups, but a series of acts by Congress led to rapid change. Creating the Northwest Territory as the sole property of the United States, these acts made settlement of the future states of Ohio, Indiana, Illinois, Michigan, and Wisconsin more attractive by banning slavery, providing for local government, forcing the Indians to move westward, and eventually offering land at prices that the small farmer could afford. The increasing scarcity and price of available land in Kentucky led to a mass migration north across the Ohio River to Ohio and especially to Indiana and Illinois. Small farmers who could not compete with the plantation system in Kentucky, and others of the poor or landless (like Abraham Lincoln's family), left Kentucky for greater opportunity in the new territories. In Illinois, this migration of Kentuckians and Tennesseans northward continued for four decades; by 1830, the population of Illinois, largely of Southern origin, was concentrated in the southern half of the state along the Mississippi, Wabash, and Illinois rivers. (Data and illustrations in this article are adapted from my monograph on Illinois speech, no. 73 in the series Publication of the American Dialect Society.) Figure 1 shows the loca-

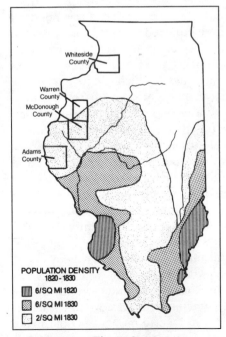

Figure 1.
Illinois Population in 1820 and 1830

tion of most of Illinois's population in 1820 and 1830. As the map shows, by 1830 the heaviest concentrations (6 per square mile) were gathered along the river valleys, while a thinner population (2 per square mile) had pretty well occupied the southern half of the state. We can use this map to represent the location of Illinois's early Southern population. As a result of this early Southern occupation, Illinois had a cultural and political system in 1830 very unlike the one it has today. The earliest laws, for example, were modeled on those of Kentucky, which had in turn been modeled on those of Virginia. And although slavery was officially forbidden by the Northwest Ordinance, a slave auction was once conducted near Shawneetown; the site remains a tourist attraction to this day.

Much other evidence of this early Southern influence remains as well. In the parts of the state that were settled during this period, some towns and villages still bear the names of Southern places: in central Illinois, for example, there are towns called Mount Vernon and Nashville. But a more dramatic Southern influence can be seen in the form of small houses that were built before the Civil War. Figure 2 shows a variety of house type that originated in the Upper South. House B has variously been called the *hall and parlor* or *single-pen* type of house; it originated in Virginia, and various versions of it can be seen throughout the southeastern United States. Similar buildings, perhaps former sharecropper cabins, have been seen abandoned in Georgia cotton fields; this house type also appears in the mountains of the South as the Appalachian mountain cabin. A larger version of this house is represented by house A, the double-pen house, which has two front doors, one for each pen. Both of these types can be found in McDonough County, Illinois (see

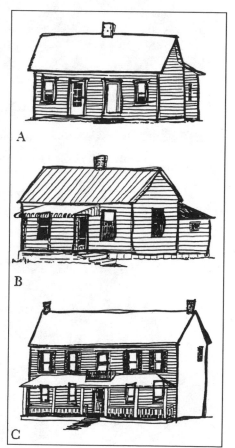

Figure 2.
Three Traditional House Types

fig. 1). The single-pen house in the first photograph (fig. 3) stands abandoned near Camp Creek in rural McDonough County, but dozens of such houses in this area are still occupied. The photograph in figure 4 shows a double-pen house in Fandon, McDonough County. A thriving village and a center

Figure 3. Single-Pen House, Camp Creek, Illinois

Figure 4. Double-Pen House, Fandon, Illinois

of stagecoach routes until the railroad came to the county in 1854, Fandon today consists of about a hundred houses, more than eighty percent of which are of the single- or double-pen variety.

This influence of Southern architecture is likewise evident throughout other parts of Illinois. Not only can single- and double-pen houses be found along the Illinois, Mississippi, and Wabash rivers, but the "I" house (fig. 2, house C)—adapted from the double- or single-pen with the addition of a second story—can also be found in these regions. The most famous example is Lincoln's home in Springfield, now something of a shrine for thousands of visitors every year (fig. 5).

Illinois's early Southern settlement is evidenced by much of its religious geography. One example is the distribution of churches belonging to the "Christian" denomination, a sect descended from the Campbellite movement (founded by former Baptists Thomas and Alexander Campbell), which began among the camp meetings of the Kentucky frontier. That this sect was brought into Illinois from Kentucky is clear in the distribution of Christian churches in Illinois today. Christian churches are most numerous in the

Figure 5. Abraham Lincoln's Home, Springfield

southern half of the state—the area of Southern settlement we showed in figure 1. Other denominations show different regional patterns. Edwin Scott Gaustad's *Historical Atlas of Religion in America,* for example, shows the heaviest concentration of Baptists to be in the extreme southern tip of the state. Since many of the original Southern settlers in Kentucky were Baptists who headed through the Cumberland Gap to escape religious persecution in Virginia, it should not surprise us to find Baptists concentrated in that part of Illinois closest to Kentucky (and the only part of the state where we find any survival for archaic Southern words like *Christmas Gift!* for *Merry Christmas* or *mosquito hawk* for *dragonfly*). Still another configuration appears on Gaustad's map of Congregational concentration in Illinois. This church, descended from New England Puritanism, was imported to the Midwest by settlers from New England and New York State; and in Illinois, Congregationalists are concentrated in the northern half of the state. Here again there is a correspondence to language: Northern words like *belly flopper* and *haycock* are largely confined to this northern part of the state.

These examples suggest an answer to the big question you might be asking: What has all this to do with language variation? Simply that the settlement patterns I have described result in many cultural patterns, the

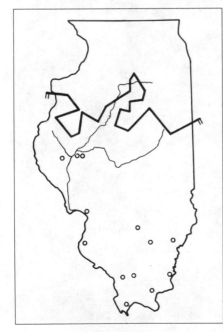

Figure 6. South and South Midland Terms in Illinois

most enduring of which is language variation. The Southern settlers in Illinois, for example, brought with them the regional dialect of Kentucky and Tennessee. This South Midland or Upper South dialect was distinguished by a number of unique regional words that survived into the twentieth century. Their distribution in Illinois conforms to the pattern of Southern settlement shown in figure 1, and the religious patterns described above; if we had a good map of single-pen houses, it would doubtless be much the same. Figure 6 shows the Illinois distribution for *pallet*, a Southern word for a bed made up on the floor. The northern boundary for this term pretty much conforms to the distribution of Southern settlement shown in figure 1 and thus to the distribution, as well, of the Southern cultural features we have discussed. Figure 6 also shows the distribution of *goober*, a Southern (originally West African) word for *peanut*. Although not quite as widespread as *pallet*, *goober* shows the same general pattern on the map. The use of other Illinois maps of this type would show similar distributions for *barnlot* (a Southern word for *barnyard* or *corral*); *pulleybone* (what Southerners call the *wishbone* in a chicken or turkey); *light bread* (an old Southern word for bread made with bleached wheat flour); and perhaps a dozen more words of Southern origin. And we would get similar maps as well if we were to plot places where Southern pronunciations of such words as *downtown, time, pen,* and *hog* were recorded.

I have presented a fairly detailed account of Southern settlement, Southern culture, and Southern language in Illinois because it offers a clear example of the relation between language and other variables, be they artifacts like nineteenth-century houses or continuing cultural patterns like religion. This does not mean, of course, that the Upper South made the only contribution to Illinois speech or folk culture. As our discussion of religion showed, settlers from New York State and New England were predominant in the northern half of the state after 1830; so were Pennsylvanians, though in lesser numbers. And after 1850, during a furious era of railroad building, thousands of Ohioans came to the previously inaccessible prairies of the central portion of the state. Each of these areas made its own linguistic contributions: *Dutch cheese*, the word for *cottage cheese* once used by my aunt, originates in New York State, while *smearcase*, used by my grandfather, originates among the Pennsylvania Germans. Some members of my family, moreover, pronounce *wash* with an *r* (hence, "warsh"), as do many Ohioans and western Pennsylvanians, while others omit the *r*, as do New Yorkers.

Such variation within a single family, however, should not surprise anyone who has examined the settlement history of Whiteside County (fig. 1), where I grew up and where all four of my grandparents came about a hundred years ago. The 1870 census shows Whiteside to have been settled mostly from Pennsylvania and New York State in roughly equal proportions. Once again, cultural evidence of Whiteside's settlement history was evident in my youth: conservative Mennonite farmers, set off by their old-fashioned clothing, could be seen visiting town on Monday nights, reminding us of the folk life of Pennsylvania, where their ancestors had first settled. And one of the most prosperous churches in my hometown was the Congregational, an artifact, as we have learned, of Northern settlement. So people in my family had two linguistic models to choose from, the dialects of either New York State or Pennsylvania.

This long exposition of state history and personal experience hasn't been just for my own fun, however; all of this has been to make a point. Language variation is related to other kinds of variation; it has roots in our history and plays a part in the human landscape. And it is important to know this because language variation, when misunderstood, can cause prejudice. For example, Chicago students at the university in McDonough County (fig. 1), where I teach, make fun of the local students' speech. One feature especially singled out for ridicule is the intrusive *r* in *wash*, the feature that comes by way of Ohio and that some people in my family use as well. The Chicagoans, assuming that people who talk this way are hicks or clods, often make life miserable for local students. Their attitude shows that language variation is not just a matter of idle curiosity; it can and often does cause human problems that require human understanding. And I suggest that we can find some of that understanding by learning why language variation occurs. Here are some of the tools that I have used for this purpose.

Next to the collection of actual language data, the most important information I obtained was about the settlement history of the counties I investigated. How can you find out about your own county's settlement history? The best place to start is with census population summaries. For my work in Illinois, I began with the published United States census summary for 1870. The short version is entitled *A Compendium of the Ninth Census*, compiled by Francis A. Walker and published in Washington by the Government Printing Office in 1872. The long version is entitled *The Statistics of the Population of the United States*, with the same publishing data. So far, I have found copies of one or the other of these volumes in all college libraries and some public libraries I have visited. The following discussion describes how one can use the tables in the government census records.

The best way to use the tables is to look for various nativities (places of birth) whose presence might account for language variation. Individual sources of population are listed at the top of each table above vertical columns of numbers; the tables on Illinois list Ohio, New York, Pennsylvania, Indiana, Kentucky, British America (now Canada), England/Wales, Ireland, Scotland, other Great Britain, Germany, France, Sweden/Norway, Switzerland, Bohemia (part of contemporary Czechoslovakia), Holland, and Denmark. Since we know something about McDonough County, let's consider its figures first. The most interesting figure is the number of Kentucky natives, 1,439. That figure might not seem significant—about 5 percent of a total population of more than 26,000. But Warren County, just to the north (fig. 1), has a Kentucky population of only 911 out of more than 30,000, and Adams County, to the southwest, has a Kentucky native population of only 1,092 out of a population of over 56,000. For Warren and Adams counties, the Kentucky population accounts for only 3 percent to 3.5 percent of the total native population, a difference that explains why there is less evidence of Southern language and culture in these counties than in McDonough. The difference between McDonough and other counties is even more striking if we go farther north and look at Whiteside, my home county. Here the

number of Kentuckians was minuscule—only 73 out of a total population
of more than 26,000. Unlike in McDonough, the influence of Southern
settlement in my home county is negligible, and the language of my family
reflects that fact.

Most of this discussion has focused on the influence of Southern settlement in Illinois, but we have already seen that other groups contributed as
well to Illinois's various language. Ohio immigration came later, and we can
find Ohioans in many Illinois counties, especially true of east-central Illinois
(see fig. 7). I constructed this map from the 1870 census tables we have
discussed by outlining all counties in which Ohioans numbered more than
10 percent of the 1870 American-born population. The map shows Ohioans
to be most widespread in the eastern part of the state, closer to Ohio itself.
But the map shows them spread as well through the north-central part of
Illinois to the Mississippi and predicts very well the appearance of some
dialect words that originated in western Pennsylvania but that reached Illinois by way of Ohio. This is true of *snake feeder*, a western Pennsylvania word
for *dragonfly*. As figure 8 shows, the distribution of *snake feeder* in Illinois

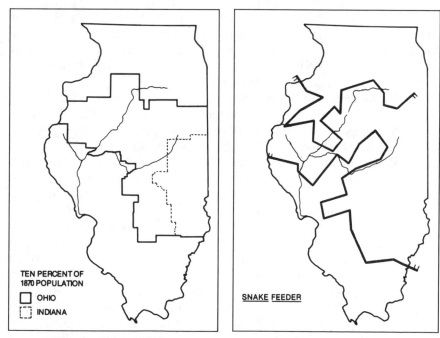

Figure 7. 1870 Population
of Illinois from Indiana and Ohio

Figure 8. Distribution
of *snake feeder* in Illinois

pretty well conforms to the outline of Ohio settlement. Similar maps would show similar distribution for words with the same regional origin: *coal oil*, for example, and *cling peach* (as opposed to *clingstone*); in this area as well we will find the *r* in *wash* and a drawled pronunciation of *coat* and *road*—still more western Pennsylvania features that reached Illinois by way of Ohio.

Teachers and students, then, can learn much about the kind of dialect variation they might expect in their own communities by looking at published census data. Summaries of census data showing the birthplaces of county populations were published for 1870, 1880, and 1890 by the Government Printing Office (published in 1872, 1883, and 1895). If you live in one of the more recently settled western states, you will want recourse to one of the later volumes. If you live in one of the older states, you can learn even more about the settlement history of your community by checking the manuscript census returns for 1850, 1860, 1870, and 1880. These manuscript census returns are copies of the family-by-family notes made by the census takers themselves; they list every resident by name and, besides place of birth, include such data as sex, race, occupation, amount of schooling, and literacy. Manuscript census returns are much used by genealogical researchers and are often now available on microfilm at public libraries. If your local librarian does not have these materials, the head of your local genealogical society or historical society might know the nearest place you can find them. State histories may provide a good overview of the settlement of your state; county and local histories, also in your local library, will be of some help as well but are not always as accurate as census data.

Marion Kaminkow's bibliography titled *United States Local Histories in the Library of Congress* is a helpful locator. Patterns of settlement are traced in Charles O. Paullin and John K. Wright's *Atlas of the Historical Geography of the United States* and Ray Allen Billington's *Westward Expansion*.

What sort of dialect project can students and teachers do together with census materials? I would suggest beginning by determining the principal source of settlers for your community. You can do so by looking at the nativities of the population of your county in the published census returns. If you want to be more specific, you can use the earliest manuscript census returns to get the actual figures for your township or municipality. If you live in a large enough city to make a total headcount impossible, do a rough random sample: count only the households at the top of every page, or every fifth page, depending on the density of the population.

Once you know the makeup of the population in your area, the next part of your project is to see if the dialect of the area matches the population. The best thing to study, of course, would be pronunciation, but this is difficult for anyone not trained in phonetics. An easier topic to cover is regional vocabulary, and an excellent way to gather this kind of material is discussed by Roger W. Shuy in his *Discovering American Dialects*. Shuy presents a mail-type questionnaire that seeks common regional words. If you have trouble finding any of those words, you might need to update the questionnaire. To do so, find out which more recent words might be appropriate to your area by consulting Craig M. Carver's *American Regional Dialects*, which lists dialect words still in use. To elicit these words in interviews, use the questionnaire format from Frederic G. Cassidy's *Dictionary of American Regional English* (1: lxi), on which Carver's book is based. Shuy, then, will provide an excellent methodology for a project of gathering dialect words, but Cassidy or Carver should be consulted in order to discover more up-to-date words.

With these research tools, teachers and students can make interesting discoveries about their own communities. And along the way, they will learn about other things of cultural interest: the prevalence of certain architectural styles or religions, for example. At this point, you probably want to get started. If you feel you still don't know enough, several publications are invaluable resources for researchers conducting studies of this sort on regional dialect items in the United States. Hans Kurath's *Word Geography of the Eastern United States* may be dated, but it remains the foundation for American word geographies. Although, as noted, *Discovering American Dialects* is also dated, it is still a good introduction for beginners. To learn about the cultural geography of America, consult *This Remarkable Continent*, edited by John F. Rooney and his coworkers. The standard guide to regional architecture and handicrafts is Henry Glassie's *Pattern in the Material Folk Culture of the Eastern United States*; religious geography (and some surprises) are treated in Gaustad's *Historical Atlas of Religion in America*.

The exercises suggested in this paper should help create a better understanding of the "why" of language variation. And understanding these differences among ourselves should, in turn, deepen our human understanding and our ability to live in peace with one another.

Questionnaire for the Study of South Carolina English

Michael Montgomery, University of South Carolina, Columbia

THE following is a brief guide to conducting a sociolinguistic interview. The five-part questionnaire, designed specifically for use in South Carolina, could be adapted for use in other states, where different questions would be more fruitful (cf. Kurath, *Word Geography*; McMillan and Montgomery). To conduct similar surveys in other states, researchers would need to examine the results of earlier studies in preparing items for the short-answer questions suggested below (part 3), because the vocabulary items one would investigate in California or Michigan, for example, would not be the same as those of interest to researchers in South Carolina. Similarly, knowledge of the regional composition of the state or area to be investigated may lead the researcher to adapt some of the general questions (part 4) and comments (part 5).

While the guidelines given here for conducting an interview should be helpful in most situations, the fieldworker must be flexible enough to make each interview an accurate record of the informant's speech. The guide does not address the question of making contact with an appropriate informant, because the nature and location of a particular project will dictate the types of informants sought—for instance, whether the informants are to constitute a cross-section of the current residents or are to be limited to long-term natives of the community, older individuals, and so on.

The fieldworker should be as accommodating as possible in the interview situation and observe social amenities. That is, the fieldworker should realize that the informants are being generous with time and attention and that what they talk about is interesting and important, at least to them. Beyond all else, the fieldworker must be a good listener and relate to the informants as people who have something to say rather than as sources of linguistic data. Usually the fieldworker is expected to explain something about the nature of the interview either before arriving or at the beginning of the interview. While it is normally unnecessary to go into great detail with all the informants, the fieldworker should always be honest in answering informants' questions and careful not to give conflicting information.

The informants should do as much talking as possible, especially for part 2 (personal data sheet) and parts 4 and 5 (general questions, comments about the state or region). Such talk helps set a relaxed tone for the interview and encourages more productive and uninhibited speech than direct, short-answer questions read by the fieldworker. To elicit spontaneous extended speech, the fieldworker should ask questions beginning with *what, why, when, where*, and *how* rather than pose queries that are likely to be answered by yes or no. The fieldworker should encourage the informants to answer at some length, if possible, and then follow up with other questions, either general or specific, on any matter that he or she wants to know about in greater detail.

While letting the informants follow their own lines of discussion, however, the fieldworker must always be in control of the interview. That is, the fieldworker listens to everything that the informants say but, at every step, knows what the next question is going to be. The fieldworker should be responsive to the informant, nodding, agreeing, or otherwise reacting. If an informant stalls or strays from the topic, the fieldworker must get the interview back on track as quickly and subtly as possible. If an interview becomes artificial because the fieldworker is no longer paying attention, it may be difficult to maintain the informant's confidence and continue eliciting data of sufficient quality or quantity.

Although the fieldworker should be responsive to the informant and ready to explore ideas and terms the informant has introduced, it is desirable that the fieldworker avoid appearing to be on the verge of asking the next question. In ordinary conversation, a significant pause often precedes a change of subject, and this pause is an opportunity for the informant to elaborate on the preceding topic of conversation. It must be understood that learning to respond to informants productively and acquiring a comfortable interview style are demanding tasks; they normally require at least one practice interview.

The fieldworker should not turn on the tape recorder immediately but prepare the informant by establishing friendly rapport and providing information appropriate for the interview. Because taping increases the formality of the informant's speech, the fieldworker should maintain a relaxed tone in the conversation after recording has begun. Responses to the entire interview must be recorded; the usual explanation, if the informant inquires, is that the interview occurs too quickly for one to take laborious notes on everything said. However, it is helpful for the fieldworker to have a notebook in hand to take down the spelling of names or unusual words the informant comments on and especially to note fine points about pronunciation or the progress of the interview that cannot be recalled from listening to the tape.

Informants may want certain information about the interview and its motivation, and the fieldworker should not disguise what the interview involves. Fieldworkers should explain that they wish to ask several general questions about the local community or town and other questions about words and phrases. Although informants will sometimes shy away and claim that they are not experts and not the best people to answer such questions, the fieldworker should express a genuine interest in what a variety of people know or in what all residents know. The fieldworker can certainly allay any apprehensions that the informant was chosen just because of a distinctive or unusual way of talking. Finally, the fieldworker ought to assure each informant that the interview will remain under a pseudonym at the fieldworker's college or university and that henceforth only the fieldworker will know the identity of the speaker.

The Interview

The interview outlined here consists of five parts and usually takes from one to two hours to complete.

Part 1: Testing the Tape Recorder (1 minute)

To ensure that the tape recorder is working properly at the proper volume, the interviewer can ask the informant to count slowly from one to ten. Then the passage can be played back and the interview begun after the numbers. (Because counting represents the careful pronunciation of several words containing variables that may differ stylistically [for example, the vowels in *five* and *ten*], it will be useful to have these to compare with more casual, conversational pronunciation later on).

Part 2: Personal Information (5 to 10 minutes)

The fieldworker asks informants for information regarding their schooling, background, travel, and other matters. If the informants are willing, these points can be explored in some detail, to establish rapport and set the speakers at ease. Some of this material will be covered in greater detail in part 4, but the fieldworker can delay part 3 and some of the questions in part 4 if it is easy and comfortable to do so. As the fieldworker asks the informant the questions, the relevant responses are entered in the personal data sheet;

details may be added to the sheet later from the recording, but as much of it as possible should be completed during the interview.

Part 3: Short-Answer Questions (10 to 30 minutes)

Informants will vary widely in how much information they can provide to these questions. Younger informants in particular may be able to provide very little. Regardless of how much information is volunteered, however, the fieldworker should ask for elaboration on specific terms that the informant offers in order to clarify their use. If necessary, the fieldworker may ask informants if they have ever heard the specific terms in parentheses after the question on the answer sheet; if the answer is yes, the fieldworker can ask where they have heard them and what they are supposed to mean. Fine distinctions must be noted for potentially ambiguous terms.

Part 4: General, Open-Ended Questions (30 minutes to 1 hour)

These very general questions, which ask about the informants and their community, begin with *what, who, why, where, when,* or *how.* They are open-ended questions because the fieldworker is free to follow up an answer with another question devised on the spot rather than move on to the next item on the questionnaire. Since the overriding goal is to get as much uninhibited, spontaneous speech from the informant as possible, regardless of the subject matter, the informant's response patterns should largely dictate the progress of this section, although the fieldworker should always have a question in reserve. Informants wanting to tell stories ought to be encouraged to do so, because anecdotes are of considerable value to folklorists who may later use the tapes. This section offers questions appropriate to informants in any community in the state. It is always up to the fieldworker, however, to come up with general questions appropriate to the particular community where each interview is conducted.

Part 5: Comments on the State or Region (5 minutes)

Sooner or later the interview will lose impetus (usually after an hour or two), and this is the fieldworker's cue to tell the informant that the interview is nearly finished by a comment like "I have only a couple of more things to ask." The questions in the sample selection are specifically about speech in South Carolina. It is important to ask about the informant's observations on how, for instance, South Carolinians in different parts of the state talk, and it is highly desirable to have informants give examples of either approved or disapproved usages, colorful local expressions, and any other terms and phrases of note. Such information tells much about the speaker and gives clues about what different communities see as the "standard." In addition, it is often interesting to compare an informant's actual usage of certain words and forms with his or her attitudes toward usage; inconsistency between the two may indicate a social bias of the informant, reveal his or her reliability in reporting local usage, or provide other useful insights.

After the interview ends, the investigator thanks the informant sincerely. It is usually a good idea not to rush off but to tarry for a few minutes to chat. This cements the relationship with the informant and makes it possible to come back or to ask advice about other informants.

Forms and Questionnaires

Personal Data Sheet

Ask the informant questions about the subjects on this sheet and fill it out yourself. Begin by saying something like "Okay, to start off, I would like to get just a little personal information about you: how long you have lived here, where your parents are from, and a little bit about where you went to school."

Interviewer	Date	
Community or city	County	
State		
Informant (initials acceptable)		
Address		
Age Sex	Race	
Place of birth		
Other places of residence		
Occupation(s)		
Education		
Amount of travel		
Ancestry		
Parents' place of birth: Mother	Father	
Parents' education: Mother	Father	
Parents' occupation: Mother	Father	

Information about grandparents

  Maternal

  Paternal

Any other relevant information about ancestry

Short-Answer Questions

Always determine the meanings of all terms the informant mentions and pin down as many distinctions as possible in the informant's speech. Ask informants if they know or have heard the terms in parentheses after each question. Unless otherwise noted, all terms in parentheses are synonyms.

1. What would you call the kind of wood you use to start a fire?
   (kindling, lightwood, lightard, fatty lightard)
   Lightwood and *lightard* are more common in the Low Country; *kindling* is general usage.
   Is there any difference between *lightwood* and *kindling*?

2. What do you call the long, skinny insect with transparent wings that you find near the water?
   (dragonfly, mosquito hawk, snake feeder, snake doctor)
   Dragonfly is general usage; *mosquito hawk* is common in the Low Country; *snake feeder* and *snake doctor* are more common in the Piedmont and the mountains.

3. What would you call the place above the fireplace where you might put a vase or a picture or something like that?
   (mantel, mantel piece, fireboard)
   Mantel and *mantel piece* are general usage; *fireboard* in South Carolina is found primarily in the Pee Dee Valley.

4. What do you call the hard-shell animal that pulls its head and feet in when you touch it?
   (turtle, cooter)
   Turtle is general usage; *cooter* is found throughout South Carolina.

5. What do you call the things that are worn over the shoulders to hold up pants?
   (suspenders, galluses)
   Is there a difference between the terms?

6. What do you call the shallow utensil with a long handle for cooking on top of the stove?
   (frying pan, skillet, spider)

Spider, found primarily in low country South Carolina, was originally the term for a frying pan with legs that sat over coals.

7. What do you call the building you store corn in?
    (corncrib, cornhouse)
    Corncrib is general usage; *cornhouse* is found primarily in low country South Carolina.

8. What is the name of the meal you eat in the middle of the day?
    (lunch, dinner)
    Do you have a different name for this meal on Sundays?

9. What do you get at the store to carry groceries in?
    (sack, bag, paper bag, paper sack, poke)
    What is a *poke*? What is the difference between a *poke* and a *bag*? between a *bag* and a *sack*?
    Poke is used primarily in the Piedmont and the mountains.

10. What is the thing that is built outside the door of a house to walk on and to put chairs on? Is there a different word if it is on the back of the house? What if it's on the second floor?
    (porch, piazza, veranda, gallery, stoop, balcony)
    Piazza is used throughout South Carolina.

11. What might you put on your hook to go fishing?
    (earthworm, redworm, rainworm, angleworm)
    Redworm is used in the mountains, *rainworm* in the North Carolina Piedmont, and *angleworm* in New England.

12. What is the name of the kind of bird that can see in the dark?
    (screech owl, shivering owl)
    Shivering owl is found primarily in the Pee Dee Valley.

13. With reference to people, what does the term *cracker* mean? To which states does the term apply? Does it apply to South Carolinians?

14. What terms are used to refer to people from South Carolina?
    (sandlapper, clayeater)
    (*For these two terms and all others mentioned, ask:*)
    Does the term refer to people throughout the state? Is it a complimentary or an uncomplimentary term?

15. What do you call the demon used to scare children?
    (boogeyman, boogerman, etc.)
    What do people sometimes think they see around a graveyard at night?
    (haint, Plateye, spook, ghost, booger)
    Have you ever heard the term *Plateye*?

16. What do the terms *Gullah* and *Geechee* refer to as far as you know? Are these terms restricted to South Carolina? Are they used for white people? black people? Are they complimentary? uncomplimentary? (*Elicit examples if possible.*)

General Questions

These questions are appropriate for informants throughout a state. You may want to devise additional questions appropriate to specific communities and specific informants.

1. Education
    When you started school, what was a typical day like?
    How big was the school and how well did you know the teachers?
    What were the teachers like? Were they especially strict?
    How do you think the schools that you went to were different from the schools today?

2. Entertainment
    When you were growing up, what sort of entertainment was there?
    What did people do on weekends or on Friday nights?
    What sorts of games did you play when you were young?
    What do people around here do nowadays when they want to have a good time?
    Are there any special events in town or in the community that you participate in or attend?

3. Religion
    When you were growing up, what were the churches (or other houses of worship) like?
    How many churches are there around here and what kinds of churches are they?
    Do most people around here belong to a church?

4. Community changes
    What was this town or community like when you were growing up (or when you moved here)?
    What would you say have been the most important or biggest changes in this town since you grew up (or moved) here?
    Do you think people around here have changed over the years? How or how not?

5. Food
    Are there any dishes or foods that are special to this part of the country?

Are there any kinds of food that used to be fixed in your family
that you haven't had in a long time?

What are the differences between the way food is prepared now
and the way it was when you were growing up?

Comments on the State or Region (Example Is of South Carolina)

(Elicit examples of specific words and pronunciations if possible.)

1. Do you think all people in South Carolina speak alike?
2. What are the different ways of talking in the state?
3. What do you think about the way people in Charleston talk?
4. People in which part of the state talk most differently from you?
   most like you?

Folk Dialect Maps

Dennis R. Preston, Michigan State University

MOST of what we read about dialects will correctly concern itself with what people have actually said. In fact, that may seem to be such an obvious requirement that we cannot imagine any study of dialect not based on actual speech. How could we determine whether people in a certain region say *branch*, *creek*, *brook*, or *run* for a small stream unless we overheard, remembered, or recorded their use? How could we tell if people in a certain area pronounce the second vowel in *pajamas* with the vowel of *jam* or *bomb* unless we studied their actual pronunciation?

Nearly all published information about dialects is derived from data collected by means of a questionnaire or a recorded conversation. In questionnaire studies, respondents report their own usage by marking a checklist or by answering direct or indirect questions posed by the interviewer, but many linguists prefer to record respondents in actual conversation, ideally in familiar settings. Each approach has weaknesses. Questionnaires may lead to reports consciously or unconsciously designed to please the interviewer or to show the respondent in his or her best light; however, the interviewer gets all the information sought. Conversations may provide actual use rather than reports of it, but the interviewer might not get all the details sought, and the respondents may be stilted or self-conscious in the presence of whatever recording device is being used.

Another approach to dialect study freely admits that respondents' conscious notions of language may interfere in research and seeks to discover what those notions are. One method of studying nonlinguists' views of language asks respondents themselves to draw maps of where they believe dialect regions are. The following text might be used by instructors to introduce students to such an assignment:

When you think of maps, you undoubtedly think first of geographical features—roads, mountains, rivers, and so on. Many maps you use, however, represent things that have no such physical reality at all. Have you noticed, when you drive from one state to another, that there are no lines actually drawn around the state boundaries, although they appear on maps? The first thing I want you to think about is the fact that maps contain information that is not a part of the physical landscape.

You might argue—and quite reasonably—that borders, equators, and such things, though not physically observable on the land itself, are reflections of physically describable objects. If you were a surveyor or a ship's pilot, you would know how to take readings from large natural features or from stars or other reference points so that divisions of the earth's space could be mathematically calculated.

Maps, then, record the presence of actual features and of mathematically calculable divisions of the land. A little reflection or observation will show, however, that you see many maps whose main point is not to show such permanent physical or mathematically determined features at all. Your newspaper and television often show maps revealing the distribution of information that does not follow political or other mathematically calculable boundaries—weather maps, maps of vegetation, or maps of the incidences of crime, suicide, or communicable diseases (although some of these facts are often shown on maps as if they covered an entire state, country, or other political division).

Traditional dialect maps are just such geographical representations of human behavior. For example, in Timothy C. Frazer's article in this volume, figure 6 shows the distribution of the South Midland term *pallet* and *goober* in Illinois, and figure 8 shows the distribution of the North Midland term *snake feeder*. The principle of dialect map construction is not different from that used to construct weather maps, maps of vegetation, or maps of other aspects of human behavior. Patterns of the incidences of terms are given geographical boundaries. From a large number of such individual items, it is possible to draw more general maps of the dialect areas of the United States. If, for example, you combine maps of homicides, suicides, muggings, rapes, robberies, and so on, you could prepare a *violence* map of the United States. Creating a graphic to depict human activity is precisely what dialectologists do when they combine

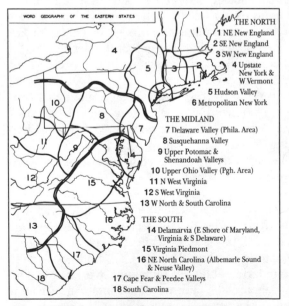

Figure 1. Dialect Areas of the Eastern United States
(Source: Kurath, *A Word Geography
of the Eastern United States*, fig. 3)

maps of many different linguistic features to produce generalizations, like the well-known map of the principal dialect areas of the eastern United States shown in figure 1, which indicates major and minor dialectal divisions in the Atlantic states from New England to eastern Georgia. You might still

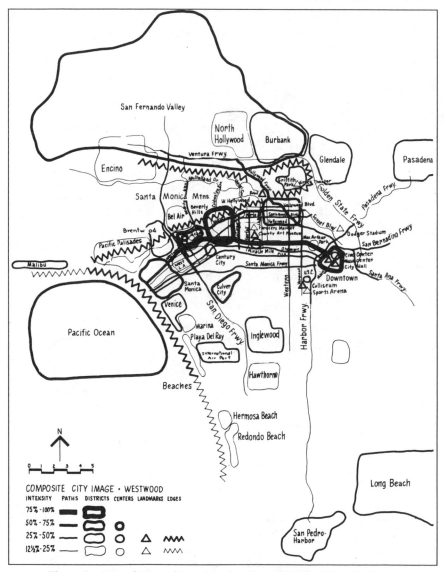

Figure 2a. Mental Map of Los Angeles: Upper-Middle-Class Residents of Westwood (Source for figs. 2a–2d: Orleans 104–06)

argue that there is a physical reality to such maps. Though the lines do not represent permanent physical features or mathematically derivable boundaries, they do represent actual behavior by people—who, after all, are spatially located when they behave. Our interests will take us even one step further in abstractness.

Figures 2a–2d display four maps of the Los Angeles area, generalized from maps drawn by local residents; all represent the same physical space,

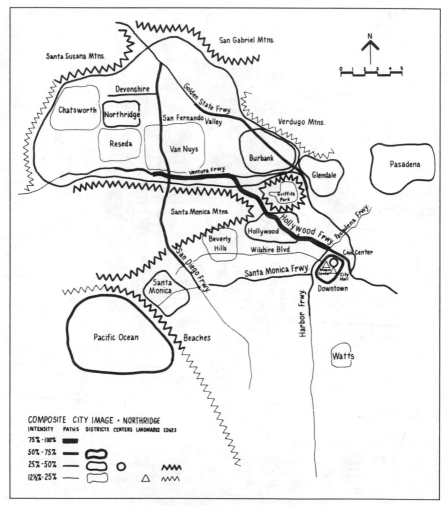

Figure 2b. Mental Map of Los Angeles:
Middle-Class Residents of Northridge

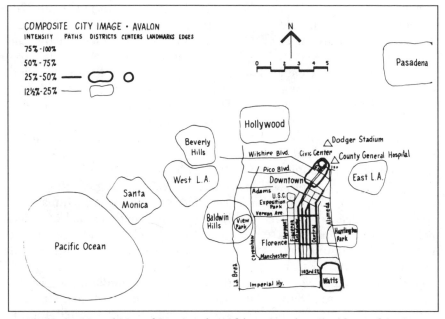

Figure 2c. Mental Map of Los Angeles: African American Residents of Avalon

but they are very different from one another (Orleans). The upper-middle-class residents of Westwood (2a) know a great deal about their own neighborhood, but they also have considerable knowledge of the beaches, airport, freeways, and areas south of the city. The residents of Northridge (2b) show no such familiarity with the south in their map, but they include many details about the north and surrounding neighborhoods and physical features lacking on the Westwood map—Chatsworth, the Santa Susana and San Gabriel Mountains, Reseda, and so on. More dramatically, African American resi-

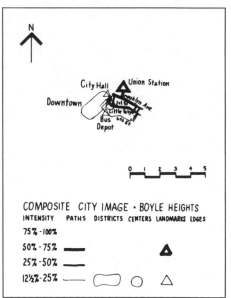

Figure 2d. Mental Map of Los Angeles: Hispanic Residents of Boyle Heights

dents of Avalon (2c) and Spanish-speaking residents of Boyle Heights (2d) see substantially diminished versions of the area; however, within their representations, they are aware of districts and even sites not mentioned in the more detailed maps (e.g., the bus station and East Los Angeles).

Such maps are completely different from all those discussed earlier; they are not maps of physical, political, or even behavioral features but of the mental images or concepts people have of an area. They have psychological rather than physical reality. You have undoubtedly disagreed with another person about where a place is or exactly how to get there. That is because your *mental maps* are different. Here I want to suggest that mental maps of dialect distribution are worth studying. If residents of Los Angeles can draw maps of their physical environments, could nonlinguists draw maps of their linguistic environments? What could we learn from such maps?

A great deal might be learned from knowing where nondialectologists believe dialect boundaries are. Consider, for example, a language attitude test in which a linguist chooses voices from Saginaw, Michigan; Fort Wayne, Indiana; Louisville, Kentucky; and Montgomery, Alabama. These voices represent the Inland Northern, North Midland, South Midland, and Inland Southern dialect areas. Suppose the pairs of traits "intelligent-unintelligent," "educated-uneducated," and "friendly-unfriendly" were selected for the study. The voices are played for respondents (usually all from one area), who then indicate on a seven-point scale how they feel about the intelligence, education, and friendliness of the speakers. After analyzing the responses, the researcher would be justified in characterizing the respondents' reactions to these voices, but there would be no justification at all in saying that the respondents believed this or that about speakers in terms of their dialect area, for in such studies it has not been usual for the researcher to ask the respondents where they think the voices are from. Information about the respondents' beliefs about dialect areas is therefore an important corollary to attitude studies.

In addition, mental maps of dialect areas might help resolve an old question in dialectology. Which dialect boundaries are most important? Are those boundaries that represent the largest number of linguistic differences the most significant ones, or is there a subjective dimension in determining the weight of a dialect boundary? I obviously believe that the subjective dimension is important and that having respondents draw maps of dialect areas is one way of determining such weight. It is curious that a dialectologist might say that there is an important speech boundary along such-and-such a line but that no nondialectologists who live on either side of the line know that it is there. It is not too much of an exaggeration, for example, to say that, for much of its distance, the Inland Northern–North Midland line is exactly such a boundary.

Although I believe that there are other research and theoretical uses for the nondialectologists' perception of dialect boundaries, I maintain, finally, that the applied linguistic dimension of these studies is perhaps the most important. Specialists in education, law, medicine, advertising, and other public domain areas who make use of dialect and language attitude studies will surely want to know how people classify language differences. If we accept only the dialectologists' classification, we may have an elegant representation of the actual differences in the linguistic items chosen for investigation but may miss many of the important classifications that the vast majority of speakers make of language and its users.

How does one go about collecting the impressions nondialectologists have of the regional distribution of language? Although there are a number of techniques, I discuss one that uses respondents' drawings of their impressions of the speech regions of an area (Preston, "Perceptual Dialectology"). Figure 3 shows the response of a young, well-educated, white female Hawaiian who was asked to outline and label the areas of the United States where people speak differently. While a great many interesting things can be learned from figure 3, it is, after all, the map of only one person. How can you generalize

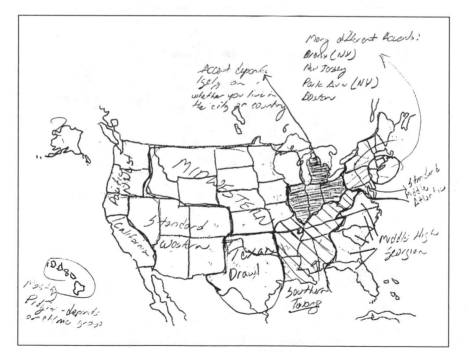

**Figure 3. A Hawaiian Respondent's Perception
of Dialect Areas of the United States**

the responses of many people? In figure 4, I have put together the perceptions of a larger number of speakers to come up with a generalization for one
region. I have copied onto one map all the boundaries drawn by different
respondents of the area I call "Northern." These responses were made
by thirty-five young, white male and female students in composition and
literature classes at Indiana University Southeast in New Albany; none had
studied linguistics or dialectology. Of course, I have not been very precise,
but where the boundaries drawn by several respondents have more or less
fallen together, I have drawn a thicker, striped, or solid line and provided
a key to indicate how many respondents think the boundary is there. This
procedure is the same one dialectologists use when they propose major
dialect boundaries. It is easy to see, in figure 4, why I suggest that Michigan,
Wisconsin, and half of Minnesota make up the area the majority of my
southern Indiana respondents regard as "Northern." Of course, you have
to look at quite a few maps to determine which areas are being drawn by a
group of respondents, and that task may be the most difficult and subjective
part of the process. As a rule of thumb, I have not generalized responses

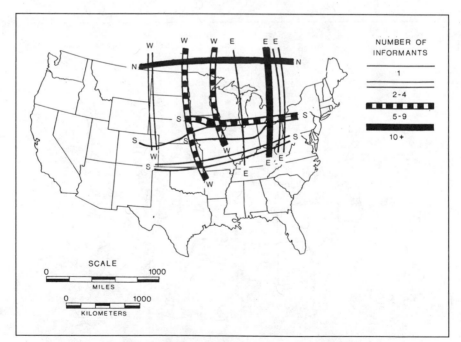

**Figure 4. Boundaries of the "Northern" Dialect Area
as Perceived by Southern Indiana Residents**

for an area unless it has been drawn by five or more respondents, but I have been working with sample sizes of thirty or forty. If you collect only a dozen or so maps, you may want to generalize regions drawn by as few as three respondents. You must be careful to pay attention to the area drawn and not the label given. For example, if two respondents outline roughly the same area and one calls it "Midwest" and another "North," you must treat the two as the same area and use a neutral geographical term of your own to describe it. Of course, you may study the labels respondents give to areas, and that is an interesting project in its own right, as I found in my study of Hawaiians' responses ("Perceptual Dialectology").

Once I have determined the majority boundaries for all the areas my respondents have drawn, I copy all the generalized areas onto a single map, such as figure 5. I am careful to identify who my respondents are—where they are from, their age, sex, social class, and ethnicity, in order to be as precise as possible about differences between the perceptions of one group

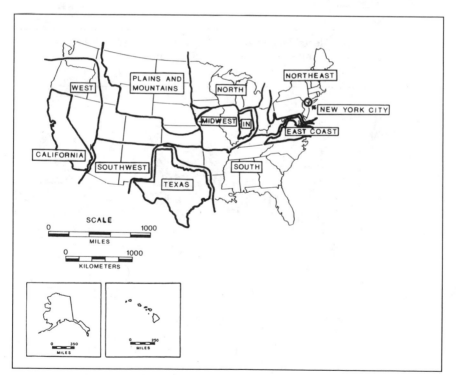

**Figure 5. Mental Map of Dialect Areas of the United States
by Southern Indiana Residents**

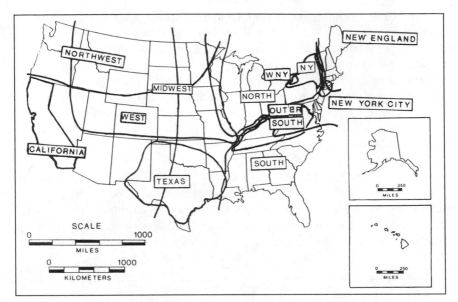

**Figure 6. Mental Map of Dialect Areas of the United States
by Western New York Residents**

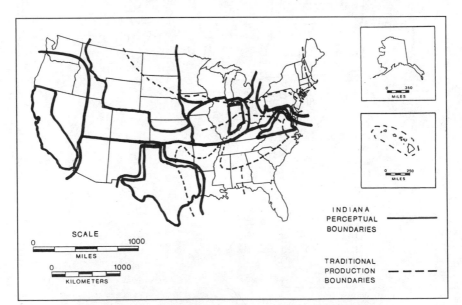

**Figure 7. Comparison of the Southern Indiana Mental Map
of United States Dialects with a Traditional Dialect Map**

and another. Figure 6, for example, is a composite map prepared in exactly the same way as figure 5, but the respondents are young college students from western New York, not southern Indiana. It is easy to see that their perceptions of dialect areas are significantly different.

Once you have completed composite maps of dialect areas, you may compare them with maps of actual dialect performance. Figure 7, for example, contrasts the perceived dialect areas as depicted in figure 5 with a dialectologist's view of the distribution of actual language features. Again, the differences are striking. The broken lines, adapted from Roger Shuy (*Discovering* 47), show the traditional boundaries of Eastern New England, Northern, North Midland, South Midland, and Southern dialects.

In addition to comparison with actual dialect distribution, the maps you derive from perception studies may be compared with other cultural geographic maps. Figure 8 represents areas of the United States designated

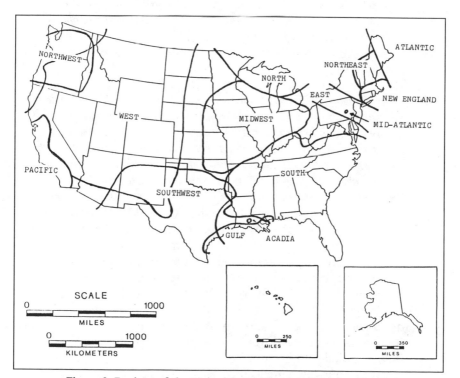

**Figure 8. Regions of the United States Based on Business Names
in Telephone Yellow Pages**
(Source: Zelinsky 14)

by names of businesses listed in telephone yellow pages advertising (e.g., "Midwest Computer Sales," "Northwest Dairy Products," "Pacific Coast Laundries"). Again, there are interesting differences and similarities. It is especially worth noting that in some ways the perception of dialects by nondialectologists in both figures 5 and 6 corresponds better to the map of regional labels from the yellow pages than it does to the traditional map of dialect areas (fig. 7). Doubtless regional stereotypes that have nothing to do with speech play a large role in the perception of dialect boundaries.

Of course, mental map dialect data can be collected by simply asking people to draw maps of their impressions of speech boundaries, but here are some hints to help you do this work on your own:

1. Remember not to use the word *dialect* in your instructions to respondents; to many people the word suggests old-fashioned or nonstandard speech. The following instructions might be helpful: *This map-drawing task is designed to discover your idea of the distribution of English in the United States. What I am after are your own opinions, based on your knowledge and experiences. The right answer is the one you have, not the answer of some expert. Please draw a boundary around each part of the United States where you believe people speak differently; if you have a name for the area you draw (or the people who live in it), please write that label on the map. You may not feel that you have been able to explain everything in writing on the map you draw, and I hope you will take time to talk to me about it. Of course, I especially appreciate your taking the time to cooperate, and I personally assure you that all the information you give me will be kept confidential. My aim is simply to find out more about language and its users. Again, thanks for your cooperation.*

2. Remember to keep a record of who your informants are by means of a personal data sheet similar to the one used by Michael Montgomery in this volume. Of course, you cannot ask people to fill in their own social-class status; but if you are interested in that distinction, you may want to consult a sociology text to help you make such decisions. I have used the system outlined in *Social Class in America*, by W. Lloyd Warner, M. Meeker, and K. Eells.

3. Use maps with at least state lines drawn in, and let your respondents consult a good road map of the United States (which you should always take with you) if they like; you do not want to test their knowledge of geography.

4. Reassure your respondents that there are no correct answers; you are interested in what they think about language distribution. If they complain that they have not visited some areas, remind them

that they may have heard speakers from other areas in person or through the media, but do not force them to draw boundaries they do not want to. In fact, people who draw only one boundary help establish those with the greatest weight. In my studies a line that divides the "South" from the rest of the United States is always the weightiest. No doubt you can think of many historical (Civil War, slavery) and popular culture (*Gone with the Wind, Dukes of Hazard,* Willie Nelson) reasons as well as linguistic ones to explain the importance of that boundary.

5.　Talk to your respondents about what they have done; if it is possible, make an audiotape of their comments. Their interpretation of what they have drawn may provide you with valuable information later on. Where did they get the information they used in drawing their maps? From actual visits to or residence in the areas labeled? From relatives, friends, or work contacts who are from the areas drawn in? From popular culture or the mass media? This information will allow discussion of the origins of such perceptions (and, perhaps, the different origins for different groups of respondents).

6.　Start your research with a homogeneous group (all the same age, ethnic group, class, and so on) so that you can make a generalized map right away. Compare this map with mine, with traditional maps of dialect divisions, with maps of other (nonlinguistic) cultural facts, and with other maps made of different subgroups from your own area. My essay "Five Visions of America" contains examples of maps drawn by respondents from five different geographical areas.

Hand-drawn maps of dialect areas and the generalizations made from them provide one example of the ethnographic record of the perception of language varieties by members of a speech community. The discovery of nondialectologists' perceptions of regional variation helps us understand the feelings and mental structures surrounding speech performance, reception, classification, and evaluation.

Suggestions for Further Reading

A good introduction to mental maps and their uses in cultural geography is Peter R. Gould and Rodney White's *Mental Maps*. Unfortunately, a good deal of the work on the perception of dialect differences has been done in languages other than English. The works listed below, however, provide a review of the field and include many references to background and related nonlinguistic geographical studies. Techniques different from the hand-drawn maps outlined here are discussed as well: Willem A. Grootaers, "Origin and Nature of the Subjective Boundaries of Dialects"; Dennis R. Preston, "Perceptual Dialectology," "Mental Maps of Language Distribution in Rio Grande do Sul (Brazil)," "Southern Indiana Perceptions of 'Correct' and 'Pleasant' Speech," "Five Visions of America," and *Perceptual Dialectology*, the last surveying the earlier studies and others. The following studies employ computer-assisted techniques: Preston, "Change in the Perception of Language Varieties," "Methods in the Study of Dialect Perception," and "Sociolinguistic Commonplaces in Variety Perception"; and Preston and George M. Howe, "Computerized Generalizations of Mental Dialect Maps."

The Use of Pictures in Collecting Regional Synonyms in the Classroom

Gordon R. Wood, Southern Illinois University, Edwardsville

THE study of regional English synonyms can enliven classroom investigations of our native tongue. Similarly, such study should have a place in courses in history, business, folklore, and social patterns. This essay explains how students can become immediately involved in finding their own local usages during single class sessions. It is hoped that such discoveries will be a livelier form of learning than that which comes from a textbook list.

The procedure to be used is to show a group of pictures of familiar objects. As the students see each picture, they write down the familiar name of the item and later in the class compare their lists. The choice of pictures given here comes from Stanley M. Sapon's *Pictorial Linguistic Interview Manual*, to which I added some pictures appropriate to word choices of the southern United States (see apps. A and B). Before we consider the adaptation of this manual to class use, it is useful for readers to know something of its background.

A conference of linguistic scholars led Sapon to devise a manual that could be used in interviewing any person regardless of degree of literacy. As the interviewer pointed to pictures of familiar objects, a respondent named them and made brief comments that were tape-recorded. The linguist later transcribed the tapes and analyzed the speech traits. Its first use for Sapon was to gather "socio-economic variables of Mexico City phonology" (3). Part 1 of the manual contains 135 simple line drawings of familiar rural and city objects; part 2 has 12 drawings of domestic animals and their young; part 3 has full-page drawings of events such as a hold-up in a city. I added pictures of vegetables, insects, and other items that were thought to have different local names in the South: *snake doctor* or *snake feeder* alongside the textbook term *dragonfly*, for example. The 161 pictures were arbitrarily assigned numbers between 1 and 999 in random order. The random numbering of the pictures was to secure a more natural pronunciation of numerals than would come from sequential counting. In my experience, numbers 100 to 199 ordinarily are pronounced as "hundred" and "hundred ninety-nine." Above that there is some variety: "two ten," "two one oh," "two hundred and ten." Regional variations have not been mapped, as far as I know.

Classroom Adaptation

Teachers can gather immediate information about the students' local word choices by asking for written rather than spoken names for the objects depicted. Let us suppose that one half of the class period is devoted to writing down the name as a picture is shown. After the final numbered picture, the students exchange lists, and the teacher asks for a show of hands. For item 116, how many lists have *skillet*? How many have *frying pan*? Does item 464 have any names other than *dragonfly*? And item 851, has it simply *rail fence* or no name at all? Discussion on other synonyms such as *spider* for a kind of skillet may or may not develop. The answers from one class can be compared with those of a later class for additional comments in other sessions.

In some courses students may interview older relatives, neighbors, friends, or others who are readily available and can provide answers that will give the student authentic data representative of a particular region or age group. If so, the teacher should furnish mimeographed copies of the pictures used in class and will probably direct the process of interviewing and reporting. Explorations of this latter sort will take several class sessions.

Small advanced classes may be able to listen to their own speech patterns. The class as a whole can go to individual booths in a language laboratory; within a given time, each student will say the numbers and names into a tape recorder. Again the teacher controls what is said by issuing the pictures and by telling the students to name the contents picture by picture. For later classroom discussion, the teacher may copy portions of each tape and play them to the entire class. After the class discussion, each student can listen to his or her entire tape and make whatever additions seem proper. The results of these taped interviews could serve as sources for term papers if appropriate for the class in which the exercise is used.

Producing the Required Pictures

As I suggested earlier, teachers should follow Sapon's and my example: draw the necessary pictures or find them in various published sources such as catalogs and magazines. A list of the numbered topics and an example of one picture come at the end of this essay. Other publications list names that may be useful and provide maps showing their local occurrence: for example, word atlases of the United States such as Hans Kurath's *A Word Geography of the Eastern United States* and Frederic G. Cassidy's *Dictionary of American Regional English*.

Some pictures should clearly depict items found in cities. Here the teacher will have to rely on experience rather than on published records. For instance, in one city a visitor may be told to go to the third *stoplight*; somewhere else it is *traffic light*; and in yet a third locality, *red light*. The object to be depicted in each instance is the same device, with three colors of lights.

For written answers, each picture should show something that has two or more names familiar to the class members.

Possible Outcomes

The presentation should obviously allow enough time for students to write their answers, exchange papers, and report what is in the lists at hand. If everything goes as planned, everyone will have a complete list. Furthermore, the class can discover an interesting variety of synonyms. Of course, if every student gives the same name to a particular picture, the teacher might want to replace it with something different in later classes.

Some pictures will produce odd responses that cannot be explained in terms of regional word choice. My evidence here comes from spoken rather than written statements. One speaker said, "That's a mighty poor picture of a lightning bug." Another picture will simply be misread. Thus an illustration with an arrow pointing to an egg yolk sometimes was named "broken egg" or "busted egg" despite the directional arrow. A third sort of response has no explanation. All but one person identified a picture as that of a grasshopper; that person said "antelope," perhaps simply pulling the name out of thin air, though the researcher can never be sure whether a single unique response represents family usage or a narrowly regional term or simply a misunderstanding. Such unexpected spoken answers hint at what now and again may occur in the students' written responses.

Privacy

Almost everyone will answer with candor, it seems to me, if privacy of response is ensured. A simple classroom precaution should establish enough privacy to reassure most students. When the students have completed their answer sheets, they put their names on the back. When the papers are exchanged, the class looks only at the front. In commenting on the word list at hand, a student can say, "This list has *rail fence* and *skillet*" or "Mine has *zigzag* and also *skillet*." And so on. In no instance should any student be named in the discussion.

Teachers who wish to publish composite class lists can do so by consolidating the counts within a class or across classes. The tabulations can be entirely anonymous:

rail fence   14
zigzag fence   9
fence   2

In some instances researchers have added such variables as gender, age, place of residence, and level of schooling. Such additional classifications do not seem to me to be appropriate in classrooms. At best, their possible usefulness needs to be weighed against the chance that these additional data will show who wrote what. Students may be hesitant if this much of their identity is revealed. But whatever the case, the aim of these studies is to arouse interest in the great variety in local word choice.

Examples

Line Drawing
The rail fence is useful for written and spoken interviews, since the fence has different regional names and the word *fence* may have several local pronunciations. The barbed wire fence is chiefly used for spoken interviews because of the local pronunciations of both *barb(ed)* and *wire*.

Numbered Word List
The numbered vocabulary items below illustrate how pictures are numbered and listed in part 1 of Sapon's *Pictorial Linguistic Interview Manual* and Wood's additions. Sapon devised the unpatterned numbering to keep informants from saying numbers in a singsong as they went from one picture to the next. The list names items that teachers might use in making their own drawings; the Sapon and Wood manuals are long out of print, and Sapon's plan for setting up a

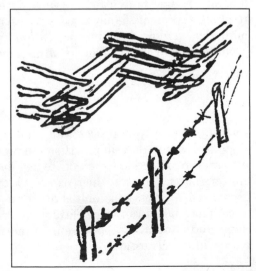

repository of taped interviews based on the drawings apparently never was fulfilled. Some responses have been set in italics to show that I have heard more than one name for the item pictured. For picture 10, names besides *woman's purse* have been *bag, handbag,* and *wallet.* Other entries than those in italics may or may not provide synonyms: for 163, *gap-toothed,* for example, I also got *snaggletoothed.*

6 locomotive; 2 handsaw; 5 cloud and lightning; 9 campfire and logs; 8 glass jug; 4 lid to milk can; 7 hammock; 3 tree leaf; 7 star shape; 20 towels drying on clothesline; 17 closed iron gate; 12 canoe at dock; 11 hand holding handkerchief; 15 face in mirror; 13 stove, oven, *burners*; 18 stork carrying baby; 16 bird's nest with eggs; 91 *yolk* of egg; 10 woman's *purse*; 14 fish in net; 30 saddle, spurs; 93 angel figure; 75 *umbrella*; 53 beer in bottle; 66 cow, milk in glass; 112 tiger; 140 medicines, mortar, pestle; 179 *traffic officer*; 196 automobile; 37 pottery jars (ollas); 108 shinbone; 42 fly, *fly swatter*; 90 block of ice, tongs; 118 wooden cross; 34 crowned queen; 133 crowned king; 188 spider, spiderweb; 115 hand-made *coffin*; 68 exploding fireworks; 40 electric iron; 86 tree stump and roots; 103 dog and fleas; 135 water from *faucet*; 60 door and door frame; 41 frog; 88 finger; 118 hand; 192 fist; 167 extended arm; 146 elbow; 50 bare feet; 79 bare foot; 151 back of knee joint; 124 measles on a face; 70 eye, lid; 163 gap-toothed; 80 eyes, eyebrows; 172 nose; 99 beard; 120 *Adam's apple*; 106 ear; 190 open mouth; 105 hands, front and back; 142 rocking cradle; 170 boat and oars; 111 wooden bench; 119 wheel; 155 house being built; 128 palm tree; 130 cottage; 101 balcony and open door; 114 comb lacking a tooth; 110 open box; 184 clump of trees; 116 *skillet*, pot; 109 swimming fish; 104 flag flying; 245 anvil and hammer; 212 three pears; 234 alligator; 200 small island; 217 rose, petal, leaves; 208 knotted rope; 300 swan; 256 roll of film; 295 three trumpets; 277 two cows; 269 royal carriage; 283 horse; 485 alarm clock; 513 knife and whetstone; 711 boy in shorts; 414 sunshine; 352 moon and stars; 408 mandolin; 510 dog; 612 ax embedded in log; 710 ears of corn, *shucks*; 316 room key; 491 city skyline; 381 bird cage; 533 submarine; 642 girl's *braids*; 481 well, pulley, bucket; 514 two *bunches* of grapes; 745 castle; 836 quill pen, ink bottle; 393 rope; 416 soldier in uniform; 619 travel trunk; 351 pearl *earrings* and necklace; 888 a bull; 792 ox and plow; 413 ox yoke and plow; 425 French bread loaf, sliced; 512 white bread loaf, sliced; 477 flower, petals, stem; 724 *eyeglasses*; 327 carrot with leaves; 516 roaring lion; 401 crossed eyes; 251 lobster; 350 old man and young boy walking; 878 pocket watch; 592 maid pushing *baby carriage*; 781 *cemetery* and *tombstones*; 333 octopus; 698 automobile accident; 843 whole and sliced apple.

Additions by Wood: 312 pliers; 466 wrench; 945 boy fishing, *fishing worm*; 433 *grasshopper*; 464 *dragonfly*; 699 wasps' nest; 650 *lightning bug*; 587 june bug; 213 *turtle*; 225 iris; 407 saw horses; 851 *rail fence*, barbed wire fence; 300 *woodpecker*; 570 wrestlers; 818 man in overalls; 535 quail; 952 owl; 887 *praying mantis*; 395 copperhead; 902 rattlesnake; 933 tomatoes; 701 *toadstools*; 801 barrel; 714 oranges; 666 lima beans; 845 *string beans*; 654 onions, squash; 775 shelled pecans.

Designing a Phonological Survey
for Students

Gilbert Youmans, University of Missouri, Columbia

POPULAR usage prefers the term *accent* to *dialect*, suggesting that, for ordinary speakers, the intuitive ability to distinguish among regional and social dialects is based largely on perceptions of systematic differences in pronunciation. Differences in syntax and vocabulary tend to be less well known and to occur less often in speech: we can talk indefinitely without using double negatives or regionalisms such as *y'all, bubbler* 'drinking fountain' and *berm* 'grassy strip between sidewalk and street,' but we cannot avoid vowels, which account for most of the variations in pronunciation among speakers of English.

Although beginning linguistics students are likely to possess greater intuitive knowledge about phonetic than about syntactic or lexical differences among speakers, phonological characteristics of dialects are harder to study rigorously in the classroom than syntax and vocabulary are. Printed surveys enable students to gather reliable data about lexical choices (*coke, fizzy drink, pop, soda, soda pop, soft drink, tonic*) and about syntactic variations such as which auxiliary verbs are preferred in conditional clauses (If I *had, would have* come . . .) or the acceptability of *anymore* in affirmative sentences (*Houses are expensive in Columbia anymore*) (Youmans). But students' judgments about the pronunciation of words such as *duty, house*, and *spoon* are too unreliable for use in published research. Indeed, even trained phoneticians are sometimes hard-pressed to decide whether the first vowel in *duty* is closer to [ɪu] or [u] in specific cases.

Nevertheless, students can learn to sharpen their perception of subphonemic differences like these, and one appropriate function of a dialects course is to teach them to do so. Such ear training refines their ability to distinguish among dialects and increases their knowledge of the phonological rules that characterize these dialects. Most students who enroll in dialects courses expect this sort of training, and they are likely to enjoy it—as long as the details do not become too minute. They want to acquire some of Henry Higgins's skill, and they are disappointed if they fail to do so.

One way for students to increase their sensitivity to pronunciation differences is by collecting and interpreting phonological data themselves. I developed a survey for this purpose based on a recording, *Our Changing*

Language (Burack and McDavid). The narrative on this recording is rather elementary, more suitable for advanced high school students than college students, but its samples of historical and contemporary dialects are useful to students at any level. The first side of the recording presents an overview of the history of English, featuring passages from *Beowulf*, the Nun's Priest's Tale, and *Julius Caesar* as they might have been read by contemporaries. The second side, focusing on English as spoken in North America, includes brief examples of the speech of twelve high school students living in the following communities: Prattville, Alabama; Redondo Beach, California; New Holland, Pennsylvania; Plymouth, New Hampshire; Chicago; San Antonio, Texas; Saint John's, Newfoundland; McClellanville, South Carolina; New York City; Salt Lake City; Marlinton, West Virginia; Edmonton, Alberta. Most of these informants read the passage reproduced in appendix 1. Other passages vary slightly, but they contain the same key words and phrases: *collar, caller; Mary, merry, character; large white house on Park Street*; and so on.

A recording such as *Our Changing Language* provides a useful introduction to regional variations in the pronunciation of white high school students in North America. (For an annotated bibliography of dialect recordings, see Linn and Zuber.) All the major dialect regions are represented, as well as some of the minor ones. The student of New Holland, for example, seems to have been influenced by Pennsylvania Dutch (that is, German) in his devoicing of the final consonants in *rug* [rʌk], *dog* [dɔk], and *cold* [kolt]. The speaker from South Carolina uses the [əʊ] diphthong before voiceless segments in *out* [əʊt] and *house* [həʊs], a dialect feature that is also found in eastern Virginia, in the New England states bordering Canada, and in Ontario.[1] Initial and medial liquids, [r] and [1], tend to shift toward [w] in the speech of the informant from New Hampshire, as in *We were very* [vɛwi]*worried* [wʌwid]; *Rover* [wovə] *was really* [wɪwi] *lost* [wɔst]. This feature occurs in the speech of the cartoon character Elmer Fudd ("You crazy [kwezi] rabbit [wæbɪt]") and the ABC newscaster Barbara Walters, parodied mercilessly as Babwa Wawa on *Saturday Night Live*. Students from states outside New England associate this unexpected [w] with baby talk, and they invariably laugh when they hear it. Their laughter provides an excellent occasion to discuss the irrationality of many of our responses to dialects, since there is obviously nothing inherently comical about the sound [w], just as there is nothing inherently ignorant about the sound of Appalachian speech, or Black English Vernacular, or whatever.

Recorded dialect samples such as those on *Our Changing Language* provide convenient reference points for defining phonetic contrasts. In dialects courses, I devote several class periods to identifying these contrasts and teaching students to identify them for themselves. Some of the differences are easy to perceive, such as the contrast between [grisi/grizi] (all of the Southerners on *Our Changing Language* say [grizi] and all of the Northerners say [grisi]). Another feature that is easy for students to recognize is the tendency in some dialects to delete [r] before consonants and at the ends of words: the informants from Alabama, New Hampshire, Newfoundland, South Carolina, and New York all show this tendency—though, interestingly enough, not in the phrase *burrs in his fur* (perhaps because of the spelling of *burrs*, with its double *r*, and the influence of rhyme in the case of *fur*).

Subtler differences require more practice to learn. On this recording, the raising of [ɛ] to [ɪ] before nasals in words such as *empty* and *then* is predominantly a South Midland feature, most obvious for the speaker from West Virginia and also clear for the informant from Texas. The predominantly Southern speaker from Alabama also exhibits this feature in her speech, but not the speaker from South Carolina, who has [ɛ] in both words, as do the speakers from the North.

The diphthong in *out* and *house* is very clearly [aʊ] for the speaker from Chicago and most other Northerners on the recording. The North Midland speaker from Pennsylvania centralizes the off-glide in these words, resulting in [aᵊ]. In extreme cases, this off-glide disappears altogether, reducing the diphthong to a monophthong—a process analogous to the change of [aɪ] to [aˈ] in words such as *white* (in the South and South Midland regions). The diphthong in *out* and *house* very clearly begins with [æ] for the speakers from New York, West Virginia, Texas, and Alabama, but with [ə] for the speaker from South Carolina. Different variations occur when the segment following the diphthong is voiced rather than voiceless. Hence this single vowel provides a rich and subtle set of contrasts for studying regional variations in pronunciation.

Another subtle, but nonetheless distinctive, contrast is evident in words such as *food* and *spoon*. Northern and Southern speakers have a high, back, rounded vowel [u] in these words that shifts toward a relatively more front, unrounded vowel [ɯˈ] in South Midland speech. (As a Northerner hearing this vowel for the first time, I mistook it for the diphthong [ɪu].) The most obvious example is in the speech of the student from West Virginia, but the speakers from Texas, Alabama, and even Salt Lake City have similar vowels.

For so short a passage, "Mary lived in a large white house on Park Street . . ." is surprisingly effective in eliciting regionally significant pronunciation differences, and initially I asked the students to use it for phonological surveys in my dialects courses. Students were unhappy, however, over their informants' complaints that the passage was "dumb, stupid, and boring." Some students also questioned the reliability of so brief a passage, since readers tended to be most nervous and stilted at the beginning of recording sessions and more natural at the end. Finally, the passage provided relatively few examples of pronunciation features that are considered especially important in Missouri—for example, the pronunciation of the name of the state itself, of words such as *forty* (which is often [fɑrʈi] in Saint Louis), and so on. At my students' request I wrote a new passage, incorporating most of the key words from "Mary lived in a large white house . . ." and adding a good many more. The result was "A Girl's Best Friend," which is reproduced in appendix 2 with many key phonological segments marked. (Naturally, these identifying markings were omitted from the copies of the story read by informants.)

Before teaching phonology in my dialects courses, I tape all my students responding to questions about their family histories, counting from one through ten, and reading "A Girl's Best Friend." I then replay the tape and discuss the distinctive features of their dialects with them. This experience helps prepare them to administer phonological surveys themselves and to understand the anxieties their own informants are likely to feel during taping.

After their own recording session, the students each recruit and tape four informants. Personal data are noted for each speaker on the form reproduced in appendix 3—including information about region (using zip codes), occupation (the first two digits of the *Dictionary of Occupational Titles* code), and the like. Also listed are typical phonetic variants in ninety-five key words in "A Girl's Best Friend." The students circle the variants that are closest to their informants' pronunciations. The results can be transferred to machine-readable test forms and collated by computer if the data are considered reliable enough for such treatment.

Students derive the most benefit from gathering and interpreting data for phonological surveys that they have helped to design, since the results often answer questions they themselves have raised about speech in their region. Sometimes these results are disappointing: for example, one student was eager to record an informant who consistently pronounced words such as *forty*, *fork*, and *Korky* with [ɑr] in his ordinary speech, but this speaker carefully shifted to [ɔr] during the recording session. The surveyor had unwittingly discovered an important fact about linguistic insecurity in Missouri, where jokes are often made about the [ɑr] pronunciation. Few people like being made the butt of a joke, especially over their speech. Hence some Missourians who normally pronounce words such as *fork* with [ɑr] are inclined to shift to [ɔr] in formal contexts (as when reading into a tape recorder for a dialect survey).

The bemusement with [ɑr] pronunciations is unusual in that it is primarily at the expense of Saint Louis speech, which is in most respects a prestige dialect in Missouri. More typical is the stigma attached to the intrusive [r] in [wɔrš] (*wash*); most Missourians associate it with the Ozarks, even though this pronunciation is found throughout the Midland dialect region (which includes nearly all of Missouri).

Missourians are also conscious (sometimes self-conscious) of the pronunciation of the vowel in words such as *white*. The boundary between North Midland and South Midland dialects divides the state roughly in half, with the North Midlanders favoring [aɪ] and South Midlanders [aˑ]. The situation is more complex than this, however, since [aɪ] also tends to be associated with urban and [aˑ] with rural speech. In Missouri this single dialect feature can thus trigger deep-seated feelings of regional and class solidarity (and prejudice).

By contrast, Missourians seem to react less strongly to differences in the pronunciation of the vowel in words such as *house*, although [aʊ] and [aᵊ] are clearly more common in northern Missouri, while [æʊ] and [æᵊ] are more common in the South. Finally, Missourians are almost wholly unaware of the distinctiveness of the relatively fronted, unrounded vowel in [spɯˤn]—perhaps because this pronunciation of *spoon* is typical throughout most of the state.

A phonological survey such as "A Girl's Best Friend" can serve as a useful exercise for beginning dialect students or as a research tool for advanced students. Such a survey can be tailored to different dialect regions by the introduction of different key words into the passage or by focusing on different key words already there. After administering such a survey, students have an increased awareness of pronunciation differences and their significance to regional and social dialectology. Indeed, most of them will never listen to speech the same way again, and this is, perhaps, the main thing.

Appendix 1

Reading passage used for samples of contemporary North American dialects on *Our Changing Language*:

> Mary lived in a large white house on Park Street with her mother and father. One day they had a caller. It was a mangy little dog. Mary let him sit on the rug in front of the fireplace in which the hickory logs were burning brightly. When she looked more closely, she saw that he was a sorry sight. He had a sore paw, many burrs in his fur, and he didn't have any collar. Mary washed the dog, but could not get him entirely clean. He looked hungry so she opened a can of food and put

it in a bowl with a greasy spoon. She also gave him some water. He ate until both bowls were empty. Just then her father came in the door. She asked if they could keep the dog instead of turning him out of the house on such a cold day. They kept the merry little character for many years. Mary and the dog had lots of very good times together.

Appendix 2

Passage written on the request of Missouri students:

A Girl's Best Fri<u>e</u>nd
1

M<u>a</u>ry Wheeler was born in a small town in Missouri, <u>wh</u>ere she lived
  2   3 4

happily wi<u>th</u> he<u>r</u> mothe<u>r</u> and fathe<u>r</u>. The <u>W</u>heelers' house was forty-four
       5   6   7   8   9

years old when Mary was born, and by the t<u>i</u>me she was t<u>e</u>n, the p<u>oo</u>r old
                                    10   11   12

building had fallen up<u>o</u>n hard times. It had a leaky r<u>oo</u>f, rotten rafters,
                  13   14

and term<u>i</u>tes in nearly every r<u>oo</u>m. One m<u>o</u>rning her father lost his t<u>e</u>mper
   15   16   17   18

and shouted that the house looked like a Color<u>a</u>do chicken c<u>oo</u>p after a
                                      19   20

spring snow sl<u>i</u>de. <u>R</u>ather than sp<u>e</u>nd <u>a</u>ny money to fix the house up, the
          21   22   23 24

Wheelers dec<u>i</u>ded to buy <u>Au</u>nt Ma<u>r</u>tha's place, which was a large <u>wh</u>ite
        25   26   27   28

tw<u>o</u>-story home on Pa<u>r</u>k Street. It was rather old, t<u>oo</u>, but it had cha<u>r</u>acter,
29   30   31   32

and Mary liked it be<u>cause</u> there was a h<u>u</u>ge climbing tree with gna<u>r</u>led
                     33   34   35

r<u>oo</u>ts in the front yard. <u>U</u>nfortunately, Park Street had a not<u>o</u>riously hi<u>gh</u>
36   37   38   39

cr<u>i</u>me rate, so the Wheelers had to g<u>e</u>t a watchdog—a German police d<u>o</u>g
40   41   42

named K<u>o</u>rky—whose d<u>u</u>ty was to look as fierce as possible wi<u>th</u>out biting
    43   44   45

any friendly c<u>a</u>llers. The dog looked mean, all ri<u>gh</u>t, wi<u>th</u> giant pa<u>ws</u>, bu<u>rr</u>s
          46   47   48   49   50

in his fur, brass studs on his c<u>o</u>llar, and saliva dripping from his bared
                                        51

fangs. Mary loved him just the same, but she was very worried about his
   52
barking and snarling, which scared away all the other little girls in the
   53
neighborhood, so they hardly ever came over to her house to play.
   54
   One day Mary was rinsing the greasy dishes in the sink in order to
   55
earn her weekly allowance. She was paid just a quarter, but she was a good
   56
little girl, so she polished the knives, forks, and spoons carefully before
   57   58   59
putting them into the drawer. After emptying the water from the sink, she
   60   61
washed her hands, then took the garbage bag outside and threw it into the
62   63
trash can beside the garage. She was about to get out a new bag, when, much
   64   65   66   67
to her horror, she heard Korky growling down by the creek behind her
   68   69
house. She ran to the creek to find out what was the matter, feeling sorry
70   71
that her family had ever bought a mangy dog like Korky and promising
   72
herself that tomorrow they'd send him on a one-way flight to Oregon, or
   73   74
maybe to a poisonous snake farm in Nevada with electrified fences guard-
   75   76   77
ing the exits. But when she rounded the corner of the house, she saw
   78   79
Korky standing with all four paws on the chest of a scruffy-looking man

who was clutching his forehead, half in fear, half in disgust. While he was
   80
squirming on the ground, her father's antique coin collection dribbled out

of his pockets onto the luxurious tall grass where he was lying. Mary ran
   81   82   83
into the house, merrily shouting to her father that Korky was a pretty good
   84   85
dog after all. When the police investigated the robber, they found that he
   86
was married to a widow from Atlanta who had nine children, so Mary's
   87   88   89

father thought it would be in<u>h</u>umane to press ch<u>a</u>rges. As for Korky, he
                 90   91
became the h<u>e</u>ro of the neighborhood. All the children br<u>ou</u>ght him left-
              92   93
over f<u>oo</u>d and bones, and he never scared Mary's friends ag<u>ai</u>n.
   94   95

Appendix 3

Answer Key to "A Girl's Best Friend"

Surveyor's name   Date

Informant (name optional)   Identifier code

Race

Sex   Age   Occupation   (*DOT* code __ __)

Father's childhood home   (Zip __ __ __ __ __)

Mother's childhood home   (Zip __ __ __ __ __)

Informant's childhood home   (Zip __ __ __ __ __)

Other home (if any)   (Zip __ __ __ __ __)

Occupation of primary breadwinner in informant's childhood family
(usually that of the father or mother)   (*DOT* code __ __)

Highest formal schooling (grade or degree)

In each item below, circle the pronunciation that is closest to the speaker's:

1. Fri<u>e</u>nd	(a) [ɛ]	(b) [æ]	(c) [ɪ]	
2. M<u>a</u>ry	(a) [ɛ]	(b) [æ]	(c) [e]	(d) [ʌ]
3. Missour<u>i</u>	(a) [i]	(b) [ə]		
4. <u>wh</u>ere	(a) [hw]	(b) [w]		
5. wi<u>th</u>	(a) [θ]	(b) [ð]		
6. he<u>r</u>	(a) [r]	(b) [Ø]		
7. mothe<u>r</u>	(a) [r]	(b) [Ø]		
8. fathe<u>r</u>	(a) [r]	(b) [Ø]		
9. <u>Wh</u>eelers'	(a) [hw]	(b) [w]		
10. t<u>i</u>me	(a) [aɪ]	(b) [aˑ]		
11. t<u>e</u>n	(a) [ɛ]	(b) [ɪ]		
12. p<u>oo</u>r	(a) [ɔ]	(b) [ʊ]	(c) [u]	
13. up<u>o</u>n	(a) [ɑ]	(b) [ɔ]	(c) [ʌ]	

14. r<u>oo</u>f   (a) [ʊ]   (b) [u]
15. term<u>i</u>tes   (a) [aɪ]   (b) [aˑ]
16. r<u>oo</u>m   (a) [ʊ]   (b) [u]
17. m<u>o</u>rning   (a) [ɔ]   (b) [ɑ]
18. t<u>e</u>mper   (a) [ɛ]   (b) [ɪ]
19. Color<u>a</u>do   (a) [ɑ]   (b) [æ]   (c) [e]
20. c<u>oo</u>p   (a) [u]   (b) [ʊ]
21. sl<u>i</u>de   (a) [aɪ]   (b) [aˑ]
22. r<u>a</u>ther   (a) [æ]   (b) [ɑ]   (c) [ʌ]
23. sp<u>e</u>nd   (a) [ɛ]   (b) [ɪ]
24. <u>a</u>ny   (a) [ɛ]   (b) [ɪ]
25. dec<u>i</u>ded   (a) [aɪ]   (b) [aˑ]
26. <u>A</u>unt   (a) [æ]   (b) [ɑ]
27. Ma<u>r</u>tha's   (a) [r]   (b) [Ø]
28. <u>wh</u>ite   (a) [hw]   (b) [w]
29. tw<u>o</u>   (a) [u]   (b) [ɯ<]
30. Pa<u>r</u>k   (a) [r]   (b) [Ø]
31. t<u>oo</u>   (a) [u]   (b) [ɯ<]
32. ch<u>a</u>racter   (a) [ɛ]   (b) [æ]
33. bec<u>ause</u>   (a) [kʌz]   (b) [kɔz]   (c) [kɔs]
34. <u>h</u>uge   (a) [hɪu]   (b) [yu]
35. gna<u>r</u>led   (a) [r]   (b) [Ø]
36. r<u>oo</u>ts   (a) [ʊ]   (b) [u]
37. <u>U</u>nfortunately (a) [ɑ]   (b) [ɔ]   (c) [ʌ]
38. not<u>o</u>riously   (a) [ɔ]   (b) [ɑ]
39. h<u>igh</u>   (a) [aɪ]   (b) [aˑ]
40. cr<u>i</u>me   (a) [aɪ]   (b) [aˑ]
41. g<u>e</u>t   (a) [ɛ]   (b) [ɪ]
42. d<u>o</u>g   (a) [ɔ]   (b) [ɑ]
43. K<u>o</u>rky   (a) [ɔ]   (b) [ɑ]
44. d<u>u</u>ty   (a) [u]   (b) [ɪu]
45. wi<u>th</u>out   (a) [θ]   (b) [ð]
46. c<u>a</u>llers   (a) [ɑ]   (b) [ɔ]
47. r<u>i</u>ght   (a) [aɪ]   (b) [aˑ]
48. wi<u>th</u>   (a) [θ]   (b) [ð]
49. p<u>aw</u>s   (a) [ɔ]   (b) [ɑ]
50. bu<u>rr</u>s   (a) [r]   (b) [Ø]
51. c<u>o</u>llar   (a) [ɑ]   (b) [ɔ]
52. j<u>u</u>st   (a) [ʌ]   (b) [ɪ]
53. sc<u>a</u>red   (a) [ɛ]   (b) [æ]   (c) [ɪ]
54. ha<u>r</u>dly   (a) [r]   (b) [Ø]

55. grea_sy   (a) [s]   (b) [z]
56. _quarter   (a) [kw]   (b) [k]
57. kn_ives   (a) [aɪ]   (b) [aˑ]
58. f_orks   (a) [ɔ]   (b) [ɑ]
59. sp_oons   (a) [u]   (b) [ɯ<]
60. _emptying   (a) [ɛ]   (b) [ɪ]
61. w_ater   (a) [ɑ]   (b) [ɔ]
62. _washed_   (a) [wɑšt]   (b) [wɔršt]   (c) [wɔɪšt]
63. b_ag   (a) [æ]   (b) [e]   (c) [ɛ]
64. bes_ide   (a) [aɪ]   (b) [aˑ]
65. gara_ge_   (a) [ǰ]   (b) [ž]
66. ab_out   (a) [aʊ]   (b) [aˀ]   (c) [æʊ]   (d) [æˀ]   (e) [əʊ]
67. n_ew   (a) [u]   (b) [ɪu]
68. h_orror   (a) [ɔ]   (b) [ɑ]
69. cr_eek   (a) [i]   (b) [ɪ]
70. h_ouse   (a) [aʊ]   (b) [aˀ]   (c) [æʊ]   (d) [æˀ]   (e) [əʊ]
71. s_orry   (a) [ɑ]   (b) [ɔ]   (c) [æ]
72. m_angy   (a) [e]   (b) [æ]
73. tom_orrow   (a) [ɑ]   (b) [ɔ]
74. Oreg_on   (a) [ə]   (b) [ɑ]   (c) [ɔ]
75. Nev_ada   (a) [æ]   (b) [e]   (c) [ɑ]
76. electrif_ied   (a) [aɪ]   (b) [aˑ]
77. f_ences   (a) [ɛ]   (b) [ɪ]
78. e_xits   (a) [ks]   (b) [gz]   (c) [kz]   (d) [gs]
79. r_ounded   (a) [aʊ]   (b) [aˀ]   (c) [æʊ]   (d) [æˀ]   (e) [əʊ]
80. fore_head_   (a) [hɛd]   (b) [əd]
                     (stressed)   (unstressed)
81. _onto   (a) [ɔ]   (b) [ɑ]   (c) [ʌ]
82. lu_xurious   (a) [gž]   (b) [kš]   (c) [kž]   (d) [gš]
83. M_ary   (a) [ɛ]   (b) [æ]   (c) [e]   (d) [ʌ]
84. m_errily   (a) [ɛ]   (b) [æ]   (c) [e]   (d) [ʌ]
85. sh_outing   (a) [aʊ]   (b) [aˀ]   (c) [æʊ]   (d) [æˀ]   (e) [əʊ]
86. f_ound   (a) [aʊ]   (b) [aˀ]   (c) [æʊ]   (d) [æˀ]   (e) [əʊ]
87. m_arried   (a) [ɛ]   (b) [æ]   (c) [e]
88. wid_ow_   (a) [o]   (b) [ə]
89. Atlan_ta   (a) [t]   (b) [Ø]
90. in_humane   (a) [hɪu]   (b) [yu]
91. char_ges   (a) [r]   (b) [Ø]
92. h_ero   (a) [i]   (b) [ɪ]
93. br_ought   (a) [ɔ]   (b) [ɑ]

94. f<u>oo</u>d   (a) [u]   (b) [ɯ<]
95. ag<u>ai</u>n   (a) [ɛ]   (b) [ɪ]   (c) [e]

Note

[1] Special symbols in this article include the following:
əʊ   dialectal variant of [aʊ], used in Ontario and eastern Virginia
ᵊ   unrounded off-glide following any vowel: e.g., [æᵊ] as a variant of [aʊ]
ˈ   slightly lengthened vowel: e.g., [aˈ] as a Southern variant of [aɪ]
ɯ<   fronted, high, back, unrounded vowel
 ̣   voicing of a consonant, as in the voiced [t] in *forty* [fɔrṭi]

Using Audio Recordings to Study Variation in International English

Charles B. Martin, University of North Texas

MANY introductory linguistics courses have at least a short unit on dialect differences in English or on language variation in general, and introductory textbooks have brief dialect descriptions (including phonetic transcriptions), dialect maps, word lists, questionnaires, and other printed aids to make the study of language variation more rewarding. Other articles in this volume mention the value of using these standard printed materials and two phonograph recordings (*Our Changing Language, Americans Speaking*) and an audio cassette (accompanying a book edited by Alva L. Davis, *Culture*) available from the National Council of Teachers of English; this article, however, suggests a slightly different approach.

One can add an interesting dimension to dialect study, at little expense, by seeking out speakers of varieties of English other than the well-known British and American dialects. With all of the inexpensive recording equipment that is available today, it is easy enough to make one's own recordings. Most of us in colleges and universities have students from other parts of the country with interesting regional dialects. With a little ingenuity, however, we can also find speakers from other parts of the world, particularly international graduate students employed as lab instructors, who would not mind reading a few sentences into a tape recorder, sentences that contain key words that usually vary in pronunciation (often in meaning as well) in the "Englishes" of the world (see, e.g., articles in Bailey and Görlach):

1. The mother wrapped the baby in a blanket and laid it in the crib.
2. You've always put butter on your bread, haven't you?
3. We need to call a plumber about a leaky faucet.
4. The thing you saw was actually a little reddish-colored dog.

A short paragraph, similar to the following, will accomplish the same purpose. Speakers should be encouraged to change the wording of the sentences or the paragraph to reflect their home dialects.

Last Tuesday Father went with us to see the haunted house. We parked the car and walked along a path which led to a creek. We could hardly

see the house for the fog. The roof was sagging; the stairs had not
been cared for; a broken cot had been left near the window. The sink
was clogged with dirt; the fireplace was full of soot. A frog croaked in
the distance. What a sorry sight!

Further samples can be collected if we ask the students to talk extemporane-
ously about themselves for a few minutes after they have read the paragraph.
We must, of course, ask some open-ended questions to get them started:
"What reasons made you decide to come to this university? What have been
some of your most interesting summer jobs? Tell me about your favorite
vacation (hobby, sport, job, etc.)."

Our dialect informants need not be students; they might be anyone
we meet at professional conferences or on vacations. The secret is to have
a pocket-size recorder handy for any unplanned interview. One summer
in Galway, Ireland, I ran across two young Presbyterians preaching in a
park to whoever would listen. Not only did I record part of their sermon,
but I got an interview afterward about their work—and in a variety of
Irish that I had not heard up to that point. Back home in a fitness program,
I met a newly arrived graduate student from England with a cockney accent. Fortunately, he had a class in my building and obligingly dropped by
my office for an interview. Most people are flattered to have their voices
recorded once you explain your interest in different kinds of speech. Indeed, there is a special value to these kinds of recordings: for whatever
reason, students are impressed by the simple fact that their teacher has made
the recordings.

If one needs samples of English from around the world but has few
opportunities to meet non-Americans, it is easy to record international English during television newscasts, talk shows, or even movies if one remembers to keep a tape recorder near the television set. Occasionally, a British
film is playing at a local theater, and students who have attended it should
be encouraged to discuss differences in British and American English.

One must not overlook community resources. In a sociolinguistics class
I taught recently, one of the assignments included an examination of a creole
language (for a more detailed study of creole language, see Mufwene, in this
volume). I enlisted the services of an international student from Suriname,
who speaks English, Dutch, and Sranan Tongo (Suriname Creole). Fortunately, he also has a beautiful voice and illustrated his creole language by
singing some folk songs as students followed a printed text. In the same
course, when we discussed the two official languages of Norway, Nynorsk
("new Norwegian") and Bokmal ("book language"), I was able to recruit a
language professor who had come to the United States from Norway and

who knew both dialects. He illustrated the differences between the two and provided printed texts that the students could follow.

With videocassette recorders becoming more plentiful in school media centers, it is also easy to play part of a film to demonstrate a point on language variation. In a class on the history of the English language, I played about thirty minutes of *Educating Rita* so that students could compare the Received Standard pronunciation of the professor with the cockney speech of Rita, a student who had decided in midlife that she wanted a university education. In a sociolinguistics class, I played the segment on English Creole from the PBS series *The Story of English*. After the students have listened to these "unusual" varieties of English, they might view *American Tongues*, a documentary highlighting differences in pronunciation and vocabulary throughout the United States, with the speakers making observations about their own speech and that of others, and then compare the variety in American English with what they have heard from other parts of the English-speaking world.

Many textbooks have samples of pronunciation and vocabulary differences throughout the country, and some, like Roger Shuy's *Discovering American Dialects*, have checklists of regional expressions. Teachers can adapt these to their own use or make up their own questionnaires. A simple exercise I have used is to give students a short list and ask them to find five informants either on campus or in their hometowns and record in phonetic symbols the pronunciations they hear. This exercise works best if the students have become proficient in phonetic transcription and have a variety of speakers to draw from. In addition to this standard exercise, students can administer questionnaires to students from other parts of the English-speaking world, such as anglophone Africa or Singapore.

The students may want to make up their own questionnaires by consulting E. Bagby Atwood's *The Regional Vocabulary of Texas*, regional atlases like Hans Kurath's *Linguistic Atlas of New England*, and Harold B. Allen's *The Linguistic Atlas of the Upper Midwest*, and publications based on data collected for the Linguistic Atlas of the Middle and South Atlantic States (Atwood, *Survey of Verb Forms*; Kurath, *Word Geography*; Kurath and McDavid, *Pronunciation of English*). The recently published first and second volumes (A–C, D–H) of the *Dictionary of American Regional English* (Cassidy) includes a questionnaire of 1,847 items used by fieldworkers to gather information for the dictionary. Such questionnaires are designed to keep the interviewer from suggesting responses. Giving the students an opportunity to do some basic fieldwork with a simplified questionnaire or word list for transcription, elementary though it may be, will teach them a valuable lesson in basic field techniques.

Materials like these make the study of language variation interesting for students. Recordings bring language variation alive. Fieldwork makes students aware of the labor that went into the great linguistic atlas projects, and live performances by skillful speakers bring the exotic into the classroom. At any rate, if teachers keep their eyes and ears open, they will encounter a number of ways to bring excitement to the study of language variation.

In recent years there has been an increasing interest in English as a world language. Articles that teachers (and students) will find useful include those of Tony Fairman; Manfred Görlach; and Braj B. Kachru ("Teaching World Englishes"); in addition, three collections contain articles of varied interest: Richard W. Bailey and Görlach, *English as a World Language*; John B. Pride, *New Englishes*; and Kachru, *The Other Tongue*. Longer volumes include the books published in the series Varieties of English around the World and works by John Platt, H. Weber, and M. L. Ho and by Peter Trudgill and Jean Hannah. Among journals on international English are *English Today*, *English World-Wide*, and *World Englishes*.

DARE in the Classroom

John Algeo, University of Georgia

EVERYONE is interested in dialects—even if we customarily think of them as the funny way other people talk. And a dictionary is the kind of book most people go to when they want to know something about language. Yet most dictionaries give relatively little information about dialect—indeed, little about any form of our language other than the standard use that appears in the straightforward prose of our leading national newspapers and publishing houses. Now, however, there is a dictionary that tells about various forms of nonstandard American English. The *Dictionary of American Regional English*, under the chief editorship of Frederic G. Cassidy, is being published.

DARE, as the dictionary is acronymously known, is a remarkable book. The making of this dictionary, the history behind it, its relationship to other dialect studies—one can read about all such matters in the introduction to the book. But one of the most remarkable qualities of *DARE* is the range of appeal it has. It is a scholarly dictionary, prepared by learned editors, to be used by the scholarly world. But in addition, it has a popular appeal unmatched by any other academic wordbook in our time. *DARE* is not only a learned book; it is a fun book. That quality makes it especially suitable for use in the classroom.

The words *DARE* records are those that interest all speakers of English—the everyday, funny expressions that make up our discourse, not as a whole people, but as the motley crew we are. *DARE* treats those portions of our vocabulary that are not part of standard use, that are limited to one or another part of the country or to one or another social group. It deals especially with "folk" words, the natural language of unsophisticated people unimpeded by an editor's notion of how they ought to be talking or writing.

The regionally and socially limited vocabulary of English interests us because we want to know whether others are familiar with the odd terms we know and what outlandish ways of talking our fellow citizens have come up with. These are not scholarly motives exactly, but they are human ones.

To try to illustrate the unscholarly, fun aspects of the dictionary is to encounter an embarrassment of riches. Here indeed is God's plenty. The first volume of *DARE* covers the letters *A–C*, and they alone are an endless source of instruction and delight. *DARE* is probably the best book in existence to use for teaching students how to browse through a dictionary—and enjoy the process. A sample of the kind of browsing that can be done with *DARE*, and of the results of such browsing, is the quiz below.

Quiz: What's That Stuff?

Match the term on the left with its meaning on the right.

a. __ Adam's ale	1. bacon
b. __ African dominoes	2. burro
c. __ African golf	3. chamber pot
d. __ Alabama wool	4. codfish
e. __ Alaska turkey	5. cornbread
f. __ Albany beef	6. cotton
g. __ Amish golf	7. craps (use twice)
h. __ Arizona cloudburst	8. croquet
i. __ Arizona nightingale	9. deck of cards
j. __ Arizona paint job	10. diarrhea
k. __ Arizona tenor	11. donkey
l. __ Arkansas asphalt	12. downpour
m. __ Arkansas chicken	13. fat pork
n. __ Arkansas dew	14. hammer
o. __ Arkansas fire extinguisher	15. large bowie knife
p. __ Arkansas lizard	16. log surface of a road
q. __ Arkansas T-bone	17. louse
r. __ Arkansas toothpick	18. mustard
s. __ Arkansas wedding cake	19. newspapers
t. __ August ham	20. noose
u. __ Aunt Jane's room	21. penny
v. __ Aztec two-step	22. pigs' feet
w. __ Boston dollar	23. privy
x. __ Boston screwdriver	24. razor-back hog
y. __ California blanket	25. rice
z. __ California collar	26. roadrunner
aa. __ California peacock	27. salmon (use twice)
bb. __ California prayer book	28. salt pork
cc. __ Cape Cod turkey	29. sandstorm
dd. __ Carolina racehorse	30. sturgeon
ee. __ Chinese grits	31. tubercular person
ff. __ Cincinnati oysters	32. unfinished surface
gg. __ Cincinnati quail	33. water
hh. __ Colorado mockingbird	34. watermelon
ii. __ Columbia River turkey	
jj. __ Coney Island butter	

The quiz was made up as follows: I went through volume 1 of the dictionary and picked out a fair sample of words that are derived from proper names, especially place names (after all, this is a dictionary of *regional* English). Then I narrowed down that selection to certain joke words—specifically, terms that ironically compare their referents to markedly superior or opposite things and associate them with places or people. I tossed out some words to keep the list at a length that would fit on one typewritten page. The result is the list of terms on the left and the list of meanings of those terms on the right. The immediate aim of the quiz is to guess which terms and meanings match. The answers are in *DARE*, but for the sake of handy reference, here is the key: $a33, b7, c7, d6, e27, f30, g8, h29, i11, j32, k31, l16, m28, n12, o3, p17, q1, r15, s5, t34, u23, v10, w21, x14, y19, z20, aa26, bb9, cc4, dd24, ee25, ff22, gg13, hh2, ii27, jj18$.

One of my own favorite terms of this kind is missing from the dictionary. It is *Confederate champagne*, meaning "Coca-Cola." But there are quite enough other words of this kind just among the letters *A–C* to make a quiz of reasonable size. If later volumes of *DARE* are also used, the supply will be very great. Students can supply other such terms, which they are likely to know but which did not make it into *DARE*. Terms of that sort can be sent to the editors of *DARE* at the Department of English, University of Wisconsin, Madison, WI 53706, for later volumes or revisions of the dictionary. In this way, even young or inexperienced students can make a contribution to scholarship.

To be sure, *DARE* is by no means limited to joke words of the sort in the quiz. There are serious terms enough amid the God's plenty of this book. But even the joke words have their serious side. They illustrate a pattern of humor—irony—that is characteristic of American life from the frontier to the urban ghetto. They tell something about us as a people. They are basically good-humored, but some of them have an edge, and some show the ethnic, racial, or regional prejudice that is also a part of American life, indeed, of human life. A class discussion of what the terms imply and what stereotypes they reflect can be profitable.

Students with little or no linguistic background—for instance, high schoolers and college freshmen—can usefully play with terms like those of the quiz. Then they can make their own quizzes by browsing through the dictionary, looking for five to ten words that have something in common, and writing a list of the terms they have found and a list of the simple definitions of the terms (like those in the sample quiz). The resulting student quizzes can be exchanged or presented to the entire class, with a following discussion on the terms, their meanings, and limitations. The purpose of such quizzes is not to test knowledge but to play with language and in the process to learn something about variation, with its social and psychological concomitants.

Another kind of class activity based on *DARE* uses the questionnaire with which much of the dictionary's oral data base was gathered. The text of that questionnaire is printed in the front matter to volume 1 (lxii–lxxxv). The questions are grouped by subject, such as "Weather," "Furniture," "Foods," "Children's Games," "Schoolgoing," and nearly another two score. The teacher can make a judicious selection from those questions, according to the age and interest of the students, and conduct a mini survey of dialect in the class to see what answers students give, for example, to items such as "To stay away from school without an excuse" or "Other ways of answering 'no': 'Would you lend him ten dollars?' '————.' " (In using the *DARE* questionnaire, keep in mind that folk speech is sometimes indelicate, hence the need for selecting judiciously according to the audience.)

Students and teachers can also jointly make a selection of questions, thereby creating their own questionnaire for use in conducting a dialect survey as a class project. The students can administer the questionnaire to their parents, grandparents, or other older people with whom they have contact. For this purpose, the questionnaire is best kept short—a dozen to a score of items works well. A comparison of older-generation usage with the students' own responses may be interesting and lead to a discussion of generation differences and changes in society.

Whatever responses are gathered by these or other such means can be checked against the alphabetical listings in *DARE* to see whether the elicited terms are included. If they are not, send them to the editors of *DARE* for their future use—and let the students know that their work can actually be of use in this way. However, the collection of data is not the main point of such exercises. The results should always be discussed in class for what they show about ourselves, our society, and our knowledge of one another.

With more advanced students, the same sorts of exercises can be used, but with increasing sophistication in the items investigated and in the analysis of the results. For naive students, the aim may be simply to make them language-aware and to help them become conscious of the implications of language variation in society. Students in a linguistics class can benefit from studying parts of the introductory matter, such as Cassidy's concise essay "Language Changes Especially Common in American Folk Speech" (xxxvi–xl) and James W. Hartman's overview of phonological variation in the United States, "Guide to Pronunciation" (xli–lxi).

DARE includes some information appropriate for the scholar's attention and other information fit for the amateur's delight. Not many books can claim to serve both readerships, and to serve them well. *DARE* is one of those few. It is therefore an ideal tool for introducing students to the study of language variation.

Student-Designed Projects on Canadian English

Lilita Rodman, University of British Columbia

∽

THE English Department at the University of British Columbia offers a thirteen-week course in language variation to third- and fourth-year students with widely varied linguistic training and interests. While some are preparing to become teachers and have no formal linguistic training, others are about to enter graduate studies in linguistics. The course considers three main topics:

1. the characteristics of the main varieties of English, with the greatest emphasis on Canadian English, somewhat less on American English, and least on British English;
2. the methods used to study language variation, together with a critical evaluation of each;
3. the relationship between language variation and linguistic theory.

There is a midterm exam and a final, but the main assignment requires each student to design, conduct, and report on an investigation of some limited aspect of Vancouver English. The purpose of this assignment is to allow the students to integrate and apply what they are learning about methods and about Canadian English and to give them a little experience in all phases of a dialect study—project design, informant selection, interviewing, data recording, data analysis, and final reporting. In learning firsthand about the problems that can arise at every stage, the students should realize that in every study there have to be some compromises. One hopes that as a result the students will become more aware of limitations in published studies and evaluate the findings of these studies more intelligently, but also that they will appreciate more fully what language variation researchers have accomplished.

The student projects can also serve as pilot probes of aspects of Vancouver English that could be explored in more disciplined studies later. The possibility of discovering useful results or of developing new methods adds interest and credibility to the assignment; students like to provide information that can actually be used. Before describing this assignment in detail, however, I will outline some of the most important characteristics of Canadian English and summarize three student projects.

Canadian English

Canadian English has received much less scholarly attention than has American or British English. Although Walter S. Avis and A. M. Kinloch's bibliography lists over seven hundred comments and articles appearing before 1975, Ian Pringle suggests that there are fewer than a dozen major studies ("Concepts" 217). Various small regional surveys led to a nationwide questionnaire of grade nine students and their parents, the Survey of Canadian English (SCE) in 1971–72 (Scargill). Since then, more intense and more rigorously designed urban surveys modeled on the work of William Labov and of Peter Trudgill have been completed in Ottawa (Woods), St. John's (S. Clarke), and Vancouver (Gregg, *Final Report*). British Columbia has been particularly fortunate to be the home of three important Canadian English scholars, M. H. Scargill and H. J. Warkentyne in Victoria, and R. J. Gregg in Vancouver. The very ambitious Survey of Vancouver English (SVEN), a 1,058-item survey of 240 informants, is the culmination of Gregg's work over the past thirty years. As a result, my students have considerable base data to work from.

In most respects, Canadian English is like American English, and publications by Avis, Richard W. Bailey, R. E. McConnell, and Pringle indicate that it appears to be remarkably uniform, especially if one excludes the Maritimes, which, of course, were settled earlier and display considerable dialect diversity. As Bailey notes, "What is distinctly Canadian about Canadian English is not its unique linguistic features (of which there are a handful) but its combination of tendencies that are uniquely distributed" (161). Canadian English is rhotic, so that there is always an /r/ in words like *car* and *cart*, and it rhymes *cot* and *caught*, usually with a low, back, rounded vowel also found in words like *pot, shone, coffee, ball*. (In all but Newfoundland, well over 85 percent of the SCE respondents have the *caught/cot* merger [Scargill 80].) The most distinctive difference from American English and the one that has received the most attention in variation literature is what is known as "Canadian raising" (J. K. Chambers, "Canadian," "Group"; Gregg, "Diphthongs"; Joos, "Phonological"; Picard; Pringle, Dale, and Padolsky; Trudgill, "New Dialect"). In words like *right* and *house* (noun), Canadians usually have diphthongs with a higher onset than in words like *ride* and *house* (verb). That is, Canadians tend to have two noticeably different allophones of these diphthongs before voiceless and voiced consonants; however, both the precise quality of these diphthongs and their distribution in linguistic environments may vary from one part of the country to another. Similar allophonic alternation is found in several areas of the eastern United States.

A frequently studied kind of variation in Canadian English is the preference for one pronunciation of a word over another. Some competing pronunciations are fairly clearly British and American, such as [šɛd] and [skɛd] for the first syllable of *schedule*, or [lɛf] and [lu] for the first syllable of *lieutenant*, while others compete within American English as well, such as [ližɚ] and [lɛžɚ] for *leisure*, or [livɚ] and [lɛvɚ] for *lever*. Although most Canadians are generally uncertain about which competing variant is British and which American, at least in British Columbia such pronunciations as [rʊf] for *roof* (instead of [ruf]), [mɑm] for *mom* (instead of [mʌm]), or [zi] for z (instead of [zɛd]) usually mark a speaker as American. (Fewer than 10 percent of the SCE informants in British Columbia chose the [rʊf] pronunciation of *roof* [Scargill 75] or the [zi] pronunciation of z [Scargill 60].)

The Canadian English lexicon, though largely the same as the American, does include such words as *fiddleheads* (the edible tips of ferns available frozen in Vancouver grocery stores) and *skookum* (meaning "large" or "good"—although *A Dictionary of Canadianisms* [Avis et al. 706] and *The Gage Canadian Dictionary* [Avis et al. 1034] do not list "good" as a possible meaning, 27 percent of the SVEN informants gave this as the only meaning [Gregg, "Local" 18]). Also, a *bluff* can be a clump of trees, and a *chesterfield* is a sofa or couch. These Canadianisms, defined as words or meanings first appearing in print in Canada, are listed in the *Dictionary of Canadianisms*, while for terms unique to Newfoundland, one can consult the *Dictionary of Newfoundland English* (Story, Kirwin, and Widdowson). Competing lexical items whose frequency of use and whose interpretation varies regionally and socially include *napkin* and *serviette; fries* and *chips; chesterfield, sofa,* and *couch; tap* and *faucet; rug* and *carpet*; no doubt there are many others that have not been investigated. Again, there are also words and expressions that will distinguish Canadians and Americans. For example, a Canadian child will say, "I'm in *grade six,*" not *sixth grade*; the youngster may bring lunch in a *bag*, but never in a *sack*; may drink some *pop* or a *soft drink*, but never a *soda*; get home at *quarter to four*, not *quarter of four*; and may go to *the States* for a five-day *holiday* or a long *vacation*, but not to *America* for a short *vacation*.

Sample Student Projects

The projects undertaken in the most recent class included an awareness survey, a survey of brother-sister pairs, and a study of verb form usage of grade six students.

Awareness Survey

Although Canadians tend to have strong attitudes about what they perceive as British or American speech, they vary in which variety they find objectionable, and, as noted, are generally not very accurate in classifying particular usages as British or as American. To examine the ability to distinguish between British and American forms, and to gather data about the attitudes to particular variants, one student surveyed ten of her friends. She used a stack of twenty-one cards on which she had printed words that have more than one pronunciation, often with one variant being preferred in British English and one in American. The informants first read the words onto tape, and then they went through the cards once more and stated whether they knew of any other pronunciations and who they thought would use them.

This study produced the following results:

1. Several times informants gave their own previous pronunciation as "another" way of saying the word. This, of course, confirms that these speakers are not particularly aware of what they do say, but it also suggests that the elicitation method produced quite relaxed, unguarded speech.

2. The subjects differed markedly in how aware they were of other pronunciations for the twenty-one items. The most aware informant noted variant pronunciations for nineteen of the twenty-one items, while the least aware noted only seven. The mean number of "other" pronunciations identified was twelve.

3. There was considerable uncertainty about which variant is American. For example, the British pronunciation of *lieutenant* (with the first syllable as [lɛf]) was classed as American by two informants and as Canadian by three. As one might predict from the SCE results, eight of the ten informants pronounced the first syllable as [lu]; only two classed this pronunciation as American.

4. Only one informant pronounced *khaki* as [kɑɚki] (like *car key*), what is commonly considered as the Canadian pronunciation (Avis et al., *Gage* 629). Two gave this as the "other" pronunciation, one calling it British and the second "Old English," while two gave [kɑki] as the "other," one gave [kæki] and called it "Canadian," and one even gave [kɔki].

Brother-Sister Pairs

A student interested in the degree of uniformity in speech within families decided to interview five brother-sister pairs among his university friends. In addition to this unusual informant sample, he also had an interesting questionnaire in which a reading passage included pictures so that it would elicit both phonological and lexical data. The pairs of informants differed in how uniform their answers were for the twenty-four items, four being the lowest number of different answers, eleven the highest, and seven the mean.

Usage Study of Elementary School Students

One student surveyed her daughter's grade six classmates in the school that serves the university community. She used a written questionnaire to check for the substitution of the preterit of some irregular verbs for the past participle after *should have, would have,* and *could have.* It included questions like the following:

> I ran five miles today. I would have ____ ten, but I was too tired.
> My sister drank all the juice. She shouldn't have ____ it because there was none left for me.

The percentages of preterits substituted for past participles were as follows:

drink	81 percent
run	78 percent
eat	57 percent
take	29 percent
do	14 percent
go	5 percent
see	—

(One may note, however, that about 60 percent of all SCE informants chose *drank* as the past participle of *drink* in the sentence "He has ____ three glasses of milk" [Scargill 32].) Although the student noted that since the children knew that this questionnaire wasn't a test, they would have been a little less attentive to correctness than they might otherwise have been, the results suggest that this feature should be studied further.

Description of the Assignment

The class knows about the assignment from the beginning of the course, but more specific explanation doesn't begin until around the fourth week, by which time we have talked about the methods of the early European atlases, the American atlas projects, and the Survey of Canadian English and have just begun to look at Labov's early work. Subsequently, one meeting a week is spent on the projects, either in class instruction or discussion, or in the students' presentation of stages of their projects for peer review, usually in groups of three or four. The group work is useful for identifying obvious errors or problems, but, more important, it involves the students in questions that their own investigations may not pose. The project unit is divided into the following subunits: defining the project, preparing and testing the questionnaire, administering the questionnaire, analyzing the results, and preparing the project report.

Defining the project. The first, most crucial, and most difficult step is to define the project; that task includes determining the aim, defining the informant sample, and selecting the elicitation method. To guard against unmanageable or predictably unproductive investigations, each project definition is first presented to the class for discussion and then handed in for formal approval.

To determine an aim, the student frames a larger question that the investigation will try to answer. For the sample projects discussed in this essay, the questions would be like the following:

How aware are university students of variant pronunciations?
How similar is the speech of siblings?
How frequently do grade six students substitute the preterit for the past participle of irregular verbs?

To minimize the interview time, students are encouraged to select easily accessible informants and to restrict their sample to ten or so, because the time needed to make arrangements and to get to and from the interview location can make even a ten-minute interview take as long as an hour. Also, since such small samples preclude legitimate comparisons between informant subgroups, the informants must be as uniform as possible for variables such as age, sex, education, social class. Finally, the students decide whether they will use a written questionnaire or a taped interview, exactly what the informants will be asked to do, and what kinds of prompts—pictures or words—they will use.

Preparing and testing the questionnaire. After the proposed project designs have been approved, the students prepare drafts of their questionnaires, submit them to peer review in class, test them on a couple of informants, revise them, and then hand them in for a final check. Again because of the limited time, there should be fewer than thirty items, and each one should be appropriate to the aim, have potential for eliciting an interesting result, and complement other items so as to make a coherent, unified questionnaire. The particular questions will be motivated either by the SCE and SVEN results or by students' own informal observation of variations that have not been studied formally. After selecting the items, they finalize the wording of each question, prepare any pictorial prompts, arrange the sequence of items, and determine the layout of the questions and responses so that the questionnaire will be relatively easy to administer and permit convenient recording and analysis of results. The group critique will usually identify unclear or ambiguous wording, and the trial interviews may reveal some unproductive questions and any difficulties in recording the responses. If the informants are filling in a questionnaire, can all responses be accommodated? If the interview is oral, can the student transcribe quickly enough? Does the tape recorder pose problems for the informant or the investigator? Can the results be tabulated easily? The students are usually surprised at how difficult it can be to produce even such a brief questionnaire.

Administering the questionnaire. If the questionnaire has been tested well, the interview step should be fairly straightforward, although there can still be problems, such as an uncooperative informant or difficulties in hearing a tape made in a noisy environment.

Analyzing the results. Since the small sample size and the great difficulty in making the samples absolutely uniform preclude a strict statistical analysis (and the students don't normally have the training needed to undertake one anyway), the "analysis" usually consists of addition, the determination of simple percentages, and the clear display of results.

Preparing the project report. The project report is first presented to the class and then submitted for grading. It must include a rationale for the investigation; a critical description of the informant sample, the elicitation strategy, and the linguistic items investigated; and a discussion of the significance of the results. All data sheets must be submitted in an appendix, and transcriptions must be supported with tapes.

The main weaknesses of these projects usually occur in their display and discussion of results. Many students are working with numerical data for the first time and may be unfamiliar with even the simplest conventions for the display of data in tables; and most do not know how to talk about the statistical—or numerical—significance of their results. Often the weaker students will make exaggerated claims that the data don't justify. The students also have to be reminded to compare their results with those of other surveys and to verify their claims about the history or regional distribution of a linguistic feature.

The main advantage of this assignment, aside from its function as the core, or focus, of much of the course, is its ability to inspire the students to do very good work. One danger, though, is that, in their enthusiasm, students will assign greater significance to these investigations than their necessarily small and relatively uncontrolled samples warrant. This means that their sense of success has to be tempered with reminders of the limitations of these projects. The other problem is that, while it is important for each student to be responsible for his or her own assignment, each phase must be monitored carefully to prevent major errors that lead to predictably flawed investigations.

Ethnic and Social
Variation

∽

Research Trends for Black American English

John Baugh, Stanford University

NEW controversy was raised during the 1980s in the field of Black English research, despite the decades that have passed since the civil rights movement heightened national attention to the plight of black Americans. The following discussion reviews three important issues that have emerged during this decade and examines their implications for the education of African Americans.

The first issue concerns the well-known "Ann Arbor trial," in which Black English usage was central to a court case on the welfare of African American students. The second concerns some complementary research among black adults in different regions of the United States. The final issue relates to the current debate regarding the nature of linguistic divergence among blacks and whites.

In contrast to the 1960s, many black scholars have now emerged as major figures in these fields, including Geneva Smitherman, Fay B. Vaughn-Cooke, Walter Pitts, Jerrie C. Scott, Delores Straker, Arthur Spears, and Wayne Williams, among others. These scholars, with doctoral degrees in linguistics, sociolinguistics, and education, have collectively offered new insights into the complexity of sociolinguistic behavior in the black community, and this author is honored to be included in their number. Indeed, William Labov's discussion ("Objectivity") of the relevance of linguistic scholarship to the Ann Arbor trial acknowledges his debt to the growing number of African American linguists who provided him with new insights into Black English Vernacular (BEV) and the corresponding speech community.

Because of the depth of the linguistic abyss between many black and white Americans and educators' limited understanding of sociolinguistics, the educational problems that have historically plagued most blacks are still with us today. However, because linguists now have a clearer sense of the nature of language usage and linguistic change, we are far better equipped to assist educators who strive to help students who speak stigmatized dialects.

The Ann Arbor Trial

Many readers of this volume may already be familiar with the Ann Arbor trial and the national attention it raised in 1979. Smitherman's volume on the trial (*Black English*) and John Chambers's edited text on the subject are useful references for readers who would like further details about the case. Labov's "Objectivity and Commitment in Linguistic Science" contains valuable information for linguists and others who seek technical information about this litigation as well as the role of linguistic testimony at the trial.

Ann Arbor had instituted a school busing plan to assist in desegregation. However, several black students who were sent to a predominantly white school were classified as linguistically handicapped. As a result of this designation, the students were placed in special-education classes, where they failed to master basic literacy skills. Through a variety of planned and fortuitous events, the plaintiffs of the trial brought suit against the Ann Arbor school district for failing to teach the children to read Standard English.

The testimony demonstrated to the presiding judge, Charles Joiner, and to the administration of the school district that Black Vernacular English is a rule-governed dialect and, furthermore, that use of this vernacular does not reflect a diminished mental capacity. Thus linguistic scholars were able to use their research on Black English to show that many African American students face specific linguistic problems in our classrooms. Judge Joiner ruled in favor of the plaintiffs, and the school district subsequently instituted special classes for their teachers with Robert Hall, a black psycholinguist, to assist them in bridging the gap in their understanding of black speech and their black students.

During a special seminar held after the trial, I had an opportunity to meet with some of the teachers who had been named in the suit; I found them to be sincere and dedicated professionals who were seeking viable solutions to the particular educational needs of their minority students. We will return to these points below; at this juncture, let it suffice to say that the Ann Arbor trial became a highly palpable reminder of the valuable research related to Black English.

Adult Style-Shifting in Black English

The educational foci of the majority of earlier Black English research created an age-biased vacuum in knowledge about the linguistic behavior of black adults. Displaying a basic misunderstanding about the sociolinguistic variation in the behavior of different age groups, J. L. Dillard (*Black English*) claimed that adults tend to speak the standard and that the vernacular was preserved by younger members of the speech community. This bias in favor of analyses of the language of younger speakers was actually a logical extension of sincere attempts to improve the education of black children. By concentrating on youth, scholars hoped to provide educators with essential insights that could rectify the perennial failure of so many black children in our schools.

Having been raised in black neighborhoods in Philadelphia and Los Angeles, I was particularly sensitive to this gap in our knowledge about adults, because I know from personal experience that social context has a great deal to do with the style of speech that both adults and young people use. This is the case for nearly everyone, but it tends to be more pronounced in vernacular Black English because of the wide range of styles employed in the community.

My fieldwork experiences are similar to those described by Salikoko S. Mufwene elsewhere in this volume. I too took the time to get to know informants on a personal basis, and I allowed them whatever time was necessary to ensure that they could trust me with recordings of their speech. Detailed discussion of my field procedures is available in my work *Black Street Speech*; however, it may be useful to address some of the concerns that have been raised about the relative naturalness of linguistic interviews (Wolfson).

The issue has to do with how the researcher makes informants feel sufficiently comfortable to talk on tape in a manner that is similar to their speaking style when they are not being recorded. In my case, I always carried a tape recorder; thus, when I met prospective informants, my research interests were obvious. In many instances, I was chided for not having a "box" with a built-in radio; most of the other young men on the street had fully equipped "jam boxes" to record popular music directly. My inability to record music was the object of considerable amusement, but it also provided me with repeated opportunities to discuss the research and my desire to conduct interviews with those who were most familiar with life in the African American community.

Because the topic of black language is of direct interest to so many prospective informants, I was fortunate to gain the cooperation of numerous adult Black English Vernacular speakers. After several years of data collection, often with the same individuals under very different social circumstances, I was able to demonstrate that adult speakers of Black English Vernacular engage in significant style-shifting. The vernacular tends to be preserved among familiar speakers, particularly if all the well-acquainted speakers are black. Race and speech community affiliation also proved to influence the fluctuation between Standard English and Black English Vernacular, albeit with slightly less effect than the familiarity, or lack thereof, of participants in any given speech event.

This research demonstrated that black adults who are active participants in the vernacular culture have considerable degree of linguistic dexterity; they monitor their social surroundings—as do most people—and adjust their speech to meet the different needs. Again, while all people engage in style-shifting between formal and informal speech, the significance of such behavior in the Black English Vernacular community stems from the greater degree of linguistic variability found there. The typical standard speaker may also change speech from one situation to another, but those shifts tend to be minor when compared with those of the typical adult Black English Vernacular speaker.

Dillard probably observed black adults in situations that they perceived as formal. Black children interviewed under similar circumstances do not yet have comparable linguistic experience, and, although the situation may be appropriate for Standard English, children do not have the same linguistic dexterity as their parents. Because the classroom is a social context in which formal linguistic behavior is not only appropriate but also demanded, it is not surprising that teachers with limited understanding of sociolinguistics did not understand that many black children's "language problem" is not that they do not know standard language but that they have not yet become adept at style-shifting.

The pattern of linguistic variability also reaffirms the value of Black English Vernacular within the community. Children observe that adults shift language as they change from one context to another and come to learn that street speech is highly prized within the vernacular community. The affirmation of black culture, which has analogies among working-class (male) groups throughout the United States—regardless of race—embodies an important aspect of the retention of vernacular culture. Black youth who demonstrate their pride in being black respect the skilled "man of words" or the ability to put together a "bad rap." This observation brings us to the controversy surrounding the concept of linguistic divergence, and the social and linguistic pressures that have led black youth in Philadelphia to reinterpret specific English inflections (see Labov and Harris; Myhill and Harris).

The Divergence Paradox

The most controversial debate among linguists regarding Black English during the 1980s centers on the issue of linguistic change and the evolution of Black English Vernacular. Labov and Wendell A. Harris, Labov ("Are Black and White"), John Myhill and Harris, and Guy Bailey ("Are Black and White") have presented different evidence in support of the position that black and white speech patterns are drifting apart. Reinterpretations of the suffix /s/ and unique usage within the auxiliary system of Black English Vernacular are cited in support of this position.

Other scholars, including Vaughn-Cooke, Walt Wolfram ("Are Black and White"), and John R. Rickford ("Are Black and White"), take strong to mild exception to the divergence hypothesis on several grounds: Vaughn-Cooke is largely concerned with limitations in the data that are used to derive the hypothesis, while Wolfram and Rickford, independently, challenge the comparability of data from unrelated studies of Black English.

Ralph W. Fasold ("Are Black and White") raises an important point, suggesting that linguists can draw different conclusions when faced with the same set of facts:

> A linguist who assumes that grammatical structure is to be discovered in language use is more likely to find a change in grammar, say between present-day and earlier records of [Black Vernacular English] speech, if a difference in use of a particular feature can be demonstrated. Other linguists, assuming that grammatical structure often stays constant while community conventions for its use change, will probably assert that the grammar is still the same, even if they agree with the first linguist that the feature is now used in somewhat different ways than it formerly was. (4–5)

My research among black adults supports a contention put forward by Guy Bailey (personal communication) that recent linguistic innovations by black youth are not the result merely of social and linguistic isolation from white Americans but a reaffirmation of pride in black culture, which is most visible through speaking style. When we consider the role of pride along with the social and economic isolation that led Labov and Harris to examine the prospects for linguistic divergence, we find that there are many forces operating within our pluralistic society that serve to accentuate class differences, particularly across racial lines.

Since the majority of black adults who are active participants in the vernacular culture tend to use Black English Vernacular in their informal speech, it comes as no surprise that their children learn this dialect as their first language. Moreover, if the immediate social environment is such that Black English Vernacular is highly prized, as is usually the case among black youth in our inner cities, then the basic grammatical structure of Black English Vernacular—which was learned at home—will be positively reinforced through the socialization process with peers as the children grow older.

Elsewhere ("Beyond Linguistic") I discuss the divergence debate in more thorough and technical detail; however, the thrust of my thesis is that linguistic change in black America is not unidirectional. When we look at black America in more comprehensive terms, we find an array of competing norms and values that defy the highly touted theories of famous linguists.

Of considerable importance to the discussion at hand, the compelling evidence in support of linguistic divergence reinforces an age-old linguistic paradox for many black Americans.

The language that is highly prized within the vernacular community is stigmatized outside of that community, especially in major institutions such as schools, businesses, and courts of law. Consequently, many black Americans, through no fault of their own, face the prospect that their speech may be perceived as ignorant or, worse, the result of diminished mental ability, as was the case in Ann Arbor.

Although linguists have the background and training to know that all dialects are logical and perfectly equal from a theoretical point of view, society does not reflect this egalitarian spirit. Some languages and dialects are clearly seen as being superior to others, and rarely does anyone reflect on the inherent political, social, and economic factors that determine which dialects are designated as "elite" or "inferior." Throughout history, the burden of linguistic and social adaptation has been placed on those who do not hold positions of wealth and political power. This is still the case today in the majority of nations, regardless of their political system.

For many black Americans we find that the manner of speech is often a reflection of personal values; as individuals mature, they come to adopt speech patterns that meet their social needs through personal interaction and aspirations. Those who seek acceptance by the majority culture strive to master Standard English; others who place a high personal value on the vernacular culture will attempt to preserve and enhance their proficiency in Black English Vernacular. Under positive conditions there may be considerable motivation to adopt particular manners of speech; however, in a hostile situation, members of socially (and linguistically) disenfranchised populations feel that they are being coerced to adopt foreign dialects or languages merely to appease those who can dictate linguistic convention by the power of their political station. We therefore find that some black Americans are eager to embrace Standard English, because they feel that all educated Americans must master this mode of speech. Others, often from similar backgrounds, reject Standard English in favor of their native dialect because of its positive role in black culture, regardless of negative attitudes about Black English Vernacular from those outside the community who lack familiarity with black culture.

These competing forces within the language and society at large are complex, but they pale in significance when compared with the herculean task of teachers who attempt to educate the children who live day to day within this linguistic tug of war.

Implications for Current Education Practice

In what ways can the linguistic research of the past decade aid in resolving the long-standing educational problems that continue to face African American youth? There are, of course, no easy solutions to this dilemma, and I will not tax your tolerance by checking off the list of clichés and platitudes that saturate so much of the educational literature on the topic.

The Ann Arbor trial reaffirmed our need to inform educators of the distinction between dialect differences and mental ability. Teachers are members of society; as such they reflect the values of the learned culture that—quite properly—recognizes the importance of literary skills and the mastery of Standard English if one hopes to take advantage of the social and economic opportunities in American society. However, because so many teachers have not been trained to address linguistic diversity in the classroom, it would be unfair to place the blame for minority educational failure on them alone. Judge Joiner's ruling discussed this dilemma in considerable detail, and interested readers are encouraged to examine his decision in detail (see Smitherman, *Black English*). In essence, the Ann Arbor trial demonstrated that we must acknowledge that some children—those who bring nonstandard English to the classroom as their native dialect—require educational assistance to master literacy skills in Standard English.

A word of caution is in order. Some school districts have begun to recognize this problem, many of them requiring their Black English students to study Standard English as if it were a foreign language. While I acknowledge the good intentions behind such efforts and the marginal value of some foreign language pedagogy, it is wrong to imply that Black English Vernacular is so different from Standard English that native speakers require pure second-language education. Those who are learning English for the first time face problems quite different from those of students who are asked to make slight modifications in their pronunciation and grammar. Thus, while selective use of second-language pedagogy may be helpful to a degree, it is no substitute for the recognition that bidialectal education (i.e., the ability to control more than one dialect of the same language) differs considerably from bilingual education (i.e., the ability to master a second language with sufficient fluency to converse with native speakers and to read it and write it.)

With this distinction in mind, we can turn to some implications of adult Black English Vernacular style-shifting. Among black adults who are active participants in the vernacular culture, we find a pragmatic reaction to different speaking circumstances. This is not to suggest that adult Black English

Vernacular speakers sound "white" in formal contexts, although some individuals have mastered the ability to do so; rather, the majority have the capacity to adopt speech patterns that shift toward Standard English in formal circumstances. The degree of linguistic style-shifting varies among speakers and is relative to their primary vernacular grammar, exposure to speakers of Standard English, and personal aspirations.

Despite the tendency to shift toward Standard English in formal speech, we should not assume that the linguistic needs of speakers of Black English Vernacular will simply fade away as the child becomes an adult. Such students require specialized instruction to identify the differences between the dialects if they are expected eventually to master Standard English. The style-shifting that we have observed among black adults in our inner cities reflects competing linguistic norms: on the one hand, there is Black English Vernacular, the language of family and community; on the other, there are the linguistic demands of the majority culture that tend to demean Black English Vernacular and—in the process—fail to acknowledge the positive value of the vernacular in native settings.

All the black parents I have interviewed across the nation over the past fifteen years share the desire for their children to receive the finest possible education. However, since many of these parents have not had the advantage of a quality education themselves, they feel reluctant to help their youngsters for fear of giving them bad academic advice. Thus, despite the hope that their children will get a good education, many believe that they are powerless to play a personal role in the process. The proliferation of private schools for privileged children, with a concomitant increase in the percentage of minority students in underfunded public schools, stands as unfortunate confirmation of the perception, if not reality, of the differential quality of education available to citizens of unequal economic means.

The linguistic style-shifting that children observe in the Black English Vernacular community reinforces and perpetuates the mixed signals of the value of the street vernacular versus Standard English. This point brings us to the relevance of the observations regarding linguistic divergence. As indicated, Labov and Harris felt that deteriorating economic and social conditions of the Philadelphia inner city have provided a cultural climate that increases linguistic divergence. The lack of jobs, poorer-quality education, inadequate housing, and so on have heightened political assertions that our society is drifting into two camps: those with adequate educational skills and members of the economic underclass. Labov and various colleagues have attempted to demonstrate that the linguistic evidence points to dwindling hope for improvement in inner-city neighborhoods.

As Dillard, in *Black English*, observed, black youth are largely responsible for the preservation of the deep vernacular, because it is a prized instrument of communication for the young men and women who use it as a marker of social status within their peer groups. Labov and Harris and Myhill and Harris suggest that this process has begun to reflect an independent linguistic change among black youth. While I do not dispute the economic observations that led Labov and his colleagues to their conclusions, I place considerable credence in Guy Bailey's observation (personal communication) that the evidence of linguistic divergence among black youth serves to reinforce their pride in black culture. The economic isolation does not stand in contrast to the importance of black pride in the preservation of the vernacular; when both factors are taken into account, we find that the conditions for sociolinguistic isolation are considerable.

This summary accentuates the need for creative solutions to the education of students who speak Black English Vernacular. Labov (*Language*) made a proposal years ago that was dismissed by many educators. He called for the use of street-wise black males in their mid-twenties to act as teacher aides. He was concerned not so much with their educational skills as with their ability to serve as positive role models in the classroom and the greater likelihood that these men would be able to minimize disciplinary problems before they caused other students to become disruptive. The resistance to this idea came from many sectors, but most forcefully from school administrators who felt that they could not justify paying "nonprofessionals" in the classroom. A program of this sort would not be viable on a voluntary basis because the best role models would have to seek gainful employment in order to survive. There are many positive attributes to Labov's suggestion, and the fact that the educational problems he identified are with us today might justify some experimentation in this direction.

If we are to educate all students, regardless of race or social background, and if we can admit that some pupils from nontraditional backgrounds have excessive rates of failure, then we must be willing to correct problems that perpetuate this situation. Even without assistance from the community, teachers have used many techniques successfully with black youth in different parts of the nation. Elsewhere ("Design," "Situational") I stress the importance of finding educational methods that motivate nontraditional students but teach basic educational skills. In pilot studies in Austin, Texas, we have used card games to introduce fundamental mathematical concepts and lyrics from popular songs to promote many literacy skills. Let us assume that an instructor is interested in the teaching of reading or the development of poetry. In the past, neither subject has elicited enthusiasm in many inner-city students. During voluntary tutorial sessions with minority students in Austin, we taught these subjects indirectly through the evaluation and creation of rap music. Moreover, rather than have students work on these topics in isolation, we formed competitive teams similar to those in athletic competition. Modest prizes (e.g., T-shirts, record albums) were awarded to members of the teams who created the best poem (rap song) or who specified the number of verbs, nouns, or prepositions in the (screened) lyrics from popular songs.

The goals are the same as that of any reading instruction, but the methods acknowledge the value of black culture and consequently have greater success with most minority students, who tend to find traditional pedagogical methods boring. This is not to suggest that Black English Vernacular students will sing their way to Standard English; but by introducing poetry and basic literacy skills through means that utilize aspects of popular culture, we provide many of these students with their first taste of academic success. As with all forms of education, we then try to build on these efforts as we make a gradual transition to traditional educational materials. My remarks here are intentionally general; while I offer specific suggestions in "Design and Implementation of Writing Instruction for Speakers of Non-standard English" on how to organize some of these procedures, I encourage teachers, parents, religious leaders, or anyone else who is interested in the educational welfare of nontraditional students to experiment along these or similar lines.

But a caveat must be introduced at this point. Having worked with educators who agreed to adopt some of the techniques, I have found that students were frustrated by instructors who used the music as a stick rather than a carrot. These methods work best with the voluntary cooperation of students when the activities are treated as natural components of instruction and are less successful when they are used as a reward for classroom silence or are postponed until the students have completed some other, less attractive assignment. Students become more enthusiastic when working with everyday examples of language rather than with the artificial language of most textbook exercises.

Parents can be provided with basic suggestions for working with their children at home; those offering recommendations should be sensitive to the fact that some parents are reluctant to help their children because they feel, as nonprofessionals, that they may cause more harm than good. In similar cases, we have found that networks of parents, or organizations like church groups or Big Brothers–Big Sisters of America, can provide support to the students and their parents and to the classroom teacher. Parents and other adults can in turn be more successful in teaching a child who already has a grasp of basic educational concepts.

* * *

I have attempted to do two things: review some of the salient issues for research in Black English Vernacular during the past decade and provide some educational suggestions that are a logical outgrowth of this research. These issues are, of course, complex; I hope that my contribution will be received in the same spirit as other articles in this collection, because we must not yield to timidity in our quest to ensure educational programs suitable for the full range of cultural backgrounds of the children in American classrooms. Research that is needed to support sound educational policy must be pursued vigorously until we no longer find disturbing statistical correlations between race or social status and the likelihood of academic success.

How to Study Black Speech in Chicago

Michael I. Miller, Chicago State University

STUDENT investigators can discover a great deal about their own speech and about the language of their communities without extensive previous training in linguistics. In particular, they can begin with the study of vocabulary. Some students may want to go on to more sophisticated explorations of grammar, perhaps even as far as minute phonetic distinctions. But while not many people are gifted phoneticians, anyone can learn how to study living speech in at least some of its aspects, and this study can provide new insight into both language and the cultures that produce language.

This discussion, which is addressed directly to students, provides them with an approach for studying black speech in Chicago. If they master the general principles described here, they should be able to transfer these techniques to other circumstances and even to other cities. The examples assume that those doing the research live on the south or west side of Chicago, attend college, and are probably black (though that is not a requirement). If these assumptions do not fit, students will have to make some changes in how they do the investigation, but the necessary changes should be pretty obvious.

An Approach

First, decide on a specific Chicago neighborhood to study. This should be either the neighborhood you currently live in or one you know well, such as one you grew up in or recently moved from. Use the Chicago *Local Community Fact Book* to identify the precise area you are interested in. This book will refer to your area as a "community" and will provide you with a brief narrative history and description, a map showing community boundaries, and several lists of statistics from census data. If you do not live in Chicago, you might have to do quite a bit of preliminary work in the library simply to define a specific community, map it, find out its settlement history and social organization, and locate pertinent population statistics. The map of your community area will be larger than the particular neighborhood you live in. Take time to explore the community: walk around it and through it; observe its public transportation systems; note which streets are used for commercial, industrial, and residential functions; try to get a feel for the people who live there and try to formulate your ideas in terms that are as objective as you can make them.

Once you have identified your study area, find out what other people have written about the speech of Chicago and possibly even the speech of your specific neighborhood. Use the bibliography that follows these instructions and the files available at Chicago State University. Consult your librarian; you might find particularly valuable the essay by Harold B. Allen, "Regional Dialects, 1945–1974." For material published since 1974, supplement Allen's bibliography with the excellent work by Wolfgang Viereck, Edgar Schneider, and Manfred Görlach, *A Bibliography of Writings on Varieties of English, 1965–1983*. For the period since 1983, you will have to dig through the various serial bibliographies.

Though sometimes omitted in studies of local speech, especially by those with a sociolinguistic bent, this search of the literature is a vital preliminary step, and you should not proceed without taking it. If you leave it out, you're likely to find yourself reinventing the wheel—or, worse, ignoring extremely useful previous work that will make your job easier, more fun, and much more rewarding.

The next step is the easiest if you live in Chicago, perhaps much more difficult if you're working somewhere else. Decide on a research instrument or questionnaire. This sounds obvious, but it is a critical element that will control the value of all your work from this point. For beginners, I strongly recommend using the checklists and questionnaires we have developed specifically for Chicago, and I'd suggest using them in the order given below. In my courses at Chicago State University, beginning students *must* start with the "Regional Vocabulary Checklist." Below is a brief discussion of research instruments.

Next, decide on a sample. This means you have to find one or more people who are willing to fill out your checklist or answer your questions. You can always begin with yourself, and in fact you should start there. After that, your best bet would be to ask members of your family to fill out copies of the checklists. Then move on to people you know through community organizations, such as your church or any other group you might belong to.

At some point, you might want to try to develop what sociologists and pollsters call a representative sample. Do not confuse this with a random sample, which requires specific mathematical procedures. For most purposes, you will be able to learn a great deal from your family and friends, without structuring a scientific sample of any sort. However, if you find that you want to take this extra step, you should consult the appropriate reference

Table 1. *Seesaw* and *Teeter-Totter* by Race, Chicago 1986

Response	Black	White	Total N
Teeter-totter	13 (22%)	23 (85%)	36
See-saw	47 (78%)	4 (15%)	51
Total N	60	27	87

Note: Chi-square signifiance at .001.

works, beginning with David L. Sills, editor, *The International Encyclopedia of the Social Sciences*, to help you structure your sample correctly.

Finally, analyze and report the results. Even if your sample consists of only one person and that one person is yourself, you can still make some interesting observations about language if you attempt to place the results of your investigation in a larger context. To do this with the local vocabulary checklist presented below, you'll want to compare your responses with the responses and the commentary provided by Lee Pederson in the articles listed in the Works Cited section at the end of this volume. See if you can find ways in which your results confirm, modify, or contradict Pederson's results. Then see if you can provide explanations for any differences between your results and his. For example, are the differences due to differences in the sample, changes in the language or society over time, or mistakes? Can you discover any social motivation for whatever change or variation you find?

If you are using a large sample, that is to say, a sample of thirty or more, you should present your data using what statisticians call a contingency table or cross-classification table, such as table 1. The reasons for using precisely this format are discussed in detail by James A. Davis and Ann M. Jacobs. Briefly, the advantages of this form are that it combines the presentation of proportional and absolute values, provides the reader with a clear means of reconstructing absolutes for all proportional values given, and gives the results of at least one meaningful test of statistical significance.

Types of Research Instruments

Necessary tools for studying grammar and pronunciation include a portable tape recorder and mastery of a finely graded phonetic alphabet. For many elements of vocabulary, however, you need only a checklist, patience, and interest in the subject. In my course, we use the following hierarchically related checklists to investigate vocabulary:

1. *The regional vocabulary.* This is the shortest of the checklists, containing not quite fifty items (see Miller, "Discovering"). Its function is to probe for the survival of the folk vocabulary of the Inland North within the City of Chicago, where many traditional folk terms survive, such as *gutters, pig sty,* and *teeter-totter.* With respect to black speech, the most important questions are (1) To what extent has Chicago's black population, derived ultimately from the plantation South, adopted the folk vocabulary of the Inland North? (2) Conversely, to what extent has the vocabulary of the plantation South influenced Chicago's current white usage?

2. *The local vocabulary.* This checklist runs to over one hundred items, is constantly undergoing revision, and is excerpted below. It focuses on the everyday speech of Chicagoans, regardless of racial subgroup. If, however, there are indeed profound differences between black and white speech not explainable as regional differences, one would expect them to show up sharply here. This checklist specifically avoids stereotypical aspects of black culture as presented in the popular media, such as public housing, remedial education, music, and drugs. These areas of experience are, of course, worth exploring, but we have adopted the view here that it is more important to place current black speech in a broad cultural context than it is to concentrate on a few stereotypes.

3. *Specialized vocabularies.* These include several shorter checklists that treat specialized sectors of the vocabulary in more detail, such as expletives, terms of abuse, sexual and excretory terms, and the language of street and playground games. Some of the sharpest differences between black and white speech show up in the language of children and in taboo language— that is, in the "intimate" vocabulary. The general character of *one* of these questionnaires may be inferred from Pederson ("Terms of Abuse").

4. *Open-ended questionnaires.* We use this approach for highly specialized looks at a city's language, such as more detailed studies of the language of food or more thorough examinations of the language of specific occupations or pastimes.

5. *Names.* Though much easier to collect than other data, at least at a superficial level, onomastic data are more difficult to analyze and require a great deal of historical and cultural background. This is an emerging field, and it seems to be most fruitful for those who already have a good grasp of linguistic, cultural, and historical contexts. Examples of current research in this area can be found in the publications of the North Central Name Society.

Using a Local Vocabulary Checklist

Following this discussion is a checklist of current local Chicago vocabulary (updated to June 1987). It is a slightly modified version of the one in Pederson's "An Approach to Urban Word Geography." The subsequent questionnaire, however, differs from Pederson's; it has been rewritten to give as possible responses those that Pederson collected in Chicago in earlier studies. The form of the checklist is based on one prepared by Alva Davis ("Word Geography"). Outside Chicago, it will be impossible to construct this sort of checklist unless you or some previous investigator has already conducted on-the-spot interviews and provided the possible answers for the checklist items.

These 106 items provide only an outline sample of the local vocabulary and are not intended to generate an exhaustive corpus. The nine semantic areas we investigate are as follows:

1. Items 1–11 involve toponymics for well-known places in Chicago.
2. Items 12–20 involve topographical terms, as distinct from toponymics, including not only well-known Chicagoisms like *prairie* for "vacant lot" and *parkway* for the "grass strip between the sidewalk and curb" but also less frequently studied terms like *oasis, centerline, cloverleaf,* and *exit ramp.*
3. Items 21–28 hark back to the topographical terms in the first section and deal with the vocabulary of city buildings and names for well-known landmarks; the term *gangway* is a characteristic Chicagoism for the passageway between buildings.
4. Items 29–51 concern various implements associated with urban life: lawn and garden tools, cooking devices, bags and containers, fasteners, garbage collection, and water distribution.
5. Items 52–75 deal with urban transportation systems, including a great deal of material on cars, trucks, and utility vehicles.
6. Items 76–83 investigate food items. This field is one of the more interesting areas of Chicago's vocabulary, but since food vocabulary needs to be surveyed in a more specialized questionnaire, the checklist focuses on only a few items known to have social significance.
7. Items 84–93 are related to those covered in 21–28 but focus on individual or family housing.
8. Items 94–99 focus on a few city types of people.
9. Items 100–06 touch on politics and city services along with terms

for mortuaries and the surprisingly rich vocabulary associated with industrial fencing.

The personal data sheet asks for information about the person filling in the checklist. It will help the researcher correlate the linguistic data with such cultural factors as sex, race, age, schooling, place of birth, mobility, occupation, and parentage. Other items could be added to this questionnaire.

Variations

In addition to the five research instruments outlined above, there are numerous variations possible as substeps within this general scheme. Some of my advanced students have adapted the questionnaire and checklist approach to develop several challenging and creative studies. For example, one of my graduate student studied the specialized vocabularies that appear in four personal environments: talk with her own children, talk among co-workers at a large insurance company, talk among teenagers in a local community band, and talk among members of her church. Another student chose a single item that appears in Chicago's black speech, the intransitive uses of *fixing* followed by an infinitive to mean "to prepare" or "to get ready." This student found a variety of pronunciations of this word in Chicago speech, including *fitn, finna,* and *finen,* none of which were found recorded in dictionaries. Still another student, using the regional and local checklists, hypothesized that the differences between the vocabulary of white and black Chicagoans will turn out to be sharper and more striking in the regional than in the local vocabulary. Our longer term results, I suspect, will prove her hypothesis correct, though not without some important qualifications.

If you begin by using the general procedures outlined here, you will be well on your way to making original and useful contributions to the study of American English in general and the speech of your community in particular.

Suggestions for Further Reading

Hans Kurath's *Studies in Area Linguistics* includes a section on Chicago speech and remains the best introduction to survey research in American dialects, urban and regional. Still useful for high school and college students—and for their teachers—is Roger Shuy's *Discovering American Dialects*. Critical bibliographies containing useful material on Chicago are Harold Allen's "Regional Dialects, 1945–1974" and Wolfgang Viereck, Edgar Schneider, and Manfred Görlach's *A Bibliography of Writings on Varieties of English, 1965–1983*. To place the study of Chicago's vocabulary in its regional context, see Alva L. Davis's "A Word Geography of the Great Lakes Region," Shuy's *The Northern-Midland Dialect Boundary in Illinois*, Timothy Frazer's *Midland Illinois Dialect Patterns*, and Craig Carver's *American Regional Dialects*. The earliest study of Chicago English is Carl Darling Buck's "A Sketch of the Linguistic Conditions of Chicago" (1904). The earliest study of Chicago black speech is Isaiah Sumner's "Some Phases of Negro English" (1926).

The one indispensable study of Chicago speech, black or white, is Lee Pederson's *The Pronunciation of English in Metropolitan Chicago*, which may be daunting to people without a background in phonology. However, Pederson also published seminal lexicological and phonological articles under the titles "An Approach to Urban Word Geography" (which forms the basis for the questionnaire used here), "Chicago Words: The Regional Vocabulary," "Non-standard Negro Speech in Chicago," "Phonological Indices of Social Dialects in Chicago," "Some Structural Differences in the Speech of Chicago Negroes," and "Terms of Abuse for Some Chicago Social Groups." To put this material in a more general perspective that nevertheless focuses specifically on Chicago, see Raven I. McDavid's groundbreaking essays "Dialect Differences and Social Differences in an Urban Society," "The Dialectology of an Urban Society," "The Relationship of the Speech of American Negroes to the Speech of Whites," written with Virginia G. McDavid, and the collection edited with William M. Austin, *Communication Barriers to the Culturally Deprived*. For a critical comparison of Pederson's methods in Chicago with William Labov's in New York, see Kurath's "The Investigation of Urban Speech and Some Other Problems Confronting the Student of American English." In Chicago, Pederson, McDavid, and Kurath are the essential trinity; everything else is secondary.

Rappin' and Stylin' Out, by Thomas Kochman, nevertheless includes pioneering work on Chicago black speech, including especially pieces by Benjamin G. Cooke, Ken Johnson, Kochman himself, James Maryland, and Annette Powell Williams. Other items of interest include Thomas Creswell's "The Great Vowel Shift in Chicago," Robin Herndobler and Andrew Sledd's "Black English—Notes on the Auxiliary," and my own summary "Discovering Chicago's Dialects." I have presented two preliminary papers on the vocabulary of Chicago's black community under the titles "Exploring Black Speech in Chicago" and "Further Explorations in Chicago Black

Speech" at meetings of the Dictionary Society of North America. In addition, an onomastic byway appears in Robert G. Noreen's and James Stronks's studies of storefront Chicago church names.

Information useful for analyzing Chicago's social characteristics can be found in the *Local Community Fact Book*, Loretto Szucs's *Chicago and Cook County Sources*, David L. Sills's *The International Encyclopedia of the Social Sciences*, and in other sources. Sociologically, Chicago may be the most analyzed city in the world. Students interested in statistical analysis and the presentation of linguistic data might refer to my pieces "Quantification of Sociolinguistic Data" and "Encoding, Data Definition, and Command Syntax for Linguistic Survey Data."

Chicago Checklist: The Local Vocabulary

Directions
1. Please put a circle around the word in each group you ordinarily use.
2. If you ordinarily use more than one word in a group, put a circle around each of the words you use.
3. *Don't* put a circle around any word you don't actually use, even though you are familiar with it.
4. If the word you ordinarily use is not listed in the group, please write it in the space after the item.
5. *The material in capitals is explanatory only.*
   Example: HARD CENTER OF A PEACH: stone, pit, seed

Checklist
1. THE CENTER CITY: the loop, downtown, the downtown section
2. MICHIGAN AVENUE NORTH OF THE CHICAGO RIVER: the avenue, North Michigan Avenue, Boul Mich, the magnificent mile, the mile, North Michigan
3. THE SMALL PARK FACING NEWBERRY LIBRARY: bughouse square, bughouse alley, bughouse row, Newberry Park
4. THE LARGE CONSTRUCTION EXTENDED INTO LAKE MICHIGAN: Navy Pier, the pier, municipal pier
5. THE LARGE STADIUM NEAR THE LAKE: Soldier Field, Soldier's Field
6. VACANT LOT: prairie, vacant lot, empty lot
7. TRISTATE TOLLWAY (I-294): highway, road, tollroad, tollway, turnpike, tristate, expressway, 294
8. SERVICE AREA ON THE TRISTATE TOLLWAY: drive-in oasis, pit, plaza, restaurant, service area, tollhouse, way station

9. EISENHOWER EXPRESSWAY: Congress Street Expressway, the Congress, Eisenhower Expressway, the Eisenhower, 290

10. KENNEDY EXPRESSWAY: Northwest Expressway, the Kennedy, Kennedy Expressway, 90–94

11. EXPRESSWAY ALONG THE LAKE: the drive, the Outer Drive, Lake Shore Drive

12. WIDE STREET IN THE CITY OR A SUBURB: avenue, drive, highway, main street, road, street, through street

13. GRASS STRIP BETWEEN SIDEWALK AND CURB: fairway, parkway, tree bank, tree lawn, grass strip

14. NEIGHBORHOOD STREET: court, dead-end street, side street, residential street, village road, village street

15. PAINTED CENTER LINE ON A HIGHWAY: center line, divider, dividing line, guideline, guiding line, marker, media, median, median line, median strip, middle line, middle strip, white line, yellow line

16. AREA RUNNING DOWN THE MIDDLE OF A STREET SOMETIMES PLANTED WITH TREES AND/OR GRASS: median, divider, median strip, boulevard

17. EXIT FROM A TOLLWAY OR EXPRESSWAY: byway, cloverleaf, cutoff, egress, exit ramp, outlet, turnoff, off ramp

18. UNDERPASS IN THE CITY BENEATH RAILROAD TRACKS: subway, tunnel, underpass, viaduct

19. DIAGONAL PARKING OF AN AUTOMOBILE: angle, crosswise, diagonal, sideways, slant, vertical, parallel

20. PARALLEL PARKING OF AN AUTOMOBILE: conventional, curb, curbside, curve, horizontal, parallel, straight, street, vertical

21. ELEVATED RAILROAD STATION: station, stop, el, el stop

22. NARROW PASSAGEWAY BETWEEN BUILDINGS: alley, breezeway, gangway, passageway

23. LARGE OFFICE BUILDING: office building, skyscraper

24. JOHN HANCOCK CENTER: the Hancock, big John, the Hancock Center, the Hancock Building

25. GROCERY STORE: grocery, grocery store, store, small store, neighborhood grocery, neighborhood store, food-shop grocer, corner store, 7–11

26. DELICATESSEN: delicatessen, del, deli

27. LARGE NEIGHBORHOOD FOOD STORE: chain store, super mart, supermarket, cooperative, chain grocery store, food mart

28. SHABBY HOTEL: dump, fleabag, flea joint, flop joint, joint, flophouse, rattrap, firetrap, seedy hotel

29. LAWN RAKE: bamboo rake, wooden rake, leaf rake, grass broom, broom rake, lightweight rake, metal rake, rake
30. GARDEN RAKE: rake, heavy rake
31. GARDEN CLAW TOOL: cultivator, fork, scratcher, claw, claw tool, hoe, claw fork
32. GARDEN TROWEL: trowel, digger, hand cultivator, spade
33. MANUALLY OPERATED LAWN MOWER: grass cutter, lawn mower, mower, push mower, grass cutter
34. POWER LAWN MOWER: electric lawn mower, power cutter, electric power cutter, power lawn mower, lawn mower, grass cutter, power mower, gas power mower
35. ELECTRIC FRYING PAN: electric cooker, electric fryer, electric frying pan, electric fry pan, electric skillet, skillet
36. MICROWAVE COOKING DEVICE: microwave, microwave oven, microwave cooker, electric oven
37. VACUUM CLEANER: vacuum cleaner, sweeper, vacuum sweeper, vacuum, carpet sweeper, duster
38. VACUUM BAG: suction bag, vacuum bag, dust bag, sweeper bag
39. TRANSPARENT POLYETHYLENE DRY-CLEANING BAG: bag, poly bag, cellophane bag, cleaner's bag, cleaning bag, clothes bag, dress bag, plastic bag, storage bag
40. SHOPPING BAG: shopping bag, schlepper, Polish suitcase
41. CLOTHES HAMPER WITH LID: hamper, basket, laundry hamper, laundry container, clothes hamper
42. PLASTIC PAIL: scrub pail, plastic pail, scrub bucket, kitchen pail, pail, plastic bucket
43. KITCHEN GARBAGE CAN: garbage can, garbage tan, rubbish can, refuse can, garbage container, corrugated garbage can, trash can
44. CONCRETE GARBAGE BOX IN ALLEY: swill box, slop box, garbage can, garbage box, garbage bin, concrete box, box
45. ROUND GARBAGE CONTAINER IN ALLEY: garbage can, barrel, garbage drum, fifty-gallon drum
46. LARGE METAL CONTAINER IN ALLEY: garbage can, dumpster, dipsy dumpster, dipsy can
47. PLACE FOR COAL STORAGE IN BASEMENT: coal bin, coal pit, coal room, coal storage room
48. RUBBER BAND: rubber band, rubber
49. PAPER CLIP: clip, clamp, paper clip
50. DRINKING FOUNTAIN: fountain, drinking fountain, hydrant, water fountain, water fount, drinking place

51. FIRE HYDRANT: hydrant, fire hydrant, water hydrant, fireplug
52. HORSEDRAWN SLED: cutter, bobsled, sleigh, sled, snow buggy
53. LARGE HILL SLED: bobsled, toboggan, toboggan sled, sled
54. SMALL HILL SLED: sleigh, sled
55. TWO-DOOR CAR WITH ONE BENCH SEAT: two-door, coupe, sports car, car
56. TWO-DOOR CAR WITH TWO BENCH SEATS: two-door, sedan, car, two-door sedan, two-door car, hardtop
57. FOUR-DOOR CAR: sedan, four-door, four-door sedan, brougham, automobile, car
58. TROLLEY CAR: streetcar, trolley car, trolley, green hornet
59. ELEVATED RAILROAD: el, el train, elevated, elevator, elevated train
60. SMALL COMMERCIAL TRUCK WITH ENCLOSED LOAD BED: compact, delivery truck, small truck, truck, panel truck, pickup, pickup truck, half-ton, half-ton truck, "B" truck, boulevard truck, light pickup, small delivery truck
61. SMALL COMMERCIAL TRUCK WITH OPEN LOAD BED: delivery, pickup, pickup truck, delivery truck
62. POLICE SEDAN: police car, squad car, squad, prowl car, squadrol, police patrol, patrol car, cop car
63. SMALL POLICE VAN: squadrol, police bus, truck, police van
64. LARGE POLICE VAN: paddy wagon, van, Black Maria, patrol, patrol wagon
65. GENERAL FIRE TRUCK: fire truck, fire wagon, fire engine, engine
66. PUMPER TRUCK: pump, hose truck, pumper, pumper combination
67. HOOK AND LADDER TRUCK: hook and ladder, hooking ladder
68. SMALL EMERGENCY TRUCK: inhalator squad, resuscitator, ambulance, pulmotor, inhalator, emergency car, fire ambulance
69. LARGE TRUCK WITH AERIAL HOSE BOOM AND BUCKET: snorkel, cherry picker
70. CHIEF'S CAR: jeep, chief's car, fire chief's sedan, fire car
71. INSTRUMENT PANEL OF A CAR: dash, dashboard, panel, instrument panel, dash panel, panel, panel board, dial board
72. UTILITY COMPARTMENT IN DASH: map compartment, glove compartment, glove box
73. EXTERIOR UTILITY COMPARTMENT: trunk, baggage compartment
74. GAS-FLOW CONTROL ON DASH: choke, throttle, hand throttle, overdrive
75. GAS-FLOW CONTROL ON FLOOR: accelerator, gas pedal, pedal
76. FRANKFURTERS: frankfurters, franks, wieners, wienies, hot dogs

77. LIGHT GLAZED DOUGHNUT: doughnut, French doughnut, Nonnesfertsliche, dewnxh-fried doughnut, raised doughnut, glazed doughnut
78. GLAZE ON A DOUGHNUT: frosting, icing
79. RECTANGULAR FROSTED DOUGHNUT: long john, fried cake, doughnut, ponchki
80. TWISTED SUGARED DOUGHNUT: twist, cruller, crawler, twister, twisted bismarck, twisted doughnut, twist roll, twist doughnut, twisted sugar roll
81. JELLY-FILLED DOUGHNUT: bismarck, jelly roll, jelly cake, sweet roll, ponchki, jelly doughnut
82. SMALL BREAKFAST PASTRY: kolacky, kilaks, Danish, Danish pastry, sweet roll
83. LARGE BREAKFAST PASTRY: stollen, strudel, streusel, kaffeekuchen, zuckerkuchen, coffee-kuchen, apfelkuchen, applekuchen, coffee cake, yeast coffee cake, Danish, prune cake, apricot coffee cake, butter coffee cake
84. ENCLOSED SUN PORCH: sun porch, sun parlor, sun room, Florida room
85. INFORMAL LIVING ROOM: recreation room, rec room, family room, playroom, TV room, den
86. LAVATORY WITHOUT BATH OR SHOWER: lavatory, powder room, washroom, half bath, bathroom, toilet
87. ROW OF HOUSES JOINED BY COMMON SIDE WALLS: town house, row house, duplex
88. COOPERATIVELY OWNED APARTMENT BUILDING: co-op, cooperative, co-op apartment, cooperative apartment
89. CONDOMINIUM: co-op, condo, condo apartment, condominium
90. APARTMENT OCCUPYING TWO FLOORS: two-story, double, duplex
91. APARTMENT OCCUPYING ENTIRE LEVEL OF A BUILDING: apartment, flat
92. GAS FURNACE: furnace, gas furnace, gas heating unit
93. OIL FURNACE: furnace, oil furnace, oil stove, oil burner, oil-fired heater
94. POSTMAN: postman, mailman, letter carrier
95. GARBAGEMAN: garbageman, garbage boy, garbage collector
96. LOAFER: bum, ne'er-do-well, goldbrick, lazy bugger, idler, lazybones, hobo, tramp, wonder boy, slacker, floater, misfit, drifter, bagman, street person
97. FEMALE WHO ROAMS THE STREET (NOT A PROSTITUTE): bag lady, street person, female bum

98. ALCOHOLIC: drunk, alcoholic, alky, sop, sot, stewpot, drunkard, souse, boozer, jughead, juicehead, rummy, stewbum, wino, toper, liquorhead, booze hound, beer belly
99. NONWORKING CITY EMPLOYEES: payrollers, city payrollers, boon-dogglers, featherbedders, loafers, tax eaters, goldbricks, slackers, goldbrickers, policemen
100. MORTUARY: funeral home, funeral parlor, undertaker's
101. POLICE STATION: police station, village hall, precinct, police head-quarters
102. POLICEMAN'S BATON: bat, club, billy club, baton, stick, policeman's club, nightstick, billy, police club
103. FIRE STATION: fire station, fire-engine house, engine house, fire-house, fire barn, fire department, barn
104. POLITICAL INFLUENCE: clout, drag, pull, connections, to have a Chinaman, to have an "in"
105. POLITICAL POWER: clout, drag, pull, power
106. INDUSTRIAL FENCING: chain fence, chain link fence, linked fence, wire fence, cyclone fence, security fence, playground fence, woven fence, wire-netting fence, steel link fence, mesh wire fence, woven wire netting, mesh fence

Personal Data Sheet

The following information will be used for research purposes only. Please help us out by answering as many questions as you can. Answer the questions without identifying yourself.

Date   Sex   Race   Age
Highest grade reached in school
Languages other than English
Birthplace
How long have you lived in Chicago?
What part of the city do you live in?
Have you traveled much outside Chicago?
Other towns, states, or countries you have lived in

Your occupation
Where was your father born?
Where was your father's father born?

Where was your father's mother born?
Where was your mother born?
Where was your mother's father born?
Where was your mother's mother born?
Have you filled out this exact same checklist before?

Investigating Gullah: Difficulties in Ensuring "Authenticity"

Salikoko S. Mufwene, University of Chicago

❦

ASIDE from Lorenzo Dow Turner, I know of no investigator of Gullah who has alerted subsequent researchers to some potential problems in the field. As those who have read Turner will soon notice, there are enough similarities between his field experience and mine to assume that these problems may be general and that future field researchers should be prepared for them. The difficulties are in some respects similar to those that students of Black English have had to overcome (Labov, *Language*; J. Baugh, *Black Street Speech*; V. Edwards, *Language in a Black Community*); it thus seems justified to consider at least some of them general for studies of basilects[1] and lower mesolects in diglossic[2] speech continua that differ from the classic cases of diglossia only in that boundaries between these nonstandard varieties and their standard counterparts are gradual rather than clear-cut.

Gullah: A Continuum of Lectal Variation

Gullah is one of numerous creoles around the world that resulted from the contacts of Europeans with non-Europeans during the mercantile and colonial explorations of the second half of the fifteenth through the nineteenth centuries. It emerged on the plantations of the coastal marshland and islands of South Carolina and Georgia, apparently a few decades after the first settlement of British colonists and their African slaves came to Charleston, South Carolina, from Barbados in 1670. The development of this language is attributed to the contact between seventeenth- and eighteenth-century colonial English, which was predominantly rural and (according to Hancock, "On the Classification") consisted of rather diverse dialects, and quite a number of typologically diverse black African languages. Being the original supplier of slaves for Georgia on into the mid-eighteenth century, coastal South Carolina may legitimately be considered Gullah's birthplace.

Originally the plantations were rather small, there were fewer slaves than colonists, and social discrimination was less harsh and rigid than in the eighteenth century. These social conditions probably gave the Africans who arrived in the seventeenth century considerable exposure to the native

English of the plantation owners; the everyday English that the earliest slaves spoke must not have been a pidgin (even though some of them may have spoken one before their arrival) but rather a nonnative variety that was fairly close to that of their masters. In the eighteenth century, the plantation industry proved to be quite lucrative, and the size of the estates, as well as the number of indentured laborers and slaves, increased drastically, making the Africans the overwhelming majority (Wood; Joyner), particularly on those plantations with more than one hundred slaves. The families of the plantation aristocracy did not increase proportionally; in fact, they some-times ran their businesses in absentia through their overseers, who spoke rural nonstandard English. The white indentured laborers, especially Gyp-sies and those from Ireland and Scotland, did not necessarily speak the native variety of the plantation aristocracy or of southern England. According to J. L. Dillard (*Toward a Social History*), the variety of English spoken on the plantations may have had some ties to the maritime or nautical English that was used on British ships (see also Dillard, *Black English*; Hancock, "On the Classification"; McCrum, Cran, and McNeil). The presence of Germans and Huguenots in the same geographic area makes the scenario even more complex.

On the large plantations, where the slave-master ratio often exceeded twenty to one, the African slaves did not interact much with native English speakers (perhaps hardly ever for many of them). Yet, given the linguistic diversity of their communities, plantation English was the prime candidate for communication not only between them and the whites but also among themselves. The Africans further restructured it into the creole now called Gullah or Geechee. Nevertheless, even though some Africans spoke a variety of the sixteenth- and seventeenth-century West African Pidgin English be-fore arriving in South Carolina, it is an oversimplification to assume that they were solely responsible for this restructuring. How many of the creole forms and structures are retentions from seventeenth- and eighteenth-cen-tury plantation and colonial varieties of European languages remains an unanswered question to date. Unlike the situation for French Creoles (see, e.g., Chaudenson's "Pour une étude" and *Les créoles*), the question has gener-ally not been addressed for English Creoles. The nonnative varieties that the European indentured laborers used and the very nature of the diverse rural varieties of English brought to the United States in the seventeenth and eighteenth centuries had a determinative role to play in the shaping of Gullah. Since some Gullah features are also attested in some rural varieties of British English (which are considered more conservative than Standard English), they were probably selected from these nonstandard varieties rather than innovated. Examples of these features include nominal plural with *dem* (*them*); durative-progressive constructions similar to *a-* prefixing of verbs (e.g., *I'm a-workin'*); relative clauses starting invariably with *what* or *where*, or without *that* even when the relative noun phrase is subject (e.g., *the man what came*); and preverbal *done* (*He done ate*) to denote completion.

We do not know for sure what difference it would have made had the Africans been exposed to a homogeneous native variety of seventeenth- and eighteenth-century English while other demographic factors remained constant. However, variation in the plantation sizes as well as stratification of the slave population into house slaves versus artisans versus field hands (Dillard, *Black English*; Alleyne; Wood; Joyner) suggests that, from the beginning, black speech was not a homogeneous phenomenon, and it varied a lot even among the Geechees (as many Gullah speakers prefer to identify themselves). The continuum that characterizes this coastal speech community today (and actually instantiates more obviously what can be observed in any language community) need not be attributed (wholly) to decreolization, the dominant explanation heretofore given by creolists such as Frederic G. Cassidy ("Some Similarities," "Barbadian Creole"); Patricia Jones-Jackson ("On Decreolization," "On the Status"); Patricia C. Nichols ("Prepositions"); and John R. Rickford ("Some Principles"). Sociohistorical accounts indicate that Gullah speech must have varied since its early days in a continuum between two poles: (1) the basilect, a projected variety that is composed of all the most nonstandard features attested among the creole's speakers but used in full by none (Mufwene, rev. of Montgomery and Bailey); and (2) any form close to local white (middle-class) English, the acrolect. If linguistic descriptions were truer to facts, it would be more accurate to say that Gullah speech must have always been mesolectal, with some varieties being very close to the putative basilect and others to the acrolect.

If for the sake of convenience we agree to characterize the varieties that are the closest to the putative basilect as basilectal, however, we are not denying that the proportion of speakers of such a language may have decreased over the years, a situation that has led a number of concerned individuals—from John G. Williams in 1895 to Jones-Jackson in 1984 ("On Decreolization"), Samuel G. Stoney and Gertrude M. Shelby in 1930 (qtd. in Reinecke 494), and Albert Stoddard in 1944 ("Origin" 188)—to assume that it was dying. Ervin L. Green's recent observation that the language is not dying is correct: Gullah may never have existed in the homogeneous form idealized by linguists for the sake of their analyses; there are still speakers around that we may nevertheless characterize as basilectal; and land developments on islands such as Hilton Head have had the side effect of developing more pride in the basilectal variety. The quasi-urbanization of some islands (Frogmore, Saint Helena) and the development of others into vacation resorts (Kiawah, Hilton Head, Tybee) or state and national parks (Jekyll,

Cumberland) have succeeded in either displacing the Geechee population (thus reducing the total number of Gullah speakers, a number that has always been a guess) or turning the language into some sort of underground variety for some speakers. But there is so far little evidence based on a systematic comparison of earlier texts with today's Gullah to indicate that the structure of the language is changing.[3]

Gullah seems to have always been a creole spoken in varieties that form a continuum from a number of levels close to the putative basilect to those closer to local white English. There are a number of similarities between Gullah, on the one hand, and Ozark and Appalachian English (Wolfram and Christian; Christian, "Relatedness"), Brandywine English (Gilbert), and Old Order Amish of Pennsylvania (Brunt, Enninger, et al.), on the other. The nature of these relationships is obscure, but all these varieties developed from varieties of rural (and maritime) English brought to the United States between the sixteenth and eighteenth centuries. As seminal as Turner has been, the work contains little grammatical description of any significance. Much research is still under way, conducted particularly by me (sponsored in 1983 and 1988 by the National Endowment for the Humanities and in 1986–88 by the National Science Foundation).

Investigating Gullah in the Field: Hunting for Gullah

Except for natives of the coast of South Carolina and Georgia, many of us have become acquainted with Gullah only through the works of Joel Chandler Harris, Charles C. Jones, Ambrose Gonzales, or Albert Stoddard. Also worth mentioning are Virginia Gerathy's poems (unpublished but often available in Charleston shops or as gifts from the author) and the record album on which she imitates the Gullah of the plantation where she grew up. Many linguists have, otherwise, learned about Gullah through Annie Weston Whitney, John Bennett, Reed Smith, Guy B. Johnson, Mamie Meredith, Claude M. Wise, Mason Crum, Stoddard, and—the turning point of studies on Gullah and Atlantic creoles—Turner. In the 1960s, studies of the vernacular speech of blacks in New York, Philadelphia, and Washington, D.C., by Labov (*Language*) and William A. Stewart ("Sociolinguistic," "Continuity," "Historical") renewed linguists' interest in the serious study of Gullah. Aside from those cited in the previous section, contemporary references include Cassidy ("Place of Gullah," "Sources"), Irma Aloyce Ewing Cunningham, Ian F. Hancock (*Further Observations,* "Gullah," "Texan Gullah"), Jones-Jackson ("Contemporary," "Gullah," "On the Status," *When Roots Die*), Mufwene ("Linguistic Significance," "Restrictive," "Number Delimitation," "Equivocal Structures," "Serialization," "Is Gullah Decreolizing?" "On the

Infinitive"), Mufwene and Marta B. Dijkhoff, Mufwene and Charles Gilman, Nichols ("Black and White," "Complementizers," "Gullah"), and Rickford ("Carrying the New Wave," "Ethnicity," "Insights," "Representativeness").

Because of the false assumptions discussed in the preceding section, undertaking field research on Gullah may entail going on location on an exploratory basis to determine for oneself where the language is still spoken and to examine the feasibility of the investigation. This is exactly what I decided to do in the summer of 1982. My first academic contacts in Charleston knew no Gullah, but one of their colleagues introduced me to one of the leaders on Johns Island (hereafter called Bill) who would be able to introduce me to native speakers. At this point, I was close to Gullah, but I still had no access to it.

The morning before I became acquainted with Bill, I drove around Johns Island and stopped to talk to some people (e.g., pretending to be lost and asking questions), but I heard no Gullah, at least nothing I could call creole in structure even though the speech was undeniably nonstandard. In the afternoon I met Bill, who is now a dear friend of mine and a big supporter of my research. The following day the black community of Johns, James, and Wadmalaw islands was having a Labor Day picnic sponsored by Budweiser on Mosquito Beach (pronounced [skito biːč]), and Bill invited me to meet the local population there, promising that I would hear plenty of Gullah. He was right: many people at the picnic spoke it, as long as they did not notice I was listening to them as they talked among themselves. As long as I did not speak, nothing gave me away immediately; my changing places from time to time as though I were looking for somebody prevented them from wondering why I was so silent. This behavior was very helpful here in establishing that Gullah still thrives. Like many other people in the United States, Gullah speakers are in most cases bilectal; in front of outsiders they switch easily from one lect to another, though in many cases the switch is only from some level closer to the basilect to another level of the mesolect. Still, I thought it best to capture the "in-group" variety of such speakers.

After I had been prepared by the literature to encounter some kind of idealized basilect, anything other than that stereotype was hard for me to take for true Gullah. The only relief for this disconcerting feeling was to hear speech that was reminiscent of the Caribbean, where I had lived a year earlier. My feast was tempered when Bill arrived and introduced me to a young man who worked for Budweiser and who enthusiastically decided to introduce the "University of Georgia professor" to people he knew spoke Gullah. Much to my disappointment, nobody admitted to speaking Gullah (even though in some cases I had heard these individuals speak that Jamaican Creole–like language variety). So there I was in the Gullah land amid its native speakers—I had heard Gullah, but I still could not make any concrete plans for field research because nobody would admit to speaking the language.

The following summer I made arrangements through the Penn Community Center at Frogmore to extend my research to Saint Helena Island. My host family seems to have been selected more out of concern for my comfort than for my academic interests; my hosts' house was air-conditioned. Although they were not middle class, they concealed their Gullah successfully. They even denied knowing anybody who spoke it, though the wife (in her 50s) conceded later that her husband "might" speak it since he "hangs out" a lot with the guys. Indeed, he did speak Gullah, and I discovered that she did too; she "slipped back to Gullah" while testifying in her church the following morning about black youths' disheartening experiences with drugs. As for her husband, I discovered that he spoke the language when he and his brother rode in my car on a tour of Saint Helena and neighboring islands after service the same Sunday. They had drunk a little bit and were talking about their childhood experiences, particularly how their deceased father used to treat them; this is the kind of thing that is done more naturally in Gullah for them. They laughed when I confronted them with the question of whether the variety they spoke was not Gullah, pretending they did not know it was called that. My host said that he knew only that they, the low country blacks, are Geechees but not that their language was called Gullah or had any special name. For him, they just speak English. Later that evening he took me out to a joint, where I came across another speaker of Gullah, whose articulation was such that, unfortunately, I could not decipher much, in part because of my limited familiarity with the language variety at the time. I was not able to record a sample of his speech either, not having made prior arrangements or knowing the people we were visiting. My experience on Saint Helena remained generally frustrating, since I hardly succeeded in establishing contacts with people who would admit to speaking Gullah and would speak it in my presence.

On a later trip to Saint Helena, a baseball game provided me with the first occasion since the Labor Day picnic on Mosquito Beach to hear a substantial number of people in one place speaking Gullah—they did not suspect that there was a stranger among them. I remained frustrated, however, in receiving no local help in establishing the kind of rapport that I had with my informants on Johns and Wadmalaw islands. Developing a trusting relationship, which Turner emphasizes, is, as I was learning, a sine qua non for collecting accurate Gullah data.

I had discovered then that Gullah is still spoken on Saint Helena, but I ended this field trip with no tape recording of data and, worst of all, no hope of better arrangements for fieldwork there. I decided to stick to Johns and Wadmalaw islands and comforted myself with the thought that, perhaps for this groundbreaking stage of my field research, *qui trop embrasse mal étreint* (roughly: I shouldn't take on more than I can handle).

Eventually Bill, the leader on Johns Island, admitted that he too grew up speaking Gullah and still speaks it, especially when interacting with the older folks. (In fact, he informed me that friends had reminded him to "watch" his speech on the air; he speaks informally and often "slips back to Gullah" ways.) Bill is quite committed to the survival of the Geechee community as a distinctive group and has always helped people who want to do nonexploitive analyses of Geechee culture. As I found out later, many other research or documentary projects on the area, including *The Story of English*, *We Got to Move*, and a project with the *National Geographic* in the summer of 1986 (in connection with which Jones-Jackson died in an auto accident), have enlisted his help. It was after meeting with him again in Atlanta in the winter of 1983, more than five months following my initial frustrating visit to Charleston, and explaining the intentions and some details of my project more explicitly that he took me more seriously and was ready to reintroduce me to the community in my terms.

As I started my project in the spring of 1983, Bill was more cooperative, taking me on a tour of both Johns and Wadmalaw islands and introducing me to several people and places I would often visit later (this time not as a linguist but as an "African brother" interested in comparing "our motherland with our new home"). He assigned his own brother, Al, to me as a guide. This made a big difference, since I would then have to do very little talking during our visits; there would be less style-shifting in the speech of my informants and the conversations would proceed fairly naturally in spite of my presence. Luckily for me, Al is also ideologically committed to Gullah (although he speaks middle-class English well), and he was very instrumental in warming up the informants and getting them to ignore me.

Some readers who have done field research on other so-called exotic languages may wonder why I did not start by learning to speak Gullah first. This is a complex question and is related in part to the element of trust I mentioned above: native speakers do not want either to admit they speak Gullah or to talk about it. Thus you cannot ask them to teach you to speak it. This is not like going to live among Indians or Africans and learning to speak their language. Although the latter groups know that their languages do not have much social prestige, nobody has told them that their languages are bad or has tried to discourage them from speaking them. Even now that my research is well under way, informants react coldly when I express any intention of speaking the language! I have to be content with passive knowledge and be grateful to my guides for being as much involved with it as they have been to date.

Collecting language in natural settings is always difficult; one cannot simply put a tape recorder on the table and ask everyone to speak. What one needs is a tape recording of a natural speech sample from which later interviews may arise. I have always been amused by fieldworkers who start with "How do you say" questions, trying to find some quick (not necessarily idiomatic) translations of things the informants say in their own languages. As a native or fluent speaker of some low-status African languages (called "dialects" by most non-linguist Westerners), I have often felt resentment when confronted with the familiar line "Can you say something in your language for me?"

Collecting Gullah Data

The only problem with Al was his tendency to dominate the conversations with his peers. Although he was good about letting the elderly speak and in prompting them to tell personal stories, it took constant reminders before our visits that he should not really go beyond encouraging the other informants to speak comfortably. Yet because Al took me to visit his relatives and friends, we had a network of about thirty people to work with, though not all cooperated to the same extent. For the sake of the project, we had agreed not to reveal that language was the main objective, to focus on gathering as large a body of natural Gullah texts as possible, and generally to postpone interviews until after many of the texts had been processed and very specific questions had arisen on topics of analytical interest. Being known as talkative, Al would have appeared unnatural had he always complied with my requests to speak less. As for me, even though the islanders liked my African accent, they tended to make accommodations when I took part in the conversations. So, without dissociating myself, I kept my own participation to a minimum and let the guides do most of the talking. This approach was particularly fruitful on first visits with informants.

There was, however, another problem on my mind, which was crucial to the continuation of the field research and called for a quick solution. As noted in the preceding section, I went to the field with the stereotypical misconception that Gullah must sound very much like Stoddard's record albums or the Jamaican Creole basilect (that is, a version close to that in Charles Jones, Ambrose Gonzales, or maybe Joel Chandler Harris). At the joints where Al took me in the beginning, the varieties I heard were more mesolectal, some of them very much influenced by urban black speech, at least prosodically. Though Al reassured me that *that* was Gullah, I asked if we could visit some older folks to obtain different samples and to determine whether age, time, or geographical distance accounted for the contrast I noticed between Stoddard's Gullah and what I heard. We did this a couple of weeks later, and the earlier generation subsequently became the focus of my investigation. The intonation of the older people sounded pretty much like that of the middle-aged guys I had met at the joints, but the grammar of the older people was more consistent, even though it was closer to the sample texts in Turner than to the so-called literary Gullah. For instance, the progressive construction with *duh* (pronounced [də]) alternates with the patterns verb plus *in'* and *duh* with verb plus *in'* (e.g., *how you duh do? how you doin? how you duh doin?*) there are almost as many past-time references with *bin* as with English-like tense inflections (however, their interpretation is trickier). The time reference system is predominantly a relative tense system, but there seem to be two coexisting systems of nominal number delimitation—one is creolelike, in that the individuated/nonindividuated distinction is prominent, and the other is quite English-like, in that the singular/plural distinction overlaps with the predominantly individuated/nonindividuated distinction (see Mufwene, "Count/Mass" and "Number Delimitation").

Older people do not all speak basilectal Gullah. Factors such as whether such people have lived for a long period of time outside their community and the roles they have played in the community may affect the language they speak. Many elderly people once left the islands to live in New York, or went to sea, and came back only to retire; they do not speak the same kind of language as those who have spent most of their working lives at home. The language the older people speak may also have been affected by their experience outside the community. How long ago they went to the city, how comfortable they felt there, and how much they like home after coming back are all factors that influence their speech. Some who have worked mostly in neighboring cities like Charleston do not speak like those who have had limited contact with city life, and those who had more education are likely to have kept only some of the basilectal features (see also Nichols, "Linguistic Change"). However, generalizations like these can be dangerous, since the personalities of individual speakers and their social relations are more important factors than level of education, though this variable is indeed an important one.

As my fieldwork progressed, I discovered that quite a few young people speak a variety of Gullah that is as basilectal as that of some older people. One of my recordings of basilectal speech around Christmas 1986 was with a couple in their late twenties and early thirties who speak this way, as do a number of their friends. I spotted them at a card game that I had organized to get people to speak naturally. In the summer of 1986, I also met a youngster who went to high school in Charleston but who continued to speak Gullah when he was back on Wadmalaw with his friends. For him, as he explained, the alternation between Gullah and urban black speech was a necessity; urban black speech protected him from mockery when in Charleston, and Gullah protected him from accusations of snobbery on the island. One of the greatest challenges in the field was to get such youngsters to speak Gullah in the presence of someone who was not a community member; they were reluctant to do so even if offered pay for interview sessions. This youngster, who happened to be very helpful for interview sessions, would not speak unless I left the room, whereupon he would converse with his father and his aunt. Such situations emphasize the need for a native guide, particularly for studies to which the investigator has not committed his or her lifetime.

In the four years of fieldwork, I found that the best alternative was to visit the informants in their homes. Appointments for these visits offered the means through which to control the number of participants. Visits by appointment also reinforced in the informants the idea that I came to see them for a special, serious reason. These visits made it easier for me to control the atmosphere, too—for instance, by asking whether the television could be turned down or off, or whether I should wait until the program was over. Such requests were usually granted, particularly if the informants were being paid for the work session. (Payment makes the Geechees feel less exploited and decreases the resentment toward outsiders who come to make money or reputations without making a contribution in return.)

Generally I found all the language varieties spoken on the islands to be relevant, since they converge to show the most dominant, persistent, or typical features of Gullah. Still, it helps to know or be told who speaks "pure Gullah" (as Al usually said) and who does not. In some cases, depending on the ideological attitude of the household, even some members of the younger generation speak "beautiful Gullah." There is no obvious evidence for assuming that Gullah grammar has decreolized over the years since Turner's study (Mufwene, "Is Gullah Decreolizing?"). Further research is needed to determine the nature and extent of changes that have occurred since the 1930s.

Processing the Data

I would hate to mislead anybody into believing that Gullah in the field is as articulate as that on Stoddard's or Gerathy's record albums. Actually, for anybody who goes to the field on the basis of the stereotype I started with and who may have not had experience with other English-related creoles, the first encounter is like meeting less-educated or noneducated native speakers of a foreign language learned in school. Conversations are often on topics that you did not see discussed in the literature, many phrases are used that for moralistic reasons may be omitted from books, articulation is frequently sloppy, and you cannot always ask speakers to repeat what they have said while a conversation is in progress—thus the need for the rather long exposure to the language in the joints or similar places before starting to collect data.

These factors certainly demonstrate how difficult it would be to process tapes if the investigator had not had enough exposure to Gullah natural speech to be able to understand it. Yet it is hard to determine the accuracy of transcriptions alone without double-checking with a native speaker. I have come to believe that there must be special cues that native speakers follow when speech is so distorted that the average nonnative cannot understand it.

When do you assume you have collected enough texts and when do you start interviews? Almost any text is enough to give you a basis for asking some questions about the language. A good one-hour tape recording can generate around one hundred double-spaced pages of transcription and should contain enough informative data about the structure of the language. However, there is a certain element of chance in speech; some features (including syntactic constructions and semantic peculiarities) may be more frequent in one speaker or on one occasion than others. Increasing the number of tapes (and speakers) increases the chances of coming across new features. Processing the tapes as the collection of data continues raises questions on features that might be expected but are at that particular point unattested. Since Gullah is stigmatized and talking about it may in itself constitute an obstacle to the investigation, I have assumed that designing new recording sessions on topics that might prompt the missing features could be productive. It is when they still do not show up that interviews become necessary. For example, it was through interviews that I collected my data on predicate clefting ("Issue"). Nonetheless, I have found patience quite an asset in regard to such features. Premature interviews often have the side effect of gearing speech toward particular features, excluding a host of alternatives that the investigator may not have anticipated. I have thus given priority to observing the speakers and analyzing their speech, making my interviews rather brief, limiting them to very specific questions prompted either by variation, by curious omissions in my data, or by features that have not been attested in other creoles. When you ask a question with enough tact (e.g., as though it were a statement that you wanted clarified rather than a request to say the construction pattern), you can almost always get a useful answer.

The most troublesome problem is to determine the norm of grammaticality in a context where most mainstream English constructions are also acceptable. For instance, the same speaker uses *all of us* as well as *all o' we*; *who chile* and *whose chile* or *child*; *his child* and *he chile*; and *he chile dem* or *nem* and *his child dem*. The last two phrases are ambiguous (Mufwene, "Number Delimitation") between "his children" and "his child and his friends or associates." I have heard at least twice the phrase *you ain' notn' fuh worry 'bout* 'you have got nothing to worry about.' Is there a mistake here, or is this idiomatic? These are the kinds of questions that I have usually included in my interviews. The situation is complicated by the low status of Gullah in a diglossic polity, the general tolerance by its speakers for English-related patterns, and the assumption by many that the basilectal way is "bad" or incorrect. I have thus avoided asking the question in terms of such qualifiers. Instead, I have opted for questions about "the customary way" of saying so and so or the ordinary intention in the use of such a phrase.

The problems outlined in the preceding two sections bear ultimately on the investigator's analysis of the language. With regard to variation, is the case of Gullah not just a more obvious instance of a reality that occurs in almost any vernacular language—French, German, worldwide Spanish? Is there a monolithic grammar shared by every (adult) native speaker in any language community? Is monolithic grammar conceivable even at the level of individual speakers? Could the Saussurean principle of "conventionality of language" be reinterpreted as the ability of speakers in a community to interpret each other's utterances without necessarily sharing all the structural analyses of the utterances? Whatever the case, all attempts to learn about language—whether through large or small projects—are worth the effort for future generations as well as for the investigator.

Notes

[1] For the sake of preciseness and for consistency with the literature on creoles, I will use some technical terms that may not be familiar to all readers: *creole, basilect, mesolect, acrolect, lexifier*. A *creole* develops when speakers of one or several languages are forced by circumstances to adopt another language without receiving formal instruction; they develop varieties of this creole as they use it in daily verbal interchange. The speakers develop a grammar that approximates that of the language of the politically or economically dominant group. The latter language also provides the vocabulary for the creole and is known by creolists as the *lexifier*. Creole-speaking communities manifest gradations of approximation to the contact language. The term *basilect* refers to a creole variety whose system is most different from that of the

lexifier, which is also commonly called the *acrolect*, although the term may in a given situation apply to any mainstream variety of the lexifier. The term *mesolect* describes any intermediate variety between the basilect and the acrolect; some creolists describe mesolects as resulting from the creole community's approximations of the acrolect. The process by which the creole speakers move closer to the acrolect is referred to as *decreolization*. This characterization applies especially to creoles such as Gullah and Jamaican Creole, which have a European lexifier and coexist with it. *Lect* is used alone or in compounds in this essay to refer to varieties of language without classifying them in more specific terms.

[2] The term *diglossia*, from which the adjective *diglossic* is derived, describes a stratification in which an individual language or lect is considered more, or less, prestigious than others.

[3] Since this manuscript was submitted in 1988, some studies have been conducted on the subject matter of decreolization in Gullah, including Mufwene ("Is Gullah Decreolizing?" and "Some Reasons") and Mille ("Historical Analysis").

Teaching Speakers of Caribbean English Creoles in North American Classrooms

Lise Winer, Southern Illinois University, Carbondale

THIS article is a guide for teachers and teacher trainers about Caribbean English, Caribbean English Creole, and the special needs of students whose first language is a variety of Caribbean English Creole. It briefly discusses some of the basic knowledge of Caribbean culture and language that teachers should have, and provides information from which both teachers and students can learn about language use in situations in which a creole language is in contact with its lexically related standard language: in this case, where English Creole speakers are in North America.

In recent years, increasing numbers of students at all levels have come into United States educational systems from the anglophone Caribbean, particularly from Jamaica and Guyana. Because they are classified as "English speakers" by teachers, by educational and psychological assessors, and by the Caribbean parents and students themselves, they are generally placed in mainstream English classes. Sometimes Caribbean students who are perceived as having "language problems"—usually because teachers find their language difficult to understand—are placed in English as a second language or speech therapy classes. Neither type of program is appropriate for most of these students. In some school systems, "ESD" (English as a second dialect) classes may be available as a transition to mainstream classes. Though the Caribbean students who need special attention may appear to be relatively few in number and are located in only a few school systems, their problems as individual students are not diminished by their small numbers. Even if there are no Caribbean-background students in a particular classroom, the approach described here can be used within a context of teaching about language variation, particularly varieties related to English. North Americans increasingly have more business, political, and tourist contacts with the Caribbean; too often, misunderstandings based on language variation arise and go unquestioned and incorrectly analyzed. The discussion below provides some basic information about Caribbean English Creole and about teaching Caribbean-background students, including suggestions for teacher preparation, classroom teaching procedures, and useful reference sources.

Characteristics of Caribbean English Creole Speakers

Not all students from the Caribbean countries where English is the official language will speak only English Creole; those who have had access to more education will tend to have greater competence in a Caribbean Standard English that varies from other standard varieties only minimally in pronunciation, vocabulary, and grammar. Within the same country, there can be enormous variation—sometimes referred to as the "creole continuum"— comprising at one end varieties that are virtually indistinguishable from Standard Englishes and, at the other end, varieties that are unintelligible to monolingual Standard English speakers. For example, in Tobago one could say *Me a go a maaket, Me goin to maaket, Ah goin to maaket, I'm going to market,* or *I'm going to the market.* In Jamaica one could say *Im a wan big uman, She is a big woman,* or *She is a grown woman.* In addition to lexical and grammatical differences, pronunciation varies among and within countries. English Creole in Jamaica, Guyana, and Barbados has a very distinctly pronounced *r,* whereas in other areas it is realized as lengthening of the preceding vowel, as in British English (e.g., *start = staat*). In Trinidad *garden* can be pronounced *gaaden* or *gyaaden.* (For a summary description of Caribbean English Creole, see Winer's "Caribbean English.")

    Differences in language may be related to such factors as the speakers' socio-economic class, level of education, degree of formality, sex, age, and geographical region (including within a country). English Creole speakers are generally well aware of such variation even when they do not control a wide range within their own English Creole but often do not realize that similar types of variation exist within the Standard English system: their Standard English usually does not include informal, colloquial, or regional Standard English registers.

    Although linguists do not agree on the exact origins of creole languages in the Caribbean, these are generally considered to have evolved through contact among African and European languages during the slave trade and plantation periods of the seventeenth and eighteenth centuries (see descriptions in Alleyne's *Comparative Afro-American*). Although much of their vocabulary is taken from European languages—English, French, Spanish, Dutch—their underlying grammars, features of intonation and stress, and a considerable part of their vocabularies are not European and come from other sources, including, perhaps, some type of "linguistic universals," local independent developments, and from Amerindian, African, and East Indian languages.

    Creoles have traditionally had very low prestige, both inside and outside the countries where they are spoken, because of their characterization as "bad" or "broken" varieties of standard European languages and their association with slavery and people of low racial, social, political, and economic status. Thus many creole speakers, especially those resident in North America for many years, will identify themselves as speaking only English. As Lawrence D. Carrington has pointed out in "The Challenge of Caribbean Language in the Canadian Classroom," students may then have very little motivation to learn English because they already perceive themselves as speaking it. When pressed, they may admit to speaking "slangs," "broken English," or "patois," none of which they consider to be a "real" language with grammatical rules. To escape such negative perceptions, many people in the Caribbean call their language "dialect," a term implying that their language is really just another legitimate version of "real" English.

The low self-esteem that results from considering oneself not a competent speaker of any real language is a significant problem even within the Caribbean. In North America, where ignorance about the Caribbean as a whole reigns, the effect on a student trying to learn language arts skills *and* other subjects only *through* Standard English can be devastating. (For descriptions of effects of non-recognition of language skills of Caribbean students and of teaching in mixed-language situations, see Coard's *How the West Indian Child Is Made Educationally Sub-normal in the British School System*, Craig's "The Sociology of Language Learning and Teaching in a Creole Language Situation," and V. Edwards's *Language in Multicultural Classrooms*.)

Rising nationalism throughout the Caribbean has been linked to increasing pride in "we own ting," including the concept of "nation language," well described in Hubert Devonish's *Language and Liberation* and E. K. Brathwaite's *History of the Voice*. The use of English Creole is now acceptable within wider circumstances than before, such as in newspaper reports and in writing dialogue in formal school-leaving examinations. Like all nonstandard languages, English Creole has had to fight against the twin stigmata of scorn for its "bastardization" and of romanticization for its "colorful charm." Until its speakers take a true and reasonable pride in their language and its history, their learning of Standard English will be greatly hampered, and until foreign listeners recognize English Creole's "normality," they will continue to perceive the language and its speakers in a distorted manner.

Linguists do not agree on whether to call English Creole a separate language or a dialect or variety of English; certainly, Caribbean English Creoles have grammatical structures and vocabulary items quite different from those of the related standard, despite the overwhelming overlap. Superficial similarities between English Creole and English hide real and fundamental differences in language. For example, in Trinidadian English Creole, the *does* in *He does go* indicates a habitual aspect marker for the verb, as in English *He goes (every day)*. In English, however, the same *does* would indicate emphasis: "He doesn't go." "Oh, yes, he *does* go. I've seen him." To North Americans, some aspects of Caribbean pronunciation sound simply British; some, particularly word-stress patterns, are not British but unique Caribbean patterns.

Most English Creole vocabulary is taken from Standard English, both British and American; in Trinidad, for example, a car generally has a (American English) *hood* and a (British English) *boot*. However, thousands of words in Caribbean English Creole are not part of Standard English, from names of plants and animals to occupational jargon and descriptions of appearance and behavior. (For descriptions of vocabulary, see Cassidy's *Jamaica Talk*, Cassidy and Le Page's *Dictionary of Jamaican English*, Rickford's *Festival of Guyanese Words* and *Dimensions of a Creole Continuum*, and Holm and Shilling's *Dictionary of Bahamian English*.) Many "false friends" exist between English Creole and English; for example, *miserable* in English Creole means "badly behaved," and *fresh* can mean "smelling slightly gamy, rotten." An understanding of one English Creole dialect may not solve the difficulties in understanding other varieties. Some words, such as *foot* 'the part of the body from toes to hips' or *study your head* 'to think hard,' are widespread; others, such as Jamaican *bammy*, a kind of fried cassava bread, or Trinidad and Tobago *macocious* 'nosy,' are found primarily in one country.

The superficial similarities between English Creole and English yield positive results for English Creole speakers learning Standard English very quickly in the beginning. Immigrant Caribbean students generally have and develop recognition and productive skills more rapidly than true ESL students, for example. But the English Creole speaker will reach crucial humps, or plateaus, at particular points and often be more frustrated and resentful than a typical ESL student. Consider, for example, that *Mind you do it* in English means the opposite in Creole and that English Creole speakers have heard the same form in the Caribbean all their lives. Years may pass before an English Creole speaker realizes that, in North America, *good night* is said only on leaving, not entering; it is difficult to judge the disconcerting effect this difference can have on monolingual English speakers. Similarly, overlaps in culture hide fundamental differences in areas such as attitudes and practices in education, child-rearing, and nonverbal behavior. (For the latter, see, for example, Fuller's "Paralanguage in Jamaican Creole.") It is impossible to understand the use of any language, including a creole one, without a close look at the social and cultural system of which it is a part. Conflicts arising from the differences between the expectations of parents, schools, peers, and the students themselves can lead to difficulties in social and educational adjustment.

Caribbean immigrant students usually face, for the first time, a situation in which many teachers truly do not understand the students' speech. Although teachers in an English Creole country may disapprove of its use, they do generally understand it. Too frequently in North American schools, however, neither students nor teachers recognize problems of linguistic or paralinguistic communications for what they are. Instead, the problems are diagnosed as an unwillingness ("behavioral problem") or inability ("deaf," "slow learner") of the student to adopt the proper behavior. For example, a well-brought-up Caribbean child receiving a *boof* 'reprimand, scolding' for not having done a *home lesson* 'assignment' is expected to remain silent and look at the ground—certainly not to be *bold-face* 'rude, aggressively challenging' by looking directly at the teacher. This behavior is often interpreted in North American schools as sullen, sneaky, insubordinate, stupid, or dishonest ("He didn't even look the teacher in the eye").

North America is also the first place in which most immigrant Caribbean students have found themselves a racial minority and the target of overt racism. Although racism exists in the Caribbean, the kind shown in North America, particularly from teachers and school administrators, is unexpected and hurtful. General ignorance of the students' backgrounds— including such simple and immediate items as the correct pronunciation of the names of the countries they or their families come from—is linked to the general foreign perception of the Caribbean as "paradise" but uncivilized. Students are often made to feel that they have nothing to offer except tourist beaches, good times, sexy calypsos, and drug-ridden reggae.

Any approach to the teaching of students whose first language is English Creole, recognized or not, must include knowledge about and acceptance of the language and its culture, contrasted specifically with English language and culture varieties. Without an awareness, on the part of teachers, administrators, and others, of the validity of creoles and an understanding of their relationship to English, the students' progress will be continually short-circuited. The approach described here is based on the availability of native English Creole speakers in the classroom or school as resources; but both community resources and audio and video recordings, as well as print sources, can be used within a context of teaching about language variation.

Suggestions for Teacher Training

The following outline lists areas that should be covered by concrete illustrations and hands-on experience. Teachers should be able to appreciate both general statements about language and culture in the English Caribbean and variation throughout the region.

I. Social, Cultural, and Political Background
    A. Overview of geography and demography of the region: names of countries and their citizens, names of languages and where they are spoken, introduction to different ethnic groups.
    B. History of the Caribbean, emphasizing English areas: influences of Amerindian, African, European, East Indian, and other cultures; slavery and indentured labor; colonial, postcolonial, and neo-colonial eras; historical and current immigration patterns. Good sources for this area are Dan Allen and Richard Hall's *New Lives in the New World*; Michael Anthony and Andrew Carr's *David Frost Introduces Trinidad and Tobago*; Tom Barry, Beth Wood, and Deb Preusch's *The Other Side of Paradise*; Brathwaite's *The People Who Came*; Morris Cargill's *Ian Fleming Introduces Jamaica*; Catherine A. Sunshine's *The Caribbean*; and Eric Williams's *From Columbus to Castro*. Olive Senior's *A–Z of Jamaican Heritage* is an excellent short encyclopedic reference work for that country.
    C. Family and social structure: the extended family network, child care, roles of family members, discipline and learning within the family.
    D. Educational system: formal school organization (types of schools, types and importance of examinations, traditional views of school and education, role of schools, role of parents); classroom behavior (teaching methods, discipline, attitudes toward use of English Creole). The most comprehensive relevant treatment of these two general areas is Elizabeth Coelho's *The Caribbean Student in Canadian Schools*, volumes 1 and 2. For a report on successful use of a Creole-language-centered approach in a United States high school, see Kathy Fischer, "Educating Speakers of Caribbean English Creole in the United States."
    E. Cultural traditions: oral traditions (e.g., story-telling), literature, drama, poetry; traditional and modern music; religions; customs; holidays; folklore; public and private behavior and manners.

    Highly recommended for both cultural and linguistic information as well as artistic merit are a number of literary works: Louise Bennett's *Selected Poems*, Paula Burnett's *The Penguin Book of Caribbean Verse*, *Caribbean Anthology* (includes audiocassettes), Michael Anthony's *Green Days by the River* and *The Year in San Fernando*, Austin Clarke's *Growing Up Stupid under the Union Jack*,

Merle Hodge's *Crick Crack, Monkey*, Evan Jones's *Tales of the Caribbean*, Paul Keens-Douglas's *When Moon Shine*, Jamaica Kincaid's *Annie John*, Earl Lovelace's *The Dragon Can't Dance*, Edgar Mittelholzer's *A Morning at the Office*, V. S. Naipaul's *Miguel Street*, Samuel Selvon's *A Brighter Sun, Turn Again Tiger*, and *The Lonely Londoners*, Olive Senior's *Summer Lightning and Other Stories*, and Anne Walmsley's *The Sun's Eye*.

Films available on videocassettes include *The Harder They Come*, about a would-be reggae singer in Jamaica, by Perry Henzell and Trevor D. Rhone; *Sitting in Limbo*, about Caribbean-background teenagers in Montreal; and *Sugar Cane Alley*, about a traditional childhood in 1930s Martinique.

Recordings by reggae artists and dub poets such as Linton Kwesi Johnson and Lillian Allen are widely available. Stephen Davis and Peter Simon's *Reggae International* is an excellent and readable history and analysis of reggae music.

II. Language
    A. Variation in English: geographical dialects, historical development, situational registers, class dialects, slang, jargon.
    B. History and development of generic creole and other languages in the Caribbean.
    C. English Creoles in the Caribbean: definition, historical development, contribution of African languages, relationship of English and English Creoles.
       • studying grammar, vocabulary, phonology, intonation, and stress
       • observing paralinguistic behavior—e.g., gestures
       • listening to oral language of various kinds from within the same country—e.g., Standard and creole Jamaican English
       • reading written forms of creoles in literature and poetry
       • examining, revising, and making dictionaries of Caribbean English Creoles

An outstanding workbooklike introduction to concepts about language, including all types of variation, is Mike Raleigh's *The Languages Book. American Tongues* is an excellent and widely usable videotape providing rich and accessible information and analysis on variation in language in the United States; it would fit well in a discussion of creole varieties. The most comprehensive classroom-oriented resource for Caribbean-background students is Coelho's *The Caribbean Student in Canadian Schools*, volume 2. In addition to the language resources mentioned above, particularly helpful classroom-oriented materials are Coelho's "An Honest Thief" (a language lesson in detail) and Nan Elsasser and Patricia Irvine's "English and Creole."

Examining Creole Language and Language Variation

It is certainly not expected that teachers become fluent in English Creole, although the teacher's own varieties of English can be a valuable resource in classroom discussion. (For an account of an English speaker's process of learning English Creole, see Winer's "Trini Talk.") Teachers should work with their students to figure out the linguistic—or other—bases of difficulties and differences, to formalize and revise hypotheses about English Creole and English. The two guiding principles throughout should be (1) *respect* the student, the student's culture, and the student's language; and (2) *suspect* language to be involved in apparent nonlinguistic problems.

Some errors in English produced by English Creole speakers can be useful starting points for discussion. For example, a student has produced the sentence *In Bloor Street have plenty shop*—in fact, a correct English Creole sentence. Typical teacher corrections might be *Bloor Street has plenty of shops* or *In Bloor Street there are plenty of shops*. The student accepts this, especially the typical focus on the missing *-s* plural marker, and then later produces *In Jamaica nice*, also grammatically correct English Creole. The teacher reminds the student of the previous correction, and the student then produces *Jamaica has nice* or *In Jamaica there is nice*. Only persistent, respectful suspicion and patient elicitation of sample sentences and discussions of "how you could say this" (e.g., both English Creole and colloquial spoken English have *Here is nice*, as in English "Where should we have the picnic?" "Well, here is nice") can reveal that structures such as *in Jamaica* and *in Bloor Street* are prepositional phrases in English but in English Creole can be locative nominalizations—that is, phrases of place acting as subjects of the sentence.

The use of pictures and the discussion of topics familiar to the students are helpful, particularly at early stages, so that the student is not struggling with both language and content at the same time, and so that students have an opportunity to show some of their own knowledge. Because of the significant differences in pronunciation, standard phonics-based approaches to reading are not very workable, except in a limited way such as the recognition of consistent consonant sounds. It is important not to attack or change the creole user's speech at first if one is attempting to establish validity of both creole and standard. Later, contextualized discussions of intelligibility and appropriateness can help students decide what they want to do in their own speech and writing.

Bilingualism and Language Variation among Chicanos in the Southwest

D. Letticia Galindo, Arizona State University

⤖

THIS paper examines bilingualism and language variation from a Chicano perspective by discussing "universals" that occur in any given bilingual community: language contact, language maintenance and language shift, and language attitudes.[1] A less-studied linguistic phenomenon that merits further attention is the variety termed Chicano English. The section "Chicano English" gives an overview of research and lists some phonological, syntactic, and lexical features of this particular dialect of American English. The last section suggests some classroom activities that draw the students' attention to variation in Chicano language use.

The following demographic data place the sociolinguistic issues surrounding bilingualism in the Southwest in perspective within larger issues in the United States:

There are more than 15 million persons in the United States of Mexican descent; 80 percent reside in urban areas (R. Sánchez, "Our Linguistic").

Of these 15 million Chicanos, 90 percent reside in the Southwest, primarily in California (40.6 percent) and Texas (36.4 percent) (Macías, "Mexicano/Chicano"; Peñalosa, *Chicano*).

Among persons fourteen years or older, 7.7 million have Spanish as their native tongue (U.S. Bureau of the Census, 1982).

Of these Chicanos, 23 percent are English monolingual (Macías, "Language Diversity").

As the largest lingual minority in the United States, the Chicano speech community is complex, heterogeneous, and dynamic.[2] The constant influx of immigrants from south of the border keeps Spanish alive for part of the population (first-generation immigrants) while maintaining a sizable number of balanced bilinguals in the Chicano community. In recent decades a third lingual group has grown in strength: the English-only generation of Chicanos who have ceased to speak the native tongue on a regular basis yet possess receptive competence in Spanish. Because of historical and social circumstances, a wide array of language varieties and language speakers exist within Chicano speech communities; the typical community is composed of three groups: Spanish monolinguals, English monolinguals, and bilingual persons (R. Sánchez, "Our Linguistic").

Thus the linguistic repertories for many speech communities consist of varieties ranging from Standard Spanish to Standard English, influenced by social variables such as age, sex, and education and by family history. In her research on language varieties and their functions within the East Austin (Texas) bilingual community, Lucía Elías-Olivares ("Language Use") found a linguistic continuum in which the distance between the two extremes is bridged by intermediate varieties, with varying degrees of borrowing and code switching. Her linguistic categories included the following: Standard Spanish–popular Spanish–mixed Spanish–Caló[3]–Chicano English–Standard English.

Language Contact

William Mackey and Jacob Ornstein define language contact as a social phenomenon that results from the meeting of peoples speaking different languages—for example, Spanish speakers coming into contact with monolingual English speakers in the Southwest. Such a situation produces interesting linguistic phenomena that were first discussed in the literature on bilingualism by Uriel Weinreich and by Einar Haugen (*Norwegian Language*). These works differ from contemporary studies of Chicano bilingualism in that they focus on the individual as opposed to the speech community; furthermore, they tend to concentrate primarily on such speakers' command of standard varieties of each of two languages. Unfortunately, the "ideal" bilingual speaker is a fiction (just as the "ideal" monolingual speaker is a fiction) and thus is never really found by researchers studying bilingual or multilingual communities. In the case of Chicano bilinguals, because many speakers are not exposed to formal instruction in Spanish, their proficiency in Spanish is primarily oral (see the publications of R. Sánchez).

What are the effects of language contact? When people speaking two different languages live in geographic proximity—like the Chicanos in daily contact with monolingual English speakers (including blacks and Anglos)—one can expect to find linguistic processes such as interference and integration taking place, especially within a bilingual context. Interference, as defined by Weinreich, is the "deviation from the norms of either language which occurs in the speech of bilinguals as the result of their familiarity with more than one language" (1). He makes a crucial distinction between *speech* and *language* interference. Speech interference is related to oral performance—that is, it involves utterances made by the bilingual speaker.

Language interference is related to competence, in that some interference phenomena become habitualized and are then established as the community's unconscious linguistic norms. Fernando Peñalosa equates interference with "cultural standardization," whereby there is widespread use and acceptance in the community of so-called speech interference mistakes (*Chicano* 55).

During the 1960s, early studies on bilingualism were based on the interference paradigm, which had its origins in foreign language pedagogy and was closely linked to error analysis and contrastive analysis. Basically, it refers to "features from one's native language which entered one's attempt to speak a foreign language and thus interfered with the second language" (Peñalosa, *Chicano* 55). Interference is equated not only with phonological differences (e.g., *bit* pronounced as *beet*) but with syntactic and semantic differences, as well as with accented speech. The interference model is viewed with disfavor by most Chicano scholars. Elías-Olivares and Guadalupe Valdés maintain that bilingual research based on the notion of interference looks at these phenomena as "deviations" from standard varieties and not as self-contained systems.

Language Maintenance and Language Shift

Calvin Veltman (*Language Shift*) states that whenever two or more language groups live in a given territory, certain outcomes will result from contact between these two groups. The two extremes are *language retention* and *linguistic assimilation*, or "anglicization." In order to comprehend the perseverance of Spanish and the transition to English among Chicano speakers, one must consider social factors that affect the processes of maintenance and shift. In her 1982 study, Rosaura Sánchez ("Our Linguistic") outlines the following factors necessary for the survival and maintenance of Spanish in urban and rural *barrios* throughout the Southwest: residential segregation, economics, geographic stability and proximity to the border, and influx of Mexicans to the United States. Low socioeconomic status and residence in segregated neighborhoods, coupled with little chance of upward mobility, have resulted in the retention of Spanish by large numbers of speakers. From a geographic perspective, there is greater opportunity for maintenance along the Mexican border, or *frontera*, because it is here that Spanish enjoys the status of the "high" language, whereby its use encompasses all domains and English is often designated as the "low" variety.[4] By far the most important factor for the continued existence of Spanish, however, is the constant migration of Mexicans and Central and South Americans into the United States. David López, in a 1978 study, observed that the retention of and loyalty to the Spanish language in Los Angeles was related to a massive influx of Spanish-speaking immigrants and to social and occupational isolation. Other factors—including nativity, age, education, and geographic locale—have a vital role in the process of language maintenance. Presently, Chicano speakers of Spanish are characterized as being first- or second-generation Americans of Mexican descent.[5] Retention of Spanish among younger generations from urban communities is not as widespread as in the past, yet varieties like *caló* are symbolic of ethnic identity and solidarity among such speakers.

Since languages are dynamic social instruments, concurrent linguistic and social processes affect the use of one language variety over another. We find that many Spanish-surnamed individuals continue to speak Spanish while an equally large number have shifted to English as their sole means of communication. Veltman, in a 1983 article, defines the language shift process among minorities in the United States as "anglicization" and describes four types of behavior that permit us to classify language practice on the continuum between minority language retention and enculturation. Figure 1 is a graphic representation of the anglicization and language shift processes he discusses (*Language Shift* 100–02):

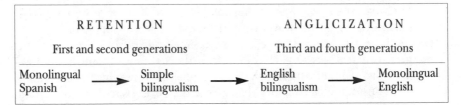

Figure 1. **Spanish-English Bilingualism and the Language Shift Process**

Minority language monolingualism—there is sole use of the native tongue

Simple bilingualism—individuals retain their native tongue as their principal language but also speak English

English bilingualism—the native tongue has been retained as a second language but English is the main vehicle of communication

English-language monolingualism—the native tongue has been abandoned or may be used only in specialized settings

Each type of lingualism depends on the language used by the previous generation and represents a degree of movement toward the monolingual

English-language group; social and historical factors influence which type of lingualism is dominant. Given this framework, it appears that age and generational differences determine whether Spanish is retained or English adopted. First- and second-generation adults are the most likely candidates for native tongue retention; the linguistic situation among third- and fourth-generation Chicanos is that, while their grandparents and parents speak Spanish, they do not. They consider themselves to be English-dominant or English monolingual instead. This is an example of intergenerational switching described by Ralph W. Fasold (*Sociolinguistics*), in which one generation is bilingual but passes on only one of the two languages to the next generation.

In the analysis of his Los Angeles data, López claims that the pivotal shift from Spanish to English occurs during the second generation. By the third generation, Spanish is hardly used at all in the home. Even in a state like New Mexico, where a high concentration of people claim Spanish as their native tongue, a gradual intergenerational process of language shift to English is occurring, especially among urban populations. By taking into account four language variables from their data—native tongue, speaking ability in Spanish, speaking ability in English, and language use in the home—Alan Hudson-Edwards and Garland Bills were able to describe and characterize the mechanism of language shift within an Albuquerque barrio.

What factors are most prominent in language shift? According to Fasold (*Sociolinguistics*), a sign that language shifts are in progress may be the tendency of a speech community to choose a new language in domains formerly reserved for the old one. For instance, Joshua A. Fishman ("Who Speaks") observed that English is taking over the home, school, and neighborhood domains in bilingual communities. In two later studies, Jon Amastae found that social mobility among university students from the Rio Grande Valley in Texas was the motivational factor to shift from Spanish to English, and Sánchez ("Our Linguistic") cited this factor and others as facilitating language shift: movement from segregated barrios to integrated, multiethnic neighborhoods, occupational mobility, education (transitional bilingual education), and social mobility and acculturation. At the present time, the linguistic situation confronting Chicanos in the Southwest is filled with contradictions; the retention and transmission processes taking place simultaneously appear to be affecting the status and distribution of Spanish and English within communities as well as within families. Spanish and its varieties will survive because it is still the informal language in the barrio and the home. To many, it is closely interwoven with culture. Also, the influx of Spanish speakers from south of the border who inhabit these ethnic enclaves

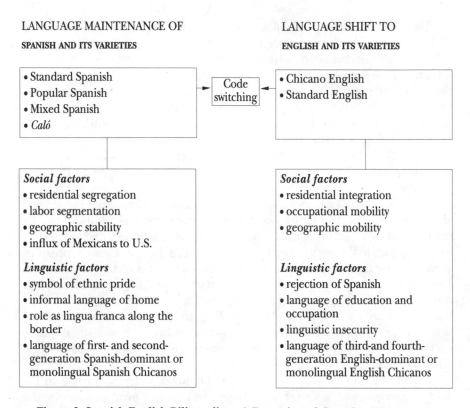

Figure 2. Spanish-English Bilingualism: A Dynamic and Complex Phenomenon
(From Lucía Elías-Olivares and Guadalupe Valdés, "Language Diversity in a Chicano
Community," and Rosaura Sánchez, "Our Linguistic and Social Context.")

promotes language maintenance. However, the lack of transmission of Spanish from one generation to another is rapidly producing offspring who rarely speak and understand the language and often assign it a subordinate status; English, in contrast, symbolizes power, upward mobility, even in-group identity. Furthermore, it is the dominant language of the school, the workplace, and other institutional milieus. Figure 2, summarizing discussions by Lucía Elías-Olivares and Guadalupe Valdés and by Rosaura Sánchez ("Our Linguistic"), provides an overview of the social and linguistic factors accompanying language maintenance and language shift.

Language Attitudes

A significant variable that correlates with language maintenance and language shift is language attitudes. When a conscious decision is made to reject

Spanish or not to hire a Chicano because he or she has a certain "accent," an evaluation is being made of a language variety or of a speaker of that variety. According to Donna Christian and Walt Wolfram, "language attitudes are generally shared by the members of a cultural group, leading to a common evaluation of certain language patterns and the people who use them" (1). Fernando Peñalosa (*Chicano*) cites several attitudinal concerns that members of the bilingual community might have: their attitudes toward their own speech (Spanish, English, code switching), other Chicanos' attitudes toward their speech, attitudes of the majority culture toward Chicano speech in general, and Chicano attitudes toward the speech of Anglos.

An overview of the Chicano situation from a historical and social perspective provides a way to conceptualize how certain attitudes and ideologies about language have come about (see esp. Acuña, *Occupied America*, and R. Sánchez, *Chicano Discourse*). Briefly, the Spanish language in the United States has been in existence since the arrival of Mexican settlers throughout the Southwest. For many years it served as a language of prestige and power in various domains. The arrival of the English-speaking settlers to Spanish-speaking areas soon diminished its function as a result of the social and economic domination imposed by these non-Hispanic immigrants; consequently, the language and its speakers were viewed as inferior by members of the dominant culture who soon took over the infrastructure. Punishment for speaking Spanish in public schools was not uncommon. Feelings of shame and linguistic inferiority began to seep into the Chicano psyche, causing many to deny vehemently their language and culture. Spanish in academic settings was considered a "foreign" language even for the Chicanos. Once these students entered secondary schools—more specifically, a foreign-language classroom—they were belittled for not knowing "proper" Spanish. Instead, they were told they spoke a bastardized version because they mixed it with English. Thus a dramatic shift to English is taking place today among third- and fourth-generation Chicanos primarily as a result of socioeconomic oppression, segregation, and discrimination experienced by their parents and grandparents.

The effects of residential patterns and school segregation resulted in a distinct variety of English for many Chicanos because of limited social interaction with native English speakers. Though this variety of Chicano English, highlighted by a Spanish accent, came to be accepted as the norm within their own communities, once the children acquired English in a formal setting such as the school, they were considered to be deficient because they spoke with a Spanish accent. The 1960s saw major changes in the way Chicanos viewed their language and culture. The Chicano movement across the Southwest was a cultural revitalization that helped instill ethnic pride and unity among second- and third-generation Chicanos. Spanish and its varieties, including code switching and *caló*, were studied in educational contexts and used by scholars in their literary works. Inez Tovar describes the attitudes prevalent through the mid-1960s:

> Those Mexican-Americans who used a mingling of Spanish and English words were classified by societal and educational standards as "disadvantaged" and "culturally deprived" and their language was considered substandard. Undoubtedly the majority of Mexican-Americans accepted this judgment for years. (64)

In the light of this overview of the linguistic history of Chicanos, we need to expand Peñalosa's points regarding language attitudes and examine some studies conducted among Spanish-speaking populations since 1970. Whenever a new paradigm comes into existence in social sciences, the majority of research efforts seem to follow its methodological procedures; studies of attitudes toward bilinguals are no exception. Since the pioneering work of Wallace Lambert and associates ("Evaluative Reactions") in Canada, the matched guise and verbal guise techniques have served as primary tools. The subjects under study have been either schoolchildren or college students. Some of the most important explorations of attitudes toward varieties of Chicano language are described here.

Concentrating primarily on midwestern bilingual communities, the research of Miguel Carranza and Ellen B. Ryan (three articles published in 1975 and 1977) examined reactions to three major varieties: Spanish, Standard English, Mexican American accented English. To distinguish two major rating dimensions of evaluative reactions, *status* and *solidarity*, they asked Mexican American and Anglo adolescents to listen to tapes employing the verbal guise technique: the subjects listened to the same voices speaking the same excerpts in English and in a Spanish translation. Mexican Americans rated Spanish higher on status and solidarity scales in a home context, English higher in a school context; English was also rated higher on both status and solidarity scales by both Anglos and Mexican Americans. In other research projects published in the 1970s, Nancy Flores and Robert Hopper asked Mexican American adults and college students to evaluate speech samples (Standard Spanish, Standard English, Tex-Mex Spanish, and accented English). Not surprisingly, evaluative ratings tended to be lower for nonstandard than for standard dialects, except for those college students who called themselves Chicanos. Employing a more direct measurement technique by means of a questionnaire, Yolanda Solé analyzed Mexican American college students' attitudes regarding language. She found that these students felt a high level of language loyalty toward Spanish and that they relegated both varieties (Spanish and English) to specific areas of appropriateness and contextualization. In a later study, Arnulfo Ramírez reported that favorable attitudes of bilingual pupils toward Spanish and English correlated highly with their scores on achievement tests in reading and in English language. He also discovered a significant correspondence between teacher attitudes and student achievement in reading: the more negative the teacher's attitudes toward the student's code-switching variety, the lower the pupil's relative gains in reading.

Two investigations focusing on Chicano Spanish and its varieties are worthy of mention because of their divergence from traditional methodology, their examination of varieties within Spanish used in the Southwest (primarily *tirilongo* and *caló*), their use of random sampling techniques within the Chicano speech communities, and their examination of language attitudes outside the educational setting. In a study in the El Paso area, Carina Ramírez's objective was to determine the extent of the use of *tirilongo* in Ysleta, Texas. This variety has historically been linked to the criminal element, especially among males. Ramírez demonstrated that selected lexical items considered to be part of this slang are recognized and used extensively among youth and adults, both males and females. Three age groups were formed, representing a cross section of people including students, homemakers, and physicians. Group 1 was composed of informants under twenty years old; group 2 had informants between twenty and forty; group 3 was comprised of informants over forty. Twenty-five sentences were used to elicit lexical usage, with the most standard form listed first and the nonstandard forms following. Sentences were read orally, and the informant completed each sentence with the term that first came to mind. The following sentence is an example:

Voy al baile y tengo ganas de . . . (bailar, borlotear, chanclear, zapatear).
I am going to the dance and I feel like . . . (dancing).

Ramírez concluded that attitudes of Spanish speakers toward the El Paso dialect varied from one age group to another. Those informants over forty with little or no education felt that their Spanish was nonstandard. Informants between twenty and forty had little academic training in Spanish; they thought that their Spanish was nonetheless acceptable if not proper. Those below twenty were better educated and cognizant of standard versus slang lexical items. They felt such terms were rapidly becoming the norm in the Ysleta area. Thus *tirilongo* has gone beyond an argot to become a variety encompassing wider usage, especially among youth who take pride in their cultural heritage. The dialect identifies them with this attitude. The other work on varieties of speech, Elías-Olivares's dissertation, focused on language among working-class Chicanos in East Austin, Texas, in 1976. Elías-Olivares discovered that heterogeneity and attitudinal differences exist, even within a family. First-generation speakers condemned *caló* and code-switching varieties, while young people did not see a need for a standard variety of Spanish. They relied on those varieties reflecting ethnic pride and bilingual agility.

Although substantial research has been done on attitudes toward Spanish and its varieties (e.g., Amastae and Elías-Olivares's 1978 study), attitudes toward accented English have constituted the bulk of research in Chicano sociolinguistics, notably the research of Flores and Hopper in 1975, Roger M. Thompson in 1975, and Eileen M. Brennan and John S. Brennan in 1981. In these projects "accented English" appears to be synonymous with "nonstandard English." It is quite apparent, then, that Mexican American English is viewed as deviating from a standard norm rather than as a systematic, self-contained linguistic entity found in many speech communities. This restricted view of language varieties and language use elicits negative evaluations, much as Vernacular Black English has, especially in a pedagogical context (see the works of Bereiter and Englemann; Labov, "Logic"; and J. Edwards). Carranza, a leading scholar in language attitudes research among Chicanos, discusses in a 1982 study the theoretical and methodological limitations that hampered early research; he advocates an interdisciplinary approach for future endeavors.

Because the Chicano speech community is a heterogeneous and socially stratified entity, it stands to reason that language choice is subjective and can be attributed to a multiplicity of social and linguistic variables. Some people associate speaking Spanish with low social status and with the older generation; others equate unaccented English with high educational aspirations or disloyalty to the Chicano community. Still others see Spanish as a symbol of ethnic identity and intimacy. To expand our knowledge of information on language attitudes among Chicanos, I used a qualitative framework to examine the views of English-dominant adolescents as they discussed their perception and use of varieties of English and their attitudes toward Anglo and Black English varieties found in Austin (Galindo, "Linguistic Influence," "Perceptions").

Summary

The preceding section presents background information on bilingual communities, summarizing important research trends in the areas of language contact, language maintenance and language shift, and language attitudes as these apply to Chicano speakers of Spanish and English in the Southwest.

To comprehend the Chicano bilingual situation, we must take historical and social circumstances into account. There was a time when one could say that Spanish was alive and well and used within all domains by both young and old alike. Its domain, however, was confined to segregated neighborhoods because speakers had little opportunity for social mobility or economic gain. Then Spanish began to assume the role of a language variety associated with those of low social class and educational status, even among its own speakers. It is not surprising today to find first- and second-generation parents rejecting all vestiges of the Spanish language and making conscious decisions not to speak to their children in the language or to encourage them to use it. This rejection may be attributed in part to the adults' own experiences of rejection and punishment when they spoke Spanish, especially in school. As a result of such experiences, they equated educational and economic deprivation with Spanish use. Parental attitudes coupled with urbanization, school integration, and pressure to assimilate into mainstream society have served as an impetus to shift from Spanish to English, creating a new, highly populous group of third- and fourth-generation English-dominant speakers.

Amid this new generation of English-dominant speakers we can be assured, nevertheless, of the continued existence of Spanish and its many varieties because of the continuous influx of immigrants. Ironically, as they boost the economy through their sweat and toil, they simultaneously promote and preserve the continuance of a language that has become associated with lack of social and financial success. The next section focuses on a language variety that also exists within the greater Chicano speech community, Chicano English.

Chicano English

Fifteen years ago, Wolfram and Fasold foresaw a need to expand our descriptive knowledge of other varieties of English, including Puerto Rican English and Chicano English. Today there continues to be an expanding research base for studying various dialects of English as a legitimate field of inquiry. Unfortunately, the work on Chicano English has not advanced to the stage that Vernacular Black English has since the 1960s and 1970s, even though it accounts for widespread usage among Chicanos in the Southwest. As Allan Metcalf succinctly stated in 1979, "Chicano English is not just an oddity to be studied by linguists but a phenomenon that must be taken into account in classrooms throughout the Southwest" (*Chicano English* 2).

How does one define Chicano English? What have been the major thrusts in research on Chicano English? Are there features that characterize this variety of English?

A Definition

Francisca Sánchez raises the question of what researchers mean by Chicano English—that of California as described by Metcalf ("Mexican-American," "Study of California") or that of Texas as described by Janet Sawyer ("Spanish-English Bilingualism")? She concludes that the issue of definition is important and that one cannot assume that the Chicano speech community is homogeneous and static. Rather, individual, group, and regional differences must be considered when one looks at varieties of English. As a result, a concrete, generic definition of what constitutes Chicano English will prove to be difficult to achieve.

In their attempt to define Chicano English, Joyce Penfield and Jacob Ornstein state that, traditionally, Chicano English has been characterized in terms of degree of approximation to Standard English. Instead of being perceived as a nonstandard variety of English, it has been labeled as an "imperfect" type of English. Bills refers to it as Vernacular Chicano English, with the term *vernacular* synonymous with "nonstandard." He poses the question "Is Vernacular Chicano English a dialect or interference?" and attempts to argue that it is indeed a dialect. While he does not substantiate his claim with empirical evidence on the topic per se, Bills advocates more descriptive research on Vernacular Chicano English, especially contributions from dialectologists.

Peñalosa ("Some Issues") sees three major varieties of English spoken in the Chicano community: English that is indistinguishable from that of Anglos, English that is heavily influenced by the speaker's Spanish, and a variety of English that shows influence from Spanish but is current in the Chicano community and often spoken by Chicano English monolinguals. For Benji Wald ("Status"), Chicano English encompasses a wide range of lingual uses: from the English of monolingual third-generation Mexican Americans to early stages of acquisition of English by adult or child Spanish speakers. Wald's is a truly ambitious and broad definition across the linguistic spectrum and will have to suffice until more research is conducted on the topic. In essence, Chicano varieties of English will include the language of both monolingual and bilingual speakers.

A complex but stable bilingual situation, constant migration, social stratification, and even region or locale are factors that make Chicano English highly diversified—so much so that one could possibly devise a linguistic continuum ranging from a standard variety of Chicano English to a nonstandard form and many varieties in between. This notion of a repertoire of

Chicano English varieties is further substantiated by Wald, who assumes that language contact with speakers of neighboring dialects of English indeed affects the types of English used by Chicanos. John Baugh ("Chicano English"), in making a comparison with the linguistic and social circumstances of urban blacks, states, "Chicano English is a more complex phenomenon in purely linguistic terms due to the combined population of monolingual Chicano English and bilingual speakers" (3).

The language variation paradigm is quite simple: because of the social parameters surrounding language use (including language contact), speakers of a community will adopt different varieties of the same language (or languages, in the case of bilinguals). Scholars such as Wolfram and Baugh have found this to be true among Puerto Ricans in New York City and urban blacks, respectively.

Research

There have been some studies of Chicano English since the 1960s, but a disproportionate amount of research has been conducted on Spanish while Chicano English remains severely overlooked by comparison. The first scholar to attest to this neglect is Peñalosa (*Chicano*). The copious bibliography compiled by Richard Teschner, Garland Bills, and Jerry Craddock in 1975 lists a small number of works on the subject, mostly from the perspective of error analysis in educational settings. The early literature assumed that linguistic differences exhibited by Chicanos were attributed to direct interference from a previously learned linguistic system—Spanish—as demonstrated in the works of Eduardo Hernández-Chávez, Andrew Cohen, and Anthony Beltramo in 1975, Sawyer ("Aloofness") in 1959, and Ricardo García in 1974. For many years Sawyer's 1957 dissertation on the Spanish-English community of San Antonio reigned as the undisputed authority on Chicano English. In addition, in a 1975 paper entitled "Spanish-English Bilingualism in San Antonio, Texas," Sawyer made this claim:

> [N]othing that could be called a Mexican-American dialect of English was found in San Antonio, Texas. The English spoken by the bilingual informants was simply an imperfect state in the mastery of English. (78)

Sawyer's arguments against assigning dialect status to Chicano English have been refuted by other research data. For instance, in 1974 Thompson described the English of Mexican Americans as a distinct entity deserving analysis in its own right. His study of Chicanos in Austin, Texas, revealed that a language shift from Spanish to English was rapidly taking place. He viewed Chicano English from a perspective quite different from Sawyer's:

"language problems will not be the result of Spanish interfering or competing with English, but of a nonstandard dialect of English conflicting with
standard English" (17). Also, Metcalf's research on Chicano English merits
serious attention. Primarily focusing on the English of southern California
Chicanos, Metcalf examined the speech of monolingual English speakers for
whom Spanish interference was not a direct issue. His work has concentrated
on distinctive features such as intonation.

Still, research needed to move beyond the interference paradigm to
one incorporating linguistic as well as social variables that contribute to the
process of dialect formation—that is, one advocating sociolinguistic theory
and methodology. Such a study was done by Beverly Hartford in 1975. Her
objective was to account for the linguistic behavior of Gary, Indiana, Mexican
American adolescents by examining selected phonological features. She
found that interference from Spanish was not the only cross-linguistic influence on variation: some variants appeared to be of a nonstandard Black
English origin as well. From a sociopsychological perspective, sex, occupational choice, and cultural attitudes also contributed to the linguistic behavior
of these adolescents. A unique dialect of English has emerged in Gary and
is seen as the "norm" by members of the Chicano speech community.

My own research utilized variable rule analysis, similar to that of William Labov (*Language*). It examined selected phonological and syntactic variables, along with the social variables of sex and language background, to
determine the range of linguistic varieties that exist among third-generation
Chicano adolescents in Austin, Texas. A major objective of the study was to
weigh the extent to which linguistic features from other monolingual English
sources, such as Vernacular Black English, affected the English of these
adolescents, especially when the groups live in close proximity. Analysis of
the intersection of linguistic and social variables showed that at least three
varieties of Chicano English are currently in existence: a variety with Span-
ish-based features, a variety based on divergent sources of Spanish and
Vernacular Black English, and a variety exemplifying little if any variability
and adhering to prescribed norms within a standard variety of English.

The sociolinguistic publications of Wald and of Maryellen García on
language use in Los Angeles have provided revealing information on the
complex situation confronting bilingual and monolingual speakers of English in East Los Angeles. García offers constructive advice to scholars desir-
ing to conduct language variation research. To study any variety of Chicano
English, the investigator must identify the speech community, designate the
social and geographic parameters, and leave the range of linguistic features
relatively open.

This brief overview of Chicano English research reveals not only the paucity of investigations conducted but also the shift in paradigms from an interference to a sociolinguistic perspective to better comprehend language variation.

Phonological and Syntactic Features

In the literature one can find a number of studies that have concentrated on phonology, fewer on syntax. Certain features seem to be widely reported in various studies and can perhaps be considered characteristic of a variety of Chicano English. They include the following:

/s/ as a realization of /z/ in word-final position (e.g., [bikʌs] instead of [bikʌz) for *because*; [ǰæs] instead of [ǰæz] for *jazz*)

/č/ and /š/ interchange (e.g., *washes* for *watches*, and vice versa)

reduction of vowel contrasts, especially between high vowels /ɪ/ and /i/ (e.g., *this* for *these*)

lowering and backing of /ɛ/ in stressed syllables followed by /l/ + /i/ (e.g., *halicopter* for *helicopter*)

Within syntax and morphology, Wald ("Status") investigated the use of embedded *wh* questions (EQW), primarily with subject-auxiliary inversion. Speakers using this sentence type produced utterances such as:

Then they asked them *where did they live*.

He also found yes-no questions embedded with *if*, as in Standard English:

We asked him *if we could go*.

In addition to the factors of convergence on subject-auxiliary inversion of embedded *wh* questions, he looked at the verbs *tell* and *ask* to introduce embedded questions of any type:

So she goes to the doctor and the doctor *tells* her *why is she nervous*.

Wald concluded that subject-auxiliary inversion in EQW and the use of *tell* and *ask* appear to be quite common among all types of speakers. He also discovered that within Chicano English syntax the use of the indirect object is different from Standard English; for example, Chicano English speakers feel comfortable saying:

They put *him* a cast (versus They put a cast on *him*).

Maryellen García discovered some morphological rules that differ from those of other nonstandard varieties of English—for example, the progressive suffix *-ing*, which in East Los Angeles English is often pronounced with a tense /i/ with no off-glide and a dental /n/, so that the word *glowing* would sound like *gloween*, as opposed to the short /I/ and dental /n/ of other nonstandard varieties of English, to produce *glowin'*. While the *-een* suffix is also heard in the speech of non-Hispanics in Los Angeles, the frequency of usage, vowel tenseness, and duration may prove to be distinctive to East Los Angeles Chicano speakers.

East Los Angeles speakers create the comparative with the *-er* suffix rather than with the prescribed word *more* (e.g. *more politely*): "I don't talk to them any *politelier* than I would anybody else."

García found usage of several lexical items considered unique to Chicano English speakers in Los Angeles, including:

All as an intensifier ("He's *all* proud.")
Use of *for reals* or *for real* ("*For reals*, did you buy it?")
Use of *barely* to mean *just* or *only* ("I *barely* have two cents.")

Intonation is yet another feature of Chicano English. Metcalf ("Mexican-American English") considers intonation as the most interesting of all the characteristics of this English variety. In Chicano English the places of greatest loudness and pitch change often and do not coincide, thus resulting in what sounds to outsiders like two separate peaks in the phrase. For example, the emphasis would be "minority GROUP" in Chicano English, whereas Anglo English speakers would tend to stress the first element of the compound, "miNORity group." Penfield has also explored this relatively uncharted area of Chicano English and found that noun compounds tend to receive the heaviest stress on the second word (e.g., "textBOOK").

What may appear as a potpourri of linguistic variables gleaned from a handful of studies indicates that much more research needs to be done to expand our knowledge of Chicano language variety. Not only is a fully satisfying definition of Chicano English difficult to obtain; we also must realize that phonological, syntactic, and lexical features found within a particular community are not generalizable to all bilingual and monolingual Chicanos. These features would simply define a variety within a particular group or community, whether it be East Los Angeles (see Wald, "Status") or El Paso (see Ornstein, "Mexican-American Sociolinguistics"). Differences across region, socioeconomic status, age, sex, and degree of bilingualism are major determinants that will affect such features. Also, the varieties and patterns of English used by upwardly mobile Chicanos is another area for investigation.

Pedagogical Strategies for Teaching about Language Variation

In the preceding discussion, we found that a linguistic continuum exists across generational and social lines ranging from monolingual Spanish to monolingual English among Chicanos in the Southwest. Bilingualism is what distinguishes Chicanos and other Hispanics (Puerto Ricans and Cubans) from monolingual populations. Furthermore, we can make the claim that Chicanos are "bidialectal" because of their ability to shift from one variety of either language to another, depending on context and interlocutors involved. The identifiable varieties within this continuum are complex linguistic systems in their own right, not varieties to be described by a comparison with the "standard" or as "deviations" from an institutional and societal norm. Only when teachers recognize the need to go beyond their language methodology coursework (comprising mainly prescriptive approaches toward grammar) and take basic courses in sociolinguistics will they be able to sensitize themselves to this view of language. Collaborative efforts between educators and linguists are needed for implementation of appropriate instructional strategies in our culturally and linguistically diverse classrooms.

If a student were to enter a classroom and speak a dialect not considered "standard" (by institutional norms), the teacher could, according to Peter Trudgill (*Sociolinguistics*), take one of several approaches: elimination of nonstandard speech, acceptance of bidialectalism, and appreciation of dialect differences. The first would presumably be achieved by presenting the standard variety as the correct model to imitate, with all students replacing their home variety of language with the school model. The bidialectalism approach recognizes the students' right to use nonstandard dialects at home and with friends in certain contexts at school; however, it advocates that students should be taught standard English as the language of reading and writing. A major prerequisite for implementing this approach is that teachers have acquired some knowledge of the linguistic features associated with the students' dialects. Finally, appreciation of dialect differences is Trudgill's version of the Utopian ideal: if children suffer because of their nonstandard language, attitudes of society as a whole toward languages of this type are the cause of their distress. Thus, if we are to follow the third approach he cites, *attitudes*, not the language, should be changed. We, as educators and scholars, should therefore try to teach society to appreciate nonstandard dialects as complex, valid linguistic systems. Once individuals or departments make a commitment to accept language diversity, they can incorporate

certain projects into the curriculum as a means of applying language variation and linguistic theory in real-life situations involving language use and
speech communities. Trudgill concludes his book by proposing a pedagogical
approach that would combine bidialectalism and an appreciation of dialect
differences.

I recommended the following projects for classes at the secondary and
college or university level, for both monolingual and bilingual students:

1. After discussing the varieties found in a speech community, students
select a situation in which a language variety can be used naturally and make
a tape (15–30 minutes long) to be examined for the following analyses:

- setting in which the variety occurred
- interlocutors involved
- function of the variety

2. Information on the different functions and contexts of language use
within a community or region is gathered, and the varieties of language used
are examined:

- the language of ballads, folk songs, *corridos*, rap music
- slang varieties among males, females, adolescents
- informal situations—greetings, departures, jokes
- stylized language use—sermons, political speeches, debates
- text analysis of poetry, prose, drama
- ritual language

3. A phonological or syntactic analysis of a variable or several variables
can be conducted from a transcribed tape of conversational data (15–30
minutes long). This project is especially recommended for undergraduates
and graduate students who have had some linguistics or field methods
coursework.

4. Students videotape people speaking different varieties and examine
what role the variables of sex, age, language background, and social class
play in the speakers' use of a variety.

5. The class conducts a poll on the attitudes toward the use (or nonuse)
of a particular language variety within the community and among different
groups. It may be appropriate, in the light of the English Only movement,
to ask people's perceptions about that particular variety.

These are a few suggestions on how to apply language variation theory outside the linguisitics classroom—whether the class consists of monolingual English students or bilinguals. Of foremost importance in such projects is the need for curricular reform, changes in instructional methodology, and a sincere commitment by teachers, department chairs, coordinators, and professors to teach objectively about linguistic diversity. Society has made great strides since the 1960s, when the federal government recognized that the varieties of language spoken by those groups left out of the mainstream are different from "standard" rather than "deficient" and that schools must provide equal educational opportunity for speakers of all varieties of language. Unfortunately, what was learned about effective language education for diverse speakers was too often ignored in the 1980s in schools with substantial enrollments of blacks, Asians, and Hispanics. Instead, groups such as U.S. English advocate the exclusion of "foreign" languages and promote English (presumably "standard") as the official and sole language. Consequently, many, including educators, perceive linguistic diversity and multiculturalism as a threat rather than an asset. The study of linguistic diversity must persevere, and we must overcome the obstacles of ignorance about language—for the welfare of all. The responsibility may well rest in the hands of language teachers who have the sensitivity and determination to make change a reality.

Notes

[1] The ethnic label *Chicano*, as used in this study, refers to Americans of Mexican descent who reside in the United States. Though the term has come to be associated mainly with militant political activism on the part of young adults, I apply the word to a group, speech community, or even language in lieu of the term *Mexican American* or the current popular label *Hispanic*.

[2] *Lingual minority* is defined by Oftedal as "a group of people whose everyday speech is definitely another language than the language or languages spoken by the majority of the population of the country in which these people live" (16). "Minority" status for the population is not necessarily determined quantitatively but rather in terms of the group's social, economic, and political status.

[3] The variety of argot or slang used among Chicano male youths of lower social class is commonly referred to as *caló* by scholars such as Ortega. In her 1965 study, Coltharp uses the term *tirilongo* for this variety of language.

[4] "High" is used in the diglossic sense proposed by Ferguson. Thus in border communities Spanish is elevated to the language of prestige in most if not all domains and by all speakers, while English is perceived functionally and socially as the "low"

variety. Fishman ("Bilingualism") also examines the Spanish-English situation as diglossic, with high status assigned to English and lesser status to Spanish. He does not take into account that Spanish is a well-known and documented language, a main criterion within the diglossia definition. One must be able to look at the community's own interpretation of language choice, because domain analysis cannot be generalizable for all speech communities.

⁵ In the literature on Chicano bilinguals, *first generation* refers to Americans of Mexican descent born and raised in Mexico; *second generation*, to those born and raised in the United States whose parents were both born in Mexico; *third generation*, to those whose parents were born in the United States (López). R. Sánchez (*Chicano Discourse*) provides a category for individuals born in the United States who have one parent born in Mexico and one in the United States: offspring of *mixed parentage* can be called second or third generation.

Language and Human Conflict: A Case-Study Approach to Language Variation

Donald W. Larmouth, University of Wisconsin, Green Bay

AT THE University of Wisconsin, Green Bay, linguistics courses are part of an interdisciplinary curriculum in broad-field communications that enrolls students in mass media, organizational communication, information and computing science, and linguistics-English as a second language, as well as students who need course work in minority-group and other multicultural studies as part of their Wisconsin teacher certification requirements. Originally, Language and Human Conflict was taught as part of the university's liberal education curriculum, and for some students it continues to serve that purpose too, even though it is a junior- senior-level course. Most students will have had other course work in linguistics; a few will have had none. Such a diversity of enrollment is probably not unusual at other universities; indeed, linguistics courses in smaller, primarily undergraduate institutions often need a broad base of nonmajors in order to survive.

As the course title suggests, Language and Human Conflict focuses on language variation in situations in which divergent and nonstandard varieties of language are a significant dimension of social and cultural conflict. The overall theme has appealed to students, but their course evaluations over the years indicate that the case-study approach itself is also attractive, especially for students who are accustomed to more passive lecture courses, because of the high level of student-to-instructor and student-to-student interaction that a case-study approach typically produces. At the same time, the case-study method is structured and organized so that the instructor can shape the discussion and keep it well focused. Taken together, the features that have made Language and Human Conflict a highly successful course for a wide variety of students suggest that the design may have application to other teaching situations.

Case Studies and "Upside-Down Teaching"

Language and Human Conflict incorporates two basic teaching strategies: case studies and "upside-down teaching." The case-study method assumes

that students can learn the important generalizations and intellectual strategies of a discipline through serious, in-depth examination and discussion of
a few particular instances—the approach is inductive and active, unlike the
lecture-discussion method, which is often deductive and passive. Case studies
are well known as a teaching technique in law school and in business courses;
they are less widely used in the liberal arts areas, where covering a subject
seems to be more important than establishing a point of view for future
learning. The case-study approach has traditionally identified "classic" cases
whose broad intellectual significance can be mined for ideas that extend to
many other situations.

The notion of "upside-down teaching" comes from Herman Epstein's
book *A Strategy for Education*, based on his experience at Brandeis University.
Epstein, a biophysicist who had never taught introductory biology, was called
on at the last minute to take over for a colleague. Instead of beginning with
the usual survey of the field, Epstein started the course by describing his
current research and giving the students scholarly articles that he and others
had written. Using the students' questions as a point of departure, he led
the class through a series of discussions of assumptions, scientific methods,
observations, and inferences, and gradually worked backward to the basic
principles underlying the discipline. In Language and Human Conflict, the
most important aspect of Epstein's approach is student discussion of primary
sources reporting on research in dialectology, bilingualism, and language
policy—the readings are not just scattered examples but institute an integral
part of the case studies that form the scaffolding for the course. In this way,
even though a case study may involve a "classic" situation, it can be continually updated and linked to analogous situations by a modification of the
background reading materials, while the core of the case study remains
intact. It is probably worth noting that the diversity of readings represents
a response to the wide range of students typically enrolled in the course.

Management of Source Materials for Case Studies

The strategy for dealing with the case-study readings has evolved from a
general reading list for everyone to a much more structured set of assignments. The class typically enrolls fifty students, divided into five groups of
ten students each. A leader is designated for each group, which is responsible
for at least twenty articles per case study. Each member of the group is
assigned two articles and must write a one-page abstract for each article (and
provide enough copies for all class members, plus one for the instructor to
grade). In addition to circulating the abstracts, students orally summarize

the articles they reported on, so that others in the group can ask questions or clarify the abstracts. The instructor makes copies of the best abstract for each article and circulates these to the group leaders. Each student must also find and read a relevant article independently and prepare an abstract, an assignment that gets the students into the library and in direct contact with the journals. Thus, while each student may read only two articles per case study in depth (plus a fifth article chosen independently), the abstract requirement creates a genuine interdependency among the students. As a result, the abstracts are typically of high quality; and because students receive an abstract for each article, they are much better acquainted with the primary source materials than if they simply read whatever they chose from the sources available. Moreover, this level of familiarity is reflected in a higher frequency of citations in the students' examinations.

Ground Rules for Case-Study Discussions

The case-study method is highly dependent on student discussion, but the discussion process is structured, not open-ended (open-ended discussion is generally unproductive, as students can quickly wander far away from the particulars of the case before they really understand them). It is important to establish ground rules, especially if the students have no prior experience with case studies. Although the design of the case study itself structures the discussion to a considerable degree, instructors should clarify procedures for discussion in advance. Following are the ground rules used in Language and Human Conflict:

1. Students are required to read the case study in advance of class discussion. Outside readings are organized around two general sections of the case study, and abstracts are prepared and circulated as those sections are developed in class.
2. Initial discussion focuses on clarification of the facts of the case, not on issues like social conflicts, race relations, or educational policy. (This approach establishes a factual base for later discussion of social issues and other topics.)
3. While references to situations outside the case study may be made along the way (and such allusions are welcome), the focus of discussion is the case study itself. (This rule is intended to minimize drift away from the case.)
4. The instructor's responses to student questions are limited to five minutes. The same rule applies to student responses to student

questions. (This rule prevents the instructor from using the students' questions as a device for minilectures; it also keeps any one student from monopolizing the discussion.)

5. Students are free to request supplementary readings, handouts, or background information from the instructor. They can also invite resource persons who might contribute to a richer understanding of the case. (Many such requests are predictable, and appropriate handouts can be prepared in advance. Others provide a basis for revising and enriching the case study when it is used again.)

While the ground rules help control the case-study process and clarify the participants' roles, the shape of the discussion varies from year to year, depending on the makeup of the class and the chemistry that evolves within it. Classes in which the students have similar backgrounds generally turn out not to be quite as lively as classes in which students represent more diverse backgrounds and academic interests. In some instances, current events involving language issues can intrude and dramatically alter the discussion, as happened in fall 1986 with the official-language referendum in California and the introduction of similar legislation in Wisconsin.

Case-Study Design: Black English in the Inner City

The case-study approach is amenable to many different topics in language variation. All that is required is that the instructor be sufficiently familiar with the particulars to write the core materials for the case study and identify relevant and accessible primary sources to support it. In Language and Human Conflict, the initial case study focuses on Black English in the inner city, because this issue is consistent with the overall theme of the course. (This theme need not be a central feature of a case-study course: the focus could just as well be on cultural diversity as on social conflict, and many other cases involving dialect variation could be used.) The Black English case study is also a good choice because there is a rich, reasonably accessible research literature as well as a variety of popular materials, commentaries on educational policies, and the like. What is more, these materials stretch back over a long period, so it is possible to show how approaches and attitudes toward Black English have changed through the years. Since the Black English case study is currently twenty-three single-spaced pages long, it is not possible to reproduce it here; the subject is well known, however, and a general outline and a representative bibliography should suggest its content.

Case-Study Outline: Black English in the Inner City

1. Origins of Black English—general principles of regional and social dialect variation; outline of dialect origins versus pidgin > creole > decreolization model.
2. Phonological features of Black English—reduction of consonant clusters; Southern regional features in Black English; length of allophones, diphthongs, and triphthongs; homophonous forms; Black English intonation; socially diagnostic features.
3. Morphological features in Black English—verb inflection (invariant *be*, contraction and deletion of *be*, present- and past-tense inflection, perfective *done*, and continuative *steady*); plural and possessive inflections; relative pronouns; further discussion of socially diagnostic features.
4. Syntactic structures in Black English—question formation (*do* deletion); pronominal repetition; double modals; embedded clauses (e.g., indirect questions with *if* or *whether* deletion); possible decreolized structures.
5. Lexical features in Black English—Southern and South Midland features; reclassification of strong verbs; semantic changes in Black English; adoption of Black English forms in white speech; verbal games in Black English (sounding, signifying, playing the dozens) as sources of innovation.
6. Educational implications of Black English—correlations among IQ scores, reading readiness, and school achievement; sources of reading and writing problems for speakers of Black English; status of nonstandard dialects in educational policy; legal issues surrounding Black English in the schools.

Readings for the Black English Case Study

The list of readings changes each time the case study is used, reflecting shifts in scholarly focus and direction. Two examples of such alterations are the reinterpretation of Black English features as evidence of possible creole origins for Black English and the possibility that Black English is diverging from Standard English. Some of the readings that address structural aspects of Black English include John Baugh's *Black Street Speech: Its History, Structure, and Survival* (chs. 6 and 7) published in 1983; Ralph Fasold's "The Relation between Black and White Speech in the South" (1981) and the earlier article by Raven McDavid and Virginia McDavid, "The Relationship of the Speech of American Negroes to the Speech of Whites" (1951); two classic articles by William Labov, "Stages in the Acquisition of Standard English" (1964) and "The Logic of Nonstandard English" (1969); Raven McDavid and Lawrence Davis's article "The Dialects of Negro Americans" (1972) and Elaine Tarone's "Aspects of Intonation in Black English" (1973). Reflecting discussion of creole origins for Black English are Kean Gibson's 1988 article "The Habitual Category in Guyanese and Jamaican Creoles," and the current discussion on divergence of Black English from Standard English is represented in an article by Guy Bailey and Natalie Maynor, "The Divergence Controversy" (1989) and papers by Labov and Fay Vaughn-Cooke from the NWAVE (New Ways of Analyzing Variation in English) panel discussion "Are Black and White Vernaculars Diverging?" (1987).

Some of the educational implications of Black English are explored in articles such as Thomas Farrell's "IQ and Standard English" (1983), Graeme Kennedy's "The Language of Tests for Young Children" (1972), Kenneth Goodman's "Dialect Barriers to Reading Comprehension" (1969), and the eighth and ninth chapters in Baugh's *Black Street Speech*. Social dimensions of Black English are discussed in articles such as John Myhill's "Postvocalic /r/ as an Index of Integration into the BEV Speech Community" (1988), John Rickford's "Ethnicity as a Sociolinguistic Boundary" (1985), Walter Pitts's "West African Poetics in the Black Preaching Style" (1989), and Thomas Kochman's chapter "Toward an Ethnography of Black American Speech Behavior" (1972). The well-known Ann Arbor case that tested the legal status of Black English and challenged basic educational policies is discussed in David Yellin's "The Black English Controversy: Implications from the Ann Arbor Case" (1980) and Labov's "Objectivity and Commitment in Linguistic Science: The Case of the Black English Trial in Ann Arbor" (1982).

The dynamics of classroom discussion of the Black English case study are generally predictable. In the early stages, students are confronted with a strategy for linguistic description that is often outside their experience. Accordingly, initial discussion focuses on the description of phonological features in Black English. The case includes a sketch of English phonology, but students will usually need clarification of particular notation. This aspect of the case study is also supported with tape recordings of Black English, so that the phonetic notation can become more tangible. The justification for such notation is easily demonstrated by showing how inaccurate "phonetic spelling" is in representing the actual features of a dialect (*wuz* vs. *was*, etc.). Student response is in sharp contrast to the usual protests of overly technical descriptions of syntactic, phonological, and lexical phenomena illustrated with some disconnected examples and a few exercises—the sort of thing one finds in introductory textbooks and course materials.

Inevitably, questions of "correct" and "incorrect" speech will come up during discussion of pronunciation, but the issue is more vigorously pursued as students examine the grammatical features of Black English. This discussion, which frequently involves allusions to nonstandard features in the students' own speech and some of the relic features of rural dialects, leads easily to examinations of socially diagnostic features. At this point, students often want to jump ahead to the educational implications of divergent dialects, arguing that such features must somehow be repaired or replaced. Instead of following their lead, however, we generally stay with the issue of variant forms, introducing the notion of inherent variability and the patterning of linguistic variation in different registers and in different social settings. This part of the case study has been quite useful in that the students are better prepared to discuss the policy implications of divergent dialects after they begin to understand this concept; they usually have progressed considerably from the attitudes they brought into the course. It is a significant step when they see dialect variation as natural and normal rather than as aberrant and deficient.

Case-Study Design: Spanish-English Bilingualism

The current version of Language and Human Conflict includes a case study on Spanish-English bilingualism, which introduces another dimension of language variation—the divergent forms produced through the transfer of features from one language to another. A case study in bilingualism is clearly related to the overall theme of the course, especially in view of current policy debates over bilingual education and the status of English as an official language. It can also be easily linked to the students' own experience, given the residue of immigrant language features found in many local dialects. Indeed, many other ethnic languages in the United States and elsewhere could form the basis for a case study on bilingualism and language variation.

It is important to note here that the discussion of the first case study, on Black English, has set up a number of reference points for this case study, and, as well, has established a vocabulary to describe phonological, grammatical, and lexical features that transfers to discussions of linguistic variants in Spanish and English. In this respect, the case-study approach is cumulative and demonstrates the broad application of basic linguistic concepts. Following is an outline of the case study in Spanish-English bilingualism. Again, because this is a fairly familiar topic, the structure of the case study is sketched in general terms here.

Case-Study Outline: Spanish-English Bilingualism

1. Historical background—early settlement patterns of Hispanics; comparison and contrast with European immigrant history and other ethnic enclaves; urban resettlement of Hispanics; more recent immigration from Cuba and Latin America; illegal immigration from Mexico and Central America.

2. Hispanic population distribution nationwide—census data; urban populations and socioeconomic profiles (per capita earnings related to fluency in Spanish and English).

3. Hispanic populations in Wisconsin—rural and urban population distribution; migrant workers in agriculture and other industries; school populations in Wisconsin and Illinois districts (can be adapted to local-area study as appropriate).

4. Dynamics of bilingualism in diglossic communities—separation of social domains in natural bilingualism, differences in functional load; code switching and social cuing (language choice as a signal of social relations); mechanisms of assimilation and language loss vs. language maintenance in diglossic communities.

5. Effects and directions of Spanish-English interference—phonetic, phonemic, phonotactic, and prosodic transfer from Spanish to English; grammatical transfer from Spanish to English (word order, inflectional patterns, question formation, article placement, etc.); grammatical transfer from English to Spanish (creolization of Spanish); lexical transfer from English to Spanish (loanwords, loan blends, loan shifts); code switching within sentences and larger discourse units; avoidance of historical Spanish loanwords in English.

6. Historical overview of language policy in the United States and in Wisconsin (or other region)—local ordinances restricting non-English-language use; the Bennett law and ethnic languages in Wisconsin; English-only laws following World War I; "nativist" and "pluralist" movements; resurgence of bilingual education in the 1970s; Wisconsin's bilingual education statute (1975) and differences between transitional and maintenance programs (assimilative and pluralistic educational programs and policies); retention and

achievement levels of bilingual students; current conflicts over language policy (U.S. English and other nativist groups, changes in federal support levels for bilingual education, etc.).

Readings for Spanish-English Bilingualism Case Study

As with the Black English case study, readings change somewhat each time the course is offered, reflecting new issues and more recent research. However, the readings here include earlier articles, again to provide a sense of the history of the scholarship and of the issues themselves. Articles should be chosen that are accessible to nonspecialist readers, so that students can read the material and prepare abstracts for distribution to other students.

One of the problems in this case study is the notion, inculcated by foreign language teachers, that language mixture results in "impure" and therefore stigmatized speech. Accordingly, the case study includes a number of readings on language mixture, such as Andrew Cohen's "The English and Spanish Grammar of Chicano Primary School Students" (1976), Rose Nash's articles "Spanglish: Language Contact in Puerto Rico" (1970) and "Englañol: More Language Contact in Puerto Rico" (1971), Rogelio Reyes's "Language Mixing in Chicano Bilingual Speech" (1976), Janet Sawyer's "The Speech of San Antonio, Texas" (1971), and Roberto Fernández's "English Loanwords in Miami Cuban Spanish" (1983). Readings also include some overview articles: James Lantolf's "Toward a Comparative Dialectology of U.S. Spanish" (1983), Carmen Silva-Corvalán's "Code-Shifting Patterns in Chicano Spanish" (1983), Roger Thompson's "Mexican-American English: Social Correlates of Regional Pronunciation" (1975), and Bernardo Vallejo's "Linguistic and Socio-economic Correlations in the Spoken Language of Mexican-American Children" (1976). The consensus of these articles is that language mixture is a natural and inevitable consequence of bilingualism.

The second major focal point in this case study, the social context for Spanish-English bilingualism, is supported by readings such as "Mexican American Language Communities in the Twin Cities: An Example of Contact and Recontact" (1983) by René Cisneros and Elizabeth Leone, Georganne Weller's "The Role of Language as a Cohesive Force in the Hispanic Speech Community of Washington, D.C." (1983), and Wallace Lambert and Donald Taylor's "Language Minorities in the United States: Conflicts around Assimilation and Proposed Modes of Accommodation" (1987). Bilingual education and the larger issue of language policy, the third focal point in the case study, are addressed in such readings as Rolf Kjolseth's chapter

"Bilingual Education Programs in the United States: For Assimilation or Pluralism?" (1972), Joshua Fishman's "Language Policy: Past, Present, and Future" (1981), A. Leibowitz's "The Terms of the Bilingual Education Act" (n.d.), Ricardo Fernández's "Legislation, Regulation, and Litigation: The Origins and Evolution of Public Policy on Bilingual Education in the United States" (1987), Frank Grittner's "Public Policies and Ethnic Influences upon Foreign Language Study in the Public Schools" (1987), and my own chapter, "Does Linguistic Heterogeneity Erode National Unity?" (1987). Since these issues are often in the news, the case study is supplemented by articles and editorials from newspapers, newsmagazines, and other current sources.

Students may begin the analysis of the second case study with somewhat greater tolerance for language variation, but they are very much entangled in current debates over the official status of English and continued support for ethnic languages—at least at the headline level. They find themselves in the classical American dilemma: they are torn between a romanticized version of their immigrant forebears' triumph and a growing suspicion of foreign "invaders." The dynamics of linguistic interference or transfer are easy to relate to relic features in some local dialects and, in the case of Spanish, to "Ceesco Keed" media stereotypes and local images of Hispanic migrant workers. Again, the strategies for accurate description of linguistic variation that occurs when languages come in contact have an obvious warrant, greater than if the same concepts and technical analyses were taught with a series of attenuated and unrelated examples in the traditional lecture-and-discussion format.

After the linguistic details have been established, the class discussion typically turns to the dynamics of code switching. Many students with dim recollections of high school foreign language classes assume that bilinguals are somehow equally fluent in the two languages—that Spanish is an inconvenient way of speaking English—and that switching from one to another is either a whimsical act or a deliberate effort to exclude Anglos. When students link the social roles of each language to differences in speakers' fluency and functional load as well as to structural differences, a rational basis for discussion of language policy begins to emerge. Typically students are prepared to advocate bilingual education and support for minority languages (somewhat sentimentally, I suspect)—only to collide with rather contradictory data concerning Hispanic students' school performance. Setting aside Snideley Whiplash villains and other unproductive stereotypes of school administrators, the students generally come to recognize that, often hidden beneath the headline-grabbing "debates" about language policy, there is a genuine, honest debate about language policy—or at least a debate that has had to confront contradictory information about the relation between language fluency and school achievement. In most discussions the contrast between this level of debate and the highly charged nativist-pluralist debate over official language policy is quite vivid; such a dichotomy usually provides the framework for generalizing to other ethnic languages, including Native American languages.

Examinations: Generalizing to Other Cases

The case-study approach is grounded in the assumption that students can generalize beyond the immediate boundaries of the case study and apply the principles it entails to other situations. Accordingly, the examinations for the course present new case studies and invite analogies and contrasts between them and those that have been discussed in class. Such explorations of similarities and differences must, of course, be supported by factual citations from the case studies and the readings. Since the students know that this approach will be the focus of the examinations, they are strongly inclined to extract general principles from the case study during its discussion, rather than simply absorb the factual material of the case study itself. The analogies and comparisons are part of the case-study discussions, but only in a limited way; that is, the case studies on the examinations have not been discussed in class. Since classes now have around fifty students, examinations are set up as essays and announced two weeks in advance to allow time for serious discussion among the students. They are permitted to bring a seventy-five-word outline to class when they write their essays. Although students may collaborate in the development of their ideas (something the whole course is designed to encourage), they write their essays in a controlled setting so that they can be individually graded.

Following is a typical essay examination question in Language and Human Conflict, coupled with an outline of an examination case study about Appalachian English as a migrant dialect in Chicago:

Sample Examination (Fall Semester 1989)

General Directions
1. Place your name on this sheet only and staple it in last; do not put your name or initials anywhere else on the examination.
2. You are permitted to bring an outline to class for the examination, but it cannot exceed seventy-five words. You must attach your outline to your exam when you turn it in.
3. You are expected to acknowledge all sources (case study, reserve

readings, interviews, and other materials) except class notes. You are permitted to prepare a bibliography in advance and attach it to your examination when you turn it in.

Examination Question

The argument has been made that the Black English case study is representative of other situations involving divergent dialects; that is, given a similar level of dialect divergence, we could expect similar kinds of problems to develop, which would in turn require a policy response (though not necessarily an identical policy response).

  This essay question is designed to test this argument by inviting you to compare the circumstances, consequences, and policy options of the Black English (BE) case study with the attached case study on Appalachian English (AE). You will note immediately that the AE case study provides information about dialect differences and some cultural and historical background, but it does not include much data about school performance, IQ scores, etc. The absence of information obliges you to project from the known (BE) to the unknown (AE) as part of the examination. Your essay should be divided into three major headings or sections, as follows:

1. Since the argument hinges on the notion of dialect divergence, you will have to develop this concept in drawing parallels between BE and AE. This task isn't merely a matter of finding superficial structural parallels; it is aimed at identifying socially diagnostic features in these dialects and the stereotypes that they trigger in the dominant culture. You should cite specific examples to clarify and support your position. (70 points)

2. The argument also suggests that consequences flow from dialect divergence, especially in the school setting. The BE case-study discussions have pointed to several kinds of problems, and the facts are reasonably clear. The AE case study is less detailed about consequences; therefore, you will have to *infer* the probable consequences for AE children, arguing by analogy with the BE case study. (70 points)

3. The third section should address the policy issue. What response should there be to the problems of BE speakers? Should there be a similar response for AE speakers, or should the response be different in some way? Whichever way you go, you must justify your position by arguing logically from the BE case to the AE case. (60 points)

Examination Case-Study Outline: Appalachian English

1. Appalachian neighborhoods in Chicago—migration patterns between Appalachia and Chicago (and other midwestern industrial
   cities); "Kentuck" settlements in northeastern Wisconsin and lower
   Michigan.
2. Phonological features of Appalachian English—replacement of
   simple vowels by diphthongs; length of allophones of /l/ and /r/,
   r-coloring of final vowels; archaic initial [h].
3. Grammatical features of Appalachian English dialects—*a*- prefixing of verbs; reclassification of strong and weak verbs; perfective
   done and other distinctive verb phrases.
4. Appalachian English vocabulary—retention of folk vocabulary in
   Appalachian speech.
5. School attendance patterns, educational levels of parents, student
   enrollments in inner-city school districts. (This section is sometimes
   deleted or reduced.)

It should be obvious that this is not the sort of reasoning one can expect
in an impromptu examination. The instructor is available for questions about
the facts of the new case but not its interpretation. In some instances, as
here, the examination case studies are incomplete by design; they require
students, reasoning from the precedents and principles of the case study
discussed in class, to predict the likely consequences of language variation.
This design has been highly productive, since other situations involving
divergent dialects or ethnic languages may not have been studied as thoroughly as the "classic" case studies and there may not be much information
about economic problems, school performance, or other consequences of
nonstandard or divergent varieties of language. Such an examination emphasizes the course's focus on application and generalization of basic principles, beyond the particular details of the case studies discussed in class.

Some Final Notes on Preparation

The instructor's preparation for a case-study course differs from preparation
for lecture-and-discussion courses. The easy part, although it may not seem
so at first, is the preparation and updating of the case studies and their
readings, a task that includes a constant search for new material that is
accessible to nonspecialist readers. The case-study document provides a basic
structure for class discussion, as well as defining and exemplifying key

concepts and serving as a bridge to the primary sources on the reading list. The reading list itself tends to get longer over time, but also more diversified, reflecting different points of view (something textbooks don't do very well) and ranging from professional to popular sources. Initially, a case study may be merely part of the total agenda for a linguistics course, but as more case studies are developed, it is possible to design the entire course around case studies, even to the point of dispensing with introductory lectures and committing substantial time to an inductive teaching strategy.

The hard part is mental preparation, especially for instructors who are accustomed to a tightly controlled teaching environment. Class discussion is structured to some degree by the case study, but the questions can still range widely. A Socratic dialogue is revered as the classical teaching style, but an instructor who uses that technique must have the ego strength to admit not knowing the answers—or must know enough about the case to show students where knowledge ends and uncertainty begins (a situation that can change when the next journal arrives in the mailbox). The approach gives instructors significantly less control than the conventional stand-up lecture, even with the discussion ground rules outlined earlier, and it results in the covering of less material. However, seventeen years of teaching with this strategy have made it clear that establishing a point of view transferable to new cases is perhaps the best kind of coverage we can hope for in any course. That conclusion may be the strongest argument for a case-study approach to language variation.

Sex, Gender, and Language Variation

Teaching about Sex Variation in Language

Miriam Watkins Meyers, Metropolitan State University,
Minneapolis–Saint Paul

❧

SINCE the early 1970s, we have witnessed increasing interest in, and scholarly work around, the topic of sex differences in language use. Though not new (Jespersen had some interesting things to say about women's speech [*Language*]), the topic had enjoyed little attention from American linguists until Robin Lakoff published *Language and Woman's Place*. Since the publication of that work, which has been criticized for being introspective and anecdotal, a veritable flood of literature has appeared, playing off Lakoff's assertions about the linguistic behavior of males and females.

The literature on the subject is diverse and has been written from a variety of points of view presented for a variety of purposes. It encompasses work in psychology, sociology, anthropology, speech communication, literature, lexicography, dialectology, sociolinguistics, and psycholinguistics, among other disciplines, cross-disciplines, and subdisciplines. Papers addressing related topics appear increasingly on the programs of professional meetings attended by scholars in these fields. National organizations, such as the Organization for the Study of Communication, Language, and Gender, have sprung up around the subject, and with them specialized journals and conferences.

Unquestionably, current changes in sex roles and the increasing number of women scholars have encouraged scholarly emphasis on topics related to sex variation in language. While only a small percentage of Americans today might identify themselves as active feminists, many more would be sensitive to language deemed "sexist" by a growing number of women. More to the point, many members of the general public hold certain beliefs about male and female language that may or may not be well founded. In this regard, sex variation is no different from other kinds of language variation: almost everyone, college students included, is a self-appointed expert on language by virtue of being a native speaker (Kramer). Since college students are accessible to us for teaching, however, they are of special interest to us here.

This essay describes an upper-level course developed for general (non-major) students enrolled in Metropolitan State University's bachelor-of-arts program. The students in question, whose average age is thirty-five, represent a growing population in higher education: adults who have returned to college or who have started college later than usual. Typically, Metropolitan State students must attend college classes in the evening, since eighty percent arc employed at least part-time outside the home and others have child-care and homemaking responsibilities during the day. Classes thus meet in three-hour blocks one evening a week or on alternative schedules. The course described in this essay was developed under these circumstances but is adaptable to a wide range of students, including majors in appropriate fields, younger "day students," and those enrolled in college-level continuing-education courses.

The course takes educational advantage of the interest in sex-linked language generated in American society by the women's movement and draws students into a careful examination of the issues raised by Lakoff, other scholars, and lay language commentators. Taking a broader approach than an inventory of research into the topic, the course aims to help students question, and not merely absorb, what they read and hear about language differences. Course objectives include

- helping students distinguish between fact and opinion, stereotype and generalization, hypothesis and research findings
- helping students support their own assertions about language with evidence that goes beyond the personal and anecdotal
- increasing students' sophistication in reading, thinking, and writing critically

More specific goals, supportive of these broader objectives, include development of skills, attitudes, and knowledge necessary to

- identify major differences in female-male communication behavior
- identify common linguistic attitudes and perceptions
- appreciate the difficulty and complexity of obtaining good information on communication differences
- understand what knowledge is and how we advance it
- be familiar with various approaches to communication behavior—in particular, those of linguistics and speech communication
- heighten powers of observation
- develop both a questioning attitude and an open mind

To accomplish—or make headway on—this ambitious agenda, we have devised a ten-week course format that involves students in a variety of activities: study of Lakoff's provocative treatise of the mid-1970s, an overview of the relevant literature, close examination of selected primary research, analysis of popular treatments of the subject, collection and analysis of data for both weekly and term assignments, and oral and written presentations of research.

The course begins with a reading of Lakoff, then some writing on each of the two parts of that book. Essentially, the assignment requires students to reiterate in writing Lakoff's assertions about "women's language" in part 1 (e.g., that women use "empty" adjectives, hedges, and tag questions after statements of feeling and opinion), and show how, in part 2, she opposes H. P. Grice's rules of conversation to her own rules of politeness to argue her position on sex differences in language use. This reading and writing assignment forms the basis for the next class, in which students' work is gone over and unfamiliar concepts encountered in Lakoff's publication, such as marking theory and the empiricism-introspection opposition, are explained. Discussion of the latter concept, in particular, lays the groundwork for the next task set for students: to look at empirical research in the field.

Students get an overview of the literature by working with a standard survey text in the field (Eakins and Eakins's *Sex Differences in Human Communication* has been used in the past). Typically, students read a chapter a week and complete an exercise that requires them to observe a particular behavior discussed in that chapter, to record what they observe, and to analyze the resulting data. Eakins and Eakins's exercises have proved to be generally well suited or easily adaptable for students in a variety of circumstances. One week students might be listening for and recording tag questions; another, they might be noting and recording how women are addressed by strangers in restaurants, grocery stores, or other public places, or how men and women use color terms, intensifiers, or profanity. They then process in class their pooled data, gathered in different settings from different kinds of subjects and under different circumstances. These discussions give ample opportunity to explore principles of data collection, variables to consider and select for investigation, and the need for careful reporting of findings. Inevitably, students see that building knowledge about human behavior is no simple matter, and they develop respect for the scholarly enterprise. They are also surprised frequently by their own findings and can get beyond their preconceptions about language behavior to see how their own perceptions may have created a personal reality unsupported by careful study.

Examination of the data collected also provides an opportunity to make students more sensitive to language *structure*. The data collected by students for a tag question exercise, for example, almost always include a number of "non-tag questions," giving the instructor a chance to teach that structural feature of English and to bring to students' attention the complex linguistic competence required to make "correct" tag questions in English, especially when tag formation rules are compared with the "cover tag" *n'est-ce pas* of French. Attempts to categorize tag questions lead into an examination of the arbitrary nature of taxonomies and the difficulty of truly knowing a speaker's motivation for any speech act. Students can then understand the influence of researcher perception and bias and thus the need for checks on one's work.

In addition to the textbook reading and exercises, students look at primary research articles on topics covered in the overview text chapters. These assignments serve partly to illustrate how complex the issues can be and how impervious they are to simple analysis and to simple one-sentence or one-paragraph summaries in survey texts. The assignments also require students to read more difficult (and, they would add, more boring) material than they would otherwise encounter. Two examples will demonstrate how supplementary articles can be used to advance the goals of the course.

During the week in which the students read the text chapter dealing with tag questions, they also work with an article published to counter Lakoff's claims regarding women's use of tag questions (Dubois and Crouch). In this article the authors argue first that Lakoff's work was inadequate on a number of counts and then present their own study of male and female tag-question behavior. As part of this assignment, students must summarize the article and critique it as a response to Lakoff.

Students raise a number of issues in the ensuing class. They have suggested, for example, that, though Lakoff's claims about women's use of tag questions center on one particular *type* of tag question, Betty Lou Dubois and Isabel Crouch lump all their tag questions together. Thus, even though Dubois and Crouch question Lakoff's basis for interpreting tag questions, their finding that men in their group produced all the tag questions does not necessarily refute Lakoff's claims. In addition to offering criticisms of the article, students detail its merits. They begin to realize that "experts" disagree on the details of language behavior and their interpretation. As they glimpse the ways in which challenge and ongoing argument are essential to the search for understanding, they see that it is through such debate that progress is made in a field and how we linguists learn what we know. Students need to know how we know; if they don't, we run the risk of keeping them slaves to the printed word, on the one hand, and only too willing to dismiss anything they read, on the other. The challenge is to help them question and understand what they read in greater depth than they have before.

The second example of the use of supplementary material to extend the text discussion of an issue—in this case, interruption behavior—involves an article published by the sociolinguist Deborah Tannen in *New York* magazine. The textbook chapter students read focuses on female and male behavior with regard to turn-taking and other conversation-management protocols. Some scholarly research on cross-sex interruption indicates that men are more likely to interrupt women in conversation than vice versa. In her work on upper-middle-class New York Jewish speech, however, Tannen has shown that ethnic and regional variables must be taken into account when studying interruption and speech overlap behavior. This particular fly in the ointment delights my midwestern students, who have always known that they were different from New Yorkers in conversation-management behavior but have typically never had such a pointed, interesting, and humane lesson on the differences.

In addition to reading, studying, and writing about material prepared by scholars, students are exposed to popular treatments of sex variation in language. Cartoons offer a rich repository of attitudes, stereotypes, and other generalizations about male and female language. Flyers inviting the "corporate woman on the move" to attend seminars to learn how to cull out so-called female speech patterns that detract from women's credibility provide additional material for analysis, as do articles from working women's magazines. Advertisements, however, constitute the most popular medium for analysis among students. Many students over the years have chosen advertisments as the source of data for their final course projects.

The weekly exercises done in connection with each text chapter are, in part, preparation for the development by each student of a term project. The course syllabus provides for the project to be done in stages; students begin the assignment by skimming the text for ideas about a project topic and move to focus their plan, conduct a limited search of the relevant literature, collect and analyze data, and present the project orally in the ninth and tenth weeks of class and in writing by the eleventh week.

Projects over the years have included such diverse male and female language behaviors as the following:

- requests and commands in recorded messages on an answering machine
- adjectives used to describe preferred winter vacation spots to a travel agent
- pronunciation of *-ing* by country-western singers
- self-deprecating remarks on comedy shows featuring couples
- color term knowledge and use
- attitudes of parishioners toward changes in liturgical language aimed at making the church more "inclusive"

- graffiti on male and female restroom graffiti boards
- references to internal states in outdoor adventure writing

Some students have been able to use their projects to investigate matters of real concern to them outside academia. One woman prepared a defense of liturgical language change for her small-town Minnesota Lutheran church. A parent of young children studied concerns his little girls addressed to him and to his wife so that he could learn what the children's perceptions were of their parents' roles. A teacher in an alternative school investigated pupils' ideas of sex-appropriate language to check out her belief that progressive educational philosophy and practice will tell in children's attitudes.

The instructor's job with regard to the term project is to help students define research goals that (1) fit the circumstances of their lives, (2) demand an appropriate level of skill and a reasonable amount of time, and (3) focus on behavior discrete enough to be amenable to investigation and significant enough for meaningful analysis. Students often overlook their best research opportunities, making their task more difficult by choosing, for example, settings that require them simultaneously to observe, record, and participate. Or they may try to observe a number of behaviors within one television program and consequently find themselves overwhelmed. A common student pitfall is to spend so much time collecting data that little time is left for reflection and "meaning-making." The instructor, therefore, needs to give regular feedback as students search out and define a research goal and methodology, so that resulting projects will both provide a learning opportunities for individual students and, through the oral class presentation, contribute to the class's knowledge.

Students receive routine information on formal aspects of preparing oral and written presentations, including background discussion of differences in the two modes of discourse and their implications. The need to "nutshell" the research project orally for an audience of peers promotes closure on the project before written reports are due, contributing to better-than-average quality of the latter. This approach to term projects has been so successful that papers from previous students are regularly distributed and used in class as models of both form and content.

A final take-home (or in-class, open-book) exam gives students an opportunity to apply what they've learned in a variety of ways: cartoons are presented for commentary; popular beliefs about male and female speech are offered for analysis and criticism ("From what you have learned in the course about actual and perceived characteristics of female and male speech, explain why women's speech may be thought more 'emotional' than men's");

a set of data, typically collected by a student in a previous class, is included for analysis and generalization; and a final question forces students to synthesize course material in some way ("Is it appropriate or important to examine sex differences in language, or should we focus instead on status and power differences? Defend your answer"). The exam tests students' ability to analyze and generalize about a set of data, to bring knowledge acquired during the course to bear on fresh material, and to use course content as evidence to argue a position.

A note is in order here about the instructor's workload in the course described. Some instructors may be unable or unwilling to carry the evaluation burden generated by weekly assignments, oral presentation, term paper, and final exam. Parenthetically, some of the work included in the course described here has grown out of Metropolitan State University's writing- and speaking-across-the-curriculum commitments. Dropping either the term project or the final exam would still leave a solid course of study, with plenty of products for evaluation. Alternatively, an instructor could split the course into two quarters or semesters, reserving the major research project for the second term.

Results of the course (and its independent study analog), with regard to both student performance and reception, indicate that nonmajors can be effectively engaged in elective courses in sex variation in language. Course evaluations show that students like the challenge, the mix of tasks, the staged research projects, and the relevance to communication issues they face daily. Even more noteworthy, perhaps, is the students' positive response to a course that builds critical intellectual skills and attitudes of a general sort. Students comment, on the one hand, on the difficulty of the work required and, on the other, on the value of that work in other classes, on the job, and in their personal lives.

Investigating Sex-Marked Language

Donald M. Lance, University of Missouri, Columbia

AMERICAN linguists began studying sex-marked language use seriously after Mary Ritchie Key published an article on language and gender in 1972 ("Linguistic Behavior") and two comprehensive studies were published in 1975, Key's *Male/Female Language* and Robin Lakoff's *Language and Woman's Place*. These works stimulated not only interest in the nature of the language each sex uses but also an awareness of sex-role stereotyping reflected in language. So many linguists, sociologists, psychologists, literary critics, and others have conducted valuable research on gender differences in language use that the bibliography in this area is now long and diverse. The issue has become important enough in American society for Casey Miller and Kate Swift to revise their 1980 handbook on nonsexist writing eight years later, now a volume of 180 pages.

In preparing the volume that she co-edited with Margaret A. Lourie in 1978, Nancy Faires Conklin wrote a chapter summarizing previous research and prepared a questionnaire for use in investigating sensitivity to sex-marked language: "Appendix F: Rating Scales for Attitudes toward Sex-Marked Language" (431). Conklin included in the questionnaire twenty-one sentences for use in determining the respondent's recognition of linguistic sex-stereotyping. Several of the sentences in the survey contain constructions discussed in Lakoff's and Key's descriptions of female and male language. Since 1981, I have used Conklin's questionnaire as either a required or an optional survey assignment in my dialects class. The original form asks the subjects only whether they think a sentence is more likely to be used by a man or by a woman or whether both would use it; I thought it would be more informative to include a "scale of likelihood" ranging from 1 (very likely) to 7 (very unlikely). I also changed the procedure to ask the subjects to indicate the likelihood ratings for members of each sex. Noting that the differences in the sentences pertained not only to vocabulary but also to level of formality, I added the latter dimension to Conklin's survey. The format of the questionnaire is as follows:

Sex-Marked Language: A Survey

Sex   Year of birth   Date   Interviewer
Occupation or major

This exercise investigates how likely it is that a male or a female would say certain sentences in a relaxed conversational atmosphere. This is the setting: Several students, all friends or at least acquaintances, are chatting in a group in a popular student-oriented restaurant like the Heidelberg, the Bengal Lair, or Brady Commons or in a student apartment. On the worksheet, indicate the likelihood that a male or female would say each of these sentences and the level of formality of each sentence when said by each sex. Underline the words or phrases that make each sentence more likely to be said by one sex or the other.

1. I had such a delicious lunch today.

female: likelihood	very likely	1	2	3	4	5	6	7	very unlikely
female: formality	very formal	1	2	3	4	5	6	7	very informal
male: likelihood	very likely	1	2	3	4	5	6	7	very unlikely
male: formality	very formal	1	2	3	4	5	6	7	very informal

2. It's hot out today, isn't it?

Instructions to interviewers are as follows:

Directions

Administer the questionnaire on sex-marked sentences to an equal number of males and females. After you have collected the questionnaires, tabulate the results to see differences between male and female responses. I will be happy to help you with the statistics if you are unsure of how to handle the numbers. If you want to compare the findings of your survey with summaries of data from earlier semesters, I can give you copies of handouts that I have prepared from previous classes. On the basis of your data and the readings that we have done for this class, write an essay of 1,200 to 2,000 words discussing what you found in your survey.

Conklin's survey has thirteen female-marked and eight male-marked sentences; in consultation with the first class that administered the questionnaire, I added five more sentences and made some minor changes in the wording of three. In her description of the assignment, Conklin indicated which sentences she considered to be more likely to be said by males and which by females. In the questionnaire I mixed the two types; the order of the sentences in my questionnaire is indicated by the numbers in the following lists. The thirteen "female" sentences include the two in the instructions above and the following additional list:

4. Would you like to help me in the garden?
7. The walls in our bathroom are mauve.

8. You have a lovely apartment.
9. How DO you do?
13. To whom am I speaking?
15. Could you please give me the time?
16. Should it rain, we would have to cancel the picnic.
18. We're feeling better today, aren't we?
21. I think I hear you saying that you feel depressed.
24. There's an eensie-weensie problem here.
25. I think you may be sitting on my magazine.

The "male" sentences in Conklin's list included the first eight in the following list. We decided that we wanted more balance in the numbers and added the two at the bottom of the list.

3. You have some pulmonary congestion, but some tetracyclines should clear it right up.
5. Get that dog out of my yard.
10. That's the worst shit I ever ate.
11. I ain't goin' with 'em.
14. They were real laid back.
19. Productionwise, we're doing real well.
22. I'll need a Phillips-head screwdriver to fix that.
26. I don't give a damn what you think.
12. Nice set of wheels ya got there.
17. Gimme a hand with these tax forms.

We also added one that we thought would be completely neutral (6), a less strong complaint about food (20), and an informal greeting commonly used by both men and women on campus (23):

6. If it doesn't snow, we can't go skiing.
20. This food tastes terrible, doesn't it?
23. How ya doin'?

In 1983 and 1984 I had approximately the same number of men (17) and women (18) in my dialects classes; since each student administered the questionnaire to two males and two females, the set of data was well enough balanced to warrant serious statistical analysis. When I tabulated the 140 questionnaires, I separated them into four groups—responses given by female subjects to male students, by male subjects to male students, by female subjects to female students, and male students to female students—because

I had a suspicion from tabulations in previous years that the sex of the student who is to analyze the data had influenced, to some extent, how students filled out the questionnaires. I asked the students merely to hand the questionnaires to the subjects and collect them later and not hover over the subjects and possibly influence their responses. I used the t-test to measure the level of significance for comparisons of the mean ratings of likelihood that each sex would say a particular sentence.

Eight of the sentences were rated as likely for females but not for males (8, 1, 7, 13, 18, 24, 16, 21,—listed here in descending order of likelihood for use by females); the differences between the mean scores for male and female ratings for likeliness were all significant at the level of $p < .0005$ (that is, with a probability of less than 5 in 10,000 that the results of the survey occurred by chance). Seven sentences (22, 12, 10, 19, 17, 14, 11) were rated as likely for males but not for females; each of these differences was also significant at $p < .0005$. Six sentences (4, 2, 25, 15, 20, 9) were rated as likely for both sexes but more likely for females; the difference in ratings for number 2 was significant at $p < .10$ and the others at $p < .005$. Three (5, 23, 26) were likely for both sexes but more so for males, each significant at $p < .005$. The sentence about skiing (6) was likely for both sexes, with mean ratings of 2.673 for both males and females. The medical sentence (3), ostensibly male-oriented, was rated as unlikely for both sexes but slightly more likely for males ($p < .05$); the unlikelihood probably occurred because the instructions did not lead the respondents to picture the speaker in a hospital or doctor's office.

Since the purpose of this article is to describe a research activity rather than to give a detailed report of the findings of my statistical analysis, only a few interpretive comments are included here. Of particular interest is the fact that when the informants were asked to indicate the likelihood that members of each sex might say each sentence, two of the tag questions (2 and 20) were likely for both sexes; though the two sentences are not strictly female-marked, informants felt that males were less likely to say them. A glance at the sentences with strongest female marking suggests that certain vocabulary items (*such a, mauve, lovely, eensie-weensie*) and overt display of personal concern ("We're feeling. . . ," "I think . . .") carry much stronger stereotyping potential than do syntactic structures such as tag questions. Readers may examine the sentences for further suggestions and either replicate my procedure or conduct similar investigations.

Suspicious that the sex of the person handing out the questionnaire might be a variable, I also used the t-test in cross-sex comparisons—the mean ratings of females' responses to male investigators were contrasted with females' responses to female investigators. Of the 312 cross-sex comparisons possible for these twenty-six sentences, 84 were different at a significance level of $p < .10$; that is, in slightly more than one fourth of the comparisons, there is at least one chance in ten that, in repeated investigations of this sort, male and female university students will adjust their responses in accordance with the sex of the person conducting the survey.

The results of the analysis of formality showed a tendency for men to speak more formally than women when they say a "female" sentence and for women to speak more informally than men when they use "male" sentences. Only two of the sentences had significant differences in formality ratings for each sex (8, $p < .05$; 24, $p < .10$). Cross-sex comparisons, however, show that men and women often give different ratings for the formality of a sentence when the investigator is of the same or of the opposite sex; of the 312 comparisons, 80 were significant at the level of $p < .10$.

I did the statistical analyses myself by setting up tables and formulas on an Appleworks spreadsheet. By analyzing the numbers myself, I was able to see some numerical patterns that raised interesting procedural questions that would not have come up if I had not worked so closely with the raw data. One factor that very graphically popped into view was the wide variation in ratings for almost every question. I concluded that, given the high levels of significance with loosely controlled data, even better results could be obtained by controlling more carefully such variables as the hypothetical setting for the language behavior being investigated.

The instructions that I now use have more clearly defined situational registers. The directions for administering the questionnaire call for the students to ask the respondent to consider four social situations: males and females in same-sex groups and each sex in mixed-sex groups. To keep the questionnaire from being burdensome, I no longer include formality but discuss this variable in class. With the new format the questions in the survey are set up as follows:

1. I had such a delicious lunch today.
      female—all female   very likely   1 2 3 4 5 6 7   very unlikely
      female—mixed   very likely   1 2 3 4 5 6 7   very unlikely
      male—all male   very likely   1 2 3 4 5 6 7   very unlikely
      male—mixed   very likely   1 2 3 4 5 6 7   very unlikely

The instructor may allow students to use a portion of the twenty-six sentences in order to keep the size of the data more manageable or may adjust wording or add other sentences to the list. There are many variations in setting that might be used, such as the presence of parents, grandparents, aunts and uncles, members of certain religious groups, total strangers, international students. Another interesting variation would be for a male instructor and a female instructor to ask their students to administer the questionnaires and subtly but clearly let the subjects know the sex of the instructor who assigned the project. The principal purpose of the exercise is to get the students to come to an awareness not only of the existence of sex-marked language but, more important, to recognize the fact that in talking about language, respondents will vary their answers on the basis of who they think is going to analyze their responses. If the instructor has the knowledge to do statistical analyses either by hand or by feeding data into a mainframe statistical package, and if variables have been controlled carefully enough and student investigators are trained sufficiently, the exercise not only may serve as serious research about human linguistic behavior but—more important—can teach the next generation of citizens, scholars, and teachers about language variation.

Variation in
Historical Contexts

Sprangorland: A Fictional Case Study in Variation and Historical Change through Cultural, Political, and Linguistic Interaction

Greta D. Little, University of South Carolina

❧

ONE of the most exasperating problems for students studying language variation and change is the lack of hard-and-fast answers to questions. Students want neat formulas that will predict specific outcomes with dependable regularity. The notion that several answers may have validity is a new and difficult concept for them to accept. While we can often provide reasonable, even likely explanations for English forms, invariably the answers are complex and impossible to verify. At best we can offer a sound hypothesis to explain the origins of certain words or expressions. There is no way, however, to predict how language will develop and change in the future. To help my students understand why the study of language change offers no clear answers, I provide them with a hypothetical region where a variety of languages are spoken and take them through its social, economic, and political history as the land becomes a nation of people speaking the same language. The students are asked to consider the options and choose a language policy, using what they have learned from studying the history of English and its growth to explain their recommendations and predictions. Their responses vary greatly, depending on where they see the similarities in the two situations. They have some general principles to guide them, but the variables, like those in real life, are immense, and no two students ever agree completely on the future of my imaginary land, Sprangorland. (See fig. 1.)

A second, unlooked-for advantage in this assignment has been its success in impressing on students the significance of nonlinguistic factors in establishing the prestige of any language. In learning how the English language developed, students often feel a sense of inevitability in the rising importance of the language. They are aware of the great body of English literature—most of them are English majors—and assume that there is something special about the language itself that makes it so influential in the world today. They see English as a naturally superior medium of communication. Even as students begin to recognize its variety and to understand that it has changed through the years, they are nevertheless reluctant to relinquish their notions of linguistic superiority. They merely begin to cite the ability of English to incorporate variety and to accept change as evidence of its superiority. However, when they approach the linguistic problems of Sprangorland, they discover that political, social, and economic events make a language important and enable it to absorb new vocabulary and structure.

The assignment itself can take several forms, but I give it as a take-home final exam. Students have about a week to prepare their answers, and on the designated day of the examination, we meet for debate and discussion about Sprangorland and its language. However, the assignment could also be a paper topic for students to prepare individually or in groups. The particular questions that accompany the description of Sprangorland can be designed to elicit a wide range of perspectives and to fit a variety of class activities.

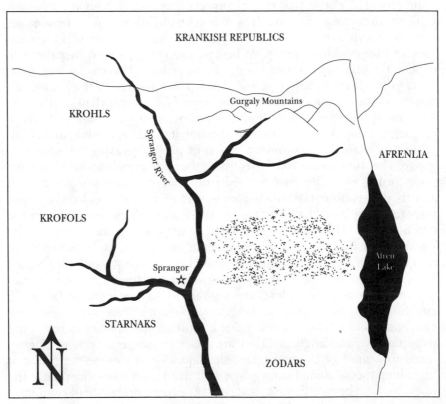

Figure 1. Sprangorland

Sprangorland

After World War II, a number of new countries all over the world emerged as people who had formerly been ruled by various empires organized themselves into national governments. Among the new nations was Sprangorland (named for the Sprangor River, which runs through the country, not for any of the languages competing for prominence). The country itself is still in the process of establishing its ethnic, cultural, and linguistic identity. The people are quite diverse and were not yet united as a nation even in 1957, when Sprangorland first came to world attention.

The People

Six identifiable groups of people live within the borders of Sprangorland: the Krohls, the Krofols, the Zodars, the Gurgs, the Starnaks, and the Afrenlians.

The Krohls. The Krohls, who make up eight percent of the population, are the educated elite of Sprangorland. Their ancestors were the feudal overlords of much of the region until the nineteenth century. Under the previous empire, Krohls held all positions of importance and more or less governed during the imperial period just before World War II. Their language is Krohlian, which has had a literary tradition rich in both poetry and recorded history since the nineteenth century. Now they tend to hold middle-management positions in the financial infrastructure of Sprangorland and in a few cities in neighboring countries.

The Krofols. The Krofols are the largest ethnic group, making up thirty-four percent of the population. They are descendants of the same civilization that spawned the Krohls. However, the Krofols were not overlords; they were the serfs. Until World War II, their lives had been essentially unchanged. Grain farmers, they were tied to the land and were ruled by the Krohls. Their language, Krofof, has the same source as Krohlian, but the years of social separation have left their mark on both languages: although they share certain features, they are no longer considered the same language. Krofols can understand Krohlian, but Krohls do not seem to understand Krofof. During the imperial period before 1939, a small group of Krofol youngsters was educated in Krohlian to facilitate communication.

The Zodars. The Zodars, representing twenty-three percent of the population, are the farmers of Sprangorland. Hard-working pragmatists, they live in a fertile southeastern area and have been supplying vegetables, meat, and dairy products to other parts of the country for several centuries. No writing system has been developed for their language. Zodarian has low social prestige because, before 1950, few Zodarians were educated, though they have an uncanny ability to pick up enough of the language of their neighbors for commercial purposes.

The Gurgs. Only eleven percent of the population of Sprangorland are Gurgs, who live in the Gurgaly Mountains in the northeast corner of the country. An aloof and independent group, they are primarily herders and make excellent woolen fabrics. Throughout history, the Gurgs have been ignored, left to pursue their own traditions. No writing system has been developed for their language, Gurgish, but the people are proud of their heritage and cherish their separate identity. They have a rich oral tradition associated with folktales and a few epics passed on by both men and women storytellers.

The Starnaks. Starnaks make up sixteen percent of the population. Descendants of the most ancient civilization known to have inhabited the region in which Sprangorland is located, today they constitute most of the nation's mercantile class. They have long been accustomed to traveling along the rivers, trading with the Krofols, Zodars, Krohls, and even some of the Gurgs. Sprangor, the largest city in the country, is populated chiefly by Starnaks. Although there is no literary tradition associated with the Starnash language, it has been written since the early 1900s and is relatively standardized.

The Afrenlians. Immigrants from neighboring Afrenlia on the east, they now constitute eight percent of Sprangorland's population. They have been leaving their own land since 1880 to settle along the Afren Lake, which forms part of the eastern border between the countries. They have settled together in small communities near the lake, where they have kept their own language and traditions. Other than Starnak traders, few people had any social contact with these Afrenlians until World War II. Even now, very few Sprangorians from other parts of the country live in or visit the area. After the war, the border between Afrenlia and Sprangorland was permanently closed.

Geography

The Sprangor River runs from north to south, separating the westernmost third of Sprangorland from the rest of the country. The Starnaks own the land along the southern part of the river valley and its western tributaries, where their fruit orchards have been productive for two centuries. The Krofols and their former overlords, the Krohls, live in the north, just south of the Krankish Republics. Krofol territory extends eastward across the country almost to the Afrenlian border. To the northeast, above the eastern flatlands where the Krofols live, are the Gurgaly Mountains. The Zodarians occupy the land along the southern border east of the Sprangor River. South of the Zodarian and Starnak region is the Republic of Zdalor.

Language Relations

Krofof, Krohlian, Zodarian, and Starnash are all related. They belong to the Starn-Krohl language family. Gurgish and Afrenlian belong to language families not related to each other or to Starn-Krohl. Krohlian and Krofof are both descended from Old Krohlian, a language of the northern branch of the Starn-Krohl family. Zodarian belongs to the southern branch, and Starnash is the sole surviving language of the western branch.

Religion

Most people in Sprangorland are Christian. They are not Roman Catholic or Protestant, but follow their own version of Christianity—the Krohlian Church. Church liturgy is in Old Krohlian, as were historical records before 1830. Old Krohlian is a dead language, but, as noted, it was the parent for both Krohlian and Krofof. Most of the education available in Sprangorland before the war was offered through the church, but schooling is now supervised by the government.

Afrenlians follow Islam, but Western scholars do not know much about the religious beliefs of the mysterious Gurgs, who allow no public display of their religious practices.

Government

Like many countries that emerged after World War II and the era of empires, Sprangorland is led by a semisocialist government. The leader of the controlling party is Henrietta P. Kabilok, who serves as president of Sprangorland. President Kabilok is actually from Zodaria, but she was raised and educated among the Starnaks until she was chosen by the Krohl governor at the time to study in Western Europe, because Sprangorland lacked institutions of higher education.

Questions

1. One of the chief problems that has faced President Kabilok and Sprangorland has been education. The first question for education concerns language. With six different languages spoken in the country, how should the government implement a policy of public education? What language(s) should be used in the schools? What problems might arise as a result of the government's language choice? As an international consultant, you have been asked by President Kabilok to advise her government about reorganizing schools and establishing a language policy. What recommendations would you make about the organization of schools, the language of instruction, and the publication and distribution of textbooks?

2. Take each of the following events and discuss how it would affect the country's language policy and the individual languages themselves. How would you expect the languages to change as a result of these events?

   a. A major rebellion breaks out among the Gurgs, who feel they are being pressured to accept the culture and customs of the Krofols, Starnaks, and Zodarians. They want to secede from Sprangorland. Guerrilla warfare continues for twenty years before a peaceful settlement is negotiated (1989–2009).

   b. The Afrenlians decide they want to annex their area of Sprangorland to Afrenlia. Demonstrations and underground agitation occur. For years the Sprangorland government has dealt with the discontent. However, now Afrenlia is lending support to its "native peoples" and is accusing Sprangorland of holding the Afrenlians against their will. Afrenlia calls for self-determination in the region and brings the problem to the General Assembly of the United Nations in 1990.

   c. In 1993 a large dam is built on the Sprangor River in the north, primarily for hydroelectric power. Consequently, industry begins moving into the area along the rivers, especially in the area populated mostly by the sedentary Krofols.

   d. Sprangorland enters into a close military alliance with its neighbors to the north, the Krankish Republics, in the mid-1990s. In 2001 the Kranks march into the capital city and take over the Sprangor government. They rule for seventy-five years, until a combination of resistance from Sprangor patriots and domestic problems in the Krankish Republics force the Kranks to withdraw.

   e. Uranium is discovered in the Gurgaly Mountains in the year 2020.

3. By the year 2300, everyone in Sprangorland speaks the same language. It is called Sprangish. The vocabulary of the language reflects its history. Below are the English glosses for several words in Sprangish. What do you think is the most probable source language for each Sprangish word? Consider the likelihood of competing forms from different languages. Explain your reasoning. Make a list of twenty additional glosses and speculate on their probable source.

a.	hoe	h.	drill
b.	pulpit	i.	power
c.	mountain goat	j.	spice
d.	caravan	k.	cereal
e.	airplane	l.	fruit
f.	baby	m.	sausage
g.	thread	n.	cheese

These are the questions I use, but of course there are many other possibilities. One (suggested by my colleague Michael Montgomery) is to assign students to the various ethnic groups and ask them to discuss their reactions to the policy decisions and consequent events. The problem of language choice in multiethnic families is also a fruitful area for exploration using the same technique. Another approach to the assignment entails students' taking on the role or perspective of different citizens of Sprangorland: the leader of the Gurg resistance, an abbot of the Krohlian Church, a teenage Zodarian tomato picker, a scion of the old Krohl aristocracy, an Afrenlian mullah, a Starnak entrepreneur, the widow of the last Krohlian governor, a Krofol farmer whose land lies along the Sprangor River. Having the students meet for discussion after they have completed the assignment helps them recognize what they have learned. They take their points of view seriously and are careful about the arguments they make. These discussions rank among the most articulate and intelligent I have managed to evoke from my students.

A Simplified Model of Language Variation and Change: A History of the Bot People

A. Wayne Glowka, Georgia College

IT NEVER occurred to me as an undergraduate that other students in my history of the English language class were not also fascinated by Grimm's law and by the Indo-European dictionary conveniently printed at the end of the first edition of *The American Heritage Dictionary* ("Indo-European Roots")—even though I was aware that only two of us showed up for Friday afternoon classes. At a later time, I scoffed secretly to myself when my dissertation director told me that he had required less and less of students as the years went on. Now, however, after teaching for a decade at a four-year college, I know firsthand that many undergraduates have little interest in intriguing subjects like the loss of nasals before voiceless fricatives in Anglo-Frisian and find the details about Indo-European and Germanic in John Algeo (*Problems* 93–111) and Thomas Cable (10–17) baffling rather than delightful—with no offense to either workbook. I have devised an entertaining chalkboard lecture that amuses my students and tricks them into thinking about the nature of language change before I ask them to read about what they like to call "the grimmest law of all."

Since my students, like many others in the United States, arrive with very rudimentary skills in a foreign language (if any), with little knowledge of geography and history, and with only two weeks' practice in phonetic transcription, an introduction to the prehistory of English seems to be as difficult as differential equations to some English majors whose main (or only) interest is contemporary literature. The extent of the difficulty of the material can be seen in the answers that some of the weaker students write on examination papers on this section of the course—for instance, that all known languages are descended from Indo-European and that the Anglo-Saxons brought the first real language to the British Isles (Latin having never caught on and Celtic being a rough sort of jargon not suited for efficient communication!). Some students encounter so much trouble in understanding the abstract phonology underlying Grimm's law that they spend hours trying to figure out "how all those letters became those other letters when they don't even look alike."

I do not abandon Grimm's law, however. It is my profound hope that a few students in each class will be excited by the correspondences that become obvious in comparisons of Germanic and Romance doublets. But because historical comparative philology is rich stuff for many of my students, I have simplified the mechanisms of historical change and geographical variation by making up an epic story of the Bot people (pronounced /bɑt/). With some basic understanding of the possibilities for language change, the students are then better prepared to comprehend relationships such as those between English and Armenian and the assumptions that make Grimm's law and other sound laws meaningful.

I start the lecture by drawing a large map on the board. The map is different every time I draw it, but I make sure that I include a great variety of topographical features, especially ones that would represent obstacles to Bronze Age people. The major portion of the map is a huge continent, littered with mountains, hills, impenetrable forests, lakes, rivers, swamps, and deserts. Off the continent, I always draw a large island, it too sectioned by mountains or forests. Sometimes I add an island far to the west of the first island. When the whole production starts to smell of J.R.R. Tolkien (and at least one of the students notices the smell), I know I am on the right track.

Into this laboratory landscape I insert a tribe of warlike, domineering people who appear on the scene from off the edges of the map. The story varies from time to time, and these people are given a variety of interesting characteristics. I call them the Bot people, the name based on a word that they use for some item. Rather than specify the item, I elicit students' speculations that it could be a fruit tree or a sacred mountain, something that might exist only in the homeland from which the Bot people emigrated or in only one area of the map, or that might even have disappeared, its specific reference forever a mystery. At any rate, in my story the Bot people find themselves growing in population, and the younger members of the tribe feel the need to expand their territory. In time, the tribe begins to spread itself over the map, sometimes killing off other people or forcing them to move elsewhere, at other times conquering but intermarrying, or simply peacefully migrating and living among people with whom they maintain little social interaction.

The movements of the Bot people leave portions of them separated by the geographical obstacles to communication. As the groups become separated, I introduce phonetic changes in the word *bot*, referring constantly to our vowel and consonant charts. Some of the changes are ascribed to the social and political contexts in which the people find themselves. Intermarriage, for example, may cause later generations of Bot people to change one or more of the phonemes of their favorite word because their mothers (from conquered people) could not pronounce those phonemes in the Bot fashion.

Further, even where intermarriage does not occur, tendencies in pronunciation among pure Bot people may, over time, change the articulation of one or more of the phonemes—analogous to the contemporary shift in pronunciation of long *o* by young people in Georgia.

The permutations in the pronunciation of the word can become exhaustingly complex. Limited to a field of, say, five cardinal vowels, the vowel of /bɑt/ can move around in the mouth, and this process becomes a simplified preview of umlaut and great vowel shifts. Slight changes in vocalization, position, and mode of articulation can turn /b/ into /p/, /ɸ/, /v/, /f/, or even /m/. Similar shifts can turn /t/ into /d/, /s/, /z/, /č/, /ǰ/, /š/, or even /k/ or /ʔ/. Either consonant or both consonants could disappear or could reverse their positions. In addition, endings could be added, with resulting accent shifts and syncopation of the /ɑ/ that could place the two consonants next to each other. The possible combinations are too great to be covered in one lecture—a brief quarter allows little time for such flights of fancy.

The purpose of this fictional social history and phonological change is to show students in a nutshell what language history and change are like. In the terms of another cliché, the purpose is to show the students what the whole forest looks like before pointing out any real trees. Principles emerge from this exercise: language changes for a variety of reasons; the changes are part of the nature of human existence.

After thirty minutes of such play with the possibilities, it is time to introduce the students to the "realities" of the study of language families and their histories. Pretending that we have not heard the preceding tale of armies, migrations, and plagues, we try to reconstruct the prehistorical account from the linguistic evidence that we have on our map. Like eighteenth- and nineteenth-century philologists, we compile a table of forms, and, feigning ignorance of the original form of the common word, we survey these forms and make decisions about the original form. Using a primitive system in which numbers of instances count, we assign a probable value to the first phoneme and then proceed to do the same to the second and third (and others, depending on how wild our changes or accretions have become). Often our posited form is not the one we started out with. We can make varying adjusted judgments based on how much of the fictional history we allow ourselves to know, but by and large we see both the limits of comparative prehistorical linguistics and the great work that went into compiling Indo-European word lists. The students come to realize, too, how far-reaching the knowledge of the old philologists was. The students are then ready to look at the family tree of the Indo-European languages, more fully appreciative both of the efforts it took to make such a representation and of the prehistory reflected in forms that give vague clues about their evolution.

Soon enough, I am sure, this method of introducing the students to Indo-European and Germanic philology will suffer from the equivalent of a computer software virus. Soon someone will tell me that English is descended from a language with one word, *bot*—in a fashion similar to the experience reported by a colleague who would get specific integers such as 1,066 to the "obvious" trick question "How many people were killed in the Great Vowel Shift?" But for the time being, the students sit engrossed in the story, following the tale and the linguistic changes with some of the same fascination that I once had when entertaining myself with Algeo's exercises on late summer evenings.

Indo-European Roots: Lexical Variation and Change through the Millennia

Donald M. Lance, University of Missouri, Columbia

EARLY in the semester in all my language classes I tell the students that there are two hard-and-fast "rules" about language and two corollaries related to them. The rules are that language always changes and that each language will always manifest variation; the corollaries are that there will always be some individuals who attempt to keep the language from changing and to keep variants ("impurities") from being used and that language will be diverse and continue to change in spite of all efforts by these well-intentioned "preservers" of linguistic heritage. The language course in which one can most convincingly present supportive data for these truths is the history of the English language.

Grimm's law is an excellent, but complex, vehicle for demonstrating evidence that variation and change have suffused the histories of languages for thousands of years without destroying the ability of human beings to communicate with each other. Because of students' seemingly ineradicable tendency to think of language primarily in written form, however, all except those at the top of the class find it a severe challenge to understand the system of Indo-European consonants and then shift their attention to what must have happened in the history of early European languages as stops (aspirated, unaspirated, voiced) and fricatives underwent several changes. Adding the s, z, and r of Verner's law to the discussion compounds the information overload. Once they have read of linguistic ancestors whose language has the consonants b^h, b, p, the students seem to visualize Cro-Magnon people writing these letters on the walls of their caves in central Europe; indeed, students write on exams that the "Indo-European alphabet" had these letters. The historical descriptions in textbooks add further complication by asking the students to "see" the phonological changes in the historical reflexes in words from Sanskrit, Old Church Slavonic, Avestan, Gothic, Lithuanian, Old Saxon, Modern English, and High German.

One of the most useful resources for data on how Grimm's law can be understood from the point of view of present-day English is the cross-referencing of Indo-European roots in the etymologies and in the appendix by Calvert Watkins in the first and third editions of *The American Heritage Dictionary*. The combination of etymologies and the index of Indo-European roots in this dictionary is particularly useful in getting students to relate historical changes to contemporary English words. In an attempt to help students comprehend relations between language change and the history of English and their knowledge of common vocabulary items, I have devised two exercises in which the students study sets of cognates consisting of native Germanic words (e.g., *two*, which underwent the Grimm change) and related borrowings from Romance and Hellenic sources (*dual, dyad*). Before asking the students to work with Grimm's law, I introduce them to language change by having them write an essay about how changes in the meanings and uses of an Indo-European root are reflected in present-day English words.

Essay on an Indo-European Root

This assignment is an essay on what has happened to a particular root as it coursed its way through the millennia in various cultures. (Later in the term I give the students an exercise that focuses specifically on Grimm's law; it is discussed below.) Before I hand out the dittoed instructions, I photocopy a different page for each student from the listing of roots in the dictionary appendix. (It is much less trouble to provide the copies than to require students to find the dictionary and make the copies themselves.) Inevitably I am faced with a barrage of complaints about how difficult the task is; however, by the class period after I hand out the assignment, some imaginative student has thought of an approach and can provide a peer-level (as opposed to "professorial") example of how one might write an interesting essay on one of the roots. This assignment, or one like it, could be based on entries in the appendix in the first edition of *The American Heritage Dictionary*, in the later edition of the roots published as a separate volume (Watkins, *American Heritage*), or in a popular book such as Robert Claiborne's *The Roots of English*. The following is an example of the kind of entry I want the students to use for their essays:

> **angh-**. Tight, painfully constricted, painful. **1**. Germanic **ang-*, compressed, hard, painful, in Old English *angnægl*, "painful spike (in the flesh)," corn, excrescence (*nægl*, spike NAIL): AGNAIL. **2**. Suffixed form **angh-os*-in Germanic **angas* in Old Norse *angr*, grief: ANGER. **3**. Suffixed form **angh-os-ti-* in Germanic **angst* in Old High German *angust*, anxiety: ANGST. **4**. Latin *angere*, to strangle, draw tight: ANXIOUS. **5**. Suffixed form *angh-os-to-* in Latin *angustus*, narrow: ANGUISH. **6**. Greek *ankhein*, to squeeze, embrace: QUINSY. **7**. Greek *ankhonē*, a strangling: ANGINA. (*American Heritage*, 1969)

The assignment asks the students to examine the Modern English words in capital letters in the entry and to write an essay based on the relationships that can be seen in the earlier and later meanings. Although the students will have to consult the main entries to understand *agnail* and *quinsy*, other relationships are rather obvious after some thought. Some Indo-European roots have undergone extremely complex historical developments, but it is not difficult to select entries on which university students can write essays. Often the etymologies in the main entries (e.g., the one for *quinsy*) pose fascinating challenges.

This activity seems absolutely impossible to students while they are trying to get started, but by the time they are finished, they feel they have written one of the most interesting compositions of their student careers. Through the critique emanating from their inevitable questions, we discuss how shifts in meaning can occur as a result of metaphorical extensions of a basic semantic reference and the adoption of these new variants into general use in the language. The variation and shift from the original is always clearest in Germanic words; it sometimes is totally obscured, except etymologically, in the more esoteric borrowings from Greek, Medieval French, or Persian (occasionally with detours through Classical Arabic).

Directions

Attached to these instructions is a photocopied page from the appendix on Indo-European roots in *The American Heritage Dictionary of the English Language* (1969). By [date], you are to choose an Indo-European root from the page that you receive and write an essay of about 500 to 700 words describing what has happened to that root as it has coursed its way through social time and geographical space during the past five and a half millennia, finding its way to us through Germanic roots or through related words borrowed from other languages. In the entries, the original meaning of the root is indicated, and each major development is briefly outlined; the words printed in capitals are Modern English words derived from the Indo-European root—that is, the words on which you are to base your paper.

You may choose any of the roots on the page that you receive, or you may choose, from another page, one that interests you more. The root you choose should have a rich history, or you won't be able to write a very interesting essay. The entry also should be no longer than 2 to 3 inches, or it will contain more information than you can fit into your essay. If you prefer, you may write on a pair of roots.

Develop your essay around some theme or unusual idea. Do not simply lay out a ploddingly dull, word-by-word string of disjointed comments that take up each capitalized word in the order of occurrence. Write something that will be interesting to read—perhaps even witty, without being cute. There is no single way to organize the essay; you will have to look for a noteworthy development or trend and use that information in your discussion of what happened to the root.

Since some of the words in the Indo-European entry will be completely new to you, you will need to look them up in the main body of a dictionary, preferably *The American Heritage Dictionary* because of its etymologies. You may also consult other sources if you like, such as *The Oxford English Dictionary*, an Old English dictionary, and so on. The entries may also refer to "zero grade" forms, "ablaut," and so on; you should ignore the more technical terms from historical linguistics and focus on the meanings of the Modern English words, though you should pay heed to the specific source of each form you discuss (e.g., "past participle of Greek *xyz*").

When you turn in your essay, include the photocopied page that contains the root on which your essay is based. If you choose a word from some other page, or if you embarrassingly befoul the page I have given you, please make another copy to submit with the essay. The reason for this requirement is simple: you shouldn't expect me to have to fumble through the pages of my dictionary before reading your essay.

If you are stuck, don't hesitate to discuss your word with another student or with me to get an idea on how to start and on what might be informative and interesting to others. I particularly encourage you to talk with each other about the roots; you'll learn more that way. But each student is to write a separate essay.

Grimm's Law and Borrowed Words

To a linguist, the most striking aspects of Grimm's law are the enormity of its effect on the Germanic sound system and the way the Grimm consonant shifts make Germanic roots so different from cognates in other Indo-European languages. In contrast, what hits the students immediately is the relatively trivial matter of nine stop consonants undergoing changes that appear almost circular; then the addition Verner's law and rhotacism in $s \rightarrow z \rightarrow r$ compounds the complexity. To assist the students in following the sound changes, I have devised the chart below. This exercise does not make Grimm's law any easier for the average or weak student, but it is of considerable value to the student with high interest in language. This approach can also reach a few more of the students who have difficulty in using only what is in textbooks; more than one approach always helps students. However much an individual student remembers of Grimm's law, this exercise gives me an opportunity to discuss systematic language changes and the corresponding differences leading to dialect and to branching within language families.

The assignment required of the students is relatively simple, with common English words borrowed from Latin and Greek rather than the Sanskrit, Gothic, and Armenian examples in traditional treatises on historical linguistics. The following is given as a handout that asks the students to fill in only a few words.

Grimm's Law

As the Indo-European dialects developed into separate languages and eventually separate language families, certain changes took place in the phonemic systems of each family and the languages within each family. The consonant changes indicated by arrows in the adjacent chart represent developments in Germanic languages from prehistoric times until some time before 300 BC; these changes are known as Grimm's law, also known as the First Germanic Consonant Shift (see 89–92 in the Pyles and Algeo text).

There is no possible way of dating the changes, but because Latin borrowings into Germanic did not undergo these changes, we can be sure that the process was no longer active during the time the Romans occupied the part of Europe populated by speakers of early Germanic dialects—that is, before about 300 BC.

(The Second Consonant Shift occurred between AD 500 and 750; it took place in the German dialects spoken in the areas away from the North Sea, particularly in the mountains of central Europe. The Second Consonant Shift is one of the primary developments that differentiate High and Low German dialects today. The Second Shift is not shown in the chart.)

Verner's law, formulated by the Danish scholar Karl Verner and published in 1875, explains some apparent exceptions to the First Consonant Shift. These "exceptions" are indicated by the rising curved lines. In *some* words the voiceless fricatives (which had developed from Indo-European /p t k/) became voiced fricatives and thus appear to be grouped with sounds that began as voiced aspirated stops (see 90–91 of Pyles and Algeo for a more complete explanation).

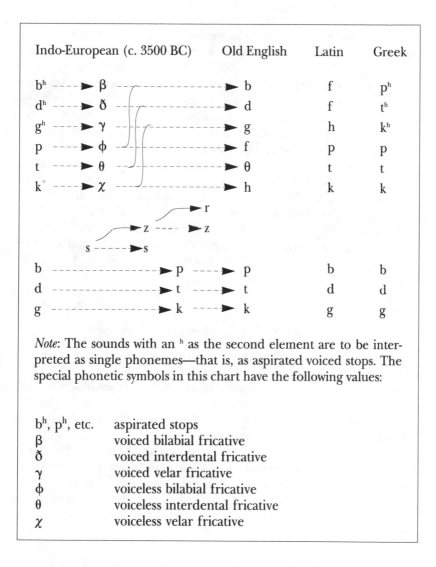

Indo-European (c. 3500 BC)		Old English	Latin	Greek
bʰ ----► β	----►	b	f	pʰ
dʰ ----► ð	----►	d	f	tʰ
gʰ ----► γ	----►	g	h	kʰ
p ----► ɸ	----►	f	p	p
t ----► θ	----►	θ	t	t
k ----► χ	----►	h	k	k
	►r			
	z ---- ►z			
s -----►s				
b --------------► p	----► p		b	b
d --------------► t	----► t		d	d
g --------------► k	----► k		g	g

Note: The sounds with an ʰ as the second element are to be interpreted as single phonemes—that is, as aspirated voiced stops. The special phonetic symbols in this chart have the following values:

bʰ, pʰ, etc.	aspirated stops
β	voiced bilabial fricative
ð	voiced interdental fricative
γ	voiced velar fricative
ɸ	voiceless bilabial fricative
θ	voiceless interdental fricative
χ	voiceless velar fricative

Verner found that the "exceptions" were not exceptions; they all occurred in Indo-European words in which the stress had shifted from the syllable following the stop to the syllable preceding it, and apparently the consonants became voiced at some stage of this shift in syllable stress. Thus the "exceptions" followed a systematic linguistic rule. Indo-European had an /s/ phoneme but no /z/; however, /s/ also became voiced under the same conditions that affected the other voiceless fricatives. The [z] that had developed from /s/ then rhotacized (became an r-like sound) in some words; this rhotacization is also considered part of Verner's law, but not of Grimm's law.

During Middle and early Modern English, thousands of words were borrowed from Latin and Greek. These words, of course, were not Germanic, so Grimm's law does not apply to them. When the French or Greek borrowing has a consonant that is different from the Indo-European source, the difference is attributable to linguistic changes in the Italic and Hellenic language families and not to Grimm's law. The sounds listed for Latin and Greek represent those of Classical times—approximately 500 BC to AD 300 for Greek, and 200 BC to AD 600 for Latin. There were also later developments in the Romance languages and in Modern Greek, as we can see in the pronunciations [s] and [k] for spelled c in the semantically related Latin and French borrowings *decade* and *decimal*. Latin did not have a dental fricative (i.e., [θ]); consequently, the Indo-European /dʰ/ became /f/ in some Latin words and /t/ in others.

Indo-European Borrowings: An Exercise

The following list was compiled from the appendix on Indo-European roots in *The American Heritage Dictionary* (1969). In many of the sets, I have listed a form in each column, but I have also inserted some blank lines for you to fill in with common, present-day words that fit the pattern. Be sure to look at the chart above to see the phonemic correspondences in Germanic, Latin, and Greek; then think of semantically related sets of contemporary words that probably are derived from the Indo-European root listed. I have filled in the correspondences that you probably would not have been able to guess. Far fewer words were borrowed from Greek than from Latinate sources, so in about 40 percent of the sets we do not have cognate Greek borrowings.

Indo-European Root	Common English Word	Latin Borrowing	Greek Borrowing
/bh/ /dh/ /gh/			
*bʰreg-	breakable	fragile	(none)
*bʰrāter	_____	friar, fraternal	(none)
*bʰel-	bloom	_____	(chloro)phyl

Indo-European Root	Common English Word	Latin Borrowing	Greek Borrowing
/bh/ /dh/ /gh/			
*dʰeu-	dust	fume	thyme
*dʰer- 'male bee'	drone	(none)	threnody
*dʰwer-	door	forum	thyroid
*dʰē-	do	fact, fashion	thesis, theme
*gʰabʰ-	give	habit	(none)
*gʰer-	garden, yard	_____	chorus (?)
*gʰend-, *gʰed-	get	apprehend	(none)
*wegʰ- 'to go'	weigh	vehicle	(none)
/p/ /t/ /k/			
*pleus-	fleece	plume	(none)
*pəter	_____	paternal	patriarch, patriot
*pūr-	fire	pure	pyrotechnic
*kaput OE heofod	_____	capital	(none)
*trei-	_____	trio	triad
*teuə-, teu- 'to swell'	thumb, thigh	tuber, tumor	tomb
*ten- 'to stretch'	_____	tenuous, tense	hypotenuse
*kannabis	_____	(none)	cannibis
*ker-	horn	coronet	carrot
*kerd-	_____	cordial, courage	cardiac
*keu-	heap	cup	cube
*kmtom	_____	_____	hecatomb, hectare
/b/ /d/ /g/			
*bak-	peg	bacillus	(none)
*beu-	pocket, poke, puff	bowl; boil (v.)	bubo

Indo-European Root	Common English Word	Latin Borrowing	Greek Borrowing
/b/ /d/ /g/			
*lep-	lip	——	(none)
*lep-	lap (of a garment)	labor	lobe
*dwō-	——	——	dichotomy
*deru- 'solid'	tree	durable	dryad 'wood nymph'
*dent-	tooth	——	orthodontist
*dekm-	——	decimal, decade	(none)
*da- 'to divide'	tide ('time')	(none)	democracy
*sed-	sit	sediment	(none)
*treud-	threat	intrude	(none)
*wed	water	undulate	(none)
*ad-	at	address	(none)
*streig-	strike	stringent	(none)
*weg-	wake	vigor	(none)
*werg-	work, wright	(none)	erg, energy, organ
*wrek-	wreak	urge	(none)
*yeug-	yoke	jugular	zygote
*gel-	club, clod	globe	gluteus
*gel-	cold, chill	glacial, gelatin	(none)
*genə-, gen-	kin, king	genus, generate	genealogy
*gwen- 'woman'	——	(none)	gynecology, polygamy

Verner's Law

*pəter	OE fæder	paternal	patriot
*bhrater	OE brodor	fraternal	
*uper	German: über	super	hyper
*deuk- 'to lead'	tug, tow	duke, conduct	
*pent- 'to tread'	find		peripatetic

Indo-European Root	Common English Word	Latin Borrowing	Greek Borrowing
	Verner's Law		
*leu-	OE leosan → forlorn		
*wes-	were		
*deus- 'animal'	deer		

[Answers, in order of occurrence: brother, flower, horticulture, father, head, three, thin, hemp, heart, century, hundred, labial, two, dual or double, dentist, ten, queen.]

Standard Language
and Questions
of Usage

∽

Standard English and the Study of Variation: "It All Be Done for a Purpose"

James H. Sledd, University of Texas, Austin

⌒⌒⌒

IF ENGLISH, rightly or wrongly, is to remain preeminent among world languages, it has to be various. It exists in the minds of its multifarious users, and its varieties mark differences among people and their multifarious purposes. Variation in English remains, and has indeed increased, despite centuries of effort to stamp it out. Its longevity results from its utility.

Yet variation is variation *from*: one thing, or one guise of a thing, varies from another. Variation in English is most often conceived and described as variation from some recognized standard, some variety of the language against which other varieties are measured. Without such a standard, the language would remain a language but not a world language. Worldwide communication presupposes a medium known everywhere.

Accordingly, the standard and nonstandard varieties of English are best studied together. Neither could exist without the other, and the tool and weapon of variation is not to be understood without some understanding of the measure by which it is judged.

For a number of years, a course with the title Standard English: Its Nature, History, and Social Functions has been taught at the University of Texas, Austin. The topical divisions of the course in one of its variations have been the nature of standard languages in general and of Standard English in particular; the history of Standard English; the present extent of variation in English, ranging from pidgins and creoles to Standard English with a posh accent ("BBC English"); and attitudes and issues, where subtopics can vary with current debates and concerns, such as the present attempts to make English the one official language of the United States. Though studies in these wide areas have multiplied recently, there is no single usable textbook, and instructors have put together their own anthologies of essays and lists of relevant though individually inadequate books and monographs. A typical procedure is for the whole class to read and discuss the essays, while individual members report on one or more of the books and lead the ensuing discussions.

So huge a subject can obviously get no profound or thorough treatment in a single course, but even under superficial treatment, the material rouses strong interest and prompts energetic debate (a result not normally attained when the literary student is led to the water of linguistics).

One device for avoiding the confusion of instant controversy is to begin with the seemingly innocuous history and to leave the attempt at defining Standard English until after the discussion both of history and of present variation. An instructor who so wished could even limit the course to history, with the other topics being developed in passing, as the history suggests. The account of standard Old English, for example, almost demands comparison and contrast with the modern standard a thousand years later.

Even so, the historically minded instructor must pick and choose from an enormous body of material: the emergence of standard written Old English toward the year 1000; its destruction in the aftermath of the Norman Conquest; the reemergence of a standard in the fifteenth century, when a Standard Scots also existed in Scotland; the spread of Standard English among the privileged in all parts of England, and the imposition of English on the Celtic periphery—Scotland, Ireland, and Wales; the contrasting decline of Standard Scots when it was no longer supported by an independent center of national power; the codification of the forms of privileged English, and the elaboration of its functions, from Geoffrey Chaucer to Samuel Johnson, whose costly *Dictionary* was immediately recognized, in the 1750s, as the English equivalent of the dictionaries of the language academies in France and Italy; the socioeconomic revolution that drastically changed Johnson's world and consequently changed the standard and nonstandard varieties of English; the rise of the British Empire, the spread of English right round the globe, and the consequent development of new national and regional standards for the language; the social turmoil attendant on two world wars, including the collapse of empires and the changed place of English in newly independent nations of Asia and Africa; the increasing salience of languages other than English in Britain and the United States, partly as a result of unprecedented movements of people; the worldwide struggle for control of revolutionary means of communication since World War II; and so on. A prudent historian might choose to begin the account with Johnson and the American Revolution, or even with World War I. What is essential is that the language should always be seen in relation to its users and uses and that both teacher and students should avoid the customary but disabling pretense of political neutrality.

The nature of the modern standard and its crucial social functions, however, are of primary concern, both in themselves and certainly in the present sketch. There is reasonable skepticism, of course, concerning the very existence of any variety of English that might be called "the modern standard." English is indeed a world language; and its dominant varieties in England and the United States, though they have been called the language's two main streams, have lost much of their authority elsewhere, especially in Asia and Africa. Even in the British Isles, in North America, and in Australia, "the tongue that Shakespeare spake" is in contact with many languages that Shakespeare never heard spoken. Teachers of English in London, for example, must deal not only with nonstandard indigenous varieties but with Caribbean creoles and with the English of children whose other languages include Arabic, Bengali, Cantonese, Turkish, Urdu, Yoruba, and dozens more—including languages whose established scripts bear no perceptible resemblance to the Roman alphabet. No course in Standard English can ignore such complexities or the voices of linguists who extend the correct denial that there is any standard for pronunciation to the total denial of any single standard for grammar, vocabulary, or any other component of the language.

It remains true that fundamental structural similarities justify the one name *English* for a multitude of varieties. Privileged speakers of English everywhere (education being one of their privileges) understand one another with no great difficulty and generally, though not always, agree in accepting or rejecting a given expression as standard, nonstandard, or debatable. Differences among the privileged are most obvious in pronunciation and vocabulary, much smaller in grammar, trickiest perhaps in areas where cultural differences cause different uses of shared linguistic forms and processes. Within the United States, though there is no national standard of pronunciation, there is a national standard for vocabulary and grammar, and there are regional pronunciation standards that are easily understood by educated people all over the world. In its written form, the American standard matches the global standard, a variety of English written by the privileged minority from London to Delhi and from Chicago to Singapore.

Standardization in what is called an advanced society changes a language. The standardized variety comes to be thought of as *the* language and sets the usual direction of accommodation, the process by which users of one variety may modify it in dealing with users of others. In the standardized variety, the potentialities of the language are most fully realized by conscious cultivation and by use as the linguistic vehicle of all the activities that the dominant choose to regulate—science, technology, government, law, and the like. For this wide range of uses, special subvarieties of the standard are developed, so that, for example, lawyers, doctors, and literary critics all have their specialized ways of talking and writing. Flexibility is therefore necessary in a standardized variety. It must meet the new demands that social change makes on it, but it must also be relatively stable—unlike (say) student slang, which students value precisely because persons beyond their years find it changed beyond comprehension.

The forces of linguistic regulation that create and govern the standardized variety of a language are familiar. In the beginning, when no variety of language has been standardized, a choice has to be made. The chosen variety is often that of a small community, an already recognized and powerful elite in a center of economic, administrative, and cultural power such as London has long been for England. It is also the powerful who control the elaboration and codification of the variety chosen for standardization. Schoolchildren, who are familiar with linguistic variation from at latest the moment when their contacts extend beyond their families, quickly learn at school that there is one variety that ranks higher than others. It is the variety that teachers teach and try to use in their teaching, the variety used and described in grammars and dictionaries, which the citizenry looks upon as law, though grammarians and lexicographers may insist that they are only describing, not prescribing. Later, young adults discover that their employers and professional colleagues make their own linguistic prescriptions, and persons of all ages undergo linguistic regulation of one kind or another by government, the mass media, and scientific, technological, and literary publications. It is essential to recognize that the regulatory institutions are parts of the established power structure. Seekers after upward mobility submit themselves most particularly to the demands of the *economically* powerful.

Not everyone, however, is submissive before the language-regulators. When the regulators agree for a long time to privilege the same linguistic forms, the standardized variety may get so deeply entrenched that it will survive decolonization or political revolution, but standard languages and even their definition and description are arenas of struggle and class conflict. A familiar example is the long debate over the common assertion by American linguists that all languages and all varieties of them are equal in complexity and value. Whatever else it may be, that assertion is a political manifesto, and characteristic of a nation where not everyone is happy with the dominance of the established powers.

Such conflict, and the demands of life itself in an advanced society, guarantee that linguistic varieties other than the established standard will survive and sometimes multiply. Among the privileged, the relatively slight variations within the highly standardized English of international communication may be cherished as marks of national identity. Singaporean officials, when they go abroad, may still want to be recognizably Singaporean in their speech, and privileged Sinhalese in Sri Lanka may refuse to distinguish /v/ and /w/ because compatriots whom they respect do not make the distinction.

For communication among the privileged within a nation, forms that would not be used internationally may be accepted and approved. Once one leaves the domain of the privileged at the apex of the socioeconomic cone, variation in English widens much further. The attempts of the upwardly anguished to master the standardized variety often leave them with what has been called a modified standard, and (especially among young males) nonstandard varieties exert their own attraction. The ability to move up and down the scale of linguistic power and prestige may itself confer social advantage. An educated West African may be able to speak a Pidgin English, and a master of Standard Caribbean English in Jamaica may also command a version of Jamaican Creole.

The vast range of nonstandard varieties of English survives and maybe grows for the simple reason already given: it is useful. That is the truth behind the political assertion that all languages and all their varieties are equal. They are equal in this—that no language and no variety would long survive if it did not serve some purposes of some people better than any other language or variety serves them. A standardized English for international use survives and is useful. Somewhat different national standards have been developed for use within nations, including nations of Asia and Africa that rightly reject the attempted imposition of a British or American standard. Pidgins and creoles, and all the varieties between them and the standards, have their uses too. The user's problem is the problem of purposeful choice. The problem of the teacher, who will usually teach some standard variety of English, is the problem of motives, of methods, and of policy toward blameless students who either cannot or will not learn and use that standard variety.

The discussion has now plainly moved from the nature and history of Standard English variation to the intensely controversial area of attitudes and issues, and a number of statements have been made that would provoke debate among teachers and among students. Teachers of the course that has here been described can easily (and often rightly) reduce their part in the conduct of a class to that of prompter, guide, and referee. English as official language, the Black English Vernacular, English Hispanicized, the language used and demanded in standardized testing, the proclamations of linguistic crisis when test results displease the testers, the English used by, to, and about women—all these and many other significantly debatable issues prompt serious thought and argument.

The argument can be informed by students' and teachers' own research, for which material is all around them, and by reading in a literature so vast that no one can master it. The twenty following books seem particularly useful to one teacher of the course. They include bibliographies that may be exhausting but cannot be exhaustive. Other teachers would choose quite differently—as they should.

Suggested Reading

Since the creation, study, and teaching of standard languages are inevitably political activities, the literature on Standard English is also inevitably political and conflictual.

Conflict is perhaps least virulent (or least obvious) in historical works, such as the old-fashioned but scholarly *A History of the English Language*, by Albert C. Baugh and Thomas Cable; the aging but still useful essays by Berndt, McIntosh, Samuels, and Dobson in Roger Lass's *Approaches to English Historical Linguistics*; and Aldo Scaglione's more wide-ranging yet uneven collection *The Emergence of National Languages*. Political conviction is visible, however, though not obtrusive, even in a less accessible scholarly work like the important *Anthology of Chancery English*, where John H. Fisher and colleagues edit early documents in what Fisher considers "an artificial written standard independent of spoken dialects."

The extent of conflict over any linguistic standard is related to the range of variation from that standard. The first chapter in *A Comprehensive Grammar of the English Language*, by Randolph Quirk and colleagues, is a good introduction to varieties of contemporary English. The linguistic situation in the United States is described in *Language in the USA*, edited by Charles A. Ferguson and Shirley Brice Heath. The companion volume *Language in the British Isles* (edited by Peter Trudgill) is generally superior to the American work but often quite technical. The past thirty years have also seen a multitude of studies of English worldwide: the periodical of that name, *English World-Wide: A Journal of Varieties of English*, published twice a year since 1980; the pioneer volume *English as a World Language*, edited by Richard W. Bailey and Manfred Görlach; numerous works written and edited by Braj B. Kachru, including *The Alchemy of English* (on "nonnative" varieties), *The Indianization of English*, and *The Other Tongue: English across Cultures*; Wolfgang Viereck and Wolf-Dietrich Bald's collection *English in Contact with Other Languages*, in which almost thirty essays consider the influence of English on other languages in Europe, Asia, Africa, and Oceania; and so forth.

Attempts to characterize standard languages in general and Standard English in particular are likely to bring political conflict more clearly into view. The merest sampling of the enormous international literature might include Renate Bartsch, *Sprachnormen: Theory and Praxis* (in Longman's Linguistic Library as *Norms of Languages: Theoretical and Practical Aspects*); *La norme linguistique,* edited by Édith Bédard and Jacques Maurais; and Einar Haugen, *The Ecology of Language,* a collection of well-worn essays which have worn well.

The literature of attitudes and issues involves all three of the preceding topics—history, the extent of variation, the nature of standard languages—and reveals them clearly as controversial. A few of many titles are Noëlle Bisseret, *Education, Class Language and Ideology*; Robert L. Cooper, *Language Planning and Social Change*; Florian Coulmas, *Language Adaptation* (esp. the last chapter, "Democracy and the Crisis of Normative Linguistics") and *Sprache und Staat: Studien zu Sprachplanung and Sprachpolitik*; Tony Crowley, *Standard English and the Politics of Language*; Jacques Maurais, *La crise des langues*; and Jacob Mey, *Whose Language: A Study in Linguistic Pragmatics.* Mey asks the oft-evaded but ultimately inescapable question "What can linguist(ic)s *do for society?*" (4).

In the years between the composition of this essay and its publication, the relevant bibliography has expanded vigorously. It has not been possible to revise the essay itself, but at least a few of the new books should be mentioned. The second edition of James Milroy and Leslie Milroy's *Authority in Language* is an accessible introduction, with a substantial bibliography. For the new series *Oxford Studies in Sociolinguistics,* Tim William Machan and Charles T. Scott have edited *English in Its Social Contexts: Essays in Historical Sociolinguistics.* Some ideas of a possible exciting future may be found in the collection of essays edited by Coulmas in 1990, *A Language Policy for the European Community: Prospects and Quandaries.*

From Standard Latin to Standard English

Mark Amsler, University of Delaware

⤬

MANY of our ideas about "standard language," "standardization," and "language variation" are based on a view of classical Latin as a single language form corrupted or altered by the dissolution of the Roman republic, or by the decentralization of the Roman Empire, or by the barbarous attempts of non-Romans to speak or write a language not their own, or by the loss of inflections and the collapse of a precise case system into a two-case system (nominative and oblique). Those who maintain this view often believe that classical Latin, the *standard* form, gave way under the pressure of less-educated speakers to Vulgar Latin, which evolved into the Romance vernaculars; classical Latin was then recovered by the Renaissance humanists from the swamp of Vulgar and Medieval Latin. English teachers have used this exemplary and nostalgic narrative to promote official schooling as the guardian of Standard English and to prescribe English usage on the model of what they regard as regular, precise, and elegant classical Latin.

But recent histories of linguistics, drawing on the detailed research of classical philology, present a different narrative of Latin grammar. As English teachers, we can learn a great deal from seeing how earlier Greek and Roman grammarians described and analyzed their own language. Moreover, through a historical case-study approach, we can discover how other English grammarians and linguists have defined a standard language or national tradition using the supposed uniformity of classical Latin as a norm. Edward Finegan's *Attitudes toward English Usage: The History of a War of Words* provides a convenient starting point for these discussions.

Although the hegemony of classical Latin as the model for a standard language has a long history in the West, that history is largely invisible to our students. I try to help my students make that history part of their knowledge about linguistics and language. For example, Joseph Priestley (1733–1804) wrote a number of linguistic texts, including *A Course of Lectures on the Theory of Language and Universal Grammar*, in which he argued that usage and custom were the only acceptable criteria for determining language standards at a given time and that grammars of modern languages should not be based on Latin models. However, Priestley's argument for usage is partially vitiated by his belief that Latin was a uniform language in the classical world. He claimed that, unlike Greek, which was a set of competing dialects used in independent city states, Latin was the language of a unified state with one written language and no dialects: "The *Romans*, having one seat of power and of arts, allowed of no dialects; which makes their language the more uniform and regular, and the more easy to be learned" (280). Priestley is referring only to written Latin and only at a certain time, but his point is more general: the strong centralized government with a single educational system standardized the proper language people used and fostered "perfect communication" (132–33). He further claimed that written language fixed the hurly-burly of spoken varieties and became the arbiter of the official standard language in both speech and writing. But when the Roman imperial government was diffused and when non-Romans attempted to speak and write Latin, classical Latin sank into Vulgar Latin and eventually evolved into the Romance vernaculars. Although he asserted that political freedom and popular control over language were interrelated, Priestley believed there was only one standard Latin from 50 BC to AD 1200, all other varieties being inferior and derivative.

Priestley's narrative of classical Latin's fall from grace is neither unique nor eccentric. Rather, such a view has been at the center of debates about standard versus nonstandard language since the Renaissance humanists promoted classical Latin as an intellectual and cultural norm. Many Renaissance scholars revolted against what they considered barbarous medieval Latin and substituted literary classical Latin as the educational standard. This model of a standard language has been applied to English in order to, in William Whitney's words, "schoolmaster the language" (qtd. in Baron 120), or to keep English from "degenerating" as its community (or communities) of speakers has changed, or to authorize the preservation of a national cultural literacy (Hirsch). Renaissance grammarians revised English spelling to foreground connections between Latin and English (e.g., *dubito > dou[b]t*). In the eighteenth century, writers such as Bishop Robert Lowth and V. J. Peyton were more prescriptive than Priestley and claimed that English grammar should be regulated by the received categories of Latin grammatical description, in that classical Latin was the exemplar for universal grammar. In the early nineteenth century, Samuel Kirkham and others continued this line of argument and corrected "false" English syntax by parsing sentences according to classical Latin paradigms; his *English Grammar, in Familiar Lectures* went through more than ten editions before 1860. It is safe to say that, until 1960, most of the grammatical categories used to describe English were drawn from those used by fourth-century Roman grammarians (see Michael).

If our students are often unaware of how Standard Latin has been used to describe Standard English, they are equally unaware of the many dissenters from the view of Standard English based on the presumed uniformity of Latin. One of the more ingenious dissenters was James Gilchrist (1783–1835), who, in *Reason, the True Arbiter of Language; Custom a Tyrant*, argued that English, a primitive language (along with Hebrew and Gothic), had become corrupted and made redundant and luxurious by changes prompted by later Latinate ideas of inflection. Other dissenters were more convincing. Besides Priestley, there was Noah Webster (1758–1843). Early in his career, Webster had labeled "Who should I see but my old friend?" as incorrect (*Grammatical Institute* 76). But five years later he observed: " '*Who* do you speak to?' '*Who* did he marry?' are challenged as bad English; but *Whom* did you speak to? was never used in speaking, as I can find, and if so, is hardly English at all" (*Dissertations* 286). Regarding his *whom* example, Webster describes the objective case form as a corruption introduced by "some Latin student" suspecting that *who* was "bad English, because not agreeable to the Latin rules" (287). Webster was by no means consistent in his condemnation of Latin-regulated English, and he very much wanted to produce a uniform Standard American English. Nonetheless, throughout his career, resisting attempts to defer to British English as a standard, he privileged contemporary usage, as well as levels and varieties of appropriateness, to describe American speech.

Reverence for classical Latin has underwritten a number of proscriptions and prescriptions for proper English usage: Standard English does not split the infinitive construction with an adverb nor use the double negative; proper English usage differentiates between *shall* and *will*; Standard English uses *who* for the subject case but *whom* for the object case (analogous with Latin oblique inflections); proper English usage prefers the ablative absolute construction *Having reached the shore*, . . . to *After having reached the shore*, . . . or *After reaching the shore*, . . . (Fries, "Periphrastic" and "Rules"). But many of these prescriptions, supposedly based on the greater rigor of Latin grammar, actually reveal how a distorted idea of Standard Latin has made invisible to our students and many others the historical development and the social stratification of elite and common forms of English. Students can learn a great deal by examining how language rules have been generated. For example, in 1640, John Wallis made his own rule about *shall* and *will*, with no reference to Latin:

> It is difficult for foreigners to know when to use the first form [*shall*] and when the second [*will*] (we do not use them both interchangeably), and no other description that I have seen has given any rules for guidance, so I thought I ought to give some. . . . In the first person *shall* simply indicates a predication, whereas *will* is used for promising or threatening. In the second and third persons *shall* is used for promising

or threatening, and *will* is simply for predication. (339; I have modified Kemp's translation.)

And surely, contra Webster, we can see some connection between the Old English interrogative pronoun *hwā* (dat. *hwǣm*) and the Modern English *whom*.

Nevertheless, the latinizing of English continues. In 1966, Wilson Follett, echoing others, underscored the "value" of English grammar based on the idea of a uniform Standard Latin:

> Those [linguists and educators] who speak so harshly against Latin do not show much familiarity with it, whereas few of those who have even a tincture of Latin deny that it throws light on both the structural and stylistic features of English. . . . For the analytic method of grammar appears all the more clearly in a language where inflections show the function of the word in the sentence, and where meaning is not so immediate as to make the form negligible. If there exists a better pedagogic device than Latin for showing how the Western languages work, it has not yet been found. (26)

For Follett, losing case marking is like unbuttoning one's shirt in public or letting one's literacy slip. Standard Latin, Follett implies, can keep Standard English dressed right.

Teachers of linguistics have several possible ways to deal with the use of Standard Latin to structure Standard English. One way is to endorse the relation, which few linguists today wish to do, though our students are not always sure why. Another is to dismiss the relation outright and then move on to "real" linguistics. This second approach, while pedagogically efficient from the teacher's standpoint, keeps students isolated from the history of linguistics and hence from the debate that the teacher's dismissal of Standard Latin as a model for Standard English is a part of. I have used a third approach in my classes. I ask students to think carefully not only about how Priestley, Webster, and others have described the relation between Latin and English but also about how Roman and humanist grammarians described and explained Latin as a living language. We can learn a great deal about how linguistics as a discourse has developed by trying to understand how Roman grammarians accounted for their own language. Through a historical case-study approach, we can also compare the Roman and humanist debates about standard language with contemporary debates about Standard English. The attitudes of Roman grammarians toward Latin raise questions regarding the role of schooling in regulating varieties of usage within a speech community, the relation of language change and language variation, the structures of diglossia and bilingualism in language contact, language attitudes and beliefs, and the correlations between language varieties and institutions, occupations, vocations, and subgroups.

Roman imperial grammarians present interesting accounts of change and variation in the Latin language from the second through the sixth centuries AD based on regional, historical, or educational factors (see surveys in Robins; Holtz). The literate bias of these grammarians was inevitable given the role of the *grammaticus* as the purveyor of literacy and elite speaking in the Roman schools (Bonner; Kaster). But the imperial grammarians did not uniformly stigmatize contemporary usage, nor did they always restrict current usage to the literary corpus defined by earlier *auctores*. Priscian, in his copious *Institutiones grammaticae*, expressly argues *against* the view that only the forms and constructions used by canonical writers are acceptable or standard in contemporary usage (see, e.g., Keil 2: 442). Similarly, Servius (Rome, fourth century AD), in his highly influential commentary on Vergil's *Aeneid*, regularly teaches contemporary Standard Latin to native speakers by pointing out the differences between Vergil's lexicon and syntax and acceptable contemporary usage.

Many imperial grammarians differentiated orthography and spelling from pronunciation, particularly in terms of older written forms and contemporary spoken forms. For instance, Velius Longus (second century AD) writes: "More refined speakers [*elegantiores*] say *vementem* and *reprendit*. . . . We say *prendo* ('grasp'), not *prehendo*" (*De orthographia*, in Keil 7: 68). Velius's remarks stand as counterevidence to the assumption that Latin orthography is always in direct correlation to Latin pronunciation. On word-final *m*, he writes, "We have to admit that [the word] is written one way and pronounced another" (Keil 7: 54). Velius's text presents contrary sociolinguistic approaches to language variation. In the first passage, he stigmatizes intervocalic aspiration (*vehementem, reprehendit, prehendo*) in favor of syncopated forms, even though *prehendo* and *prendo* exist side by side in written texts from Plautus to Apuleius. (Curiously, many modern Latin dictionaries do just the opposite and list *prendo* as an alternate form, or refer the reader to *prehendo*.) But in the second passage, Velius distinguishes written forms from spoken forms without stigmatizing either one or placing them in a normative hierarchy. The postmedieval distinction between classical and Vulgar Latin as two discrete spoken or written versions is based on one of two assumptions: either that in the later empire elite ("correct") classical Latin existed alongside less prestigious ("popular") Vulgar Latin in a diglossic situation (cf. Ferguson; Lloyd) or that Vulgar Latin was an ungrammatical version of Standard Latin. Neither assumption can be fully supported.

Students can discover much about the concept of regional and institutional dialects by looking at how different Standard Latins evolved or were described in various regions or linguistic communities. Irish Latin was not a corruption of a classical or more standard continental Latin but a version of Latin as a second language whose sound and spelling system and morphology were partly influenced by Old Irish and Old English. In the seventh century, Isidore of Seville, archbishop and intellectual leader of the Spanish episcopal see, described the four stages of the historical development of Latin as "Ancient, Latin, Roman, and Mixed" (9.1.6–8). Isidore characterizes the language of the Roman republic and the early empire as *Romana* while he refers to his own Latin as *Mixta* (see Wright). He associates the latter variation with the expansion of the Roman Empire and the corruption of the proper nature of words by solecisms and barbarisms ("integritatem verbi per soloe-cismos et barbarismos"). Sociolinguists are well acquainted with the practice of stigmatizing foreigners as those who corrupt (*corrumpens*) the integrity of a linguistic system by using the language imperfectly according to native standards (e.g., Gumperz; Kachru, *Alchemy*). But what did Isidore mean by "corrupting"? Did Isidore really believe that his own language was an inferior variant of classical Latin? Or did he distinguish between vernacular speech and an elite Latin that conformed more closely to classical Latin as described in imperial grammars and that was preserved in monastic culture? Recent work on imperial and early medieval Latin indicates that the second possibility (that there were two linguistic norms, Latin and several kinds of Romance, in seventh-century Europe) was probably not the case. The first possibility, that Isidore stigmatized his own language in favor of an antique school Latin, is even less likely, though he may have been distinguishing a spoken standard from a written one. Since *corrumpo* can never have a positive value, Isidore's description of the stages of Latin is ill fitted to the received grammatical metalanguage whereby a language is presumed to derive or decline from a pure original form.

The case of Isidore's description of language development can help students of English understand the relation between linguistic categories and language attitudes. Students often encounter two arguments based loosely on a nonhistorical, nondevelopmental view of Standard English or Standard Latin: that Black English Vernacular is not a dialect at all but an impoverished version of Standard English and that an elite, learned dialect must necessarily be intellectually superior to a less prestigious or "everyday" ("vulgar") dialect. These are politically and emotionally controversial beliefs in English-language studies. But sometimes historical case studies and cultural distance let us focus on sociolinguistic presuppositions and reflect on analogous arguments at the present time in a mediated way. Students can, one hopes, use such case studies to conceptualize and theorize the question of standard language and language varieties and to reflect on how language attitudes, including their own, emerge.

Because Renaissance humanism has strongly influenced our ideas about Standard Latin and standard vernaculars, I also introduce students to some of the texts assembled by Mirko Tavoni from the fifteenth-century Italian humanists' debates over the question of what language the ancient Romans spoke. The debate was carried on by some of the leading intellectuals of the time. One side argued that "a kind of *vulgaris sermo* was characteristic of the *illiterati*, and that it must have been sharply distinct from the *litteratus sermo* as the vernacular of their own times was distinct from the Latin of clerks and scholars." The other side claimed that in Rome's golden age, people of the lower social strata used the same language as the orators and writers: "Latin was the language of the whole society, an integrity not compromised by the obvious distinctions in lexical quality and style, depending on the different cultural levels of the various speakers" (Tavoni 237). These texts concretize for students some of the historical contexts of problematic linguistic terms (for example, *litteratus, illitteratus, vulgus*) often used in discussions of "cultural literacy" or Standard English. They also illustrate how particular groups' views on language variation can set the direction of future linguistic work. For instance, the view that ancient Rome was essentially diglossic, with the elites using one language and the common people another, was a version of the humanists' self-imposed separation from other ordinary citizens by virtue of the fact that they used learned Latin while the other citizens used the vernacular. The humanists' debate also reveals how discussions of elite or standard language vary depending on the status the grammarian or linguist accords to ordinary people and common speech.

In the humanist linguistic tradition, classical Latin was often understood as a uniform language "without dialects" (Priestley) whose usage was regulated by a community of educated, cultured, elite speakers and writers. Late Latin and early medieval grammatical writings present a different view, in which antique usage did not necessarily override contemporary usage and in which geographical and institutional variation accounted for different Latin standards. The humanists rewrote the linguistic past with a particular reformist educational program in mind. If we model our debates about Standard English on a presumed uniform Standard classical Latin, we naively fall into the view of those fifteenth-century humanists sitting in the antechambers of the pope, for whom standard usage was elite, educated usage as described by the institutional authority of schooling and a corpus of canonical texts. But through historical case studies of language variation, we can uncover some deep-seated and misleading assumptions about language standardization. By comparing notions of standard language in Latin and English, teachers and students can consider standardization as an activity with a history and as operating across languages—that is, as a social construction rather than an essential linguistic feature. If so, then teaching about language variation and varieties of English will have been partly successful, and English teachers can come down from the antechambers to listen to the voices in the street.

Attitudes toward Language Variation

Donald M. Lance, University of Missouri, Columbia

SINCE 1973, I have regularly taught a course entitled Regional and Social Dialects of American English. Of the many activities I have assigned to students, those that seem to have been most valuable require the students to investigate their own and others' attitudes toward various aspects of language use. Some of the assignments are interview-research projects; others are conducted within the classroom. This article presents guidelines for three of these activities. I always offer the students a variety of term projects from which to choose, but I will include here only those that are substantially different from projects described in other articles in this volume.

In classes at all levels of education, students are often exposed to teacher attitudes that conflict with what dialectologists know about the nature of language variation. Paramount in the literacy industry is the persistent, lingering notion of a single standard that either presently exists or can come into being if students will learn what they are taught in English and speech classes. Composition handbooks and basal readers depend on the continued institutionalized belief in the notion of a single standard, and most popularizers of language study treat it as a given. Because the idea of "standard" generally applies to a finite—and relatively small—set of linguistic items, it is not difficult for teachers to focus on the troublesome "errors" about which they are most concerned. When students investigate actual use of language by their peers and themselves, they are surprised by the diversity in what people tell them about language and in what they discover about their own attitudes toward the item included in debates about what is "correct." Students are often either amused or disturbed to find that they are oblivious to heated disputes over certain "standard" or "nonstandard" usages (e.g., *hopefully*), that many problematic items are too difficult to remember or even to explain, and that there is considerable disagreement about several items that they have always regarded as "standard" or "nonstandard." They want to know what can be done to rectify the situation—"We *must* have standards in order to be understood!" They persist in repeating this dictum even though their research reveals surprisingly few instances of a lack of understanding resulting from the (mis)use of the questioned forms.

In their research, students may support and supplement their investigation by consulting such books as Edward Finegan's history of usage in England and America since 1500 and Dennis Baron's analysis of the development of standard language in America. They can find additional resources in the bibliographies of these two publications—including "classic" works such as those of George Krapp, Otto Jespersen, John S. Kenyon, Charles Fries, and others. Overviews of dialect study in Europe and America are available in W. N. Francis and Lawrence M. Davis. One of the most useful resources for both teachers and students is the anthology *A Pluralistic Nation: The Language Issue in the United States*, edited by Margaret A. Lourie and Nancy Faires Conklin; particularly useful for teachers are the eight appendixes.

Questionnaire: Attitudes toward Speech

Lourie and Conklin include in their book a linguistic attitude questionnaire (427–28), which the authors adapted from William Labov's *Social Stratification of English in New York City* (600). I give my students dittoed copies of the questionnaire and ask them to administer it to a few people and then write an essay of six to eight pages summarizing their findings and generalizing on the experience. I also distribute copies of a personal data sheet much like those included in other articles in this volume. Below are the instructions and the questionnaire for the assignment. Questions 1–9 and 11 are virtually the same as the ten items in Lourie and Conklin's questionnaire, with some minor or sometimes major changes in wording; I have added items 10 and 12 to their list because students find that these questions often elicit information that is helpful in analyzing other data from the questionnaire.

For this assignment I do not insist on a precise definition of "speech," because most of the undergraduates in the class have not studied much linguistics. Lourie and Conklin are not specific about what they mean by the term, nor are my students, but the exercise works well nevertheless. For a term paper or thesis by a graduate student, I would require much more rigor in determining the variables being investigated. Often, in class discussions following this exercise, students report that the respondents or the investigators themselves have had difficulty deciding exactly what is meant by "speech" in the questionnaire; I use these opportunities to discuss how vague and misleading popular definitions of linguistic terms are.

Attitudes toward Speech

Instructions: Administer the linguistic attitude questionnaire to at least three people but not more than five. There are no restrictions on the type of person to select, but you should have an explainable reason for choosing your interviewees. The interview must be conducted in person so that you can catch nuances of attitude that cannot be detected unless you are present when the respondent attempts to answer the questions. If possible, you should tape-record the interview to make sure you get the small details that you cannot write down in brief notes. You must get permission to make the recording; do not use a concealed microphone. Conduct the interview orally rather than in writing so that you will have spontaneous answers rather than a combination of spontaneous responses and afterthoughts.

Give the interviewee a reason for the interview—for example, that you are collecting the information for a term paper in an English class; that you are currently teaching English composition (if you are a graduate TA) and need more information about students' ideas concerning language; that you are planning to teach English in the public schools and are collecting information on the effective use of language. Do not give a false reason. The reason you give will provide a frame of reference for the interviewee. The way you present your reason may depend on the type of person you have chosen to interview. There are numerous approaches that you might choose: you may give the same reason to all your interviewees, or you may express the reason slightly differently for each interview, to investigate the effects of diverse preconceived mind-sets. Give serious thought to the way you introduce the interview.

Ask each interviewee to fill out the personal data sheet. You will need this information for the analysis of the data, though some of it may not turn out to be directly relevant to your analysis.

For each of these questions, first answer the questions yourself and record the answers. Then ask the questions of others and record their answers. By answering the questions yourself, you will become familiar with the task and will develop ideas on how you want to pose the questions for others.

After you have collected the information from your subjects, write an essay of 1,200 to 2,000 words. There is no prescribed form for the essay; because you are advanced students, I assume you can write coherent essays with central theses, footnotes where necessary, and so on. What you say and how you say it will depend on the information you have.

Questionnaire

1. What do you think of your own speech?
2. Have you ever tried to change your speech? What particular features have you tried to change?
3. Have you ever taken any courses in speech? What did the teacher mention in connection with pronunciation?
4. What do you think of the speech of your home area?
5. When you have traveled or lived elsewhere, were you picked out as being from your home area? Why or why not, in your opinion?

6. Do you think people from other places like the speech of your home area? [may be varied depending on interview] Why or why not? What do they say?

7. What do you think of the speech of people from particular cities or areas of the state or country? Missourians? St. Louisans? Kansas Citians? people from the Ozarks? Chicagoans? Southerners? New Englanders? recent immigrants? [may also be varied for race, specific foreign accent, etc.]

8. Have you noticed the speech of ____, ____, and ____? How do you like the speech of each—irrespective of politics or professional position? What do you think others feel about these people's speech? Which one is more similar to your own? Whose speech is better? How so? [*For this question the interviewer should select two or three individuals such as former President Ronald Reagan, the current or a former governor of the state, former President Jimmy Carter, the head of the college or university, the mayor of the locality, the professor, any other professor at the college or university, or anyone else whose speech the interviewee is likely to know and find interesting. No more than three people should be considered in this item.*]

9. Try to remember the kind of speech you usually heard from the age of about five through fifteen. Did most of your friends talk the same way as your parents, brothers and sisters, aunts and uncles, grandparents, and others? What do you think was the main influence on your own speech?

10. When you were younger, did you have any friends of a different race or friends who spoke with a foreign or regional accent? Did you particularly notice the differences between their speech and your own at that time? What effect did their speech have on either your or other people's attitudes toward them?

11. Can you remember—either in your youth or in secondary school or now—serious arguments about the right way to say words?

12. Who do you think are more concerned about the way a person speaks—men or women? mothers or fathers? teachers or parents? employees or employers? others?

Attitude toward Pronunciation:
An Index of Linguistic Insecurity

Lourie and Conklin also include a questionnaire that can be used in an investigation of "linguistic insecurity" as it relates to the pronunciation of certain words (428–29), another activity based on Labov's 1966 study of vernacular speech in New York City (601). In my assignment I include the same forty words that they have in their questionnaire, but I have more specific questions for the students to ask of their subjects. As with the preceding activity, students soon become aware of the fuzziness of popular notions about language, but this exercise makes them want to know more about the intricacies of verbal and cultural interaction. The goal of the exercise is not to find the truth about language but to open the students' minds to the potential consequences of making hasty judgments about people based on gut reactions to hearing them speak. Students become aware that their popular notions of "speech" are an amalgam of judgments about regional, social, occupational, and ethnic "dialects" and reaction to voice quality, idiosyncratic pronunciations that reflect idiolect rather than dialect, about unanalyzed notions of "correctness," and a variety of other factors.

Lourie and Conklin's questionnaire insists on the term "correct" in regard to the pronunciations of the forty words—a term that linguists find of limited usefulness. Though I do not use the word as a technical linguistic term, I retain it in this exercise for pedagogical reasons: the students have come into the class believing strongly that each word has *one* "correct" pronunciation, and they must use this term in an activity such as this exercise to see how complex the issue of "correctness" is.

The implications of linguistic insecurity are too often overlooked in the classroom, particularly if the teacher has a high degree of personal linguistic insecurity or has worked hard at overcoming the stigma of a strong family dialect without studying dialectology. Below are my instructions to the students and the questionnaire that they are to administer. Because some of the students have not had much training in linguistics, I must keep the instructions somewhat simple; for a graduate seminar, if I used this exercise at all, I would insist that the students establish specific criteria for the exercise and use technical terminology very carefully.

Survey: Linguistic Insecurity

Lourie and Conklin call this questionnaire a "test of linguistic insecurity," which is designed to measure the discrepancy between individuals' own pronunciations and what they assume to be "correct." The alternative pronunciations used in this survey are regional variants, some of which are stigmatized and some of which are not, but all of which could be commonly used by the speaker's family and peers. Thus all the pronunciations can be considered "correct" to some degree. What counts is whether the form designated as "correct" is the same as the one designated as "what I use." The measure of insecurity is the frequency with which the informant considers one pronunciation to be "standard" but admits to using the other. Linguistic insecurity can be found in the attitudes of groups as well as individuals; it is often prevalent in speakers whose own dialect is socially stigmatized.

Instructions: Select about half the words in the list to use in your survey, choosing words whose alternates you can say convincingly. When you administer the survey, read the alternative pronunciations aloud in a natural voice, trying not to show any preference yourself. Be sure that the forms differ in only one sound. Speak slowly but naturally, pausing between words, saying each set no more than three times. Always say the words in pairs (or sets, if there are three or more alternates); do not isolate individual variants, because the test focuses on one or sometimes two phonemic contrasts in each set. Have a worksheet for each person you interview. Mark two pronunciations: the one that the informant claims to use and the one that the informant considers to be "correct." The two may be the same or different for a given interviewee. In your interaction with the informant, listen carefully for any clues that suggest differences between what the informant claims and actually does. Also note any additional comments; they might be informative when you analyze your data. If possible, you might tape-record the interview (getting permission first) so that you don't miss any subtleties in what the informant says as you discuss the items in your list.

Introduce the list by suggesting a natural setting for the pronunciations, such as "If a friend is working on a report for a history class and asks you which of these pronunciations is correct, how would you try to help the friend? You probably would need to consider both what you would say and what you think is correct." Another possible ploy would be to say, "There are a lot of words that people pronounce in different ways around here. I have a list of them and was wondering if you could tell me what you think." You should tell the informants that you are collecting the material for a report for a linguistics class (not English or speech) and that "linguistics is sort of like sociology—you know, concerned with what people actually do and say—dialects, that sort of thing."

Interview three to five individuals and write an essay of 1,200 to 2,000 words describing and commenting on the responses. Ask each informant to fill out a personal data sheet to provide background information for your report. The organization and content of your report will depend on the kind of information you collect in your survey.

Pronunciation of Individual Words: An Interview Questionnaire

Date
Name of person interviewed

Name of interviewer

[Give the following instructions:]

1. I am going to give you two or more pronunciations of each word. First I'd like you to tell me which pronunciation you normally use and then which one you consider to be "correct." You may or may not use the one that is generally considered "correct"; that's part of what I'm interested in. I want to know what you say; then I want to ask you some more questions. [Place "S" beside the transcription that the interviewee says, and place "C" beside the transcription that the interviewee says is the "correct" one. Phonetic transcriptions are provided on the worksheet; if the respondent claims to use another pronunciation, or mentions one that is not listed, transcribe it.]

2. Do most of your friends or family use pronunciations that are the same as or different from yours? Which ones are the same and which ones different? [You might need to suggest alternative pronunciations.]

3. What do we mean by "correct"? Pick several of the words and tell me why one particular pronunciation is "correct." [If necessary, list some of the words that the interviewee might discuss.]

4. If you or someone else says one thing but the other pronunciation is actually considered "correct," can you give any reasons why this might happen? What would you want your own children to say? [Ask about several specific words if the interviewee does not volunteer much information.]

The words to be pronounced are listed on a worksheet with alternative pronunciations given for the convenience of the student, as follows:

1. Joseph   a. /ǰosɪf/   b. //ǰozɪf//
2. catch   a. /kæč/   b. /kɛč/

The remainder of the words in Lourie and Conklin's list are as follows: *tomato, diapers, aunt, often, garage, humorous, vase, length, February, catsup, avenue, half, escalator, singing, Missouri, this, sure, car, greasy, roof, calm, wash, poor, house, egg, across, sock, rouge, ask, hanger, marry, get, iron, Mary, overalls, police, comparable, pecan.* Other words may be added to the list, either by the instructor or by the students.

Semantic Differential Analysis of Reactions to Tape-Recorded Speech

Labov's research in New York City in the early 1960s led a number of linguists and educators to conduct investigations on how individuals and groups respond subconsciously to various features of a person's speech. Because Labov's work coincided in time with the civil rights movement and concern for equal educational and economic opportunities for all social and ethnic groups in America, much of his colleagues' research was related to teachers' attitudes toward the language of their students. Negative attitudes can affect not only judgments of students' classwork and their potential for educational success but also their employment opportunities after they have completed (or voluntarily ended) their schooling. In 1976, Frederick Williams published a monograph summarizing such research. Shorter summaries appear in Finegan (147–57) and in Fasold (*Sociolinguistics* 147–79).

Before discussing such studies in my courses, I conduct an in-class exercise similar to a survey conducted by Gary N. Underwood in the 1970s. I usually indicate on the syllabus that there will be an important in-class activity, but I give no details about the exercise lest the students come to class with preconceived ideas. At the beginning of class, I hand out the worksheets described below and then have the students listen to a tape of eighteen speakers reading a passage used for the phonograph recording *Americans Speaking*. The tape consists of the six readings from that record and twelve others recorded on our campus in 1973; unfortunately, we do not have specific city or county locations for each speaker or information about how long the speakers lived in the locations listed as their "homes." The speakers are from Topsfield, Massachusetts (female); eastern New England (female); Hartford, Connecticut (male); New York City (female); the Bronx, New York (male); Philadelphia (male); Prattville, Alabama (female); Savannah, Georgia (male); Macon, Georgia (male); Greenville, South Carolina (male); northern Florida (female); Mission, Texas (male); London, Kentucky (male); Galesberg, Illinois (female); Pike County, Missouri (male); Madison, Wisconsin (male); Australia (male); Yorkshire, England (male). They all read the following passage:

> My grandfather put his poor old Ford car out to pasture in 1940, and for fourteen years he rode the train four mornings and four afternoons a week, getting up at 5 A.M. on Tuesdays and Thursdays to light the sooty old oil burner, boil his pot of coffee, and catch the dairy route man as he drove past to get his orange juice and daily bottle of milk.

I play only nine to twelve of the recordings, because the exercise is very tiring, but I need data on about ten speakers in order to make informative comparisons. I give the students dittoed copies of the instructions and worksheets and then play the passages one at a time, stopping the tape player after each speaker, pausing long enough to allow all students to complete the worksheets. I usually play the first speaker twice so that the students can get a "feel" for the activity; thereafter I play each passage only once. (On two occasions I played each selection twice but found no noticeable difference in students' apparent comfort between the double exposure and a single playing of the passages.)

Subconscious Response to Speech

Instructions: I am going to play a tape for you, and, as you listen to each person on the tape, you will tend to develop an idea of what kind of person is speaking. Relax and let free association develop. After each speaker has been played, the tape will be stopped while you fill out a questionnaire. You will be asked to give your impressions of the speaker's speech, of the speaker as a person, and of the speaker's physical appearance.

You are to use the scales listed below to indicate your impressions of the speaker. You may look at the scales as you listen, but please wait until the tape player is stopped before you begin writing down numbers. Do not mark on this sheet, because you will need to use it for each speaker, and you wouldn't want notations about one speaker to affect your responses to another speaker.

After each passage is played, fill in the appropriate numbers on the worksheet in the columns of spaces below speaker numbers. Try to respond to each category for each speaker.

Evaluation Scale

Impression of speaker's speech

Very • Quite • Slightly • Neutral • Slightly • Quite • Very

a. good	1	2	3	4	5	6	7	bad
b. sloppy	1	2	3	4	5	6	7	careful
c. ugly	1	2	3	4	5	6	7	pretty
d. smooth	1	2	3	4	5	6	7	harsh
e. awkward	1	2	3	4	5	6	7	graceful
f. nasal	1	2	3	4	5	6	7	nonnasal
g. fast	1	2	3	4	5	6	7	slow

Impression of speaker as a person

Very • Quite • Slightly • Neutral • Slightly • Quite • Very

h. dumb	1	2	3	4	5	6	7	smart
i. poor	1	2	3	4	5	6	7	not poor
j. friendly	1	2	3	4	5	6	7	unfriendly
k. city	1	2	3	4	5	6	7	country
l. lazy	1	2	3	4	5	6	7	industrious
m. rich	1	2	3	4	5	6	7	not rich
n. polite	1	2	3	4	5	6	7	rude
o. conceited	1	2	3	4	5	6	7	not conceited

Impressions of speaker's physical appearance

Very • Quite • Slightly • Neutral • Slightly • Quite • Very

p. tall	1	2	3	4	5	6	7	short
q. light hair	1	2	3	4	5	6	7	dark hair
r. stocky	1	2	3	4	5	6	7	thin
s. dark com-plexioned	1	2	3	4	5	6	7	light com-plexioned

ANSWER WORKSHEET

Information on respondent

Sex   Hometown
Year of birth   Parents' occupations

After hearing each passage, fill in the appropriate numbers in these columns:

	Speaker									
	1	2	3	4	5	6	7	8	9	10
Speech										
a. good—bad	—	—	—	—	—	—	—	—	—	—
b. sloppy—careful	—	—	—	—	—	—	—	—	—	—
c. ugly—pretty	—	—	—	—	—	—	—	—	—	—

This activity usually takes most of a seventy-five minute class period; in the few remaining minutes at the end, we briefly discuss how the students felt as they responded to the task. If I have time—and I always try to find the time—I calculate the mean ratings of each characteristic for each speaker so that the reactions of the class to the speakers may be compared; within a week or two we look at the results. The polarities in the rating sheets are "scrambled" so that "most positive" is sometimes 1 (e.g., polite-rude) and sometimes 7 (e.g., lazy-industrious). I forewarn the students orally that they must pay close attention to the numbers, but I do not say anything about polarities. Before I tabulate the results, I change the ratings on the students' worksheets so that "most positive" is always 7. Some of the pairs of terms have no apparent evaluative polarity (e.g., light or dark hair).

I make separate tabulations of ratings given by men and women, because there are always some interesting differences in male and female responses to some of the speakers. In every class so far, if both men and women rate a female speaker positively on the polar traits, the men tend to perceive her as having a slightly lighter complexion and slightly darker hair than the women raters do. The men also give decidedly higher ratings to southern women than the women raters do. I also tabulate the international students' responses separately because these students usually respond quite differently from the Americans—they tend to give even lower ratings to southern speakers than American women do. When I have done statistical analyses of these differences, however, I have never found a level of significance approaching $p < .10$ on any comparisons (i.e., statistical analyses have never indicated that the probability is less than one in ten that the results occurred by chance). Since the late 1960s, dialectologists have found that their discussions of sociolinguistic variation have been more informative if standard measures of statistical significance are used to evaluate and interpret their data (L. Davis 69–127).

Class discussions of what the students actually think about the exercise are highly informative, revealing wide variation in response patterns. In using the questionnaire over the years, I have changed some of the adjectives and added others because of comments made in class. One interesting change was that I began having doubts about whether *rich* and *poor* were polar opposites in students' "feelings." I changed the questionnaire to have the affirmative and negative of each of these traits. As I suspected, neither individual nor group responses to *poor* and to *rich* are mirrored in the polarity of the numerical ratings; some speakers are rated as both "not poor" and "not rich."

Unfortunately, I do not have foreign accents or ethnic dialects on the tape. The voices of several of the speakers reveal nervousness, and students admit that this feature can cause them to give the speaker more negative ratings. Several of the readers make false starts and manifest temporary "disfluencies." If the speaker has a "pleasant" voice, in the opinion of the rater, the vocal "stumble" appears to have no effect on the rating; but if the speaker displays nervousness or also is perceived as having a vocal feature such as a "nasal twang," less fluent readings compound negative ratings.

Though this activity does not seem to be a scientifically valid procedure because the variables cannot be adequately controlled, the students learn more about themselves than from any other activity during the term. Some admit that they would have denied any biases but can no longer make such a claim. Some find that they try hard not to "make judgments" and consequently mark 4 (neutral) most often but feel awkward doing so. Though we do not rate an ethnic variant of speech, I always bring up the question of how they would have responded to a reading in Black English or a foreign accent. I also have them read Underwood's article on the responses of residents of northwest Arkansas to a similar group of speakers, one of them speaking in southern black dialect. When we discuss Underwood's finding that all his raters assumed the South Carolina white to be black, some class members admit to having made a similar assumption about one or more of the southerners on my tape.

Though the objectivity of the activities in these three exercises on attitudes is not high, the pedagogical value is considerable. The impact of recognizing hidden biases can be seen in the somber looks on the faces of most of the students in the class as we discuss the results of these investigations. My experiences with these exercises have convinced me that all current and future teachers should be required to participate in studies that force them to be aware of biases in their attitudes toward others' speech.

Investigating Disputed Usages

Charles F. Meyer, University of Massachusetts, Boston

IN AN Ann Landers column in the late 1980s, a reader wrote to complain about the usage of *pled* instead of *pleaded* as the past-tense form of *plead*: "I can't believe," the reader remarked, "how often I hear this mistake." In her reply to the letter, Landers politely called her reader's choice of *pleaded* "incorrect" and advised him to consult his dictionary, where he would find *pled* listed as the correct past-tense form of *plead*. Had Landers and her reader taken the time to consult a reputable dictionary—*Webster's Third New International Dictionary* or any of its collegiate spin-offs—they would have found that both forms exist and that both forms are acceptable.[1]

The exchange between Landers and her reader is one illustration of a disputed usage: a disagreement over what is the "correct" linguistic form to use in a particular situation. Disputed usages, and the emotional and impassioned debates they inspire, are a relatively recent phenomenon in the history of the English language, dating back only as far as the eighteenth century. Before that time, there was no established standard dialect of English and little concern with correctness: "We can speculate that nobles and peasants [of the medieval and early Renaissance periods] recognized that they spoke different versions of the same language, but if discussions about the goodness or badness of peasant versus noble usage occurred, it seems not to have appeared in print" (Stalker 41).

In the eighteenth century, however, we find ample documentation of a rising concern over the perceived deterioration of the English language, a concern reflected, as Thomas Pyles and John Algeo note (209–10), in the works of the greatest minds of that century: in Jonathan Swift's *Proposal for Correcting, Improving, and Ascertaining the English Language* and Robert Lowth's *Short Introduction to English Grammar*. The goal of these scholars was to fix the English language in its then-current state, and their attempts to do so gave rise to many disputed usages still evident in contemporary times. For instance, it was common in the eighteenth century to attempt to model the English language after Latin, a language that held great prestige during this period. As a result of this attitude, eighteenth-century grammarians condemned split infinitives, such as *to vigorously defend*, on the grounds that if infinitives cannot be split in Latin, by analogy they should not be split in English. Although split infinitives have become more acceptable in the twentieth century, many people continue to object to the practice.

While there was much scholarly apprehension in the eighteenth century over the "decline" of the English language, today such concern is reflected more in the popular media than in scholarly writing. Journalists like Edwin Newman and John Simon have written books on the decline of the English language, and, as Algeo notes, public awareness of usage is evident in some of the mail newspapers and magazines receive: "Readers of the popular press do not flood their favorite publications with letters on usage, but there is a steady trickle" ("Mirror" 61).

Language scholars of the twentieth century, however, have sought to demonstrate that the belief that the English language is declining is based on subjective opinion rather than on sound linguistic principles; for as Thomas J. Creswell has pointed out in his book on English usage, every disputed usage "is an instance of a regular, normal process or tendency in English, other instances of which occur and have occurred without arousing question or bringing down disapproval" (131). For instance, while many object to the use of *hopefully* in a sentence such as *Hopefully, it won't rain tomorrow*, this usage is not unusual or bizarre. Detractors of the construction claim that *hopefully* dangles—that it is not logically connected to any word in the sentence to which it is attached. Those objecting to this usage, however, fail to consider that *hopefully* dangles in this example no more than *frankly* does in the sentence *Frankly, the dinner was terrible*. Moreover, *hopefully* has entered the language through a common word formation process—functional shift—and has shifted from a manner adverb (*We waited hopefully* [i.e., in a hopeful manner] *for their arrival*) to an attitudinal disjunct. This class of adverbs includes words such as *probably*, *fortunately*, and *certainly*, words expressing the point of view of the speaker or writer. Any objections to *hopefully* are therefore purely subjective and emotional and have no linguistic justification. By 1982, with the publication of the second college edition, the editors of the *American Heritage Dictionary* had softened their position on this issue:

> The use of *hopefully* to mean "it is hoped," as in *hopefully, we'll get there by dark*, is grammatically justifiable by analogy to the similar uses of *happily* and *mercifully*. However, the usage is by now such a bug-bear to traditionalists that it is best avoided on grounds of civility, if not logic.

(For a thorough discussion of the use of *hopefully*, and of its status as a shibboleth, see the article by Whitley.)

The conflict between scholarly and popular attitudes toward English usage in the twentieth century has on occasion led to some bitter disputes, particularly among dictionary makers. Because so many objections to certain usages are based on whims and prejudices, editors of *Webster's Third New*

International Dictionary decided, in 1961, to drop from its inventory of status labels the tag under which many disputed usages have been classified: *informal*. Webster's decision caused a tremendous controversy between those who wanted dictionaries to prescribe correct usage and those (such as the editors of *Webster's Third*) who felt that dictionaries should simply describe usage as it existed (see, e.g., Sledd and Ebbitt). The controversy ultimately resulted in the creation of an entirely new dictionary, *The American Heritage Dictionary of the English Language* (1969). To provide a "definitive" view of usage, editors of this dictionary put together a panel, a group of one-hundred "experts" on the English language, that was asked to comment on the usage of a number of words. The panel's reactions to a given word were calculated in percentages and were included in the entry for that word. Here is what the panel has to say about the word *hopefully*:

> *Hopefully*, as used to mean it is to be hoped or let us hope, is still not accepted by a substantial number of authorities on grammar and usage. The following example of *hopefully* in this sense is acceptable to only 44 per cent of the Usage Panel: *Hopefully, we shall complete our work in June*.

Although the *American Heritage* panel may seem to be a good way of determining appropriate usage, there are several problems with its approach. First, the members of the panel are not fully representative of American society: most are white, middle-aged, and male. Hence the views of the panel are those of only one segment of our society. Second, even if we accept the one-sided nature of the panel, however, the inconsistency of the replies given by the panel members raises questions. In his survey of the responses of the panel to a number of usages, Creswell found little consensus in their replies: "Why," he inquires, "if the opinions of such groups are really authoritative, is there so little agreement on such a small number of items?" (*Usage* 127). A much better way to determine appropriate usage, he argues, is to observe how language is really used: to collect samples of written and spoken English from such diverse places as student writing, black newspapers, or recorded dialogue (139). The findings of the empirical research can then be analyzed and appropriate standards for usage implemented.

Although usage is, as the previous discussion has illustrated, a topic that has inspired much disagreement, the average undergraduate comes to the typical language class feeling that there is one absolutely correct way to speak and write. The assignments described here are intended to debunk this myth: to acquaint students with what the authorities have to say about usage and to help them experience firsthand the extent of disagreement that exists.

Assignment 1

The purpose of assignment 1 is to familiarize students with the notion of level of usage, to acquaint them with the various status labels that dictionaries use to depict these levels, and to demonstrate that various dictionaries contain different labels and define similar labels (such as slang) in quite different ways. Although this assignment can be developed into a writing activity, it will be most successful if it is first done orally in class.

Before students are sent out to do assignment 1, they should be given one dictionary's inventory of status labels to serve as a basis of comparison for the exercise. One good volume for this purpose is *Webster's Third New International Dictionary*. Students should be instructed to compare Webster's status labels and their definitions with those in any other hardcover dictionary. They can use either their family dictionary or any one of many available in the school's library. Students need not be told to use only newer dictionaries for the assignment; older dictionaries work equally well and are quite good at revealing how attitudes toward usage have changed over time. However, students should avoid paperback dictionaries, since they tend to be too brief for the purposes of this task.

Students will make two important discoveries while doing this assignment. First, they will realize that, as noted, different dictionaries include different status labels. While *Webster's Third* lacks the status label *informal* (or *colloquial*), most dictionaries contain this identification tag. And this discovery leads quite nicely into a discussion of why the label is lacking in *Webster's Third* and of the subsequent controversy that this omission caused. Second, students will find that dictionaries differ in the way they define similar status labels. *Webster's Third*, for instance, defines *slang* very precisely and objectively as informal language confined to a particular region or interest group. Other dictionaries (particularly older ones), however, define *slang* in very mean-minded terms, calling it an instance of vulgar or abusive language.

Status Labels in Dictionaries

Directions
In the introductory sections of most dictionaries you will find a section that explains how the dictionary is set up. This section will include, for instance, explanations of the pronunciation symbols the dictionary uses, the kinds of etymological information it gives, and the abbreviations it uses to define words it contains. Look in this first section of any hardcover dictionary—the dictionary your family uses or any of the

many that you can find in your college library. Find the section in the dictionary labeled "usage." In this section there should be a number of status labels similar to the ones listed below. Compare and contrast the labels you find in your dictionary with those listed below, from *Webster's Third New International Dictionary* (1986). Does your dictionary contain similar labels but with different definitions? When you are selecting dictionaries for this exercise, avoid those that list, but do not define, the status labels they use.

STATUS LABELS

1.   The temporal label *obs* for "obsolete" means that no evidence of standard use since 1755 has been found or is likely to be found.

2.   The temporal label *archaic* means standard after 1755 but surviving in the present only sporadically or in special contexts.

3.   The stylistic label *slang* is affixed to terms especially appropriate in contexts of extreme informality, having usually a currency not limited to a particular region or area of interest, and composed typically of clipped or shortened forms or extravagant, forced, or facetious figures of speech.

4.   The stylistic label *substand* for "substandard" indicates status conforming to a pattern of linguistic usage that exists throughout the American language community but differs in choice of word or form from that of the prestige group in that community.

5.   The stylistic label *nonstand* for "nonstandard" is used for a very small number of words that can hardly stand without some status label but are too widely current in reputable context to be labeled *substand*.

6.   The regional label *dial* for "dialect" when unqualified indicates a regional pattern too complex for summary labeling usually because it includes several regional varieties of American English or of American and British English.

7.   The combined label *dial Brit* and the combined label *dial Eng* indicate substandard currency in a provincial dialect of the British Commonwealth or England.

8.   A standard word requiring a specified regional restriction in the U.S. will have one of the seven labels *North, New Eng, Midland, South, West, Southwest,* and *Northwest.*

9.   A regional label that names a country indicates standard currency in the named part of the whole English language area.

Assignment 2

Assignment 2 is a short writing task that gives students practice doing library research and comparing and contrasting secondary sources. In addition, it is effective at impressing upon students the notion that so-called authorities disagree about what constitutes "correct" usage. This is an important discovery for most students, since many will have come to class thinking that there is only one correct way of speaking or writing.

This assignment requires a paper of two to four double-spaced pages. Essentially, students should look up their disputed usage in any of the guides or handbooks listed in assignment 3. They should define the problem at the start of their papers and then describe how their sources treat the problem. At the end of the paper, they should synthesize their findings and state which of the authorities they have consulted gives the best advice on usage. Alternatively, students can argue that none of their sources gives good advice and then provide advice of their own.

Students will learn from assignment 2 that authorities on usage not only disagree about what is "correct" and "incorrect" English but frequently base their prescriptions on fallacious, arbitrary, prejudiced, and unenlightened arguments. For instance, students who consult William Morris and Mary Morris's *Harper Dictionary of Contemporary Usage*, a dictionary containing quotes from members of the American Heritage Usage Panel, will find that one member of the usage panel, Phyllis McGinley, thinks that *hopefully* used as an attitudinal disjunct "is an abomination and its adherents should be lynched" (312). Yet if the students turn to Theodore Bernstein's *Do's, Don'ts, and Maybes of English Usage*, they will encounter a more enlightened discussion of *hopefully*. While Bernstein acknowledges that some people object to its use, he notes that it is parallel to words such as *fortunately* and states that its use "in no way distorts or corrupts the first meaning of the word ['in a hopeful manner']" (105).

Disputed Usages: Short Paper

Directions
Select one of the disputed usages from the list given below. Look up the usage in any three or four books on usage, and write a paper in which you (1) define the disputed usage, (2) summarize what three or four sources have to say about it, and (3) argue that either one or none of the sources you have consulted provides the best solution to the use of the usage. If you feel that none of the sources gives a good solution, propose a solution of your own.

You may select a disputed usage not on the list, but clear your choice with me first. Some examples of books on usage are given in the bibliography on usage, though you may use a book not in the bibliography. Your paper should be approximately 2–4 double-spaced typed pages, with an additional bibliography page.

Topics
1. positioning of *only*
2. *can* in permission sense
3. *slow* as an adverb
4. subject-verb agreement with *data* and *media*
5. *hopefully* as a sentence modifier
6. *between you and I*
7. *ain't*
8. *these kind of, these sort of*
9. *awhile* and *a while*
10. *feel bad* and *feel badly*
11. *play good* and *play well*
12. *due to* as a preposition
13. *the reason why*
14. *aren't*
15. *among* and *between*
16. *graduated* and *was graduated*
17. *contact* as a verb
18. *each other* and *one another*
19. *from whence*
20. *hanged* and *hung*
21. *human* as a noun
22. *dove* and *dived*
23. *whose* in reference to nonpersons
24. *further* and *farther*
25. *-wise* as a suffix for adverbs
26. *alright*
27. *nauseous* and *nauseated*
28. *disinterested* and *uninterested*
29. *imply* and *infer*
30. *flaunt* and *flout*
31. *affect* and *effect*
32. *use to* and *used to*

Assignment 3

Assignment 3 is similar to assignment 2 in that it involves library research and comparison and contrast of sources. However, because the topics for assignment 3 are more general than those for assignment 2, they lend themselves to a more in-depth paper; in addition, they provide students with the opportunity to perform elicitation experiments, whose purpose is to draw out opinions on a disputed usage from native speakers of the language.

Assignment 3 is outlined below, with a sample elicitation form. Before beginning the experiments, students should be told to clearly define their disputed usage and to survey the opinions of three or four books that discuss the usage. After this preparation, students should set up their elicitation experiments. The experiment has two parts: a section asking for general biographical information and a series of sentences testing instances of subject-verb agreement (such as agreement in sentences headed by existential *there*) that typically produce variable responses. This is only one type of elicitation test format; other formats can be found in Sidney Greenbaum and Randolph Quirk's *Elicitation Experiments in English.*

There are two ways in which students can organize a paper based on their survey of the literature and on their elicitation experiments. They can either discuss first what the authorities have to say about the usage problem and then detail the results of their experiments, or they can break the paper up into sections, discussing in each section both the opinions of authorities and the results of their experiments. This latter method of organization tends to lead to more effective papers. For instance, a student writing a paper on subject-verb agreement could divide the paper into sections on subject-verb agreement in sentences with existential *there*, in sentences with plural subjects (such as *linguistics*) taking singular verbs, and so on.

Students will learn from this assignment that what the authorities have to say about a usage problem differs considerably in many situations from what the average person will say. While usage authorities may prescribe a singular verb with the indefinite pronoun *each*, for example, students will find that many people—even those who are highly educated—prefer *Each of them have to leave* to *Each of them has to leave*. This discovery clearly illustrates that innovation and change in language occurs first in the general population and appears only later in usage books.

Disputed Usages: Lengthier Paper

Directions
Select a disputed usage or a series of usages from the list below. Write a paper in which you (1) define the disputed usage(s), (2) report what

three or four sources have to say about it, (3) conduct a survey of opinions on the usage. Report the results in detail. Include biographical information about your subjects (age group, educational level, areas in which they lived, etc.). You may want to compare two groups. Survey at least twenty subjects. And (4) relate your two sets of findings and draw conclusions.

You can select a disputed usage not on the list, but clear your choice with me first. Some examples of books on usage are given in the bibliography on usage, though you may use a book not on the list. The paper should be approximately 6–8 double-spaced pages, with additional pages for table(s) and bibliography.

Topics
1. Pronoun agreement with indefinite pronouns (e.g., *everybody . . . his*)
2. *Like* as a conjunction
3. Case with a gerund (e.g., *my reading the book* vs. *me reading the book*)
4. *And* and *but* at the beginning of a sentence
5. Sentence fragments
6. Run-on sentences
7. Comma splices
8. Comparatives with three or more (the *better* of the three sisters) and superlatives with two (the *best* of the two sisters)
9. Uses of *who* and *whom*
10. Subject-verb agreement
11. Multiple negation
12. Sexism in language
13. Uses of alternative verb forms (e.g., *dived, dove; proved, proven*)
14. Uses of the subjunctive mood
15. Dangling, misplaced, and squinting modifiers
16. Confusing adjectives and adverbs (e.g., He feels *good/well*)
17. Preposition at the end of a sentence
18. Split infinitives
19. Uses of the verb *get*
20. Uses of *shall* and *will*

Survey on Subject-Verb Agreement

1. Age 17–22   23–30   31–40   40+   (Circle one.)
2. Sex
3. Areas of country lived in

4. Highest level of school completed: High school ____ One year of college ____ Two years of college ____ Three years of college ____ Four years of college ____ MA ____ PhD ____ (Check one.)
5. College major (if any)

Please circle the answer you would use in formal writing.

1. The United States (has/have) not been in an armed conflict since the Vietnam War.
2. There (is/are) two reasons why the epidemic has not reached Massachusetts.
3. One of the people who (is/are) in my history class plans to major in history.
4. The committee (plans/plan) to issue a joint recommendation.
5. Either the husband or the wife (plans/plan) to attend the meeting.
6. The instructor, as well as her students, (is/are) going to the museum.
7. Driving in large cities (is/are) a real nightmare.
8. One pair of glasses (is/are) all I plan to buy.

Books on English Usage

Usage has been studied from various perspectives. To best research this assignment, you should attempt to consult books by authors in all three of the areas described below.

First of all, usage has been the focus of scholarly inquiry by professionals in the field: Margaret Bryant, Roy H. Copperud, Thomas J. Creswell, Bergen Evans and Cornelia Evans, Margaret Nicholson, and Robert C. Pooley. Although these writers all offer advice on usage, their advice tends to be less biased and emotional than the recommendations of those who write popular books on usage.

The following write for the general public and are journalists, educators, editors, and authors: Sheridan Baker, Theodore Bernstein, Thomas E. Berry, Wilma R. Ebbitt and David R. Ebbitt, Wilson Follett, Walter E. Meyers, William Morris and Mary Morris, and Eric Partridge.

Finally, usage is often discussed briefly in handbooks written for freshman composition classes. Frequently, authors of these books are teachers and composition theorists: Charles Brusaw, Gerald J. Alred, and Walter E. Oliu; Jim W. Corder; Langdon Elsbree and Frederick G. Bracher; Hans P. Guth; John C. Hodges et al.; Glenn Leggett, C. David Mead, and Melinda G. Kramer; Porter G. Perrin and Jim W.

Corder; Floyd C. Watkins and William B. Dillingham; and Hulon
Willis.

Note

[1] I wish to thank Sidney Greenbaum for suggestions about the assignments in
this paper, and Gene Boyles for doing background research.

Using the Word *Ain't* to Introduce the Study of Dialects to High School Students

Harry Homa, Morris High School, South Bronx

MORRIS High School in the South Bronx may seem an unlikely place to present the principles of linguistics to secondary school students. All the woes of inner-city life are reflected in the dropout rate of 74 percent. Low reading levels, low family income, and high single-parent-household membership characterize the student body, which is about 60 percent Hispanic and 40 percent black. Fortunately, for a number of years I have instructed College Bound tutorial classes in English. These draw the best students, many of whom read near grade level—some above it. Even among these students the prevailing speech pattern is nonstandard, however, and various Black English forms are also used by a number of Hispanic students. About 10 percent of the students are unable or unwilling to switch to a variety of standard when assigned written work. But these students have youth. These youngsters are much more open to linguistic ideas than are several of my middle-age colleagues who learned "all there is to know about language" at an earlier period in their education.

In this setting I feel very comfortable introducing a month-long unit on dialects by intensely studying the word *ain't*. After all, the students know the word; many use it dozens of times daily. And the word has been scorned by many of their previous teachers. Often, when I present the pretest that follows, some wit will laughingly comment, *"Ain't* ain't a word." The word *ain't*, then, is an ideal springboard for diving into controversy. Without forewarning, I begin the term with this pretest.

Word Pretest

Objective: This short quiz will tell you whether or not you know what makes a word a word.

Directions: Put a check in the true or false column.

	True	False
1. *Ain't* is a word.	____	____
2. Millions of people use *ain't* in their everyday speech.	____	____

	True	False
3. You will find *ain't* in the *New York Times, Times, Newsweek, Sports Illustrated,* and other respectable newspapers and magazines.	____	____
4. *Ain't* has meanings, even to educated people.	____	____
5. Like any other word, *ain't* must have a history, an origin.	____	____
6. *Ain't* is in almost all the big dictionaries.	____	____

(I've given this pretest to over one thousand students—I also teach at Washington Irving Evening High School in Manhattan. The average score on this pretest is about three correct. Perhaps 1 percent or 2 percent of the students mark all six items correctly.)

Before I give the answers to the pretest, I ask the students if *OK* is a word, as in "I'm feeling *OK*." When they say that it is, I ask them why it is. Once they draw on their experience to give a justifiable explanation, I ask if anyone knows the history of the word. No one ever does, so I summarize H. L. Mencken's account (*American Language: Supplement I* 269–79). When somebody states that being in the dictionary makes *OK* a word, I counter with one of the newer words drawing attention in the mid-1980s: *break dancing, caplet, preppie,* or *crack* in its new meaning. Students then realize that words appear in speech and print long before they appear in dictionaries.

Now I ask students if in their experience *ain't* has been around long enough to be in the dictionaries. Then they relate where they hear *ain't*: in everyday conversation, on TV shows, in songs, in movies. Of course, everybody has heard it in conversation; some recall lyrics; others name specific TV programs or movies. Some have a dim memory of seeing the word in print. Nevertheless, the students need the confirmation of a dictionary. At this point, I direct them to nine different dictionaries I have in the classroom (see the appendix). Others are sent to the school library, which has *Webster's New International Dictionary* (2nd ed.), *Webster's Third New International Dictionary, Random House Dictionary* (unabr. ed.), *Grolier International Dictionary,* and *World Book Encyclopedia Dictionary.* The instructions for the students are to copy the full name and latest printing date of any three dictionaries and copy what each one has at the entry *ain't,* including usage notes. If a dictionary has no entry, they are to write "nothing." For this lesson I bring in *Webster's Ninth New Collegiate Dictionary,* which has added citations and "fixed phrases" to the comments on *ain't* in *Webster's Third.*

On completion of this work, I show clippings from newspapers, magazines, and ads that demonstrate that *ain't* has meanings to the educated. We summarize our findings: what makes a word a word is that it is used in speech. Once it is widely circulated in writing—as with a neologism—it is destined to appear in a dictionary. Later, when we study social dialects, the students discover that one meaning of *ain't* is not in dictionaries: *didn't*, as in *I ain't do it*.

As a homework activity, students are required either to cut an article out of a newspaper or magazine with the word *ain't* in it and to record the name of the publication, its date, and the page number, or to bring in a novel, poem, or play with the word in it.

Our next objective is to examine the etymology of *ain't* and to trace its use in the United States. To begin, I ask, "Was *ain't* invented in the South Bronx? Was it created ten, twenty, fifty, or two hundred years ago? Did the British or the Americans coin the word?" Since none of the students know, I present the origins of *ain't* as recorded in *The Oxford English Dictionary*. But first I dwell on the uniqueness of this publication, since no one has ever heard of it. The information in the *OED* illustrates how language may change: *ain't* replaced *an't* and *han't*, terms that the students declare are now "played out." Then I tell them that according to *Webster's New World Dictionary*, second college edition (xxi), *ain't* was used in the "best circles in New England" in the early 1800s. Next I cite Stuart B. Flexner's findings in *I Hear America Talking* that, once *ain't* took on additional meanings in the 1830s, the word went out of fashion among many educated speakers but still appears in educated speech in parts of the South (5).

The students conclude that *ain't* has been a useful word for more than two hundred years. Like many other words, it has drawn the interest of serious scholars. Research demonstrates that the use of *ain't* has survived while *an't* and *han't* have become obsolete. Also, as the meaning of the word changed, *ain't* became "played out" among the educated, though it is often used today by educated speakers in the United States, Britain, and Australia.

A third objective is to evaluate the status of *ain't* among educated people today. I ask the students what, if anything, other teachers, adults, or friends have told them about using *ain't*. It seems that in every class at least one or two students have been told by a teacher in the past that *ain't* is not a word. Then we examine the usage notes found in the *Random House College Dictionary* and the *American Heritage Dictionary* (paperback ed.). Next we contrast the chronological entries of Merriam-Webster in the second and third editions of *Webster's New International Dictionary* and in the *Ninth New Collegiate*. Now we are ready to examine the students' findings on the use of *ain't* and the evidence of our clippings of *ain't* in print.

We conclude that while many educated persons still shun *ain't*, the word—used with care—is popular in speech and writing. The students also realize that the word is inappropriate in some situations but not in others.

A related objective is to trace the history of *gonna* in print and to demonstrate, again, the influence of a nonstandard form on informal speech and writing. The procedures used with *gonna* are similar to those used with *ain't*. To substantiate my claims, I present the findings on *gonna* rendered in the 1972 supplement to the *OED*, *Random House Dictionary* (unabr., 2nd ed.), and *Webster's Third* at the entry for the verb *go* and collected in the written and taped citations that I've gathered. A conclusion we reach is that *gonna* is not in all the dictionaries—yet. The students observe that this nonstandard form has risen to common use in educated, informal speech. The students tentatively conclude that *ain't* has yet to receive the colloquial acceptance that *gonna* has.

This lengthy examination of nonstandard forms opens the door to the study of regional and social dialects, levels of usage, vulgarity, language changes, and case histories of dialect switching. Moreover, since I have a class set of the *Barnhart Dictionary Companion*, the students have the opportunity to approach new words with sharpened eyes. And, of course, they are a little more critical of many of the regular dictionaries.

We also explore grammatical, phonological, and lexical features in literary dialects. (There are those who scoff at literary dialects. Yet the *OED*, the *American Dialect Dictionary* [Wentworth], and the *Dictionary of American Regional English* [Cassidy] include citations from literature.) We read the poetry of Langston Hughes and passages in the works of William Faulkner, John Steinbeck, and Stephen Crane. To experience artistic renditions of standard and nonstandard varieties of black speech, we read black militant Martie Charles's 1970 one-act play "Job Security." Since we are New Yorkers, we also read Thomas Wolfe's short story "Only the Dead Know Brooklyn" and a scene from Sidney Kingsley's play *Dead End*, both of which capture many features of the metropolitan New York dialect of fifty years ago. And all these writers find *ain't* useful. We also listen to varieties of English spoken by blacks as we watch productions like the ABC-TV drama *Cindy* (the Cinderella story set in Harlem). This examination of literary dialects encourages the students to be expressive in writing dialogues in which they depict the way people they know actually speak. More important, the students realize that literary giants—as well as novices—find great value in attempting to capture nonstandard (and standard) speech variations in their works. In sum, the students recognize that for Faulkner and other writers, verisimilitude is impossible without a rendition of nonstandard forms.

For this activity, the traditional homework assignment—the book report—is given another dimension. As usual, the students are directed to read novels and write book reports. However, one assignment is to have students focus their attention on the dialogue found in the novels. The students copy a stretch of dialogue and label it standard or nonstandard. Next, the students comment on the importance of dialogue in an author's characterization technique and on its fidelity to actual speech.

Our work on dialects, then, merely begins with the lengthy study of *ain't*. The goal is for the students to reach two major conclusions: (1) Non-standard speech has dignity and vigor; it will always be useful to those who choose to remain in the South Bronx. (2) Those students who aspire to function successfully in wider worlds—college, office work, the professions—need to learn varieties of the standard dialect.

Appendix: The Dictionaries in My Classroom

American Heritage Dictionary. Paperback. 1976.
Doubleday Dictionary. 1975.
New American Webster Handy College Dictionary. Paperback. 1981.
Random House Dictionary. Paperback. 1980.
Thorndike-Barnhart High School Dictionary. 4th ed. 1965.
Webster's Dictionary. Paperback. 1973.
Webster's New Collegiate Dictionary. 8th ed. 1976.
Webster's New Secondary School Dictionary. 1961.
Webster's New World Dictionary of the American Language. Student's ed. 1976.

A Critical Approach to Questions of Usage

Harry Homa, Morris High School, South Bronx

MANY schoolbook grammars shortchange students by ignoring the history from which disputed usages emerge. Knowledge of this history heightens students' language awareness, for divided usage arises from linguistic change. Documented shifts in usage, in turn, suggest that every language will continue to evolve as people speak and write it. However, a prescriptive grammarian, instead of weighing evidence on divided usages, characteristically inhibits discussion with a simplistic view of "right" and "wrong" English. For example, in the 1958 edition of his widely used grammar book, John Warriner has a detailed admonition on the "misuse" of *like, as,* and *as if*:

> **like, as**. *Like* is a preposition and introduces a prepositional phrase containing an object. *As* may be a conjunction introducing a subordinate clause. EXAMPLES He fought *like* a tiger. He fought *as* a tiger fights. One of the most common violations of standard usage is the substitution of *like* for *as*. Remember that *like* is followed by a noun or pronoun—never by a verb. . . .
>
> **like, as if**. . . . WRONG He treats Phyllis like she were a princess. RIGHT He treats Phyllis as if she were a princess. (184–85)

The conjunctive use of *like* has been the subject of much discussion. Students should sample different observations on this usage, as in the following citations:

> **like** Do not use **like** as a conjunction in the sense of *as, as if*. CORRECT *B as in Boston* (not "like in Boston"). *Speak as if* (not "like") *you mean what you say*. . . . (Witherspoon 102)

> **like** . . .—*conj*. In the same manner or to the same extent or degree as. *Now chiefly in dialect and popular speech. Like*, introducing a complete clause (he took to figures *like* a duck to water), is common colloquially but is usually replaced by careful writers by *as*. (*Webster's Collegiate Dictionary*, 5th ed.)

> **like**. Should not be used as a conjunction. Substitute *as* or *as if* . . . (Wykoff and Shaw 464)

> **Like, as** . . . *Like* as conjunction is commonly heard in informal speech, but it is still not acceptable in standard formal usage. (Warriner 184)

> **like** . . . **Usage** LIKE as a conjunction meaning "as, in the same way as" . . . or "as if" . . . has been used for nearly 500 years and by many distinguished literary and intellectual figures. Since the mid-19th century there have been objections,

often vehement, to these uses. Nevertheless, such usages are almost universal today in all but the most formal speech and writing. . . . (*Random House Dictionary*, unabr., 2nd ed.)

like, as, as if. . . . To summarize the controversy: *like* has been in use as a conjunction for more than 600 years. Its beginnings are literary, but the available evidence shows that it was fairly rare until the 19th century. A noticeable increase in use during the 19th century provoked the censure we are so familiar with. Still, the usage has never been less than standard, even if primarily spoken. . . . (*Webster's Dictionary of English Usage*)

By contrasting findings presented in such works with their own experience, students will understand how important actual usage is when dictionary editors are trying to decide on how to label words and expressions with disputed usage. Moreover, they will discern the gulf between prescriptive and descriptive approaches to linguistic observations.

At the outset, then, it is useful to make students aware that every usage problem has a history. To this end, the teacher may use our greatest resource, the *Oxford English Dictionary*. The version I use is the *Compact Edition (COED)*. Citations found here often startle students. Many are surprised when they see English's most famous playwright listed as using *me* as a predicate nominative:

me. . . . 6. For the *nominative.* **a.** Chiefly predicative; as subject now only *dial.* and *vulgar.* . . . 1591 SHAKS. *Two Gent.* II, iii, 25 Oh, the dogge is me, and I am my selfe. . . . **b.** After *as, than.* 1606 SHAKS. *Ant. & Cl.* III, iii, 14 Is she as tall as me?

Further, *they* in reference to a singular indefinite noun, is dated to 1526:

they. . . . **B.** Signification. . . . 2. Often used in reference to a singular noun made universal by *every, any, no,* etc., or applicable to one of either sex. . . . 1526 *Pilgr. Perf.* (W. de W. 1531) 163b Yf. a psalme scape ony persone, or a lesson, or else yᵗ they omyt one verse or twayne.

The *COED* also prescribes: *me* as a "subject [is] now only *dial.* and *vulgar.*" This sort of injunction from our prime historical source contributes to a lively discussion, for among dictionaries disagreeing with this finding are these more recent ones: *Webster's Ninth New Collegiate Dictionary* (1983); *Random House Dictionary*, unabridged, second edition, (1987); and *Webster's New World Dictionary*, third college edition (1988). This work also draws student interest with its assertion that *disinterested* originally meant "not interested" early in the seventeenth century.

To engage young minds in usage issues, then, the teacher may begin

with citations—and prescriptions—found in any version of the *OED*. Following this activity, the teacher describes the prescriptions laid down by grammarians, usage panelists, and self-appointed language guardians in the last
forty to fifty years. Once students test the depths of usage problems, they
are more likely to stand on firmer ground when arriving at practical solutions
to assorted questions of usage. In my classroom, I have single copies of nine
different dictionaries and a classroom set of the eleventh-grade version of
Warriner's grammar. Occasionally I bring in other reference works and let
students do research during class time. The dictionaries that I generally use
are listed at the end of the preceding article, and the reference works that
I keep in my classroom are cited in this essay and included in the works-
cited list at the end of this volume. All of us share the joy of discovery as we
use these reference works cooperatively in the classroom. The remainder of
this article briefly discusses the kinds of exercises that may be used to direct
students' attention to the vagaries of usage rules.

The teacher may begin the study of usage by giving an example of the
pronoun *their* with a singular antecedent, by asking the students this question: "Can *their* mean *his* or *her*?" The teacher can then ask the students to
supply the missing pronoun in a statement such as the following:

a. Each student is to hand in ＿＿ report by Friday.
b. Mother said that someone called but ＿＿ didn't leave ＿＿ name.
c. Everyone in this class should ask ＿＿what ＿＿ want(s) from
    education.

The students should write their versions of the sentence before they are
asked for oral responses. After a sufficient number of oral responses are
elicited from the students (*his, their, his or her, his/her*), some of the students
can read aloud the rulings of the Barnhart dictionaries, the Random House
dictionaries, the various Webster's dictionaries, the two editions of *The American Heritage Dictionary*, and other dictionaries that students may bring to
class; usage dictionaries such as Margaret M. Bryant's *Current American Usage*,
the *Harper Dictionary of Contemporary Usage* (Morris and Morris), Alexander
M. Witherspoon's 1943 listing of "common errors," and newer usage dictionaries published by Merriam-Webster and Webster's New World (Randall);
and popular commentaries such as those by Theodore Bernstein, Edwin
Newman, and John Simon.

When a student reads a dictum that only *his* is correct, members of the
class can consider whether they object to that statement. Why does the
women's movement object to *his*? Bernstein declares that *his or her* sounds
"awkward." Does it sound awkward or natural to the student? Individual

students should be encouraged to explain or justify their answers. The instructor may want to list the responses on the chalkboard if the class is especially perceptive.

Following this discussion, students can examine the view that the absence of a genderless singular pronoun to refer to an indefinite antecedent is a defect in our language—summarized in Raven I. McDavid's abridged edition of H. L. Mencken's books on American language (545–46).

A comparison of Mencken's observations with comments made during the class discussion and with their own experience produces a number of questions. What do students hear teachers, parents, and TV notables using? What do they see in print? In which contexts does *everyone* have the feel of a plural? What is the rationale for the acceptance of *they* in informal contexts but not in formal ones? What are some practical solutions for avoiding problems with indefinite antecedents?

A useful passage to copy as a handout is the entry for *everyone* in *The American Heritage Dictionary*, second college edition, in which the editors conclude that "the entire matter is properly outside the scope of grammar." An appropriate written assignment as a conclusion to this unit would be to have the students contrast and compare the *COED* or the *American Heritage* entries on *they, themselves, theirs,* and *them* with those in other general dictionaries of the 1940s through the 1980s, and to formulate conclusions about usage and levels of style and the linguistic contexts in which these pronoun problems arise. The assignment could be introduced by suggesting paper titles such as "Grammar, People, and Logic" or "People vs. the Authorities on Usage."

An ambitious teacher with an enthusiastic class could take on other issues. More work with pronouns can be done with *It's I/me, It's he/him, It's she/her, It's they/them, It's we/us.* And indeed a great number of usage issues could become the focus of a critical approach to usage: semantic shifts, function shifts, productive affixes like *-ize,* variation of prepositions in idioms like *different from/than/to,* sexist and nonsexist language, and a variety of terms proscribed in usage guides. Following class activity in making up sample sentences, the students could devise their own usage panel by polling faculty members and other students. Students might include a questionnaire asking for age, sex, and educational level. The students' findings could be compared with the comments in the *Harper Dictionary* (Morris and Morris). Students would then be armed with additional data for judging the acceptability of particular items, and in the process they could learn something about thinking for themselves.

Studying Phonological Variation through Photography

Kathryn Riley, University of Minnesota, Duluth
Frank Parker, Louisiana State University

☙

BEGINNING students of language variation sometimes have difficulty in recognizing the pervasiveness of social and regional dialects, in understanding their rule-governed nature, and in collecting and analyzing data.[1] As a way of introducing students to these concepts, the teaching unit described in this essay shows how photographing nonstandard spelling can be a useful method for collecting data that reflect predictable patterns in phonology and, secondarily, morphology. More specifically, photography is used in two ways: as a medium of classroom instruction and as a medium through which students collect and analyze data as part of a fieldwork project.

The discussion focuses on three points: first, a rationale for having students collect written data from local sources and for using photography; second, suggestions about implementing the teaching unit, based on a junior-senior level course at Louisiana State University on social dialects; and, third, ideas about adapting the activities to other courses that deal with the study of language.

When discussing language variation, teachers have traditionally relied on either tape-recorded or published data (for example, as presented in a linguistic atlas, article, or textbook). While these time-proven methods are certainly sound, several arguments exist for supplementing data from these sources by having students collect "local" written data—that is, instances of language variation obtained from the students' own surroundings.

First, by collecting and studying local data, students can gain a better sense of the extent and diversity of language variation than they might by relying exclusively on published sources. For example, one of the works used in the Louisiana State class was Walt Wolfram and Ralph Fasold's excellent introductory text, *The Study of Social Dialects in American English*. However, much of the data presented in this text was collected in New York City, Detroit, and Washington, D.C. Exposed only to this material, students might incorrectly conclude that language variation occurs primarily in certain regions or among particular demographic groups. Analyzing samples they have collected from their immediate surroundings provides students with a firsthand perspective on the types of language variation that exist closer to home. We believe that this perspective can help counteract the popular misconception that a dialect is "what somebody else speaks."

Second, collecting data from their print environment can provide students with a manageable introduction to fieldwork. The task of personally gathering data from informants—for example, through interviews—is not only time-consuming but requires extensive training in fieldwork methods, sampling techniques, and accurate transcription. The task of photographing data, in contrast, is a reasonable one for students who lack training and experience in fieldwork.

Third, data obtained using a visual medium such as photography can illustrate vividly how phonological and morphological processes may affect written forms and thus can complement tape-recorded data or transcribed spoken data. An awareness of how language variation influences writing is important because students of the English language are often preparing for careers in fields such as education, English as a second language, basic writing, and composition. Practitioners in these areas need to know specific facts about different varieties of English in order to understand the relation between linguistic systems and the written language.

The teaching unit may begin with several sessions that introduce students to basic concepts and principles of phonology to enable them to analyze phonological variation. Two or three sessions can be devoted to instruction in phonemic transcription, with special attention to the variability between phonological representations and alphabetic spelling in English. The students may submit homework assignments requiring both phonemic transcriptions and descriptions of phonemic segments in terms of place, voicing, and manner of articulation.

The following are excerpts from sample exercises in phonemic transcription and segment analysis:

1. Transcribe the following words in phonemic transcription. Example: *chow* /čaʊ/
   a. through   b. rough   c. blink   d. foot. . . .
2. Identify each of the following English phonemes in terms that are sufficient to distinguish it from other segments. Example: /i/ high, front, tense vowel; /b/ voiced bilabial stop.
   a. /l/   b. /k/   c. /w/. . . .
3. Identify the English phoneme(s) described by each of the following terms.
   a. back, nonround, low vowel   b. velar stop. . . .

The next several sessions of the class should be devoted to common phonological processes. Instruction here should include the distinction between phonemic and phonetic representation, as well as formal conventions for stating phonological rules. Aspiration, flapping, and phonemic alternations of the past-tense morpheme are typical phonological rules of English that may easily be covered in class. Phonological processes common to English and other languages can also be discussed. Sample phonological exercises are given below; similar exercises appear in many introductory textbooks (Akmajian, Demers, and Harnish; Demers and Farmer; Parker; Parker and Riley; Schane and Bendixen; and Wolfram and Johnson).

1. Flapping in English. Consider the following data:

said	tire	raider	caddy
daughter	catty	Easter	spender
attack	attic	right	candy

   Questions for discussion:
   a. Which words are pronounced with a flap [D] rather than a clear [t] or [d]?
   b. What is the phonetic environment for flapping?
   c. State in words the flapping rule.
   d. State the rule using formal notation. Make the most general statement possible.
2. The morphophoneme //D//. The past-tense forms of some regular verbs in English are given below.
   thrashed, loved, knitted
   a. Transcribe each word phonemically.
      Example: thrashed /θræšt/
   b. Determine what controls the phonemic form of the morphophoneme //D//. What environments trigger /t/, /d/, and /əd/? State these generalizations in words.
   c. Based on your answer to b, write phonological rules that describe the phonetic data.

At this point, the instructor can discuss the potential effects of phonological and morphological processes on spelling. In the Louisiana State class, these effects were illustrated by showing the students slides of nonstandard spellings that we had found on signs and bulletin boards. Examples of these are listed here, with target forms in parentheses.

1. Consonant cluster reduction: the deletion of the second member of a consonant cluster (typically a stop)

    a. Mother Gray, *Spiritulis* (Spiritualist) Reader and Advisor

    b. Please do not go *pass* (past) this point.

    c. I need an *experience* (experienced) babysitter.

2. Unaltered base form: the addition of a derivational suffix without a change in the root

    a. *Carpentery* (Carpentry): Cabinets, hot tubes [sic], remodeling

    b. Two bedroom townhouse with *centeral* (central) air conditioning

    c. Cedar Grove Campground *Registeration* (Registration)

3. Syncope: the deletion of an unstressed vowel between two consonants

    a. *Astroid* (Asteroid) Den—a video game arcade

    b. Cuccia *Choclates* (Chocolates)

    c. *Restraunt* (Restaurant) and Lounge

    d. No *loitring* (loitering)

4. Misspelling of a neutralized vowel: the tendency for unstressed vowels to reduce to schwa ($[\mathrm{\partial}]$) and to resist accurate reconstruction in spelling

    a. Job opening: *Flexable* (Flexible) hours

    b. Blue Grass Jamboree—*Augest* (August) 3–9

    c. 1983 Mazda RX7—under *warrenty* (warranty), *excellant* (excellent) condition

    d. Motorcycle with *helmut* (helmet)

5. Assimilation: the tendency for a segment to acquire one or more of the voicing, manner, or place characteristics of an adjacent segment

    a. For rent—1 bedroom . . . call (phone number) for *imformation* (information)

6. Progressive nazalization: the tendency to insert a nasal consonant after a nazalized vowel

    a. 1980 Suzuki GN 400×, 2 full face *helments* (helmets)

    b. *Clemantis* (Clematis) Street

    Slides can also be used to illustrate several other principles, such as the distinction between phonological and morphological deletion (Wolfram and Fasold 125–27). For instance, the examples of consonant cluster reduction listed above reflect a phonological process that presumably operates independently of the morphological status of the deleted segment (e.g., the /t/ in *experienced* represents the past participle morpheme, whereas the /t/ in *spiritualist* is nonmorphemic). But the omission of the morphophoneme //Z// (e.g., *-s* in *pats* [plural noun], *Pat's* [possessive noun], *pats* [verb]) cannot be analyzed as phonological deletion, since this segment is deleted with different frequencies depending on its function (as a plural, possessive, or third-person singular inflection). Sample data illustrating morphological deletion include the following:

    a.   Our *biscuit* (biscuits) have the majority vote.
    b.   Registered *guest* (guests) only
    c.   *World* (World's) Fair *gift* (gifts)

    Moreover, consonant cluster reduction does not necessarily result in a stigmatized written form. For example, *ice tea* freely alternates with *iced tea*, suggesting that the former is perhaps interpreted as a compound noun, similar to *ice cream, grape juice,* and *ice milk*. (However, the different stress patterns in *ice téa* and *íce crèam* indicate that the first phrase has not been fully reanalyzed as a compound, while the second one has.) Yet when consonant cluster reduction leads to a form such as *experience babysitter*, the reduced form is not readily interpretable as a compound noun and consequently is considered a nonstandard spelling.

    Following the preparatory sessions, the students are ready to begin collecting their data themselves. Before this process begins, however, the instructor should discuss possible sources for finding data close to campus, in order to accommodate any students who do not have cars. Potential sources include bulletin boards in dormitories and the student center, as well as public signs in the commercial areas near campus.

    Once prepared, the students should first locate and photograph data illustrating the effects of phonology or morphology on spelling and then provide a brief written analysis of the process underlying each misspelling. Students may work individually or in groups while collecting data, in order to accommodate students who do not own cameras. Slides are preferable to prints for presenting the data to the class as a whole. For each piece of data obtained, the students should provide a form such as the following:

Information Sheet

Instructions: Complete an information sheet for each piece of data
    that you collect.
Full text of sign or notice
Misspelled form and phonemic transcription
Target form and phonemic transcription
Phonological process involved
Location of sign (e.g., street or building)
Date collected

    About three weeks should be allowed for the students to photograph data, have their film developed, and complete the information sheets to accompany the slides. At the end of the data collection period, a slide presentation may be scheduled so that each student's findings can be shared with the entire class. Some of the specific forms photographed by our students are given below.

1. Consonant cluster reduction
   a. *Package* (Packaged) liquor
   b. *Chop* (Chopped) beef
   c. *Screen* (Screened) porch
   d. *Can* (Canned) soft drinks
   e. Classes for beginner, intermediate, or *advance* (advanced) taught by certified instructors
2. Unaltered base form
   Found—a piece of *jewelery* (jewelry)
3. Epenthesis: insertion of a vowel between two consonants
   Fresh baked European *pasteries* (pastries)
4. Syncope
   Baton Rouge *Monoply* (Monopoly)
5. Misspelling of a neutralized vowel
   a. Truck Stop *Resturant* (Restaurant)
   b. *Carberator* (Carburetor)
6. Lack of distinction between /ɛ/ and /ɪ/ before nasals in Southern dialects
   a. Reward for stolen *simi-automatic* (semi-automatic)
   b. Neat as a *pen* (pin)

In addition, some students may find data that reflect the deliberate use of "misspelled" and dialectal forms to evoke a regional aura, as in this example from a Baton Rouge restaurant specializing in Cajun cooking: "Cajun Crawfish say, 'Eat dat tater.' " This message reflects several processes. The form *say* (instead of *says*) demonstrates omission of the third-person singular morpheme and the subsequent tensing of the lax vowel. The form *dat* (for *that*) illustrates the phonological process of stopping—that is, the substitution of a stop (e.g., /d/) for the corresponding fricative. The form *tater* (for *potato*) exemplifies the phonological process of aphesis, in which an unstressed initial syllable is deleted, as in *'rithmetic* for *arithmetic* and the brand name *Lectric Shave*. Other examples of dialectal "misspellings" are the names of two Southern restaurants, *Podnuh's* and *Po Folks*, both of which reflect the absence of postvocalic [r].

All the students in the pilot class were successful at finding and analyzing written forms reflecting phonological or morphological variation. As a more precise measurement of their ability to identify such forms, part of the final examination required the students to identify dialect-related errors in a passage adapted from Mina P. Shaughnessy (247). The passage contains several types of errors, some that can be analyzed as resulting from social or regional dialect influence (e.g., *involve* for *involved*) and others that cannot (e.g., *discus* for *discuss*). Eighty percent of the students were able to differentiate dialect-related errors from other types of errors with one hundred percent accuracy and also to explain the specific processes involved in the dialect-related errors. Thus it appeared that, by collecting and analyzing local data, the students gained skills that they could apply to new material.

Although the teaching unit we have outlined was first implemented as part of a course on social dialects, similar activities are adaptable to other courses such as phonetics, phonology, regional dialectology, and fieldwork methodology. In addition, a project of this type could be used in courses pertaining to research in education, English as a second language, composition, and basic writing.

Data similar to those discussed in this essay can also be collected from other sources—for example, nonstandard written forms occur frequently in freshman writing. Newspapers are another potential source of spelling data, especially in the classified ads. Because such ads are often placed by phone, their spelling may reflect what the ad taker perceived, rather than what the advertiser said: witness an ad we saw recently for a *ten-year track position* at a university.

Regardless of the particular method used, we believe that collecting and analyzing written data from local sources can be a valuable exercise for students of language variation. By completing a project such as that outlined here, students are introduced to fieldwork, gain experience in analyzing the relationship between spoken and written forms of English, and develop an awareness that language variation exists, so to speak, right in their own backyards.

Note

[1] A version of this article was presented by Kathryn Riley, Frank Parker, and Nick Macari at the American Dialect Society, Washington, D.C., 1984. The pilot study was funded by a joint grant from the National Education Association and the Kodak Cameras in the Curriculum Program.

Language Variation
and Composition

⸙

Accommodating Nonmainstream Language in the Composition Classroom

Jerrie Cobb Scott, Central State University, Ohio

HOW can language differences be accommodated in the composition class-room? This question arises most poignantly when teachers must deal with the "intrusive" role that nonmainstream varieties of English play in the development of writing skills. In planning writing instruction, we also need to consider ways in which spoken language may be used to facilitate writing; heretofore, dialect-based instructional programs have tended to focus on contrasting the "standard" and "nonstandard" forms that linguists have de-scribed. Researchers and teachers should attend to differences in the re-gional and ethnic dialects of their students and, also, to differences between and variation within spoken and written styles. In developing teaching meth-ods, we also have to consider what composition researchers and theorists have learned about specialized instruction for classes with a mix of speakers of standard and nonstandard dialects. Both concerns are addressed in this paper.

One of the purposes of this essay is to show that dialect-accommodating instruction need not—indeed should not—focus exclusively on the intrusive effects of students' naturally acquired language patterns on their mastery of skills taught in school. Instead, the language strategies learned outside of school can be linked to those targeted for development within school. An-other purpose is to illustrate that dialect-accommodating instruction ought not to be presented as special or remedial but should be integrated into the basic classroom framework. Information from both applied linguistics and composition theory can help educators design pedagogically sound methods for determining which language differences actually pose challenges and thus must be accommodated. In keeping with these aims, the first part of this article reviews the literature on studies of "intrusive effects" of nonmain-stream varieties of English on the production of Standard English in school, and the second part takes a more positive view of the student's home dialect: how language acquired outside of school can facilitate the development of literacy.

This essay focuses on nonmainstream language used by African Ameri-can students, but the principles discussed can be adapted to the challenges of teaching writing to speakers of other nonmainstream dialects who have difficulty learning the "school dialect" in composition classes.

Intrusive Spoken Language Patterns

Studies of dialect variation and writing have focused on testing the dialect interference hypothesis that speakers of nonmainstream varieties of English automatically transfer features from their spoken dialect to their writing in school. From this theory special instructional methods for teaching writing have evolved, the most popular of which is the contrastive analysis method. Basically, students are taught to see the differences between the forms used in their particular variety of English and those typically found in standard written English. Specific guidelines for teaching these contrasts vary from broadly based instruction on the history and development of varieties of present-day English to more narrowly focused grammar exercises. Judging how well the various dialect-accommodating techniques work is complicated. For one thing, programs employing such techniques have not been given a fair test. A perusal of the literature will show that little research has been conducted to determine how dialect-focused instruction affects the quality of students' writing performance, and the question of pedagogical efficacy is usually lost in the debate over whether dialect should be corrected in compositions. Obviously, this debate cannot be resolved here. Rather, I briefly review some representative viewpoints on the issue to identify features that frequently occur in the writing of speakers of nonmainstream dialects. After identifying the features, I propose guidelines for treating the features within the regular instruction sequence.

Of the studies designed to test the transfer of dialect patterns to writing, only three will be referred to here: Marcia Farr Whiteman, Marilyn Sternglass, and Jerrie C. Scott. Whiteman compared features in the writing of black and white nonstandard dialect speakers. She identified five features that occurred frequently in the writing of both groups.

1. Verb -s absence: He walk_ to school every day.
2. Plural -s absence: They walk down the street their radio_ in their hand_.
3. Possessive -s absence: Then he went over to my girlfriend_ house.
4. Verb -ed absence: He miss_ the bus yesterday.
5. Present be absence: She_ so calm.

Whiteman concluded that dialect accounted for some, but not all, occur-
rences of nonstandard features in these students' writing.

In a study of black and white students' writing, Sternglass found six
features that appeared more often in the writing of black students.

1. Absence of past-tense and past participle forms
2. Absence of forms of *be*
3. Incorrect subject-verb agreement patterns
4. Incorrect uses of articles (e.g., *a* for *an*)
5. Incorrect uses of prepositions
6. Incorrect pronoun inflections

Since the two groups differed quantitatively but not qualitatively in their use
of dialect features, Sternglass concluded that separate language materials
for white and black students were unnecessary.

In my own study of the relationship between dialect patterns in the
oral and written language of black students, I found some of the same
features in writing, though of course not in the writing of all black students.
The five features that occurred most commonly in writing are listed below
in the order of frequency.

1. Plural -*s* absence: Mr. Haley knew that many volume__ of book__
   could be found on the topic.
2. Verb -*ed* absence: First of all he travel__ to Gambia where he talk__
   to many elderly Africans.
3. Copula *be* absence: The most touching thing in the passage __
   where he tried to figure out the anguish of his great grandaddy.
4. Participle -*ed* absence: Alex Haley being a determine__ person
   wanted to find out. . . .
5. Possessive -*s* absence: Alex Haley__ research then comes to Africa.

I discovered that while some nonstandard features occurred in both writing
and speech, others occurred in writing only, and still others in speech only.
In addition, not all the features could be classified as dialect. Some were
better classified as intralectal patterns: some features corresponded to neither of the varieties commonly known as "African American" and "General
American," or "Standard," English. I concluded that the dialect interference
hypothesis accounts best for the unconscious transfer of spoken dialect features to writing, but at least three other processes were in evidence: (1)
monitoring, the formation of idiosyncratic rules that resulted in the production of intralectal patterns; (2) editing, the conscious application of learned

Standard English rules; and (3) controlling, the unconscious application of learned Standard English rules. The unconscious transfer of spoken dialect features to writing tends to yield the largest number and most consistent use of nonstandard features in writing. The number declines and usage continues to vary as students move toward the controlling process. It is quite likely that not all features undergo these processes simultaneously or that a single feature suddenly changes. Instead, forms change in an orderly manner, moving from one syntactic and semantic environment to another, appearing to be more sporadic in their presence and absence than they actually are. Students are not simply remembering and forgetting the Standard English forms. They are learning rules for producing Standard English forms in writing. It is important to note that the four processes outlined here involve not just the matching of forms but also the learning of rules.

Consider, for example, the intralectal pattern *There were so many information to be obtained.* This pattern is structurally incorrect by the standards of both edited written English and African American English. The verb *were* agrees with the plural quantifier *many*, but the verb does not agree with the headword *information*, a noncount singular noun. This structure is further complicated by the inverted word order of the subject and verb in existential sentences. The student who wrote this sentence had not mastered all the constraints on the application of the subject-verb agreement rule. This same student might, however, write *Many books were found, The book was found,* as well as *There was some books to be found.* The point is that the writer's use of *was* and *were* will vary until the constraints on subject-verb agreement rules are fully understood. Thus, for such a student, the familiar rule "a singular subject takes a plural verb" is not only confusing (since verbs technically are not marked for plurality) but also inadequate (since the rule does not explain the full range of structures that govern the Standard English rules for subject-verb agreement). To accommodate dialect differences, teachers must be prepared to explain constraints on rule application in accordance with the needs of students from various language backgrounds. Moreover, students must be able to detect contrasts not only between surface forms but also between the rules of different varieties of English.

Many questions about how spoken language affects writing remain unanswered. There are those who reject the dialect interference hypothesis, as well as related "corrective" pedagogy. Patrick Hartwell, for example, reasons that features such as those listed above occur because of partial mastery of the print code and can be attributed more to reading than to speech. After all, regardless of one's spoken dialect, it is necessary to learn a different code in order to write. Hartwell does not, however, consider the large body of information on dialect interference and reading in his discussion. I disagree with his total rejection of the dialect interference hypothesis but agree that sources other than the student's dialect must be considered. One such source is speech; indeed, the writing of inexperienced students often sounds like spoken language written down.

Colette A. Daiute has identified several speech patterns that cause problems when transferred to writing (11–12). Sentence fragments, for example, often go unnoticed in spoken language but are evident in written language, particularly in student writing. Although Daiute's work was directed toward understanding writing as a derivative of basic speaking processes, his analyses yielded descriptions of syntactic errors that are not often treated in composition textbooks but that I have found in the writing of black students. Short-term memory, Daiute argues, makes these errors difficult to recognize, especially when they occur in speech. The relation of these syntactic errors to the speech behaviors of particular social-class or ethnic groups has not, to my knowledge, been investigated. The three most frequently occurring constructions in Daiute's study were fragments, overlapping sentences, and distant modifier sentences. Unpracticed writers from any language background are likely to produce these errors. Nonstandard dialects will complicate, but not necessarily cause, the errors.

Another characteristic of unskilled writing is described by James L. Collins and Michael M. Williamson, who argue that, when oral communication has been highly dependent on abbreviated meanings, the communication pattern may be carried over to the written language as abbreviated syntax. They discuss two types of semantic abbreviations, exophoric references and formulaic expressions, which they describe as "inadequate representation of situational and cultural contexts of language" (23). Examples of exophoric reference are personal pronouns (*I, you,* and *it*) and demonstrative pronouns and deictic adverbs (*this, that,* and *there*) used in a context that does not provide a clear referent. Formulaic expressions include clichés, adages, and other words or phrases considered to be vague or trite. Collins and Williamson's "semantic abbreviations" are similar to usage patterns that Basil Bernstein examined in formulating his theory about elaborated and restricted codes—the latter code, he claimed, being used by members of lower socioeconomic groups who are accustomed to communicating only in informal social settings in which shared knowledge makes the explicit expression of context unnecessary. Citing data derived primarily from oral language, Bernstein argues that the cognitive processes of lower social-class groups, including nonmainstream ethnic groups, are constrained by the use of restricted codes. Focusing on the written language of unskilled writers, Collins and Williamson suggest that "strong writers are more able than weak writers to vary the extent to which their writing represents situational and cultural contexts" (33). Thus weak writers, they assert, may—regardless of ethnic or social background—depend heavily on the semantics of spoken language, causing their writing to sound simplistic and immature. Given Bernstein's premise that restricted codes and the language socialization processes of lower-class groups are causally related and Collins and Williamson's implied premise that restricted codes cause the abbreviated semantics of weak writers, syllogistic logic would lead one to the conclusion that the transfer of oral language patterns to writing is a source of the writing problems of students whose public language behavior manifests a "restricted code." This hypothesis was investigated by Marcia Farr and Mary Ann Janda.

Using the case-study approach, Farr and Janda set out to test the hypothesis that the writing difficulties of an African American male student were the result of the transfer of oral features to writing. Among the features examined were those identified by Wallace Chafe in his attempt to distinguish between typically oral and typically written discourse constructions. Chafe offers the following characteristics of informal spoken language: initial coordinating conjunctions, first-person references, references to a speaker's mental processes (*I remember*), statements that monitor information flow (*I mean, you know*), emphatic particles (*just, really*), direct quotes, and fuzziness. Characteristics of formal written language include passive voice, nominalization, participles, attributive adjectives, conjoined phrases, nouns in series, sequences of prepositional phrases, complement clauses, and relative clauses.

Farr and Janda concluded that the difficulties experienced by "Joseph" (the fictitious name given to the subject) evidenced many literate, or typically written discourse, features, though his oral language reflected conventional uses of many spoken language features. Also, in the more global qualities of his discourse, Joseph showed a highly literate orientation: "[H]is oral language was topic centered, explicit, and decontextualized" (80). Yet Joseph's writing was not acceptable. Why? Farr and Janda explain that while the form was there, evidence of Joseph's functional attempt to communicate was absent: "[H]is writing contained terse, unelaborated statements and inexplicitly expressed logical relationships" (81). If his school experiences are typical, they reason, "Joseph may not have had much instruction which called for the meaningful use of writing or for writing which required more than a sentence at a time" (81). Evidence of Joseph's functional attempt to communicate can also be found in settings outside the formal school environment, language experiences that should be used by teachers in facilitating his development of literacy, a point to which I shall return in the next section. Before moving to the facilitative effects of oral language on writing, we should take a closer look at writing instruction relevant to the intrusive effects of oral language on learning.

We have looked at writing in relation to dialect patterns, semantic abbreviations, and distinctive textual features of oral and written discourse. Most would agree that the patterns targeted for language-accommodating instruction thus far could be treated in the revising-editing part of composition. Once viewed as a type of readiness for or prerequisite to "real" writing, revising-editing instruction consisted primarily of threatening reminders: "Don't forget to proofread" or "Points will be deducted for errors." Nowadays, it is not unusual to find statements such as "revision provides a window into the cognitive operations which occur when a writer writes" (Birdwell 220) or "writing is rewriting" (Murray 56). Researchers and writing theorists have come to recognize the importance of revision to the composing process. Likewise, revision has become an integral part of writing instruction, one that should lend itself well to dialect-accommodating instruction.

What do researchers tell us about the editing-revising behaviors of writers? Poorer writers revise most at the "surface" level of word choice, sentence form, punctuation, and so on (Birdwell). Persistent revising during the first draft is a sure sign of writer's block (Rose). Blacks make more mechanical changes in their writing than their white peers (National Assessment). As noted above, researchers have found that speakers of nonmainstream varieties of English tend to make more mechanical errors (especially dialect-related deviations from standard written English) than speakers of mainstream varieties (Sternglass) and that black and white speakers of nonmainstream dialects use similar nonstandard features in their writing (Whiteman). We can say, then, that speakers of nonmainstream dialects are sensitive, perhaps hypersensitive, to the need to monitor their written expressions; and if they are unpracticed writers, they tend, like other inexperienced writers, to focus their revisions on surface-level features. Their concentration on surface-level monitoring should come as no surprise, since teachers often lead students to believe that they must demonstrate mastery of the smaller units of language before being taught about higher-level aspects of composing. The problem, of course, is that despite the perceived ease with which teachers can correct smaller units of language, students' effective manipulation of these units depends greatly on message content and writing context. Far too often, forms and expressions are treated in isolation or through exercises in grammar and mechanics that focus more on error detection than on error correction and not at all on contextualization of language structures.

Clearly, the elevated status of editing and revising will require more finely tuned instructional methods and greater understanding of variation in spoken and written styles. Currently, we know better what does not work than what does. We know, for example, that grammar exercises do not yield the expected results. Students often do not transfer their error-detecting skills to their writing. Similarly, the contrastive analysis approach to dialect-based writing instruction helps students to detect differences—and this is probably useful—but it does not guarantee the transfer of this information to their writing. We also recognize that detecting errors in connected written discourse is more difficult, but more beneficial to students, than spotting errors in isolated sentences. Finally, we know that it is more difficult to detect and correct errors in one's own writing than in the writing of others.

Guidelines for Improving Writing Instruction

We can now move toward more specific guidelines for accommodating language differences within the editing-revising component of writing instruction. I propose first that provisions be made to construct editing-revising exercises using the types of errors that students actually produce in their writing. Second, the errors targeted for instruction should be presented in context. Third, attention must be given to students' strategies for both detecting and correcting errors in context. Fourth, students must be given practice to help them make the transition from editing and revising the work of others to editing and revising their own work. The following guidelines embrace these four points.

1. Using features that actually occur in students' writing, teachers can construct an essay or paragraph for students to edit. They can assign students a topic to write about in a limited period of time, collect error sentences from the essay, and then construct a text, paragraph or essay, with the error sentences incorporated into the text. Alternatively, the teacher may select a student essay that contains a representative sampling of the common errors of members of the class, or may compose a text that is not directly based on essays by the class. The rationale for using sentences actually produced by students is to ensure that errors are analyzed within the syntactic and semantic environments in which they tend to occur. Following is a sample editing exercise I constructed for use in a research project:

> I like watching the soaps. General Hospital is my favorite. The reason why General Hospital is my favorite show is because it tells you what goes on in a hospital and how the doctors react. It also tell you and show you on General Hospital when doctors are married how they

react to each others problem and how they solve the problem between there selves. I like General Hospital a lot because it sho things we are suppose to see.

This passage was constructed from the writing of African American students, sixth graders of different writing levels. The students had been asked to write about their favorite television programs. Similar exercises could be composed with representative "errors" made by any group of students whose writing manifests cross-style influence.

2. The class can discuss the cues students use in detecting errors and their strategies for correcting errors in sample passages such as the preceding one or in their own writing. This discussion could lead to either a student- or a class-constructed writing handbook.

3. Teachers might assign impromptu writing with specified time limits for both writing and editing and then discuss with the students their experiences in doing the timed writing and editing assignment.

4. Peer-editing workshops can be held in which students use their class-constructed writing handbook as an editing-correcting reference book.

5. Students' editing-revising performance should be graded separately from their writing. This approach encourages the students to concentrate on completing a first draft, then on editing and revising the draft. The point here is that attempts to produce correct forms in the first draft often result in numerous false starts, fewer complete drafts, and serious cases of writer block. Assigning separate grades elevates the status of editing-revising strategies for students.

These guidelines serve as examples of how dialect-accommodating instruction can be treated within the framework of the regular composition classroom. As they improve their methods for teaching revision, instructors should focus more easily on differences in oral and written language within the revising-editing part of composition instruction.

The Facilitative Role of Oral Language in Writing

Researchers are now examining how language patterns that are developed outside of school are employed in the attainment of skills targeted for instruction in school. In this section of the paper, I briefly describe two related studies that investigated the facilitative effects of language patterns acquired outside of school on students' reading performance. I then describe my own explorations with lessons designed to draw on nonschool language in the teaching of writing.

At the outset, we should note that the success of students who already have command of the mainstream language of the school—whether they are white, black, or Hispanic—has been linked to similarities between language behaviors practiced in the home and those valued at school. For these students, the language behaviors learned in the home are accepted and expanded in school; contrarily, for nonmainstream groups, language patterns learned in the home are devalued in the school. Since schools are designed to meet the needs of the former group, when substantial numbers of this group fail, the system receives the blame and is immediately placed under investigation. Yet when nonmainstream students fail, blame is placed on their home environments. Researchers apparently have heretofore seen no reason to investigate aspects of the students' informal language and literacy patterns in order to discover means to facilitate the development of academic literacy. The research discussed below illustrates the need for a shift from "corrective" to language-accommodating instruction.

Marsha Taylor-Delain, P. David Pearson, and Richard Anderson explored the hypothesis that teachers can use "the rich and varied experience of black youth with figurative language outside the school" to "enhance their understanding of figurative language in school texts" (155). They found that skills in "sounding" had a positive effect on students' comprehension of figurative language. Sounding is a verbal game played by many black youth; if African Americans do not engage in sounding or other "street language," they are at least familiar with it unless they have had little contact with users of these language styles. It involves the exchange of ritualistic insults that cannot be interpreted as literally true and makes use of such figurative language devices as hyperbole, irony, and metaphor. (See the work of Mitchell-Kernan and of Smitherman [*Talkin and Testifyin*] for fuller descriptions of similar African American discourse patterns.) The work of Taylor-Delain and her coauthors shows that skills acquired "in the street" do transfer to school settings. They go on to say that "teachers need to appreciate differences in communication strategies in order to foster an environment in the classroom that capitalizes on the strengths of all children" (171).

In a related study, Andrew Ortony, Terence J. Turner, and Nancy Larson-Shapiro examined cultural and instructional influences on the comprehension of figurative language by elementary school children. In opposition to the cognitive-constraints view of language learning (i.e., that "the ability to properly understand metaphorical language is primarily constrained by the child's level of cognitive development" [25]), these researchers found support for a language-experience view of learning (i.e., that "a child's ability to understand metaphorical language is primarily dependent on the extent to which the child has had exposure to such language" [26]).

All students in this study were exposed to figurative language through instruction in creative writing. The researchers concluded that while such instruction improved students' comprehension of figurative language, "the use of figurative language in sounding tends to enhance Black school children's ability to understand the more literary uses of metaphor and simile encountered in the classroom" (34). Both studies point to the facilitative role that language acquired outside of school by a nonmainstream group can have on the development of skills taught in the schools.

More of this type of research is needed. I believe, though, that even without further empirical proof, we can safely assume that the degree of school success attained by any group is directly linked to the degree of bridging that takes place between naturally acquired and school-taught language and literacy patterns. When the school succeeds in teaching, it does so because it has either purposely or accidentally provided mechanisms for linking the naturally acquired to the school desired language behaviors and goals.

The exploratory work described below was an attempt to bridge another popular form of communication, rapping, to language behaviors targeted for development in the composition classroom.

> Come up with a topic and write a few lines about it. Make sure they rhyme. Now create a rhythm—bang it out on a tabletop if you have to. Then put it all together, kind of like you're Muhammad Ali with a backbeat. That's rap. (Graff B1)

What Gary Graff describes in this 1986 *Detroit Free Press* article is the rock music version of a form of communication that has it roots in the African American speech community. "Rap is what its name implies, a music of language, an evocative talk-singing in rhythmic, rather melodic, patterns accompanied only by a spare beat" (B1). He traces the roots of rap back to the street poetry of the late 1960s, but almost any middle-aged African American can tell you that this form of communication has been used in both sacred and secular contexts for as long as we can remember (see Smitherman, *Talkin and Testifyin*). Origins aside, the rap's former appeal to African American teenagers, especially males, had been expanded to adolescents of both sexes and various ethnic and social groups, including many whites, by 1990. As an instructional tool, the rap has been employed by songwriters as a mnemonic device to aid in the teaching of, for example, the eight parts of speech. My interest in the use of the rap stemmed from my amazement at the spontaneity with which rappers could construct messages that were sound in content and aesthetically pleasing. For instance, I observed an African American male end a student debate session with a rap. Amazingly, not only was the rap rhythmic, but it contained the major issues of the debate as well as congratulatory remarks to the winning team. Admittedly, it was the rapper's summary strategies that interested me most, perhaps because I was at the time treating summaries in my composition course. I wondered what other educational benefits the rap might serve.

In an exploratory study of the rap, I discovered that many of the concepts taught in composition could be covered using the rap as source materials, much as we regularly employ reading selections to illustrate various strategies used by writers. In what follows, I provide a sample of a rap and discuss it in relation to a variety of composing tasks. It was produced spontaneously by an African American male, "Lo the Pro," who was asked to create a rap in response to the question "What do you think of the recent presidential election results?" The rap was collected about two days after Reagan's reelection, in 1984. The rapper was a tenth grader, and this exploratory work was conducted in a tenth grade class.

M to the R with a Capital L: Mr. Reagan and His Spell

Now I see Mr. Reagan won again,
And Mondale felt like a lost man.
So he turned around and started to weep
Cause Reagan almost had a 50 state sweep.
Mr. Reagan began to brag to those who were sad:
  I'm—too hot to freeze,
      too cold to burn,
      too young to seize,
      too old to learn;
      too much ahead
      to lose the race
         and
      too far in front
      for second place.
Cause I'm a M to the R with a capital L.
  And I got you Americans under my spell.
So rock on to the bell of my spell.
  Rock on to the bell of my spell. Ha-ha.

Since the rap was presented orally, the first task was to transcribe it. This is my written version of the rap. Students varied greatly in their written presentations, from the use of a poetic to a prose representation. The task turned out to be an excellent way to get students to pose questions about the relationship between punctuation and intended message.

Most composition textbooks contain, indeed often begin with, a section on invention strategies—helping students generate ideas for writing. Following the process models of composition, textbooks often provide exercises in freewriting, such as brainstorming, nonstop stream-of-consciousness writing, focused freewriting. These exercises, like the rap, engage the student in spontaneous language production. There is no reason why the rap could not be included among the various types of invention strategies.

We also might consider the rap in relation to discourse planning, often referred to as outlining. To illustrate, I asked students to present in outline form three major ideas from the rap above. Three examples of student generated outlines follow.

Sample A: I. Feelings of Mondale and Reagan
            II. Reagan's Attitude toward Mondale
            III. Reagan's Attitude toward Americans
Sample B: I. No Contest in the Election
            II. No Reason for Reagan to Change
            III. No Use for People to Resist Reagan's Spell
Sample C: I. Mondale Didn't Have a Chance
            II. The People Can't Change Reagan
            III. Reagan's Power Is like Magic

While these simplistic outlines do not represent the ultimate in discourse planning, they do help students to see that effective raps, like effective essays, contain an orderly sequence of ideas. Furthermore, the outlines show the move from spontaneous to more carefully planned processes for selecting ideas.

The rap also permits wide-ranging analyses of rhetorical strategies. In response to the question "How does the rapper keep your attention?" students responded in interesting ways. One student wrote:

I liked the different types of ways to express the same feelings in the rap. To say that Reagan was confident the rapper said too hot to freeze, too cold to burn, too young to seize, too old to learn. The description given by the rapper from my point of view is that Mr. Reagan knows he's untouchable and no one can stop him.

It took very little probing to get the students to see the use of parallel structures and opposites as devices that kept their attention. Another student wrote:

The rapper keeps my attention by keeping on striving for his main point. I do that whenever I open up a speech. All he said was that Reagan knew he was going to win cause Americans are stupid.

In more formal terms, the rap attains unity through the repetition of ideas.

Still other students attempted to make a connection between the title, "M to the R with a Capital L," and the rapper's strategy for keeping the audience's attention. The most interesting example follows:

> In this rap, he strangely but naturally changed himself into Mr. Reagan. (In another rap, the rapper had called himself "M to the R with a capital L, Mr. Lo the Pro.") But then the M to the R with the capital L could also mean Mondale to Reagan lost.

This analysis of the ambiguity of the title led to a highly informative discussion of the function of titles.

Frequently mentioned was the alliteration of this rap—the repetition of *l* as a device used to keep the audience's attention. One student pointed out that he would have reversed the last line of the rap to produce another type of double meaning:

> So rock on to the bell of my spell.
> Rock on to the bell of my spell. Ha-ha.

to be changed to

> So rock on to the bell of my spell.
> Rock on the spell of my bell. Ha-ha.

My point here is not to be exhaustive but merely to illustrate that the methods frequently used to teach students the importance of keeping the audience's interest can be expanded to include strategies that the students quickly recognize in a popular form of communication but often do not grasp in the more formal language of the composition textbook.

Obviously, the rap falls under the general rubric of poetic language. Many of the students admitted that they were not as good at rapping as "Lo the Pro" but that they could and occasionally did intersperse such patterns into their oral language, essentially to get attention.

When, we might ask, does a writer try hardest to get the audience's attention? Again, we can point to an area typically treated in composition textbooks—introductions and conclusions, or openers and closers. Students were asked to write papers using the outlines generated from the rap and some interesting strategies discussed for openers and closers found in the rap. This assignment, however, was given after students had been instructed to define and supply examples of metaphors, similes, narrative patterns, parallel structures, and repetitions in the forms of words, phrases, and idea units. They were required to select the examples from both their textbooks and their collection of raps. No attempt was made to measure the effect of these lessons on students' actual writing performance. It was clear to me, however, that the writing evinced a functional attempt to communicate, the quality found missing from the writing of Joseph in the Farr and Janda study. And this, I believe, is as important in learning to write as any other factors that have been empirically demonstrated.

What students produced in this instructional sequence was a rough draft. The next logical step in the sequence was to revise and edit. I believe that beyond the editing done during the construction of the first draft, it is wise to delay closer readings until after students have had the chance to figure out what they have to say about a given topic and how they can manipulate language to express their ideas clearly, concisely, and effectively. If my initial observations are borne out, the teacher can expect the first drafts to read like speech written down (i.e., the writing is personal). As students learn to accept the notion that revising and editing are essential parts of preparing writing for presentation to larger audiences, they will begin—with assistance, of course—to bridge the gap between personal and transactional writing. Their bridging, then, provides the evidence that the teacher, too, has made a giant step toward accommodating nonmainstream language in the composition classroom.

Dusty Books and Dense Contracts: Exercises That Involve Students in Language Research Projects

Jeutonne P. Brewer, University of North Carolina, Greensboro

PERHAPS too often we think of classroom teaching as the public agony (or ecstasy) required to impart a specific set of details about language. Too often we think of analysis and research as the secluded agony (or ecstasy) required to collect and then order our data, the result being a class presentation, an article to signal our success in a given area, or possibly a thesis to admit us to membership in academe. Perhaps too seldom do we reflect on how we learned about language, how we learned to conduct successful research, and how we mastered the necessary steps. As teachers, we should consider what first sparked our interest in language. Drawing on this understanding of how our interest in language developed, we should involve our students in the study of "real" language in everyday contexts, as these relate to the teaching of language and the teaching of writing.

Every teacher faces a major problem in trying to meet the goals of sharing knowledge of language and involving students in research—finding or designing projects that are brief enough to be usable yet adequately challenging to be interesting. Recognizing that problem, I have designed exercises that have been useful in my classes and that I hope will be helpful for other teachers.

I have used the five exercises discussed in this paper with two courses: an introduction to the English language and an American dialects course. Students who enroll in these courses typically have diverse backgrounds, various majors, and no particular experience in studying language. Because my university offers an undergraduate interdepartmental major in linguistics, some students may have studied linguistics before enrolling in these courses, but they are the exception. Majors in English, communication studies, physical education, elementary education, and business constitute the majority of the students. I suspect that my situation is similar to that of many—probably most—instructors who teach undergraduate language courses in such departments as anthropology, speech, English, foreign languages, and psychology.

The number of exercises I use in a semester depends on the topics included in the course and the amount of time I plan for introducing the topic and guiding the students through the research and writing process. A useful guide is one or two exercises per semester.

Language Attitudes and Dusty Books

After presenting the historical background of language policy in this country and explaining shifts in language attitude during the nineteenth century (based on Heath, "A National Language Academy?"), I give the students a handout containing the following information: a statement that we will investigate the possibility that language attitudes became more prescriptive after 1850; a list of nineteenth-century periodicals in our library; directions for them to find articles about language attitude, with at least one article published before 1850 and one published after 1850 (the initial collection should include three to four articles); directions about how to write note cards, bibliography cards, and an abstract card for each article; directions for writing a brief paper on the topic. After the students have collected their material, they write a brief paper in which they discuss the attitudes of the writers, the writers' arguments about language, and change (or lack of change) in writers' attitudes during the nineteenth century. These papers provide the basis for class discussion of their findings.

The students then place their note cards, bibliography cards, and abstract cards in a file box I have placed on reserve in our library. Their first papers on language attitude can also be placed on reserve, making each student's research available to all students in the class. Starting with the sources they have collected and drawing on all the information on reserve in the library, the students continue their research on the question of a shift in language attitude; they search for additional articles and review the findings of other students. They then write a second paper discussing language attitude and any shift discernible in their ongoing research.

One major advantage and problem with this exercise is that it is collaborative. The teacher must make sure that the students understand the nature of appropriate collaboration, as distinct from inappropriate use of others' ideas. However, the project provides an opportunity to teach students how to recognize and give credit to other students' findings. While the students' major complaint about this exercise has been that the books are musty and dusty, the librarians, of course, have been pleased that such books are being used.

Names

An examination of place names, personal names, or product names appears in several of the introductory language texts and readers. After reading about and discussing place names and personal names, including Thomas Pyles's article "Bible Belt Onomastics or Some Curiosities of Anti-pedobaptist Nomenclature," I give the students a handout with these directions:

1. There are three lists of names of UNCG students on reserve in the library.
2. Select twenty names from each list. (For example, you may select the first twenty names in the list or every third name in the list. Use the same method for selecting names from each list.)
3. Classify the names into categories.
4. Write a paper in which you explain the purpose of your project, the method by which you selected the names discussed in your paper, and the categories of names you developed. Compare your categories with those presented by Thomas Pyles and discuss ways in which the categories are similar to or different from Pyles's categories.

This project is particularly interesting and easy to design. I provide one list of names from an early decade of the university, the second list from the middle period, and the third list from a recent decade. Because the University of North Carolina, Greensboro, was formerly the Woman's College of North Carolina, the names are primarily those of female students, a helpful simplification for comparisons and discussion.

Dense Contracts and "Plain" English

Starting with President Jimmy Carter's executive order in 1978 requiring the government to write documents in plain English, I discuss with the class some examples of bureaucratic language and the advantages and disadvantages of using plain English. I include an examination of readability formulas and a brief exercise in the use of these formulas (Flesch; Klare, *Measurement* and "Second Look"); the class then explores some of the problems in using a readability formula as a measure of plain English. I hand out copies of sample passages from several types of writing: textbooks, fiction, memoranda, directions from Internal Revenue Service tax publications, dissertations, rental contracts, and bank loan agreements. Students and community contacts often provide the best examples for discussion. A major insurance company whose home office is in Greensboro sent copies of before-and-after versions of contracts that had been rewritten in plain English. One semester a student who worked for a realty agency brought in copies of realty contracts. After we identify phrases, sentences, and passages that are difficult or impossible to understand, the discussion leads quickly and rather easily into a grammatical analysis. We focus particularly on agentless passives, passive adjectives, and nominalized constructions. We evaluate the before-and-after versions of insurance policies and realty contracts rewritten in simplified language. That is, we want to discover what the effects of the rewording are.

A guest lecturer from an insurance company described how he went about rewriting the insurance policies the students have studied. He explained to the class that he was an actuary who had been assigned the task of rewriting insurance policies in plain English. As a mathematician with a new and, for him, very different assignment, he decided to use a common-sense approach. His procedure was to read the old contract, ask himself exactly what meaning was intended, rewrite the section, and then ask other employees to read his new version. After noting that the company had also redesigned the format of the insurance policy to make it less intimidating to the policy buyer, he discussed the before-and-after versions of the work and outlined an unexpected problem that arose. Sometimes policy buyers did not realize that the policy they received in the mail was their insurance contract; it did not have the intimidating appearance of such a document! The company had to print the contract with the words "THIS IS A CONTRACT" in large type with a reminder that the policyholder should file the contract with other important papers.

Then the students select a section of the insurance policy or of the realty contract and analyze the grammatical differences between the before-and-after versions. Finally, the students write a paper in which they present the results of this analysis.

Rental agreements, leases, and bank loan agreements provide equally useful examples of attempts to reword legal documents. The directions written by the Internal Revenue Service always prompt lively class discussion. A timely candidate for analysis is the new W-4 form. I often ask the students to provide examples for their papers. Banks and realty firms are located near campus. Students who live off campus have probably signed a rental contract or lease. Although this collection may seem to be a motley mess of legal documents, it provides an interesting and challenging set of legalistic papers that are important to the students: each student works with one type of document. Also, it provides examples I can use in introductory class sets in later semesters.

Tag Questions

The fourth exercise involves a questionnaire designed to elicit items for tag questions. Without prior discussion of tag questions, the class participates as subjects by supplying tags for the eighty-five items in a questionnaire I have prepared. I present the material with a tape that includes explanations and the questionnaire; there are two versions available, one with a female voice and one with a male voice. We discuss the kind of knowledge that speakers must have in order to use tag questions and the variation in their use of pronouns in the tags for constructions like *Neither John nor Sue will come*. Then each student collects data from two subjects using my tape-recorded explanations and questionnaire.

With some classes, I show students how to enter their data into a computer. I combine the students' data with the database already on file in the computer from previous classes and analyze the entire set with SPSS (Statistical Package for the Social Sciences). I print cross-tabulations of the data for each verb and pronoun used in the tags and place the printouts on reserve in the library. I show the students how to read a cross-tabulation table so that they can consider not only the gross tabulation but also the percentage of use of a tag in relation to social variables. The students have available information on the use of each tag in relation to such social factors as age, sex, region, and level of education. The printouts also contain means, standard deviations, chi square, and degrees of freedom. Although most students do not have the background to use these measures, they are available to students who have adequate training.

Each student then selects five related items from the questionnaire that illustrate variations such as the use of verb forms or pronouns. In their papers, the students list the items they will analyze, select the social factors that might influence the use of tags, explain how and why they chose those items, and analyze the variation in the use of verb forms or pronouns in relation to their selected social variables.

Two other approaches, however, do not require students to learn to use the computer. Students can analyze the data collected with previous classes. In another approach, the students analyze only the data from three (or more) questionnaires completed in the introductory exercise. Each student selects five related items from the questionnaire, analyzes the verb or pronoun form used in the responses, and considers how English grammar can account for those facts. This approach is limited to the use of tabulations but adds the more general question about the form of the grammar.

Where Do All Those Neat Tables Come From?

In their reading, students encounter tables and figures suggesting that data in the "real" world come in neat packages. They can easily assume that language data are as neat and regular as those tables. Researchers know better.

Like many other teachers, I require students to conduct a tape-recorded interview, preferably with a subject forty years of age or older. They use a written questionnaire that I have developed with the questionnaire in Walt Wolfram and Donna Christian's *Appalachian Speech* as a guide. They tape-record their interview and analyze that recording.

Sometimes I play selections from the tape-recorded material from my research so that the students can hear an actual example of field research. One selection I have found useful is a sample of six Lumbee Indians from Robeson County in southeastern North Carolina, in which students can hear the use of the Tidewater diphthong as well as other speech characteristics. Another informative selection is a sample from the few hours of tape-recorded interviews with ex-slaves, collected by the Archive of Folk Song in the 1930s and 1940s (available from the Library of Congress), in which students can hear examples of invariant *be*.

Their assignment is to analyze variation in the subject's use of phonological or syntactic features selected from their interview, a sample selection I provide them from my research tapes, or a copy of an ex-slave interview recorded by the Archive of Folk Song. They write a paper presenting their analysis. The project can be kept within manageable proportions by setting an upper limit on the number of examples the student must include in the analysis or by limiting the extraction of data from a set number of minutes at the beginning, the middle, and the end of the tape. The student must explain the method used in deciding which data to select for the paper.

The table on the use of *chick, girl, woman,* and *lady* appended to Frank Anshen's *Statistics for Linguists* can be used effectively to analyze variation in the use of lexical items. I ask the students, "What can you say about the use of these terms by looking at the table?" Very quickly the students begin to analyze the data in relation to the sex and age of the subjects.

Purpose of Projects

Projects provide a way for students to write shorter papers while trying to learn analytical procedures. They benefit from the experience of working with "real" problems, "real" data—and, if we are fortunate, from sharing our enthusiasm for the project. We benefit by stating a problem in a clear, organized form for the students and sometimes by gaining new perspectives about language and language research. With our students as colleagues, we can delve into topics that are related to our primary interests in language, although perhaps not central to them—those areas we might investigate if time and energy permitted, as they seldom do.

I propose that projects such as these are ways to spark student interest, as well as to maintain our own interest in the courses we teach semester after semester and year after year.

Variation in Written English: Punctuation

Greta D. Little, University of South Carolina

EVEN among the linguistically sophisticated, the assumption that punctuation is uniform and allows the writer few options is common, yet any casual survey of written language in its many forms shows a great variety in both the frequency and placement of punctuation marks without any accompanying loss of meaning. Examining variation in the placement of different marks of punctuation across time and in a wide range of written media gives students a good opportunity to learn firsthand the flexibility of language use. Such activities provide an accessible and interesting corpus of data for students both because samples are easy to collect and because one can immediately make comparative analyses. Although no special equipment or new skill is required of the students, gathering examples of punctuation remains a challenge. What makes that task difficult is precisely what makes it valuable. People rarely pay very much attention to marks of punctuation in everyday reading; they assume the marks are where they have been taught to expect them and only occasionally realize that those expectations have been violated. In fact, those expectations are frequently not met, especially in the casual texts of signs, billboards, fliers, and announcements. When students collect these kinds of data, they become more aware of variation and of how often usage they have been taught is wrong is tolerated and even accepted in nonscholastic, informal circumstances.

Collecting Examples

My own interest in punctuation as an area of investigation was sparked by looking at the apostrophe, an excellent mark for a first exercise. I have approached the issue in a variety of ways, but one of the most amusing for my students is to survey restroom signs within a given area. The data are readily available and easily accessed. Further, only a limited number of responses are possible, so the collection task is quite simple. The results, however, provide fruitful ground for discussion. Some labels will be fairly clear, like *Women*; others will be definitely possessive, like *Men's*. A few will be obvious violations of school rules: *Mens* or *Ladie's*. A number will be unclear, however. If the door has a sign reading *Ladies*, do we think of the word as possessive or not? Frequently, I expand the assignment to include all signs identifying or labeling areas. I ask the students to pay particularly close attention to areas marked by more than one sign, making sure that they collect any variation that might show up there. Inevitably they will find clear examples of inconsistency: *Women's Locker Room* and *Womens Locker Room*. I want to make certain that the students consider the impact of such variation on learners who are attempting to unravel the meaning of that little curly mark before or after an *s*. I also ask the students to look for examples of other symbols being used to do the work of the apostrophe—the asterisk in *Macy*s* or the ice cream cone in *Steve♥s Ice Cream*.

I have students in a wide range of courses gather examples of punctuation use. In my freshmen classes, we look at sentences the students have collected from printed texts so that we can *see* the punctuation in use. For classes in English grammar and history of the language, I frequently assign projects that involve collecting a large sample of sentences that use one particular mark of punctuation. The students are asked to examine their collections and develop a set of generalizations to describe where the marks are used. Sometimes the generalizations conform pretty much to the patterns prescribed by handbook rules, but exceptions do occur. For instance, students collecting colons discover sentences like "Tom Selleck: Sexy, Sane, and Single" (*McCall's*) and "Its mandate: to settle disputes between nations" (*Newsweek*). The sentence pattern is fairly common in reputable publications, but it is not mentioned in most handbooks. Thus students can discover for themselves examples of "nonstandard" usage that is not stigmatized. They can also investigate the role of context in the appropriateness of forms and structures that do carry clear stigmas. Collecting examples of periods has turned up surprising numbers of fragments in published texts and can contribute to informed discussions about the acceptability of incomplete sentences in formal and informal English.

Comparing Frequency

In classes where linguistic change is important, my students have examined patterns of usage in comparable texts from different time periods. These comparisons have revealed a greater frequency of most marks of punctuation in nineteenth-century texts. We have also compared texts using the variables British or American, male or female, and fiction or nonfiction. For these assignments, we use a technique introduced by George Summey, author of two studies on punctuation usage. Using a text with 100 sentences, we count the marks of punctuation occurring within that sample and divide by 100 to discover the average marks per sentence. If a sample has a total of 342 marks, it will have an average 3.42 marks per sentence.

Because I am convinced that casual written English is as deserving of attention as its more formal counterparts, I have encouraged students to look at advertisements as well as more conventional texts. Not surprisingly, they have discovered that fashion has prompted varied punctuation in advertising contexts. Another example of unconventional texts that have proved a fruitful ground for investigating variation of this sort are children's books. My classes have investigated paragraphing and capitalization in books for youngsters and have found the patterns of usage to be distinctly different from what we had expected. Many of these books do not have paragraphs at all. Some have only a single paragraph or sentence on each page, and some will designate a new paragraph by extending the first line to the left instead of indenting. Sentence length and punctuation frequency in nineteenth- and twentieth-century children's books also show quantifiable differences. For these assignments, I have had students use primitive methods such as counting punctuation by hand as well as more sophisticated tools such as computer analysis.

Style Sheets

In some of my assignments, students rely on their knowledge of handbook rules to recognize departures from the prescribed norm. In others, they are asked to see how patterns are changing. Yet another type of assignment I use is one in which students are asked to produce rules (or style sheets) for writing found in highly specific contexts. The first example of this kind of assignment concerns comic strips. The text is not connected prose and consequently requires its own rules. I make a list of the various strips available in local newspapers and allow students to choose the one they would like to follow. Over a three-week period the students pay close attention to their strips, the manner in which they are written, and the conventions that are used for the text. At the end of the three weeks, they submit a style sheet that could guide a substitute cartoonist. In class, we compare the ways in which various functions are performed, developing a taxonomy, as it were, of comic strip styles. The last time I used the assignment, we discovered three different ways of indicating the end of a declarative sentence: the expected period; either the bubble or nothing; or exclamation points, dashes, or ellipses. None of the three was significantly more common than the others.

In a similar exercise, students are assigned to watch the news on local stations, major networks, and cable news stations. The students' task is to develop a style sheet for the people in charge of the captions that appear on the screen during news broadcasts. This task is far from simple without a VCR, because the captions are always on the screen for only a brief time, and students, like ordinary viewers, are more concerned with the content of the news than with the form of the captions. Nevertheless, the results are well worth the effort. Students discover that some networks feature patterns of usage that are drastically different from what they had expected. What is most revealing is that students had frequently watched such broadcasts for years without ever noticing the differences. Copy in television ads and in the captions used for sports events can also offer fruitful ground for similar investigations.

I am particularly fond of these assignments in which students observe patterns of usage that they have seen over and over again without noticing the lack of conformity with what they have learned in school. Even English teachers are often surprised to discover that rules they hold sacred are violated again and again without the predicted loss of meaning.

Unpunctuated Text

My last assignment on the general topic of punctuation is another that is especially interesting when English teachers are involved. I provide students with two or three copies of an unpunctuated text printed completely in uppercase letters, such as the following:

ALL THE CHILDREN WERE AFRAID THAT AMY MIGHT DIE WHILE THE DOCTOR WAS THERE MR TISDALE TOOK THE CHILDREN DOWNSTAIRS TO THE KITCHEN

To make sure that they understand that the exercise is not some sort of test, I tell them to ask friends, relatives—even former teachers—to provide the necessary marks of punctuation. In class, we divide into groups and compare the results. The outcome is fascinating because there are both areas of agreement—mostly at sentence boundaries—and areas of frequent variation. Much of the variation, on close examination, appears to be motivated by differences in intended interpretations of the text. And, finally, there are a number of careless errors—errors made by both those who are learned and those who are not. My students, of course, enjoy the mistakes made by English teachers most of all.

All this attention to punctuation may seem excessive, but I believe that understanding how readers and writers deal with punctuation is an important, and often overlooked, step in understanding literacy. Furthermore, exploring how such marks are learned will help us see if connections between spoken and written language exist and how the two modes interact. Assignments like these enable students to contribute to our general understanding of language, but the most important fact is that this exercise teaches them more about punctuation than they ever learn from traditional instruction based on partially complete descriptions of everyday uses of punctuation marks.

Using Language Study
in Freshman Composition

Lynn K. Varn, Belmont Abbey College
George Dorrill, Southeastern Louisiana University
Gloria Jones, Winthrop College

HAVING heard for years the complaints of composition teachers that freshmen are not only voiceless on issues but deaf to language, we decided to test the validity of these assertions by trying a sensitizing experiment: to have freshmen do research on the talk going on around them and to write about language on the basis of firsthand observation. This article describes the three types of open-ended designs that the three authors used in their sections of Writing 102, a research-based composition course at Winthrop College in Rock Hill, South Carolina. Throughout the experiment, we probed for the answers to these questions:

1. Is a language focus in composition stimulating enough for our freshmen?
2. Can students at this level extend themselves as researchers—go from library sources to assertions based on evidence they uncover in the language around them?
3. Can students who are uninitiated to language study grasp enough of the differences in the use of language to make valid observations?
4. Will any assumed increase in sensitivity to language measurably affect their writing competence?

As three of us have presented this language-alert model to more than a dozen sections, we feel confident in sharing some preliminary findings. Most of the students have been able to equip themselves for empirical study of language after reading some assigned essays and participating in class discussions on linguistic theories, linguistic controversies, and ethnography. The student evaluations have indicated that, after some time for adjustment, the new topic of language freshened the students' attitudes toward research and the enterprise of composition. Their papers (with topics from sound symbolism in advertising to movie ratings and titles, New Journalism, and language in the courtroom, in protest music, in dormitories, and on the golf course) have reflected independent, critical thought and an awareness of culture and its speech communities, especially the professions. The students were able to find issues—real for themselves—in language everywhere and came to understand how people use language differently for different purposes.

We were struck with the hyposensitivity to language among students in a culture filled with high-tech communications. They had few skills as listeners and no idea that they suffered any disadvantage with their ears turned off. In the beginning, their writing lacked spontaneity, and classroom debate did not seem to be regarded as a resource for student and teacher in gathering data for research papers.

Our objectives for Writing 102 were to stimulate students to think for themselves, to do research for their own purposes, and to write for themselves. We felt that undergraduates who would never take another English course could learn how to observe their own and others' use of language, think critically about their observations, and conclude that the analysis of language had extrinsic value for everyday life, not just for classroom assignments.

We cast the students in the role of observer-inquirers themselves, their own analysts: they would observe the language around them, and we would observe the students. Quite recursively, some students would observe us. We also "weighted" (Bean, Drenk, and Lee) certain assignments, building the students up to committed arguments: What right have companies to use the terms *health foods, natural, organic* so loosely? How are sports metaphors undermining meaning in our world, rendering everything a game? How should one view what the press deemed a propagandized translation of *The Oxford English Dictionary* published in the Soviet Union? Should we violate the pornographer's right to free speech? What system of movie rating symbols would work better for a concerned public? Such matters, if the students had never taken notice, could become their personal controversy, stimulating genuine interest in the use of deliberative writing and research on a topic for a term paper, the only department requirements.

Four textbooks were selected for our sections of the course over a period of three semesters, with each teacher permitted to choose the reading selections that would best suit the needs of particular assignments: Linda A. Morris, Hans A. Ostrom, and Linda P. Young (*Living Language*), Gary Goshgarian (*Exploring Language*), Paul Eschholz, Alfred Rosa, and Virginia Clark (*Language Awareness*), and Peter Farb (*Word Play*).

Course Design 1:
Ethnography of Communication
by George Dorrill

In preparing a design for my two sections of Writing 102, I relied on an eclectic combination of influences and resources: the work of Dixie Goswami (Goswami and Stillman) and Shirley Brice Heath (*Ways with Words*) in adapting the ethnography of communication to the classroom; Marie Ponsot and Rosemary Deen's insistence on writing directed to the class and on having everyone in the class comment orally and in writing on the topic at hand (with writing preceding the oral discussion); distinctions between informative and deliberative writing made by Walter H. Beale, Karen Meyers, and Laurie L. White (and by Aristotle); Laurence Behrens and Leonard Rosen's and Robert Day's models for formal academic writing; and my own experience as a linguist and a composition teacher.

I designed the course so that a sequence of steps would lead students to present to the class, at the end of the semester, a paper on some aspect of human communication. This paper would be based on data gathered and analyzed by the student and would include a review of previous research on the subject. The first half of the semester was concerned with informative writing, including a formally documented synthesis of research on an individually chosen topic. The second half of the semester concentrated on deliberative writing, including a second research paper. This last assignment, based on the students' own empirical research, fit into Beale's notion of interpretative deliberation—creating knowledge rather than transmitting knowledge.

In addition to the two research papers, the students turned in written assignments that complemented the research topics. The first paper the students wrote was a diagnostic essay, an essay on public lying, which they rewrote toward the end of the semester. The first graded assignment was a summary of a chapter in Farb's *Word Play* or of one of the essays in *The Living Language* (Morris, Ostrom, and Young). The students then wrote a synthesis based on at least two sources from *Word Play* or *The Living Language*. This exercise led to their first research paper, formally documented literature reviews on selected research topics. The research topics varied considerably, but most could be subsumed under the following general headings: nonverbal communication, onomastics, language variation, specialized languages (including slang and occupational or recreational languages), and language development. As part of the course, I held weekly conferences, to keep track of each student's progress and provide individual guidance for reading and research.

The types of research also varied. Many students did ethnographic or observational research of one kind or another—hand and arm positions in the lunch line, courtship gestures at fraternity parties, gaze and eye contact in elevators and fast food restaurants, and language on the golf course, in grocery stores, and at the gym. Others did survey research—attitudes toward slang, interpretations of photographs of facial expressions and sound-symbolic words. Still others did textual and quantitative studies—the most popular given names at Winthrop, surnames in a small-town telephone book, pet names in Rock Hill, differences between British and American spelling, the uses of the semicolon. Some conducted dialect interviews and case studies of language development.

In the second half of the semester, students kept one another informed of their progress in classroom group sessions. Following the suggestions of Ponsot and Deen, we read all the essays aloud in class. Everyone wrote comments on each essay and read the comments aloud to the class. I wrote and read along with the students: my own research project was how linguistics could be applied to the composition classroom, using observations of my own classes.

Course Design 2:
The Language of Contemporary Issues
by Gloria Jones

Because many of the readings used in other writing courses are not necessarily relevant to student experience, the students' initial reaction to the idea of writing about language was obvious apprehension. Students later were surprised when they realized that what they would study, research, deliberate on, and write about was an integral part of their lives that they had always taken for granted: news broadcasts, political speeches, sports broadcasts, conversations in grocery store aisles, conversations in the dorm, lectures in classrooms, sermons from the pulpit, and even song lyrics.

The vehicle for our language exploration was class discussion generated by our readings. The essays in Morris, Ostrom, and Young; Goshgarian; and Farb provided the foundation for the discussion, but they frequently had to be supplemented with additional readings. Since there are many viewpoints on specific language topics, I wanted the students exposed to some of these differing opinions. Often the supplemental essays simply reinforced hypotheses that the class had ventured on its own. The class discussions had the effect of group brainstorming with the formulation of deliberative essays as the result. Working within the overall guidelines for the course of 4,200 graded words, the students submitted essays approximately every ten days.

An examination of both the subtle and more obvious manipulative power of language seemed to be an excellent starting point. The objective was to demonstrate that we—as consumers, citizens, friends, students, and teachers—were not only victims of this manipulative power but users of it as well. We began with readings on public lying, advertising "catch words," and the psychology of advertising, and we progressed to analyzing a magazine or newspaper ad. We then exercised our new awareness by composing an ad of our own, enticing vacationers to visit a most unpleasant resort by employing language that portrayed it as anything but (no lying allowed).

After reading several essays on the use of sports terminology by politicians, business executives, and even educators, the students formulated a list of other areas in which sports jargon was prevalent. The men in the class admitted that they commented on their success or failure with their dates by borrowing sports idioms: "Did you score?" "I couldn't get to first base." "I hit a home run."

Evidence that real critical thinking was taking place was demonstrated when the students began speculating on why we, as a nation, have such a preoccupation with sports terminology. This conjecture made students cognizant, perhaps for the first time, of the relation between our language and our culture, a relation further investigated in areas of their choosing: kinship terms, sexism in language, political doublespeak, censorship, and the evidence that there is real correlation between the linearity of language and our art, our music, our most popular sports, the way we perceive time, and our manner of mathematical computation.

In the three years that I have used this approach, student input has increased. We have now expanded the political doublespeak section to include "nukespeak." The students read, at their choice, some rather technical essays on nuclear armament and disarmament, the possible effects of nuclear attack, and the language used to influence the reader. This work culminates in a policy paper that is generally the finest essay of the term.

The freshmen in my sections submitted anonymous evaluations at the end of each semester. Some students were more enthusiastic than others, but most stated that, given the choice, they would take the language track again. One student summed it up well: "This course has accomplished the difficult but admirable task of getting me involved in language investigation *and keeping* my interest level wonderfully high. I have become one hundred percent more proficient in observing and recognizing the subtleties of our language. It has forced me to be more critical of my own style and writing habits."

Course Design 3:
Speech Communities within the Classroom
by Lynn K. Varn

Attached to my Writing 102 class throughout this project has been a title, "Language Alert: Talk Is Not Cheap; or, The Language of Argument and the Argument of Language." Such a title indicates that the course operates on the deliberative principle and that papers—long and short—are meant to afford opportunities for choice and commitment to thought. The readings in our texts feed into observations and writing; of the spare and especially of the overly scholarly essays, the students are rightly critical.

For our complex of objectives and a new subject of inquiry, language, the course needed some machinery not ordinarily employed in composition classes, although the department requirements of a term paper and at least several 400- to 600-word essays were to be upheld. The following are the key devices I have used consistently with my eight sections of language researchers, to date 225 students, both advanced-placement and regular sections.

Organization of the Class into Speech Community Groups

To get the students to think of language as a system and subsystem of circuitry and to understand that they have speaker identity and power with certain groups through dialect, I divide the class into speech communities, with different groupings for each topic. Some common topics covered in the course are media, sports, consumerism, education, technology, family, evangelism. In group discussions, the students share mutual concerns, try the defensibility of each other's arguments and strategies, generate ideas for topics and support, comprehensively test each design from blueprint to documentation, and act as sharpened editors on topics that have something in common and about which they are an informed audience. Some students get started on their research papers in early discussions in these group sessions, and others have used the discussions to solve writing problems while working on their papers.

Questionnaires

I administer three to four questionnaires during each semester as part of my own research on the classroom community; the questionnaires also prime the students to be less reluctant to express their own opinions. Furthermore, this approach is designed to demonstrate the utility of empirical evidence, rarely part of the secondhand research that students traditionally do for term papers. The first questionnaire constructs a kind of linguistic profile of each student—our language values, the authorities we acknowledge, the dialects we feel comfortable with. The second questionnaire, administered after the semester is well under way, deals with class discussion, revealing to the students some of the variables in speech acts in the classroom: preparation for class, dynamics among students and between teacher and student, time of day, the shape of questions posed to students, prior experience in other classes with exchanges between students, expectations derived from former English classes. These early questionnaires open the research community to poll taking, in addition to recording and managing quotations of others' opinions. After the class members are engaged in their long-term researched arguments, the third questionnaire plumbs their writing processes and airs their anxieties about writing.

The fourth questionnaire comes at the close of the course as an evaluation geared to our specific goals about language and argumentation and the general end of writing: "Where did the idea for your researched argument come from: the reading, conferences, speech community group? Did this course make you any more alert as a speaker, listener, consumer, reader, voter, writer? How?" Most of the responses to the fourth questionnaire have indicated that the students in an array of majors (mostly outside the humanities) have become more alert as writers, and ninety-five percent have said that they have also improved as listeners. Most commented on more than one process in their writing as having improved markedly: sixty percent have answered that primary-data collection widened their concept of research and intensified their interest; seventy-five percent have said that they could now readily make a decision on an opinion and devise a plan of action based on that decision.

The Microargument

To poise the students for issuing opinion inferred from observation from the first day of class, I use a ten- to twenty-minute kernel response writing, which I call the microargument. In one paragraph, students can parlay a specific given fact—a statistic, an utterance, an example from the readings or class discussion—into opinion. Or, working in the other direction, they can find bases for their impressions of the core meaning of the reading selection.

The microargument has also been useful as a preliminary to the required research paper. For instance, if student researchers are examining the jargon on Internal Revenue Service forms or assessing themes in music lyrics, they can begin by writing down their separate and atomized observations instead of attempting to bundle the strands together before they get a chance to examine them.

The microargument is again a vehicle in research paper writing. Each student has to turn in cards containing primary data (one observation or statistic each) and a comment or inference (microargument) so that I can be sure the students are doing more than just scooping up nuggets of information when they should be formulating opinions, no matter how limited or qualified. These microarguments then are not just a way of making the students accountable for assignments or research reading; they provide a specific apparatus for the student and teacher in the processes of observing and analyzing the currents of language around them and in the readings. The procedure has kept class discussion alive and provided a bridge between the research of others in the community and the student's own discovery and reflection. These essays-in-miniature are the practical "leverage" that is defeatingly absent from traditional assignments connected with reading and research: "a small amount of writing is preceded by a great deal of thinking" (Bean, Drenk, and Lee 28).

Following are some microargument starters for which students are expected to generate conclusions, predictions, implications—the germ for a developed essay and a more complete vision of reasoning:

Microarguments drawing inference:

> If English possessed a mere 1,000 nouns (such as *trees, children, horses*) and only 1,000 verbs (*grow, die, change*), the number of possible two-word sentences therefore would be 1,000 × 1,000, or one million. . . . One linguist calculated that it would take 10,000,000,000,000 years (two thousand times the estimated age of the earth) to utter all the possible English sentences that use exactly twenty words. Therefore it is improbable that any twenty-word sentence a person speaks was ever spoken previously and the same thing would hold true, of course, for sentences of greater length, and for most shorter ones as well. (Farb 253)

> Initially, the language spread with the British Empire. After WWII, English with a twist—American jargon—circled the globe, boosted by

U.S. economic and political power. Finally, the language captured the lead in the knowledge explosion: English is the medium for 80% of the information stored in computers around the world. (McBee 49)

The doctor's *we*, by the way, is of special interest. Medical pronouns are used in special ways that ensure that the doctor is never out alone on any limb. (D. Johnson 58)

Microarguments establishing value:

Do the Miss Fidditches of this world really do any harm? (Farb's old schoolmarm "would rather diagram a sentence grammatically than eat." [83])

Are we more susceptible than ever to propaganda, the kind of language that Orwell says makes "lies sound truthful and murder respectable"? (Goshgarian 71)

Is it better for southerners if their dialectal differences are leveled, as Cleanth Brooks has observed is happening because of miseducation? (53)

Have we become a "nation of liars," as purported in *U.S. News and World Report*? (McLoughlin, Sheler, and Witkin)

On the topic of language in the courtroom, a student noted the use of particular verbs by lawyers; ultimately, she wrote, the degree of statement could register exclusively in the verb (*smash* instead of *hit* for measure of violence or force)—a key factor in the language control exercised by speakers in charge. (Travis)

The use of the microargument cards has translated into more fluid discourse, papers showing connections and greater momentum drawn from fact. The students discover their own authority in moving discretely from fact to idea in each case. They seem more involved in the semester's assignment than previous writing classes once they have negotiated a topic; consequently, I have less of a problem with late research papers than I have had in years and less resistance to using a required oral component. Many students have told me that it was at the level of the data card with microargument that they were struck with the manner of induction and argumentation for the first time.

Comments on Our Experimental Classes on Language

Obviously, there are certain caveats any experienced teacher could point out at the outset. Students will need conditioning and stroking because of the newness of the mode in the composition class, though once they have practice looking, they see and hear linguistic rhythms from their culture all around them. Much linguistic research is high-level, seasoned scholarship whose effulgence could vex young eyes and blind them to the basic purpose of the course: to have them train themselves for writing. Therefore, beginning students of language need general, panoramic texts from which they can absorb scope, not much detail. Farb, for instance, can guide students to a coherent understanding of what language is, how it behaves, and what it can mean to us as individuals in linguistic pluralism. That is distance enough. The instructors will have to put forth a never-ending parade of examples, cases, and curiosities for linguistic arguments, so that the students can see applications they too must make with their own data. And instructors must stretch to be open to new sources of data: insurance forms, cereal boxes, menus, telephone books, news broadcasts, billboards, questionnaires and interviews, and the classroom itself. Conferencing can get individual students over certain obstacles of syntax, phonology, and complex concepts that might discourage a student working alone. The students cannot and need not go deeper into technical analysis than is required by their purpose for the writing assignment.

Using a classroom research community breathed new life into the old enterprise. The students and we were working creatively and jointly with a purpose, and a new one at that: language and how it works for and against us. What Shirley Brice Heath had said in her 1985 CCCC keynote address about collaborative learning about language had been realized:

> By enabling students to become inquirers or re-searchers of language which surrounds them, we strip away terms, fixed practices, expectations, routinized predictors of our own behaviors and our students'. We replaced these with a spirit of intuition and intuitive knowledge— the stuff of which we as language-makers are made. Drawing out students' intuitive knowledge about language depends heavily on having them recognize the oral and written language they command. They come to this recognition as they collect, record, and analyze these data. All students can become experts, for they own the knowledge from which the group works together to determine what is in the data and what the data say about their system, its features, and their relevance to other kinds of data. For students in mixed-language or mixed-dialect

classes, there is the extra bonus that the study of the various systems and repertoires of language uses enhances a sense of language as a vastly varied and versatile instrument. ("Student")

Who of us would say there is no future in this kind of exercise for these students? At least here they were performing analytical tasks for writing, collecting information, and evaluating its significance and direction, probing the dialects of audience—acts fundamental to writing across the disciplines and the world of work. All of us were surprised at some of the acute language impulses that were unleashed in students who, green as they were, could sniff out examples and conclusions. So until another idea for Writing 102 comes along that charges us, we will be forestalling burnout with this one.

Sneaking Linguistics into the Freshman Comp Classroom: Compiling a "Dictionary of Slang"

Karen McFarland Canine, Scott Community College

AS A "typical" freshman English teacher, I am always searching for ways to interest and motivate students who occupy my classroom only because they are required to. A number of years ago I devised a writing project—a "dictionary of slang" compiled by my students—that has not only maintained most students' interest but also allowed me to "teach" *my* interest, linguistics: at a minimum, an awareness of levels of language usage and variation in spoken and written English; at best, a crash course in etymology, code switching, language communities, sociolinguistics, occupational jargon, geographical and social dialects, gender tags, idiom, speech-act theory, and classifications of slang-formation strategies.

What exactly is slang? In his preface to *The Dictionary of American Slang*, Stuart Berg Flexner discusses slang for page after page before finally concluding (rather inconclusively) that "any cultural sub-group develops its own personal cant and jargon which can later become general slang. All of us belong to several of these specific sub-groups using our cant and jargon" (181). For the reading and research part of the dictionary-of-slang assignment, I have my students study Flexner's preface. Along with it, students read three other selections included in one section of Paul Eschholz, Alfred Rosa, and Virginia Clark's fourth edition of *Language Awareness*: "Vogue Words Are Trific, Right," by William Safire; Roger Shuy's "Differences in Vocabulary," showing some of the ways a speaker's vocabulary may reveal age, gender, occupation, or geographical region; and S. I. Hayakawa's "How Dictionaries Are Made." Each of these pieces is followed by discussion questions that point up the relations among *slang, jargon, idiom*, and *dialect*. With this background, I encourage my students to arrive at their own definition of *slang*. However, the definition is secondary to my objectives in this unit. I want students to see that there are many varieties of English, that English changes over time, and that English has a sociolinguistic aspect that includes speakers using a nonstandard "code" (or slang) to define their inclusion in (or exclusion from) a group.

In fact, the dictionary-of-slang assignment began as a way to meet the "definition mode" requirement (present in many composition curricula) while simultaneously challenging my students to question the prescriptivist notion that slang is taboo. In the process of designing the assignment, I found that writing an essay defining a slang term could involve using all the traditional modes—comparing and contrasting synonymous slang terms; classifying slang terms according to function or degree; writing a narrative prompting use of the slang term; describing people, things, or conditions that merit the label or the term; showing the effects of using the slang term; arguing for or against the acceptance of the particular slang term into Standard English. In addition, defining a slang term forces students to examine the speech they use every day and to observe language patterns and accompanying extralinguistic behaviors (gestures, intonations, facial expressions, etc.). And the way I set up the assignment often leads students to a concrete understanding of grammatical form and categories, even if they do not have a precise vocabulary to discuss them.

Other benefits of this writing project for students include their realization that observing and analyzing language can give them a new kind of insight and knowledge; their learning the difference between primary and secondary sources, since they must not only observe speakers but also do research in the library; and their seeing that "essays" can be written to entertain and enlighten readers.

This assignment also provides benefits for the teacher, of course. Not only do I receive a set of papers more interesting than usual to read, but the students keep me up to date on current slang, gathered by those who are right in the middle of all that linguistic creativity. Although I designed this assignment because I am interested in linguistics, colleagues who have no such affinity have used the dictionary-of-slang assignment with great success—it was fun for both teachers and students, and it resulted in some good students essays.

Also, the dictionary-of-slang unit can reinforce a number of skills that students need to practice: critical thinking, analysis, research, synthesis (including incorporation of quotations), and writing for a particular purpose and audience. Depending on the sophistication of the class, each step of this assignment may be expanded or narrowed in its coverage of technical information, terminology, methodology, and readings from linguistics; in some circumstances, a whole semester can focus on language variation.

There are many ways that the dictionary-of-slang assignment can be introduced to classes. In general, I lead into it after a unit on diction, which includes exercises on connotation and slanting, euphemism, and jargon. There are so many examples of jargon at any college or university that by listing a few well-known local terms, the instructor can open up a deluge of examples of many types from the students. A good starting point is terminology associated with computers.

One of my favorite handouts for a jargon unit is a piece by Russell Baker, first published in the 1970s, "Little Red Riding Hood Revisited: Why Senior Citizen, What an Enlarged Oral Cavity." This Nixon-era bureaucratese translation of the Little Red Riding Hood tale contains allusions to "making one thing perfectly clear" and "at this point in time" and other such phrasings that my students don't get at all. Their failure to grasp the meaning inevitably leads us to a discussion of diachronic change. My handout analyzing *freak* (at the end of this article) provides an example of outdated slang; students like to talk about such exotic words as *hippie* or *groovy*, especially since every campus seems to be equipped with a resident Dead-Head on whom the sarcasm of current students using those words is lost. *Fox* is another example I usually bring up, since its meaning has changed in the past six or seven years.

All this talk of outdated terms can be used to get into a discussion of code switching, showing how each of us, no matter how inept we think we are at writing or speaking, possesses the ability to shift our tone and style depending on our audience and purpose. Sometimes I have students write letters requesting money, first to friends and then to parents, so that they will see the difference. I sometimes distribute a packet of newspaper articles on male-female speech differences to generate discussions about such patterns. And we talk about regional dialects by brainstorming for vocabulary items learned through experience. Discussing rap songs and other popular music is a good way to bring in Black English and its related extralinguistic gestures, sounds, and behaviors. And, if time permits, we view part 1 of the PBS series *The Story of English*, which shows students just how "various" the English language is.

The next step is to demonstrate that a definition can be more than the formula "*X* belongs to class *Y* and shows characteristics *ZZ*." Any standard dictionary uses many methods to define words or terms: description, comparison and contrast, classification, cause and effect, and especially examples and etymology. I stress to my students that I am most interested in knowing what the slang term means to them and that, in order to get the meaning across, they should use as many methods to define as they need. We talk about the importance of context to when and how language—especially slang—is used; I encourage the students to describe and to tell stories about the kinds of situations and people that are associated with the term they are defining. And I urge them to try to find the origin of the slang term, so that we as a class can see the many ways that new terms are formed.

It is important for composition students to realize that there is a whole world of scholarship devoted to the observation of language patterns. If the students are especially open-minded or bright, or if the semester will cover more readings and assignments on language use beyond the dictionary of slang, I show and discuss with them other academic studies of language communities. Robert L. Chapman's *New Dictionary of American Slang* includes a comprehensive "history of slang lexicology" as well as an extensive definition of *slang* and a reprint of Flexner's preface. The journal *American Speech* is an excellent resource for analysis of individual slang terms and idiomatic expressions. In addition to her recently published dictionary, *College Slang 101*, students should look at Connie C. Eble's two reports in *The SECOL Review* on her "ongoing study of the semantic intricacies of productive processes at work in slang" with items contributed from her Modern English grammar course at the University of North Carolina at Chapel Hill ("Scenes" 74). Her "Scenes from Slang" discusses slang formation in terms of semantic shift (generalization, specialization, amelioration, pejoration) as well as of rhetorical categories (metonymy, synecdoche, metaphor, and irony). Her 1986 essay ("Slang") reports on the complex etymologies of slang terms and gives attention to allusions, "because one of the functions of slang is to bring about or to confirm group identity." According to Eble, "Another complicating factor in analyzing the semantics of slang is that the meaning of a slang expression often relies on rather specific references to extra-linguistic facts" (9). This observation is confirmed in minute detail in the chapter "How to Ask for a Drink" in James P. Spradley and Brenda Mann's *The Cocktail Waitress*, an ethnographic study of a bar. Students should read this chapter, especially if they are skeptical of being able to complete questions on the guidelines sheet or fulfill the requirements for the essay listed on the definition assignment sheet (appended to the end of this article). "How to Ask for a Drink" includes a clear discussion of speech acts, with case-study examples showing how speakers' underlying assumptions and perceptions affect the situation, as well as a chart of the waitresses' slang labels for customers or particular speech events.

These preliminary sessions discussing "theory" are necessary to show students that current slang is a legitimate field for study. The next step in the dictionary-of-slang assignment is to have students brainstorm so that they can select the term or terms they want to define in their essays. Students are sometimes reluctant to share "their" language with classmates they don't know well, much less with the instructor. Providing them with the theoretical concepts of language change helps them to open up. I usually distribute the definition assignment sheet explaining what I expect from students for the dictionary of slang after introducing the background materials (although it can be handed out before discussing the background materials as a way to introduce the entire unit on slang). The assignment sheet itself can serve as a trigger to brainstorming. I suggest that the students brainstorm for slang terms as homework and bring in their lists to share with classmates in small groups that later report to the entire class.

At this point, some students are still completely turned off by the idea of slang, claiming that they never use slang and don't associate with anyone who does. Also, students for whom English is a second language may have trouble coming up with a term they can define. In these cases, I suggest that such students write about an idiomatic expression, a geographical dialect item, an occupational jargon term, or some other word or phrase that strikes them as "strange" and therefore appropriate for analysis, particularly etymological analysis. I have had students complete essays, for example, on *hushpuppy* and *knucklebuster*. One especially good student essay was a treatise on *get* as a productive particle (*all getout, getup,* etc.); other possibilities are the way particles such as *out, up,* and *in* can entirely change the meanings of the noun and verb phrases to which they are attached. Other suggestions have included words and phrases like *polka dot, jukebox, lame duck, eat your heart out.* Most texts on the history of the language contain chapters tracing the derivations of borrowings and compounds; J. N. Hook's *History of the English Language* is an especially good source of noncurrent slang topics.

Once students have brainstormed for a term to define and have discussed alternative choices with classmates in their groups, they should complete the guidelines sheet. This activity stimulates their thinking about what meaning the term holds for them as well as its grammatical form, its derivation, and its speech-act context. They are also required to consult dictionaries, especially the *OED* or slang dictionaries.

Before students bring in drafts of their essays to be peer-edited, I distribute and discuss with them newspaper articles about slang. These are not hard to find: Erma Bombeck's humorous observations about how people use language underscore the point that essays can be written both to entertain and to enlighten; James J. Kilpatrick and Russell Baker, although lamenting the current state of usage, provide good examples of reflections on derivation and language change. Every semester I find so many new ruminations about slang that I have a hard time choosing the few that my class will have time to read during the unit on the dictionary of slang. Currently, I distribute two 1989 articles published in the *Des Moines Register*—"Why Slang Is Winner of Language Wars" (Vandermey) and "From 'Tush-Ups' to 'Odoralls,' Families Have Special Words" (Kahn). A favorite is Doug Marlette's 1987 series of *Kudzu* comic strips in which "whitest white boy in Bypass," Nasal Lardbottom, is trying to master the intricacies of "jive." In short, writers and journalists, because they play with language for a living, love to write about language.

I also like to present examples of student essays to my classes—before they bring in rough drafts, as well as during the content, style, and mechanics editing sessions done with my reviewing and editing sheet.

Finally, I insist that students make an extra copy of their final draft for me to keep. This collection of student essays provides not just examples to use in future classes but a documentation of change and variation in current usage. From the first time I presented the dictionary of slang in my composition course, I intended to have the class make a "real" dictionary, a bound booklet, as incentive for producing polished, publishable essays, but teaching the assignment as only one unit during the semester imposes time constraints on such a project.

Though I have not produced a "real" dictionary yet, some success stories have grown out of the slang dictionary project. Some students' essays have been published in campus newspapers. One of the most successful applications of the dictionary-of-slang assignment occurred in my journalism class. I asked the students to produce a reflective column about current slang for the newspaper. Since these students had already had composition courses, I did not insist on the rigors of completing the guidelines or the editing sheets as I do with the freshman writers, who expect more structure built into their writing assignments. Nevertheless, the journalism students responded with the kind of insightful observations about language that I always hope to receive. In my favorite, a student moved from confusion about current slang she had heard at work to a self-conscious realization about language in general: our speech communicates who we are and what language community we belong to; and the more varieties we can decode and assimilate, the more enriched we become.

Definition Assignment

Situation: Your instructor is off on one of her hare-brained schemes again. It seems that she just came back from a convention of linguists (you are not sure what a "linguist" is, but it must have something to do with studying language) that inspired her to compile a "dictionary of slang," using student essays about language. Her idea is not only to publish a book for other students but to try to get individual essays published in newspapers and magazines, so that people in general will become more aware of how inventive speakers of English are and how language is changing all the time.

Your assignment is to write an interesting essay defining a slang (nonstandard) or idiomatic term—one word, a phrase or sentence, or a group of related terms.

Your entry may define any slang expression except those that are considered dirty, obscene, or racially or sexually offensive (see your instructor if you have questions). It may be a *dialect* term (e.g., *yonder, homeboy, might could, Chucks*). It may be a term that you have made up. It should be a term that is recent or unusual—not common nonstandard terms like *ain't* and *darn.*

Your underlying purpose is to enlighten readers (entertaining them along the way) about the language you use every day. This means that your thesis should be a general point about how interesting it is to become aware of and analyze the way spoken language is used, focusing on one of your favorite slang terms.

Procedure

1. Brainstorm
   a. Make a list of all the slang terms you can think of—those you use or have heard others use.
   b. If your mind goes blank, listen to your friends, classmates, or co-workers talk among themselves; observe how language is used on TV or in movies. Good resource categories for finding slang terms include these:
      greetings
      exclamations and expletives
      descriptions of physical conditions (intoxication, illness)
      descriptions of leisure activities (parties, barhopping)
      descriptions of emotional states (anger, ecstasy)
      labels for people (e.g., *airhead, nerd, fox*)
      descriptions of nonleisure activities (work, study, sleep)
2. Answer the questions on the guidelines sheet.
   a. For one-word terms, determine the part of speech.
   b. For phrases, categorize according to use (greeting, label, etc.).
   c. Make sure you consult
      a standard dictionary (or, if the word is not listed, a slang dictionary)
      The Oxford English Dictionary (in the library)
3. Write a rough draft. Make sure your essay contains (although not necessarily in this order)
   a. a thesis
   b. examples of how the term is used, and a discussion of the contexts (who, when, where, why) in which it is used (as well as any nonverbal behavior—such as gestures—that go along with the term)

    c. a discussion of what the term means to you and those who use it

    d. a discussion of how the term came about (rely on conventional dictionary meanings, or speculate)

    e. a comparison and contrast with similar slang terms, either current or past

4. Consult the editing sheet to help you shape your draft. (Hint: When you discuss terms as words, <u>underline</u> them.)

5. When your final draft is due, turn in

    a. cover sheet with a catchy title for your essay

    b. self-evaluation

    c. typed draft, with title on the first page

    d. editing sheet

    e. edited draft

    f. guidelines sheet, *completed*

    g. *extra* typed copy for instructor to keep

Guidelines

Select several words in common use and answer the following questions about them:

1. How many grammatical forms can the term take? For example, consider these three terms:

	freak	*mess*	*stone*
Noun	freak	mess	a stone?
Verb	to freak	to mess	to stone
Particles	to freak *out*	to mess *up, in, around*	to stone *out*
Past participle	be *freaked* out	be *messed* up	be *stoned*
Active	I freak out.	Drugs mess up your mind.	The music stoned me.
Adjective	freaky	messy	stoned
Complements	He freaked *me* out.		He was stoned *on drugs.*
	I freaked out *on drugs.*		Drugs stoned *him.*
	I freak out *at concerts.*		
	He freaked out *in the theater.*		

a. Make another chart like this one, but with different words.
b. What are the dictionary definitions of these terms or of the main part of the expression?
c. What does this term mean to you?
d. Does a conventional dictionary give the idiomatic or slang definition of the term? If so, what is it?
e. By referring to how you've heard it used and what you've found in the dictionary, speculate on how you think this term came into being.
f. According to the *OED*, when did this term come into English? What did it mean then?
g. What is the derivation—where does it come from, and how did it get into English?
h. Is the term used only by your generation, or do many different ages and classes of people use it?
i. How has this expression changed in meaning over the past five or ten years (e.g., *fox*)?
j. In what different situations or contexts would you use this term?
k. What are the different meanings of this term?
2. What alternative terms—also idiomatic—might you use in place of this particular term? In what situations and why?

To help the students organize information for their essays and to provide a mechanism for "cooperative editing" of early drafts of their essay, I hand out the editing sheet for them to use in analyzing each other's work.

Editing Sheet

1. What term is being defined?
2. If more than one term is discussed, what do the terms have in common?
3. What methods of defining does the writer use?
Specified meaning in context
Listing characteristics or parts
Etymology (or history) of the word
Synonyms
Dialogue
Dictionary definition
History and background of the item
Familiar examples of the item
Comparison

Description
Contrast
Metaphor
Stating functions
Analysis of parts

4. What additional methods might the writer use to strengthen the paper? Would any other methods of development add interest to the paper? Comment on the overall development of the paper.

5. Is the subject matter and level of writing suitable for the audience? If no, what suggestions can you make to help the writer modify the paper?

6. What is the purpose of the definition? Does the writer achieve the paper's purpose effectively? If no, please make appropriate suggestions.

7. What is the thesis? Write it here:
    Is the thesis well supported? Are you convinced of the writer's point? Why or why not?

8. Have you heard the term(s) before? If the term means something different to you from what the writer has defined, explain it here:

9. Has the writer used any outside sources to help uncover the meaning of the word? If no, would such definition help your understanding of the term?

10. What kind of framework or context does the writer use to discuss the term?

11. Is the introduction interesting?
    If *no*, check below what might make it more grabbing.
    _____ narration about how the term first came to mind
    _____ description about how the term first came to mind
    _____ description of the term itself, or where it can be heard
    _____ dictionary definition
    _____ rhetorical question
    _____ quotation
    _____ dialogue using the term
    _____ list of more familiar synonyms for the term

12. Does the writer need to use more examples? If yes, suggest some.

13. Is the pattern of organization clear? If no, how could the essay be organized better?

14. On the paper, point out where more transition is needed.

15. On the paper, point out any words or terms that need more explanation.

16. On the paper, point out any sentences that don't sound right.

17. On the paper, point out any errors in grammar, spelling, or punctuation.
18. On the paper, point out any repetitive terms or words that the writer needs to find alternatives for.
19. Has the writer structured sentences effectively? If no, check the following suggestions that apply:
    _____ Use more variety in kinds of sentences.
    _____ Use more variety in sentence length.
    _____ Vary your sentence openers.
    _____ Combine sentences to show relationships between ideas.
    _____ Use more variety in choice of verbs and verb forms.
20. Is the ending conclusive? If no, suggest ways that the conclusion could be improved.
    _____ Return to the context of the introductory framework.
    _____ Make a "play on words" about the expression.
    _____ Provide a quotation.
    _____ Offer advice for the audience.
    _____ End the paper with an anecdote.
21. Make a general comment at the end of the paper, including what you thought was good about it.
22. What have you learned from this essay?

Works Cited

Acuña, Rodolfo. *Occupied America: The Chicano's Struggle toward Liberation.* New York: Harper, 1972.

Akmajian, Adrian, Richard A. Demers, and Robert M. Harnish. *Linguistics: An Introduction to Language and Communication.* 2nd ed. Cambridge: MIT P, 1984.

Algeo, John. "The Mirror and the Template: Cloning Public Opinion." Greenbaum 57–64.

———. *Problems in the Origins and Development of the English Language.* 4th ed. New York: Harcourt, 1993.

Allen, Dan, and Richard Hall, eds. *New Lives in the New World.* London: Collier, 1975.

Allen, Harold B. *The Linguistic Atlas of the Upper Midwest.* 3 vols. Minneapolis: U of Minnesota P, 1973–76.

———. "Regional Dialects, 1945–1974." *American Speech* 52 (1977): 163–261.

———. "Teacher-Training in the English Language." *English Journal* 27 (1938): 422–30.

Allen, Harold B., and Gary N. Underwood, eds. *Readings in American Dialectology.* New York: Appleton, 1971.

Alleyne, Mervyn C. *Comparative Afro-American: An Historical-Comparative Study of English-Based Afro-American Dialects of the New World.* Ann Arbor: Karoma, 1980.

Amastae, Jon. "Language Shift and Maintenance in the Lower Rio Grande Valley of Southern Texas." *Bilingualism and Language Contact.* Ed. F. Barkin et al. New York: Teachers Coll. P, 1982. 261–77.

Amastae, Jon, and Lucía Elías-Olivares. "Attitudes towards Varieties of Spanish." *Fourth LACUS Forum 1977.* Ed. M. Paradis. Columbia: Hornbeam, 1978. 286–302.

———, eds. *Spanish in the United States: Sociolinguistic Aspects.* New York: Cambridge UP, 1982.

The American Heritage Dictionary of the English Language. Boston: Houghton, 1969. 2nd college ed., 1982. 3rd ed., 1992. Paperback ed. New York: Dell, 1976.

Americans Speaking. Recording. Prepared by John T. Muri and Raven I. McDavid. Urbana: NCTE, 1967.

American Tongues. Videotape. Prod. Andrew Killer and Louis Alvarez. New York: Center for New American Media, 1987.

Anshen, Frank. *Statistics for Linguists.* Rowley: Newbury, 1978.

Anthony, Michael. *Green Days by the River.* London: Heinemann, 1967.

———. *The Year in San Fernando.* London: Heinemann, 1965.

Anthony, Michael, and Andrew Carr, eds. *David Frost Introduces Trinidad and Tobago.* London: Deutsch, 1975.

Arahill, Edward J. *The Effect of Differing Dialects upon the Comprehension and Attitude of Eighth-Grade Children*. Diss. U of Florida, 1970.

Ashley, Leonard. *What's in a Name? Everything You Wanted to Know*. Baltimore: Genealogical, 1989.

Atwood, E. Bagby. "*Grease* and *Greasy*: A Study of Geographical Variation." *Studies in English* 29 (1950): 249–60.

———. *The Regional Vocabulary of Texas*. Austin: U of Texas P, 1962.

———. *A Survey of Verb Forms in the Eastern United States*. Ann Arbor: U of Michigan P, 1953.

Avis, Walter S. "The English Language in Canada." *Current Trends in Linguistics*. Ed. Thomas A. Sebeok. Vol. 10, pt. 1. Hague: Mouton, 1973. 40–74. 14 vols.

Avis, Walter S., and A. M. Kinloch. *Writings on Canadian English, 1792–1975: An Annotated Bibliography*. Toronto: Fitzhenry, 1978.

Avis, Walter S., et al., eds. *A Dictionary of Canadianisms on Historical Principles*. Toronto: Gage, 1967.

———, eds. *The Gage Canadian Dictionary*. Toronto: Gage, 1973.

Bailey, Guy. "Are Black and White Vernaculars Diverging?" *American Speech* 62 (1987): 32–40.

———. Personal communication.

Bailey, Guy, and Natalie Maynor. "The Divergence Controversy." *American Speech* 64 (1989): 12–39.

Bailey, Guy, Natalie Maynor, and Patricia Cukor-Avila, eds. *The Emergence of Black English*. Amsterdam: Benjamins, 1991.

Bailey, Richard W. "The English Language in Canada." Bailey and Görlach 134–76.

Bailey, Richard W., and Manfred Görlach, eds. *English as a World Language*. Ann Arbor: U of Michigan P, 1982.

Baker, Russell. "Little Red Riding Hood Revisited: Why Senior Citizen, What an Enlarged Oral Cavity." *So This Is Depravity*. 1980. *Elements of Argument*. Ed. Annette T. Rottenberg. 2nd ed. New York: St. Martin's, 1988. 177–78.

Baker, Sheridan. *The Complete Stylist and Handbook*. 3rd ed. New York: Harper, 1984.

Barnhart, Clarence L., ed. *Barnhart Dictionary Companion*. 4 vols. Cold Spring: Lexik, 1982–85.

———, ed. *The Third Barnhart Dictionary of New English*. New York: Wilson, 1990.

Barnhart, Clarence L., Sol Steinmetz, and Robert K. Barnhart. *The Barnhart Dictionary of New English since 1963*. Bronxville: Barnhart, 1973.

Baron, Dennis E. *Grammar and Good Taste: Reforming the American Language*. New Haven: Yale UP, 1982.

Barry, Tom, Beth Wood, and Deb Preusch. *The Other Side of Paradise: Foreign Control in the Caribbean*. New York: Grove, 1984.

Bartlett, John R. *Dictionary of Americanisms*. 4th ed. Boston: Little, 1877.

Bartsch, Renate. *Norms of Language: Theoretical and Practical Aspects*. Ed. Mark Anderson. London: Longman, 1988. Trans. of *Sprachnormen: Theorie and Praxis*. Tübingen: Niemeyer, 1985.

Baugh, Albert C., and Thomas Cable. *A History of the English Language*. 4th ed. Englewood Cliffs: Prentice, 1993.

Baugh, John. "Beyond Linguistic Divergence in Black American English: Competing Norms of Linguistic Prestige and Variation." A. R. Thomas 175–86.

———. *Black Street Speech: Its History, Structure, and Survival*. Austin: U of Texas P, 1983.

———. "Chicano English: The Anguish of Definition." Ornstein, *Form* 3–13.

———. "Design and Implementation of Writing Instruction for Speakers of Nonstandard English." *The Writing Needs of Linguistically Different Students*. Ed. Bruce Cronnell. Los Alamitos: SWRL Educational Research and Development, 1981. 17–44.

———. "The Situational Dimension of Linguistic Power in Social Context." *Language Arts* 64.2 (1987): 234–40.

Beale, Walter H., Karen Meyers, and Laurie L. White. *Real Writing*. Glenview: Scott, 1982.

Bean, John C., Dean Drenk, and F. D. Lee. "Microtheme Strategies for Developing Cognitive Skills." *Teaching Writing in All Disciplines*. Ed. C. W. Griffin. New Directions for Teaching and Learning 12. San Francisco: Jossey-Bass, 1982. 27–38.

Bédard, Édith, and Jacques Maurais, eds. *La norme linguistique*. Québec: Conseil de la langue française, 1983.

Behrens, Laurence, and Leonard Rosen. *Writing and Reading across the Curriculum*. 2nd ed. Boston: Little, 1985.

Bell, Alexander Melville. *Visible Speech: The Science of Universal Alphabetics; or, Self-interpreting Physiological Letters for the Writing of All Languages in One Alphabet*. New York: Trübner, 1849. Rpt. 1863, 1867.

Bennett, John. "Gullah: A Negro Patois." *South Atlantic Quarterly* 7 (1908): 332–47; 8 (1909): 39–52.

Bennett, Louise. *Selected Poems: Jamaica Labrish*. Ed. Mervyn Morris. Kingston: Sangster's, n.d.

Bereiter, Carl, and Siegfried Englemann. *Teaching Disadvantaged Children in the Preschool*. Englewood Cliffs: Prentice, 1966.

Berger, Marshall. "Accent, Pattern, and Dialect in North American English." *Word*, 24 (1968): 55–61.

Bernstein, Basil. "A Sociolinguistic Approach to Socialization with Some References to Educability." Gumperz and Hymes 465–97.

Bernstein, Theodore M. *The Careful Writer: A Modern Guide to English Usage*. New York: Atheneum, 1965.

———. *Do's, Don'ts and Maybes of English Usage*. New York: Times, 1977.

Berry, Thomas E. *The Most Common Mistakes in English Usage*. New York: McGraw, 1971.

Billington, Ray Allen. *Westward Expansion*. 3rd ed. New York: Macmillan, 1967.

Bills, Garland. "Vernacular Chicano English: Dialect or Interference?" *Journal of the Linguistic Association of the Southwest* 2.2 (1980): 30–36.

Birdwell, Lillian S. "Revising Strategies in Twelfth Grade Students' Transactional Writing." *Research in the Teaching of English* 14.3 (1980): 197–222.

Bisseret, Noëlle. *Education, Class Language and Ideology*. London: Routledge, 1979.

Bloch, Bernard. "A Set of Postulates for Phonemic Analysis." *Language* 24 (1948): 3–46.

Bloomfield, Leonard. *Language*. New York: Holt, 1933.

———. "A Set of Postulates for the Science of Language." *Language* 2 (1926): 153–64. Rpt. in *Readings in Linguistics*. Ed. Martin Joos. Washington: American Council of Learned Societies, 1957. 26–31.

Bolinger, Dwight. *Language—the Loaded Weapon: The Use and Abuse of Language Today*. London: Longman, 1980.

Bonner, Stanley F. *Education in Ancient Rome: From the Elder Cato to the Younger Pliny*. Berkeley: U of California P, 1977.

Bowen, J. Donald, and Jacob Ornstein, eds. *Studies in Southwest Spanish*. Rowley: Newbury, 1976.

Brathwaite, Edward K. *History of the Voice*. London: New Beacon, 1984.

———, ed. *The People Who Came*. 3 vols. London: Longman Caribbean, 1970.

Brennan, Eileen M., and John S. Brennan. "Accent Scaling and Language Attitudes: Reactions to Mexican American English Speech." *Language and Speech* 24 (1981): 207–21.

Bronstein, Arthur. "The Pronunciation of English." *Random House Dictionary of the English Language* xxiii–xxiv.

Brooks, Cleanth. *The Language of the American South*. Athens: U of Georgia P, 1985.

Brunt, R. J., W. Enninger, et al. "The English of the Old Order Amish of Delaware." Meeting of the American Dialect Soc. U of Delaware, 10 June 1983.

Brusaw, Charles T., Gerald J. Alred, and Walter E. Oliu. *The Business Writer's Handbook*. New York: St. Martin's, 1982.

Bryant, Margaret M. *Current American Usage*. New York: Funk, 1962.

Buck, Carl Darling. "A Sketch of the Linguistic Conditions of Chicago." *The Decennial Publications of the University of Chicago*. First Series 6. Chicago: U of Chicago P, 1904. 97–114.

Burnett, Paula, ed. *The Penguin Book of Caribbean Verse*. Harmondsworth, Eng.: Penguin, 1986.

Cable, Thomas. *A Companion to Baugh and Cable's* History of the English Language. Englewood Cliffs: Prentice, 1983.

Cargill, Morris, ed. *Ian Fleming Introduces Jamaica*. London: Deutsch, 1965.

Caribbean Anthology. London: ILEA, 1981.

Carlson, Helen S. *Nevada Place Names: A Geographical Dictionary*. Reno: U of Nevada P, 1974.

Carranza, Miguel. "Attitudinal Research on Hispanic Language Varieties." *Attitudes towards Language Variation*. Ed. Ellen Ryan and Howard Giles. London: Arnold, 1982. 63–83.

Carranza, Miguel, and Ellen B. Ryan. "Evaluative Reactions of Bilingual Anglo and Mexican American Adolescents toward Speakers of English and Spanish." *International Journal of the Sociology of Language* 6 (1975): 83–104.

Carrington, Lawrence D. "The Challenge of Caribbean Language in the Canadian Classroom." *TESL Talk* 14.4 (1983): 15–28.

Carter, Jimmy. Executive Order 12044. *Weekly Compilation of Presidential Documents*, 23 Mar. 1978: 558–64. Washington: Office of the Federal Register.

Carver, Craig M. *American Regional Dialects: A Word Geography*. Ann Arbor: U of Michigan P, 1987.

———. *A History of English in Its Own Words*. New York: Harper, 1991.

Cassidy, Frederic G. "Barbadian Creole: Possibility and Probability." *American Speech* 61 (1986): 195–205.

———, ed. *Dictionary of American Regional English*. 2 vols. to date. Cambridge: Belknap, 1985–.

———. *Jamaica Talk*. London: Macmillan, 1971.

———. "Language Changes Especially Common in American Folk Speech." Cassidy, *Dictionary* xxxvi–xl.

———. "The Place of Gullah." *American Speech* 55 (1980): 3–16.

———. "Some Similarities between Gullah and Caribbean Creoles." Montgomery and Bailey 30–37.

———. "Sources for the African Element in Gullah." *Studies in Caribbean Language*. Ed. Lawrence Carrington. St. Augustine, Trinidad: Society for Caribbean Linguistics, 1983. 75–81.

Cassidy, Frederic G., and Robert Le Page. *Dictionary of Jamaican English*. 1967. Rev. ed. Cambridge: Cambridge UP, 1980.

Chafe, Wallace. "Integration and Involvement in Speaking, Writing, and Oral Literature." *Spoken and Written Language: Exploring Orality and Literacy*. Ed. Deborah Tannen. Norwood: Ablex, 1982. 35–53.

Chaika, Elaine. *Language: The Social Mirror*. Rowley: Newbury, 1982.

Chambers, J. K. "Canadian Raising." *Canadian Journal of Linguistics* 18 (1973): 113–35. Rev. and rpt. in *Canadian English: Origins and Structures*. Ed. Chambers. Toronto: Methuen, 1975. 83–100.

———. "Group and Individual Participation in a Sound Change in Progress." Warkentyne, *Papers* 119–36.

Chambers, John, ed. *Black English: Educational Equity and the Law*. Ann Arbor: Karoma, 1983.

Chapman, Robert L. *New Dictionary of American Slang*. New York: Harper, 1986.

Charles, Martie. "Job Security." *Black Theater USA: 45 Plays by Black Americans 1874–1974*. Ed. James Hatch. New York: Free, 1974.

Chaudenson, Robert. *Les créoles français*. Evreux: Nathan, 1979.

———. "Pour une étude comparée des créoles et parlers français d'outre mer: Survivance et innovation." *Revue de linguistique romane* 37 (1973): 342–71.

Christian, Donna. *American English Speech Recordings: A Guide to Collections*. Washington: Center for Applied Linguistics, 1986.

———. "Relatedness among Varieties of English: Irregular Verb Forms in Ozark and Appalachian Speech." Southeastern Conference on Linguistics. Duke U, 1984.

Christian, Donna, and Walt Wolfram. *Exploring Dialects*. Washington: Center for Applied Linguistics, 1979.

Cisneros, René, and Elizabeth Leone. "Mexican American Language Communities in the Twin Cities: An Example of Contact and Recontact." Elías-Olivares, *Spanish* 181–209.

Claiborne, Robert. *The Roots of English: A Reader's Handbook of Word Origins*. New York: Doubleday, 1989.

Clark, Thomas L. "The Environment of Names in the Classroom." *Elementary English* 49 (1972): 1061–63.

———. "Noms de Felt: Names in Gambling." *Names* 34 (1986): 11–29.

Clarke, Austin. *Growing Up Stupid under the Union Jack*. Toronto: McClelland, 1980.

Clarke, Sandra. "Sociolinguistic Variation in a Small Urban Context: The St. John's Survey." Warkentyne, *Papers* 143–53.

Coard, Bernard. *How the West Indian Child Is Made Educationally Sub-normal in the British School System*. London: New Beacon, 1971.

Cockeram, Henry. *The English Dictionarie; or, An Interpreter of Hard English Words . . . By H. C. Gent*. London: Printed for Edmund Weauer, 1623. New York: Huntington, 1930.

Coelho, Elizabeth. *The Caribbean Student in Canadian Schools, Book 1*. Toronto: Carib-Can, 1988. *Book 2*. Markham: Pippin, 1991.

———. "An Honest Thief." Ed. Lise Winer. *Branching Out: TESOL Newsletter*. Supplement 2 (June 1985): 9–11.

Cohen, Andrew. "The English and Spanish Grammar of Chicano Primary School Students." Bowen and Ornstein 125–64.

Collins, James L., and Michael M. Williamson. "Spoken Language and Semantic Abbreviation in Writing." *Research in the Teaching of English* 15.1 (1981): 23–35.

Coltharp, Lurline. *The Tongue of the Tirilones: A Linguistic Study of a Criminal Argot*. University: U of Alabama P, 1965.

Compact Edition of the Oxford English Dictionary. 2 vols. New York: Oxford UP, 1971.

Conklin, Nancy Faires. "The Language of the Majority: Women and American English." Lourie and Conklin 222–37.

Cooke, Benjamin G. "Nonverbal Communication among Afro-Americans: An Initial Classification." Kochman, *Rappin'* 32–64.

Cooper, Robert L. *Language Planning and Social Change*. Cambridge: Cambridge UP, 1989.

Copperud, Roy H. *American Usage and Style: The Consensus*. New York: Van Nostrand, 1979.

Corder, Jim W. *Handbook of Current English*. 7th ed. Glenview: Scott, 1985.

Coulmas, Florian, ed. *Language Adaptation*. Cambridge: Cambridge UP, 1989.

———, ed. *A Language Policy for the European Community: Prospects and Quandries*. Contributions to the Sociology of Language 61. Berlin: Mouton de Gruyter, 1991.

———. *Sprache und Staat: Studien zu Sprachplanung und Sprachpolitik*. Berlin: de Gruyter, 1985.

Craig, Dennis R. "The Sociology of Language Learning and Teaching in a Creole Language Situation." *Caribbean Journal of Education* 5.3 (1978): 101–16.

Craigie, William A., and James R. Hulbert. *A Dictionary of American English on Historical Principles*. 4 vols. Chicago: U of Chicago P, 1938–44.

Creswell, Thomas J. "The Great Vowel Shift in Chicago." *Festschrift in Honor of Virgil J. Vogel*. Ed. Edward Callary. Dekalb: Illinois Name Soc., 1985. 176–89.

———. *Usage in Dictionaries and Dictionaries of Usage*. Pub. of the American Dialect Soc. 63–64. University: U of Alabama P, 1975.

Crowley, Tony. *Standard English and the Politics of Language*. Urbana: U of Illinois P, 1989.

Crum, Mason. *Gullah: Negro Life in the Carolina Sea Islands*. Durham: Duke UP, 1940.

Cunningham, Irma Aloyce Ewing. "A Syntactic Analysis of Sea Island Creole." Diss. U of Michigan, 1970.

Daiute, Colette A. "Psycholinguistic Foundations of the Writing Process." *Research in the Teaching of English* 15.1 (1981): 5–22.

Davis, Alva L., ed. *Culture, Class, and Language Variety*. Urbana: NCTE, 1972.

———. "A Word Geography of the Great Lakes Region." Diss. U of Michigan, 1949.

Davis, James A., and Ann M. Jacobs. "Tabular Presentation." Sills 15: 497–509.

Davis, Lawrence M. *English Dialectology: An Introduction*. University: U of Alabama P, 1983.

Davis, Stephen, and Peter Simon. *Reggae International*. New York: Random, 1982.

Day, Robert. "What Is a Scientific Paper?" Morris, Ostrom, and Young 412–20.

Demers, Richard A., and Ann K. Farmer. *A Linguistics Workbook*. Cambridge: MIT P, 1986.

Devonish, Hubert. *Language and Liberation*. London: Karia, 1986.

Dictionary of Linguistics. Ed. Mario Pei and Frank Gaynor. New York: Philosophical, 1954.

Dictionary of Occupational Titles. Washington: GPO, 1986.

Dillard, J. L. *Black English: Its History and Usage in the United States.* New York: Random, 1972.

———. *Toward a Social History of American English.* New York: Mouton, 1985.

Doubleday Dictionary. Garden City: Doubleday, 1975.

Dubois, Betty Lou, and Isabel Crouch. "The Question of Tag Questions in Women's Speech: They Don't Really Use More of Them, Do They?" *Language in Society* 4 (1975): 289–94.

Duran, Richard P., ed. *Latino Language and Communicative Behavior.* Norwood: Ablex, 1981.

Eakins, Barbara W., and R. G. Eakins. *Sex Differences in Human Communication.* Boston: Houghton, 1978.

Ebbitt, Wilma R., and David R. Ebbitt. *Writer's Guide and Index to English.* 7th ed. Glenview: Scott, 1982.

Eble, Connie C. *College Slang 101.* Georgetown: Spectacle Lane, 1989.

———. "Scenes from Slang." *SECOL Bulletin* 5 (1981): 74–78.

———. "Slang: Etymology, Folk Etymology, and Multiple Etymology." *SECOL Review* 10 (1986): 8–16.

Edwards, John. *Language and Disadvantage.* London: Arnold, 1979.

Edwards, Viv. *Language in a Black Community.* San Diego: College-Hill, 1986.

———. *Language in Multicultural Classrooms.* London: Batsford, 1983.

Elasser, Nan, and Patricia Irvine. "English and Creole: The Dialectics of Choice in a College Writing Program." *Harvard Educational Review* 55.4 (1985): 399–415.

Elías-Olivares, Lucía. "Language Use in a Chicano Community: A Sociolinguistic Approach." *Sociolinguistic Working Paper 30.* Austin: Southwest Educ. Dev. Laboratory, 1976. 1–21.

———, ed. *Spanish in the U.S. Setting: Beyond the Southwest.* Rosslyn: Natl. Clearinghouse for Bilingual Educ., 1983.

———. "Ways of Speaking in a Chicano Speech Community: A Sociolinguistic Approach." Diss. U of Texas, Austin, 1976.

Elías-Olivares, Lucía, and Guadalupe Valdés. "Language Diversity in Chicano Speech Communities: Implications for Language Teaching." *Bilingual Education for Hispanic Students in the United States.* Eds. Joshua Fishman and G. Keller. New York: Teachers Coll. P, 1982. 151–66.

Elsbree, Langdon, and Frederick G. Bracher. *Heath's Brief Handbook of Composition.* 9th ed. Lexington: Heath, 1977.

Epstein, Herman. *A Strategy for Education.* New York: Oxford UP, 1970.

Eschholz, Paul, Alfred Rosa, and Virginia Clark, eds. *Language Awareness.* 4th ed. New York: St. Martin's, 1986.

Evans, Bergen, and Cornelia Evans. *A Dictionary of Contemporary American Usage*. New York: Random, 1957.

Fairman, Tony. "Teaching the Englishes." *International Review of Applied Linguistics* 26 (1988): 115–26.

Farb, Peter. *Word Play: What Happens When People Talk*. New York: Knopf, 1974.

Farr, Marcia, and Mary Ann Janda. "Basic Writing Students: Investigating Oral and Written Language." *Research in the Teaching of English* 19.1 (1985): 62–83.

Farrell, Thomas J. "IQ and Standard English." *College Composition and Communication* 34 (1983): 470–84.

Fasold, Ralph W. "Are Black and White Vernaculars Diverging?" *American Speech* 62 (1987): 3–5.

———. "The Relation between Black and White Speech in the South." *American Speech* 56 (1981): 163–89.

———. *The Sociolinguistics of Society*. London: Blackwell, 1984.

Ferguson, Charles A. "Diglossia." *Word* 15 (1959): 325–40.

Ferguson, Charles A., and Shirley Brice Heath, eds. *Language in the USA*. Cambridge: Cambridge UP, 1981.

Fernández, Ricardo. "Legislation, Regulation, and Litigation: The Origins and Evolution of Public Policy on Bilingual Education in the United States." Van Horne and Tonnesen 90–123.

Fernández, Roberto G. "English Loanwords in Miami Cuban Spanish." *American Speech* 58 (1983): 13–19.

Finegan, Edward. *Attitudes toward English Usage: The History of a War of Words*. New York: Columbia UP, 1980.

Fischer, Kathy. "Educating Speakers of Caribbean English Creole in the United States." Unpub. ms. Evanston Township High School, Evanston, IL.

Fisher, John H., Malcolm Richardson, and Jane L. Fisher, eds. *An Anthology of Chancery English*. Knoxville: U of Tennessee P, 1984.

Fishman, Joshua A. "Bilingualism with and without Diglossia: Diglossia with and without Bilingualism." *Journal of Social Issues* 2 (1967): 29–38.

———. "Language Policy: Past, Present, and Future." Ferguson and Heath 516–26.

———. "Who Speaks What Language to Whom and When?" *Linguistics* 2 (1965): 67–88.

Fitzpatrick, Lilian L. *Nebraska Place Names*. Lincoln: U of Nebraska P, 1960.

Flesch, Rudolph F. *How to Test Readability*. New York: Harper, 1951.

Flexner, Stuart B. *I Hear America Talking*. New York: Touchstone, 1976.

———. Preface. *The Dictionary of American Slang*. Ed. Harold Wentworth. New York: Crowell, 1975. Rpt. in Eschholz, Rosa, and Clark 180–90.

Flores, Nancy, and Robert Hopper. "Mexican American's Evaluations of Spoken Spanish and English." *Speech Monographs* 42 (1975): 91–98.

Follett, Wilson. *Modern American Usage: A Guide.* Ed. and comp. Jacques Barzun, with the collaboration of Carlos Baker, Frederick W. Dupee, Dudley Fitts, James D. Hart, Phyllis McGinley, Lionel Trilling. New York: Hill, 1966.

Francis, W. N. *Dialectology: An Introduction.* London: Longman, 1983.

Frazer, Timothy C. *Midland Illinois Dialect Patterns.* Pub. of the American Dialect Soc. 73. University: U of Alabama P, 1987.

Fries, Charles. "The Periphrastic Future with *Shall* and *Will* in Modern English." *PMLA* 40 (1925): 963–1024.

———. "The Rules of Common School Grammars." *PMLA* 42 (1927): 221–37.

Fuller, Maud. "Paralanguage in Jamaican Creole." *TESL Talk* 10.4 (1978): 21–24.

Galindo, D. Letticia. "Linguistic Influence and Variation on the English of Chicano Adolescents in Austin, Texas." Diss. U of Texas, Austin, 1987.

———. "Perceptions of *Pachuquismo* and Use of *Caló/Pachuco* Spanish by Various Chicana Women." Master's thesis. U of Texas, Austin, 1982.

García, Maryellen. "Parameters of the East Los Angeles Speech Community." Ornstein, *Form* 85–98.

García, Ricardo. "Toward a Grammar of Chicano English." *English Journal* 63 (1974): 34–38.

Garvin, Paul, and Peter Ladefoged. "Speaker Identification and Message Identification in Speaker Recognition." *Phonetica* 9 (1963): 193–99.

Gaustad, Edwin Scott. *Historical Atlas of Religion in America.* Rev. ed. New York: Harper, 1976.

Gerathy, Virginia. *Maum Chrish' Chaa'stun.* Record. 1979.

Gibson, Kean. "The Habitual Category in Guyanese and Jamaican Creoles." *American Speech* 63 (1988): 195–202.

Gilbert, Glenn G. "The English of the Brandywine Population: A Triracial Isolate in Southern Maryland." Montgomery and Bailey 102–10.

Gilchrist, James. *Reason, the True Arbiter of Language: Custom a Tyrant.* London, 1814.

Glassie, Henry. *Pattern in the Material Folk Culture of the Eastern United States.* Philadelphia: U of Pennsylvania P, 1968.

Gonzales, Ambrose. *The Black Border.* Columbia: State, 1922.

Goodman, Kenneth. "Dialect Barriers to Reading Comprehension." *Teaching Black Children to Read.* Ed. Joan C. Baratz and Roger W. Shuy. Washington: Center for Applied Linguistics, 1969. 14–28.

Görlach, Manfred. "English as a World Language: The State of the Art." *English World-Wide* 9 (1988): 1–32.

Goshgarian, Gary, ed. *Exploring Language.* 4th ed. Boston: Little, 1986.

Goswami, Dixie, and Peter R. Stillman, eds. *Reclaiming the Classroom: Teacher Research as an Agency for Change.* Upper Montclair: Boynton, 1987.

Gould, Peter R., and Rodney White. *Mental Maps.* New York: Penguin, 1974.

Graff, Gary. "Rock Music." *Detroit Free Press* 12 Mar. 1986: B1–2.

A Grand Dictionary of Phonetics: A Comprehensive Store of Neo-macro-phonetics. Supervisor Masao Onishi. Tokyo: Phonetic Soc., 1981.

Gray, Charles, and George A. Kopp. "Voice Print Identification." Unpub. report. Bell Telephone Laboratories, New York, 1944.

Green, Ervin L. Interview. *Chapel Hill Newspaper* 24 Apr. 1987: 5B.

Greenbaum, Sidney, ed. *The English Language Today.* Oxford: Pergamon, 1985.

Greenbaum, Sidney, and Randolph Quirk. *Elicitation Experiments in English.* Coral Gables: U of Miami P, 1970.

Greet, Cabell. "American Speech." Record. Victor and Victrola 65–76. 1940s.

——, pronunciation ed. Introduction. *American College Dictionary.* New York: Random, 1947. xxiv.

Gregg, R. J. "The Diphthongs əi and ai in Scottish, Scotch-Irish, and Canadian English." *Canadian Journal of Linguistics* 18 (1973): 136–45.

——. *Final Report to the Social Sciences and Humanities Research Council of Canada on "An Urban Dialect Survey of the English Spoken in Vancouver."* U of British Columbia. 1984.

——. "Local Lexical Items in the Sociological Survey of Vancouver English." *Canadian Journal of Linguistics* 28 (1983): 17–23.

Grice, H. P. "Logic and Conversation." *Syntax and Semantics.* Vol. 3 of *Speech Acts.* Ed. Peter Cole and Jerry L. Morgan. New York: Academic, 1975. 41–58.

Grittner, Frank. "Public Policies and Ethnic Influences upon Foreign Language Study in the Public Schools." Van Horne and Tonnesen 189–210.

Grolier International Dictionary. 2 vols. Danbury: Grolier, 1981.

Grootaers, Willem A. "Origin and Nature of the Subjective Boundaries of Dialects." *Orbis* 8 (1959): 355–84.

Gudde, Erwin G. *California Place Names.* 3rd ed. Berkeley: U of California P, 1969.

Gumperz, John J. "Types of Linguistic Communities." *Anthropological Linguistics* 4 (1962): 24–40.

Gumperz, John J., and Dell Hymes, eds. *Directions in Sociolinguistics: The Ethnography of Communication.* New York: Holt, 1972.

Guth, Hans P. *Concise English Handbook.* 4th ed. Belmont: Wadsworth, 1977.

Hancock, Ian F. *Further Observations on Afro-Seminole.* Soc. for Caribbean Linguistics Occasional Paper 7. St. Augustine, Trinidad: U of West Indies, 1977.

——. "Gullah and Barbadian: Origins and Relationships." *American Speech* 55 (1980): 17–35.

——. "On the Classification of Afro-Seminole Creole." Montgomery and Bailey 85–101.

——. "Texan Gullah: The Creole English of Brackettville Afro-Seminoles." *Perspectives on American English.* Ed. J. L. Dillard. Hague: Mouton, 1980. 305–32.

Hanley, Miles L. *Handbook to the Linguistic Atlas of New England.* Providence: Brown UP, 1939.

Harder, Kelsie B. *Illustrated Dictionary of Place Names.* New York: Nostrand, 1976.

———, ed. *Names and Their Varieties: A Collection of Essays on Onomastics.* Lanham: UP of America, 1986.

The Harder They Come. Videocassette. By Perry Henzell and Trevor D. Rhone. Prod. and dir. Henzell. Intl. Films, 1972. 93 min.

Harris, Joel Chandler. *Uncle Remus.* New York: Houghton, 1880.

Hartford, Beverly. "The English of Mexican-American Adolescents in Gary, Indiana: A Sociolinguistic Description." Diss. U of Texas, Austin, 1975.

Hartman, James W. "Guide to Pronunciation." Cassidy, *Dictionary* xli–lxi.

Hartwell, Patrick. "Dialect Interference in Writing: A Critical Review." *Research in the Teaching of English* 14.2 (1980): 101–18.

Haugen, Einar. *The Ecology of Language.* Stanford: Stanford UP, 1972.

———. *The Norwegian Language in America: A Study in Bilingual Behavior.* Philadelphia: U of Pennsylvania P, 1953.

Hayakawa, S. I. "How Dictionaries Are Made." Eschholz et al. 192–93.

Heath, Shirley Brice. "A National Language Academy? Debate in the New Nation." *International Journal of the Sociology of Language* 11 (1976): 9–43.

———. "Student Writing: Myths and Ethnography." Keynote address. CCC Conference. Minneapolis, 22 Mar. 1985.

———. *Ways with Words: Language, Life, and Work in Communities and Classrooms.* New York: Cambridge UP, 1983.

Hempl, George. "Grease and Greasy." *Dialect Notes* (1896): 438–44.

Hernández-Chávez, Eduardo, Andrew Cohen, and Anthony Beltramo, eds. *El Lenguaje de los Chicanos.* Arlington: Center for Applied Linguistics, 1975.

Herndobler, Robin, and Andrew Sledd. "Black English—Notes on the Auxiliary." *American Speech* 51 (1976): 185–200.

Hirsch, E. D., Jr. *Cultural Literacy: What Every American Needs to Know.* Boston: Houghton, 1987.

Hodge, Merle. *Crick Crack, Monkey.* London: Deutsch, 1970.

Hodges, John C., et al. *Harbrace College Handbook.* 10th ed. San Diego: Harcourt, 1990.

Holm, John A., with Alison W. Shilling. *Dictionary of Bahamian English.* Cold Spring: Lexik, 1982.

Holtz, Louis. *Donat et la tradition de l'enseignement grammatical.* Paris: CNRS, 1981.

Hook, J. N. *History of the English Language.* New York: Ronald, 1975.

Hubbell, Allan F. *Pronunciation of English in New York City.* New York: Kings, 1950.

Hudson-Edwards, Alan, and Garland Bills. "Intergenerational Language Shift in an Albuquerque Barrio." Amastae and Elías-Olivares, *Spanish* 135–53.

392 WORKS CITED

Isidore of Seville. *Etymologiae sive origines.* Ed. W. M. Lindsay. Oxford: Clarendon–Oxford UP, 1911.

Jespersen, Otto. *English Phonetics.* Copenhagen, 1950. Trans. of *Engelsk fonetik.* Copenhagen: Nordisk, 1912 (rpt. 1921, 1936, 1945).

———. *Language: Its Nature, Development, and Origin.* 1921. New York: Norton, 1964.

———. *The Philosophy of Grammar.* 1924. London: Allen, 1963.

Johnson, Diane. "Doctor Talk." *The Living Language: A Reader.* Morris, Ostrom, and Young 55–59.

Johnson, Guy B. *Folk Culture on St. Helena Island, South Carolina.* Chapel Hill: U of North Carolina P, 1930.

Johnson, Ken. "The Vocabulary of Race." Kochman, *Rappin'* 140–51.

Johnson, Samuel. *A Dictionary of the English Language.* 2 vols. London: Knapton, 1755.

Jones, Charles C. *Negro Myths from the Georgia Coast.* Boston: Houghton, 1888.

Jones, Daniel. *Cardinal Vowels.* Gramophone recording. B 804. London: Linguaphone Inst., c. 1940.

———. "Concrete and Abstract Sounds." *Proceedings of the 3rd International Congress of Phonetic Sciences.* Ghent, 1938.

———. *An English Pronouncing Dictionary.* London: Dent, 1917.

———. *An Outline of English Phonetics.* 4th ed. Cambridge: Heffer, 1932.

———. *The Pronunciation of English.* 4th ed. Cambridge: Cambridge UP, 1966.

Jones, Evan. *Tales of the Caribbean.* 4 vols. Aylesbury: Ginn, 1984.

Jones-Jackson, Patricia. "Contemporary Gullah Speech: Some Persistent Lingusitic Features." *Journal of Black Studies* 13 (1983): 289–303.

———. "Gullah: On the Question of Afro-American Language." *Anthropological Linguistics* 20 (1978): 422–29.

———. "On Decreolization and Language Death in Gullah." *Language in Society* 13 (1984): 351–62.

———. "On the Status of Gullah on the Sea Islands." Montgomery and Bailey 63–72.

———. "The Status of Gullah: An Investigation of Convergent Processes." Diss. U of Michigan, 1978.

———. *When Roots Die: Endangered Traditions on the Sea Islands.* Athens: U of Georgia P, 1987.

Joos, Martin. *Acoustic Phonetics.* Language Monograph 23. Baltimore: Waverly, 1948.

———. "A Phonological Dilemma in Canadian English." *Language* 18 (1942): 141–44.

Joyner, Charles W. *Down by the Riverside: A South Carolina Slave Community.* Chicago: U of Illinois P, 1984.

Kachru, Braj B. *The Alchemy of English: The Spread, Functions, and Models of Non-native Englishes.* Oxford: Pergamon, 1986.

———. *The Indianization of English: The English Language in India.* Delhi: Oxford UP, 1983.

———, ed. *The Other Tongue: English across Cultures*. Urbana: U of Illinois P, 1982.

———. "Teaching World Englishes." *ERIC/CLL News Bulletin* 12.1 (1988): 1–4.

Kahn, Aron. "From 'Tush-Ups' to 'Odoralls,' Families Have Special Words." *Des Moines Register* 6 June 1989: T1+

Kaminkow, Marion J. *United States Local Histories in the Library of Congress: A Bibliography*. 4 vols. Baltimore: Magna Carta, 1975.

Kane, Joseph Nathan, and Gerald L. Alexander. *Nicknames and Sobriquets of U.S. Cities and States*. 2nd ed. Metuchen: Scarecrow, 1970.

Kaster, Robert. *Guardians of Language: The Grammarian and Society in Late Antiquity*. Berkeley: U of California P, 1988.

Keens-Douglas, Paul. *When Moon Shine*. Port-of-Spain: Keensdee, 1975.

Keil, Heinrich, ed. *Grammatici Latini*. 8 vols. Hildesheim: Olms, 1961.

Kennedy, Graeme. "The Language of Tests for Young Children." Spolsky, *Language* 164–81.

Kenyon, John S. *American Pronunciation*. 1924. 10th ed. Ann Arbor: Wahr, 1950.

Kenyon, John S., and Thomas A. Knott. *A Pronouncing Dictionary of American English*. Springfield: Merriam, 1944.

Key, Mary Ritchie. "Linguistic Behavior of Male and Female." *Linguistics* 88 (1972): 15–31.

———. *Male/Female Language*. Metuchen: Scarecrow, 1975.

Kincaid, Jamaica. *Annie John*. New York: NAL, 1983.

Kingsley, Sidney. *Dead End. Twenty Plays of the Modern American Theatre*. Ed. John Gassner. New York: Crown, 1957.

Kirkham, Samuel. *English Grammar, in Familiar Lectures*. 2nd ed. Harrisburg: S. Wiestling, 1824.

Kjolseth, Rolf. "Bilingual Education Programs in the United States: For Assimilation or Pluralism?" Spolsky, *Language* 94–121.

Klare, George R. *The Measurement of Readability*. Ames: Iowa State UP, 1963.

———. "A Second Look at the Validity of Readability Formulas." *Journal of Reading Behavior* 8 (1976): 129–52.

Kochman, Thomas, ed. *Rappin' and Stylin' Out: Communication in Urban Black America*. Urbana: U of Illinois P, 1972.

———. "Toward an Ethnography of Black American Speech Behavior." Kochman, *Rappin'* 241–64.

Kramer, Cheris. "Perceptions of Female and Male Speech." *Language and Speech* 20 (1977): 151–61.

Krapp, George Philip. *The English Language in America*. 2 vols. New York: Century, 1925.

Kurath, Hans. "The Investigation of Urban Speech and Some Other Problems Confronting the Student of American English." *Publication of the American Dialect Society* 49. University: U of Alabama P, 1968. 1–7.

————, ed. *Linguistic Atlas of New England*. 3 vols. in 6 parts, with Handbook. Providence: Brown UP, 1939–43.

————. *Studies in Area Linguistics*. Bloomington: Indiana UP, 1972.

————. *A Word Geography of the Eastern United States*. Ann Arbor: U of Michigan P, 1949.

Kurath, Hans, and Raven I. McDavid, Jr. *The Pronunciation of English in the Atlantic States*. Ann Arbor: U of Michigan P, 1961.

Labov, William. "Are Black and White Vernaculars Diverging?" *American Speech* 62 (1987): 5–12.

————. *Language in the Inner City: Studies in the Black English Vernacular*. Philadelphia: U of Pennsylvania P, 1972.

————. "The Logic of Nonstandard English." *Florida Foreign Language Reporter* 7 (1969): 60–74, 169. Rpt. in *Georgetown Monograph Series on Language and Linguistics* 22. Ed. James Alatis. Washington: Georgetown UP, 1970. 1–44.

————. "Objectivity and Commitment in Linguistic Science: The Case of the Black English Trial in Ann Arbor." *Language in Society* 11 (1982): 165–201.

————. *The Social Stratification of English in New York City*. Washington: Center for Applied Linguistics, 1966.

————. *Sociolinguistic Patterns*. Philadelphia: U of Pennsylvania P, 1972.

————. "Stages in the Acquisition of Standard English." *Social Dialects and Language Learning*. Ed. Roger Shuy. Champaign: NCTE, 1964. 77–103.

Labov, William, and Wendell Harris. "De Facto Segregation of Black and White Vernaculars." Sankoff 1–24.

Lakoff, Robin. *Language and Woman's Place*. New York: Harper, 1975.

Lambert, Wallace, Robert C. Hodgson, R. C. Gardner, and S. Fillenbaum. "Evaluative Reactions to Spoken Language." *Journal of Abnormal and Social Psychology* 60 (1960): 44–51.

Lambert, Wallace, and Donald Taylor. "Language Minorities in the United States: Conflicts around Assimilation and Proposed Modes of Accommodation." Van Horne and Tonnesen 58–89.

Landers, Ann. Newspaper column. *Boston Globe* 4 Mar. 1987.

Lantolf, James P. "Toward a Comparative Dialectology of U.S. Spanish." Elías-Olivares, *Spanish* 3–20.

Larmouth, Donald. "Does Linguistic Heterogeneity Erode National Unity?" Van Horne and Tonnesen 58–89.

Lass, Roger, ed. *Approaches to English Historical Linguistics*. New York: Holt, 1969.

Lawson, Edwin D. *Personal Names and Naming: An Annotated Bibliography*. Westport: Greenwood, 1987.

Leggett, Glenn, C. David Mead, and Melinda G. Kramer. *Prentice-Hall Handbook for Writers*. 9th ed. Englewood Cliffs: Prentice, 1985.

Leibowitz, A. "The Terms of the Bilingual Education Act." *The Bilingual Education*

Act: A Legislative Analysis. Rosslyn: National Clearinghouse for Bilingual Educ., n.d. 15–42.

Linn, Michael D., and Maarit-Hannele Zuber. *The Sound of English: A Bibliography of Language Recordings*. Urbana: NCTE, 1984.

Lloyd, P. "On the Definition of Vulgar Latin." *Neuphilologische Mitteilungen* 80 (1979): 110–22.

Local Community Fact Book. Chicago: U of Illinois, n.d.

López, David. "Chicano Language Loyalty in an Urban Setting." *Sociology and Social Research*, 62.2 (1978): 267–78.

Lourie, Margaret A., and Nancy Faires Conklin, eds. *A Pluralistic Nation: The Language Issue in the United States*. Rowley: Newbury, 1978.

Lovelace, Earl. *The Dragon Can't Dance*. London: Deutsch, 1979.

Lowth, Robert. *A Short Introduction to English Grammar*. 1762. Facsim. ed. Menston, Eng.: Scolar, 1967.

Machan, Tim William, and Charles T. Scott, eds. *English in Its Social Contexts: Essays in Historical Sociolinguistics*. Oxford Studies in Sociolinguistics 2. New York: Oxford UP, 1992.

Macías, Reynaldo F. "Language Diversity among U.S. Hispanics: Some Background Considerations for Schooling and for Non-biased Assessment." Paper Presented at the Invitational Symposium on Hispanic Diversity, Michigan State U, East Lansing, 14–15 Mar. 1981.

———. "Mexicano/Chicano Sociolinguistic Behavior and Language Policy in the United States." Diss. Georgetown U, 1979.

Mackey, William, and Jacob Ornstein, eds. *Sociolinguistic Studies in Language Contact*. Hague: Mouton, 1979.

Marckwardt, Albert H. *American English*. New York: Oxford UP, 1958.

Marlette, Doug. Kudzu. Comic Strip. *Des Moines Register* 21, 22 Jan. 1987.

Martinet, André. *Elements of General Linguistics*. Trans. Elisabeth Palmer. U of Chicago P, 1964. Trans. of *Eléments de linguistique générale*, 1960.

Maryland, James. "Shoe-Shine on 63rd." Kochman, *Rappin'* 209–14.

Maurais, Jacques, ed. *La crise des langues*. Québec: Conseil de la langue française, 1985.

McBee, Suzanna. "English: Out to Conquer the World." *U.S. News and World Report* 18 Feb. 1985: 49–52.

McConnell, R. E. *Our Own Voice: Canadian English and How It Came to Be*. Toronto: Gage, 1978.

McCrum, Robert, William Cran, and Robert McNeil. *The Story of English*. New York: Viking, 1986.

McDavid, Raven I., Jr. "Dialect Differences and Social Differences in an Urban Society." *Sociolinguistics*. Ed. William Bright. Hague: Mouton, 1966. 72–83.

——. "Dialect Geography and Social Science Problems." *Social Forces* 25 (1946): 168–72.

——. "The Dialectology of an Urban Society." *Communication et rapports du premier congrès internationale de dialectologie générale*. Ed. A. J. Van Widckens. Louvain: Centre International de Dialectologie Générale, 1960. 68–80.

McDavid, Raven I., Jr., and William M. Austin, eds. *Communication Barriers to the Culturally Deprived*. Chicago: US Dept. of Health, Educ., and Welfare, 1966. ERIC ED 010 052.

McDavid, Raven I., Jr., and Lawrence Davis. "The Dialects of Negro Americans." *Studies in Honor of George L. Trager*. Ed. M. Estellie Smith. The Hague: Mouton, 1972. 303–12.

McDavid, Raven I., Jr., and Virginia G. McDavid. "The Relationship of the Speech of American Negroes to the Speech of Whites." *American Speech* 26 (1951): 3–17. Rpt. in *Dialects in Culture*. Ed. William Kretzschmar, Jr. University: U of Alabama P, 1979. 43–51.

McLoughlin, Merril, Jeffrey L. Sheler, and Gordon Witkin. "A Nation of Liars." *U.S. News and World Report* 23 Feb. 1987: 54–60.

McMillan, James B., and Michael Montgomery, eds. *Annotated Bibliography of Southern American English*. University: U of Alabama P, 1989.

Mencken, H. L. *The American Language*. 1919. New York: Knopf, 1936. Ed. Raven I. McDavid, Jr. 1963. New York: Knopf, 1979. *The American Language: Supplement I*. 1945. New York: Knopf, 1966.

Meredith, Mamie. "Negro Patois and Its Humor." *American Speech* 6 (1931): 317–21.

Merriam-Webster Dictionary of English Usage. Springfield: Merriam-Webster, 1989.

Metcalf, Allan. *Chicano English*. Language in Education: Theory and Practice 21. Arlington: Center for Applied Linguistics, 1979.

——. "Mexican-American English in Southern California." *Western Review* 9.1 (1972): 13–21.

——. "The Study of California Chicano English." *International Journal of the Sociology of Language* 2 (1974): 53–58.

Mey, Jacob. *Whose Language: A Study in Linguistic Pragmatics*. Amsterdam: Benjamins, 1985.

Meyers, Walter E. *Handbook of Contemporary English*. New York: Harcourt, 1974.

Michael, Ian. *English Grammatical Categories and the Tradition to 1800*. London: Cambridge UP, 1970.

Mille, Katherine W. "A Historical Analysis of Tense-Mood-Aspect in Gullah Creole: A Case of Stable Variation." Diss. U of South Carolina, Columbia, 1990.

Miller, Casey, and Kate Swift. *The Handbook of Nonsexist Writing*. 2nd ed. New York: Harper, 1988.

Miller, Michael I. "Discovering Chicago's Dialects." *Field Museum of Natural History Bulletin* 57 (1986): 5–11.

———. "Encoding, Data Definition, and Command Syntax for Linguistic Survey Data." *Journal of English Linguistics* 22 (1989): 142–48.

———. "Exploring Black Speech in Chicago." Dictionary Soc. of North America. Philadelphia, 1987.

———. "Further Explorations in Chicago Black Speech." Dictionary Soc. of North America. Cleveland, 1989.

———. "Quantification of Sociolinguistic Data." *Studies in English Literature and Linguistics* 14 (1988): 137–48. [Published by Dept. of English, Natl. Taiwan Normal U]

Milroy, James, and Leslie Milroy. *Authority in Language: Investigating Language Prescription and Standardisation.* 2nd ed. London: Routledge, 1991.

Mitchell-Kernan, Claudia. "Signifying and Marking: Two Afro-American Speech Acts." Gumperz and Hymes 161–79.

Mittelholzer, Edgar. *A Morning at the Office.* London: Heinemann, 1950.

Montgomery, Michael, and Guy Bailey, eds. *Language Variety in the South: Perspectives in Black and White.* University: U of Alabama P, 1986.

Morris, Linda A., Hans A. Ostrom, and Linda P. Young, eds. *The Living Language: A Reader.* San Diego: Harcourt, 1984.

Morris, William, and Mary Morris. *Harper Dictionary of Contemporary Usage.* New York: Harper, 1975.

Mufwene, Salikoko S. "The Count/Mass Distinction and the English Lexicon." *Papers from the Parasession on Lexical Semantics.* Ed. David Testen et al. Chicago: Chicago Linguistic Soc., 1984. 200–21.

———. "Equivocal Structures in Some Gullah Complex Sentences." *American Speech* 64 (1989): 304–26.

———. "Is Gullah Decreolizing? A Comparison of a Speech Sample of the 1930's with a Speech Sample of the 1980's." Bailey, Maynor, and Cukor-Avila 213–30.

———. "An Issue on Predicate Clefting: Evidence from Atlantic Creoles and African Languages." *Varia Creolica.* Ed. Philippe Maurer and Thomas Stoltz. Bochum: Brockmeyer, 1987. 71–89.

———. "The Linguistic Significance of African Proper Names in Gullah." *New West Indian Guide* 59 (1985): 146–66.

———. "Number Delimitation in Gullah." *American Speech* 61 (1986): 33–60.

———. "On the Infinitive in Gullah." *Verb Phrase Patterns in Black English and Creole.* Ed. Walter Edwards and Donald Winford. Detroit: Wayne State UP, 1991. 209–22.

———. "Restrictive Relativization in Gullah." *Journal of Pidgin and Creole Languages* 1 (1986): 1–31.

———. Rev. of Montgomery and Bailey. *Journal of Pidgin and Creole Languages* 2 (1987): 93–110.

———. "Serialization and Subordination in Gullah: Toward a Definition of Serialization." *Working Papers in Linguistics.* Columbus: Linguistics Dept., Ohio State U, 1990. 91–108.

———. "Some Reasons Why Gullah Is Not Dying Yet." *English World-Wide* 12 (1991): 215–43.

Mufwene, Salikoko S., and Marta B. Dijkhoff. "Notes on the So-Called 'Infinitive' in Creoles." 6th Biennial Meeting of the Soc. for Caribbean Linguistics. U of the West Indies, St. Augustine, Trinidad, 1986.

Mufwene, Salikoko S., and Charles Gilman. "How African Is Gullah, and Why?" *American Speech* 62 (1987): 120–39.

Murray, Donald. "Teach the Motivating Force of Revision." *English Journal* 67.7 (1978): 56–60.

Myhill, John. "Postvocalic /r/ as an Index of Integration into the BEV Speech Community." *American Speech* 63 (1988): 203–13.

Myhill, John, and Wendell A. Harris. "The Use of the Verbal -S Inflection in BEV." *Diversity and Diachrony.* Ed. David Sankoff. Amsterdam: Benjamins, 1986. 25–31.

Naipaul, V. S. *Miguel Street.* Harmondsworth, Eng.: Penguin, 1958.

Nash, Rose. "Englañol: More Language Contact in Puerto Rico." *American Speech* 46 (1971): 106–22.

———. "Spanglish: Language Contact in Puerto Rico." *American Speech* 45 (1970): 223–33.

National Assessment of Educational Progress. *Write/Rewrite: An Assessment of Revision Skills: Selected Results from the Second National Assessment of Writing,* 1977. ERIC ED 141 826.

Negus, V. E. *The Mechanism of the Larynx.* London: Heinemann, 1929.

New American Webster Handy College Dictionary. Paperback. New York: NAL, 1981.

Newman, Edwin. *Strictly Speaking: Will America Be the Death of English?* New York: Warner, 1974.

Nichols, Patricia C. "Black and White Speaking in the Rural South: Difference in the Pronominal System." *American Speech* 58 (1983): 201–15.

———. "Complementizers in Creoles." *Working Papers on Language Universals* 19 (1975): 131–35.

———. "Gullah and Caribbean Creole English." American Dialect Soc., South Atlantic MLA Convention, Atlanta, 1983.

———. "Linguistic Change in Gullah: Sex, Age, Mobility." Diss. Stanford U, 1976.

———. "Prepositions in Black and White English of Coastal South Carolina." Montgomery and Bailey 73–84.

Nicholson, Margaret. *A Dictionary of American-English Usage.* New York: Oxford UP, 1957.

Nilsen, Alleen Pace. "Guidelines against Sexist Lanuage: A Case History." *Women and*

Language in Transition. Ed. Joyce Penfield. Albany: State U of New York P, 1987. 37–64.

Noreen, Robert G. "Ghetto Worship: A Study of the Names of Chicago Storefront Churches." *Names* 13 (1965): 19–38.

Oftedal, Magne. *What Are Minorities? Lingual Minorities in Europe.* Oslo: Norske, 1969.

Orleans, Peter. "Differential Cognition of Urban Residents: Effects of Social Scale on Mapping." *Science, Engineering, and the City.* Publication 1498. Washington: Natl. Acad. of Sciences, 1967. 103–17.

Ornstein, Jacob, ed. *Form and Function in Chicano English.* Rowley: Newbury, 1984.

———. "Mexican-American Sociolinguistics: A Well-Kept Scholarly and Public Secret." *Sociolinguistics in the Southwest.* Eds. Bates Hoffer and Jacob Ornstein. San Antonio: Trinity U, 1974. 91–131.

Ortega, Adolfo. *Caló Tapestry.* Berkeley: Justa, 1977.

Ortony, Andrew, Terence J. Turner, and Nancy Larson-Shapiro. "Cultural and Instructional Influences on Figurative Language Comprehension by Inner City Children." *Research in the Teaching of English* 19 (1985): 25–36.

Our Changing Language. Recording. Prepared by Evelyn Gott Burack and Raven I. McDavid, Jr. Urbana: NCTE, 1965. 50 min.

The Oxford English Dictionary. Ed. James A. H. Murray, Henry Bradley, W. A. Craigie, C. T. Onions. 12 vols. London: Oxford UP, 1961. *Supplement to the Oxford English Dictionary.* 4 vols. Oxford: Clarendon–Oxford UP, 1972–86. *Compact Edition.* 2 vols. New York: Oxford UP, 1971. 2nd ed. Ed. J. A. Simpson and E. S. C. Weiner. 20 vols. Oxford: Clarendon–Oxford UP, 1989.

Paher, Stanley W. *Nevada Ghost Towns and Mining Camps.* Berkeley: Howell-North, 1970.

Parker, Frank. *Linguistics for Non-linguists.* New York: Little, 1986.

Parker, Frank, and Kathryn Riley. *Exercises in Linguistics.* Boston: Little, 1990.

Partridge, Eric. *Usage and Abusage.* Harmondsworth, Eng.: Penguin, 1963.

Paullin, Charles O., and John K. Wright. *Atlas of the Historical Geography of the United States.* Washington: Carnegie Inst. and American Geographical Soc., 1932.

Pederson, Lee A. "An Approach to Urban Word Geography." *American Speech* 46 (1971): 73–86.

———. "Chicago Words: The Regional Vocabulary." *American Speech* 46 (1971): 163–92.

———. "Non-standard Negro Speech in Chicago." *Non-standard Speech and the Teaching of English.* Ed. William A. Stewart. Washington: Center for Applied Linguistics, 1964. 16–23.

———. "Phonological Indices of Social Dialects in Chicago." McDavid and Austin.

———. *The Pronunciation of English in Metropolitan Chicago.* Pub. of the American Dialect Soc. 44. University: U of Alabama P, 1965.

———. "Some Structural Differences in the Speech of Chicago Negroes." *Social*

Dialects and Language Learning. Ed. Roger W. Shuy. Champaign: NCTE, 1964. 25–51.

———. "Terms of Abuse for Some Chicago Social Groups." *Publication of the American Dialect Society* 42 (1964): 26–48.

Peñalosa, Fernando. *Chicano Sociolinguistics.* Rowley: Newbury, 1980.

———. *Introduction to the Sociology of Language.* Rowley: Newbury, 1981.

———. "Some Issues in Chicano Sociolinguistics." Duran 3–18.

Penfield, Joyce. "Prosodic Patterns: Some Hypotheses and Findings from Fieldwork." Ornstein, *Form* 49–59.

Penfield, Joyce, and Jacob Ornstein. *Chicano English: An Ethnic Contact Dialect.* Varieties of English around the World Series 7. Philadelphia: Benjamins, 1985.

Perrin, Porter G., and Jim W. Corder. *Handbook of Current English.* 4th ed. Glenview: Scott, 1975.

Peyton, V. J. *The History of the English Language.* 1771. Facsim. ed. Menston, Eng.: Scolar, 1970.

Picard, Marc. "Canadian Raising: The Case against Reordering." *Canadian Journal of Linguistics* 22 (1977): 144–55.

Pitts, Walter. "West African Poetics in the Black Preaching Style." *American Speech* 64 (1989): 137–49.

Platt, John, H. Weber, and M. L. Ho. *The New Englishes.* London: Routledge, 1984.

Ponsot, Marie, and Rosemary Deen. *Beat Not the Poor Desk: Writing—What to Teach, How to Teach It, and Why.* Upper Montclair: Boynton, 1981.

Pooley, Robert C. *The Teaching of English Usage.* 2nd ed. Urbana: NCTE, 1974.

Potter, Ralph, George Kopp, and Harriet Green. *Visible Speech.* New York: Van Nostrand, 1947.

Prescott, Robin B. *Some Descriptive Features Observed in Cry Sounds of Infants in the First Ten Days and the Second Half Year of Life.* Diss. Wayne State U, 1967.

Preston, Dennis R. "Change in the Perception of Language Varieties." *Historical Dialectology: Regional and Social.* Ed. Jacek Fisiak. Berlin: de Gruyter, 1988. 475–504.

———. "Five Visions of America." *Language in Society* 15 (1986): 221–40.

———. "Mental Maps of Language Distribution in Rio Grande do Sul (Brazil)." *Geographical Bulletin* 27 (1985): 46–64.

———. "Methods in the Study of Dialect Perception." A. R. Thomas 373–95.

———. *Perceptual Dialectology.* Dordrecht, Netherlands: Foris, 1989.

———. "Perceptual Dialectology: Mental Maps of United States Dialects from a Hawaiian Perspective." Ed. Preston. *Working Papers in Linguistics* (Dept. of Linguistics, U of Hawaii, Manoa) 14 (1982): 5–49.

———. "Sociolinguistic Commonplaces in Variety Perception." *Linguistic Change and Contact.* Ed. K. Ferrara, B. Brown, K. Walters, and J. Baugh. Austin: Dept. of Linguistics, U of Texas, 1988. 279–92.

——. "Southern Indiana Perceptions of 'Correct' and 'Pleasant' Speech." Warkentyne, *Papers* 387–411.

Preston, Dennis R., and George M. Howe. "Computerized Generalizations of Mental Dialect Maps." *Variation in Language: NWAV-XV at Stanford.* Ed. K. M. Denning, S. Inkelas, F. C. McNair-Knox, and J. R. Rickford. Stanford: Dept. of Linguistics, Stanford U, 1987. 361–78.

Pride, John B., ed. *New Englishes.* Rowley: Newbury, 1982.

Priestley, Joseph. *A Course of Lectures on the Theory of Language and Universal Grammar.* 1762. Facsim. ed. Menston, Eng.: Scolar, 1970.

Pringle, Ian. "The Concept of Dialect and the Study of Canadian English." *Queen's Quarterly* 90 (1983): 100–21. Rpt. in Dialect and Language Variation. Ed. Harold B. Allen and Michael D. Linn. Orlando: Academic, 1986. 217–36.

Pringle, Ian, R. H. Dale, and Enoch Padolsky. "Procedures to Solve a Methodological Problem in the Ottawa Valley." Warkentyne, *Papers* 477–94.

Pringle, Ian, and Enoch Padolsky. "The Linguistic Survey of the Ottawa Valley." *American Speech* 58 (1983): 325–44.

Pugh, Lee G. *An Assessment of Teachers' Social Perceptions of Dialectal Differences among Junior-High-School Males.* Diss. U of Miami, Coral Gables, 1973.

Pullum, Geoffrey K., and William A. Ladusaw. *A Phonetic Symbol Guide.* Chicago: U of Chicago P, 1986.

Pyles, Thomas. "Bible Belt Onomastics or Some Curiosities of Anti-pedobaptist Nomenclature." *Names* 7 (1959): 84–100.

——. *Words and Ways of American English.* New York: Random, 1952.

Pyles, Thomas, and John Algeo. *The Origins and Development of the English Language.* 4th ed. New York: Harcourt, 1993.

Quirk, Randolph, Sidney Greenbaum, Geoffrey Leech, and Jan Svartvik. *A Comprehensive Grammar of the English Language.* London: Longman, 1985.

Raleigh, Mike. *The Languages Book.* London: ILEA, 1981.

Ramírez, Arnulfo. "Language Attitudes and the Speech of Spanish-English Bilingual Pupils." Duran 217–46.

Ramírez, Carina. "Lexical Usage of and Attitudes toward Southwest Spanish in the Ysleta, Texas, Area." *Problems in Applied Educational Sociolinguistics.* Ed. Glenn Gilbert and Jacob Ornstein. Hague: Mouton, 1978. 43–53.

Ramsay, Robert L. *Our Storehouse of Missouri Place Names.* Columbia: U of Missouri P, 1952, 1973.

Randall, Bernice. *Webster's New World Guide to Current American Usage.* New York: Webster's New World, 1988.

Random House College Dictionary. 1968. Rev. ed. New York: Random House, 1975.

Random House Dictionary. Paperback ed. New York: Ballantine, 1980.

Random House Dictionary of the English Language. Unabridged ed. New York: Random, 1966. 2nd ed. 1987.

Random House Webster's College Dictionary. New York: Random, 1992.

Read, Allen Walker. "The Challenge of Place Name Study." *Elementary English* 48 (1971): 235–36.

———. Dictionary of Briticisms. Work in progress, 1938–93.

———, British and American usage ed. Introduction. *American College Dictionary.* New York: Random, 1947. xxx–xxxi.

Reinecke, John Ernest. "Marginal Languages: A Sociological Survey of the Creole Languages and Trade Jargons." Diss. Yale U, 1937.

Reyes, Rogelio. "Language Mixing in Chicano Bilingual Speech." Bowen and Ornstein 183–88.

Richmond, W. Edson. "The Value of the Study of Place Names." *Indiana Names* 1 (1970): 1–10.

Rickford, John R. "Are Black and White Vernaculars Diverging?" *American Speech* 62 (1987): 55–62.

———. "Carrying the New Wave into Syntax: The Case of Black English *bin*." *Analyzing Variation in Language.* Ed. Ralph Fasold and Roger W. Shuy. Washington: Georgetown UP, 1975. 162–83.

———. *Dimensions of a Creole Continuum.* Stanford: Stanford UP, 1987.

———. "Ethnicity as a Sociolinguistic Boundary." *American Speech* 60 (1985): 99–125.

———, ed. *A Festival of Guyanese Words.* Georgetown: U of Guyana, 1978.

———. "Insights from the Mesolect." *Pidgins and Creoles: Current Trends and Prospects.* Ed. David DeCamp and Ian Hancock. Washington: Georgetown UP, 1974. 92–117.

———. "Representativeness and Reliability of the Ex-slave Materials, with Special Reference to Wallace Quaterman's Recording and Transcript." Bailey, Maynor, and Cukor-Avila 191–212.

———. "Some Principles for the Study of Black and White Speech in the South." Montgomery and Bailey 38–62.

Robins, R. H. *A Short History of Linguistics.* 2nd ed. London: Longman, 1979.

Rooney, John F., Wilbur Zelinsky, Dean R. Louder, John D. Vitek, eds. *This Remarkable Continent: An Atlas of the United States and Canadian Societies and Cultures.* College Station: Texas A & M UP, 1982.

Rose, Mike. *Writer's Block: The Cognitive Dimension.* Studies in Writing and Rhetoric. Carbondale: Southern Illinois UP, 1984.

Ryan, Ellen. "Ingroup and Outgroup Reactions toward Mexican-American Language Varieties." *Language, Ethnicity, and Intergroup Relations.* Ed. H. Giles. London: Academic, 1977. 59–82.

Ryan, Ellen, and Miguel Carranza. "Attitudes towards Accented English." *College English and the Mexican-American.* Ed. P. Walcott and Jacob Ornstein. San Antonio: Trinity U, 1977. 52–58.

Safire, William. "Vogue Words Are Trific, Right?" Eschholz et al. 164–68.

Sánchez, Francisca. "The Chicano English Dilemma: Deficit or Dialect?" *La Red* Apr. 1984: 2–8.

Sánchez, Rosaura. *Chicano Discourse: Socio-Historic Perspectives.* Rowley: Newbury, 1983.

———. "Our Linguistic and Social Context." Amastae and Elías-Olivares, *Spanish* 9–46.

Sapir, Edward. *Language: An Introduction to the Study of Speech.* New York: Harcourt, 1921.

———. "Speech as a Personality Trait." *American Journal of Sociology* 32 (1927): 892–905. Rpt. in *Selected Writings of Edward Sapir.* Berkeley: U of California P, 1951. 533–43.

Sapon, Stanley M. *A Pictorial Linguistic Interview Manual.* Columbus: privately printed, 1957.

Sawyer, Janet. "Aloofness from Spanish Influence in Texas English." *Word* 15 (1959): 270–81.

———. "A Dialect Study of San Antonio, Texas: A Bilingual Community." Diss. U of Texas, Austin, 1957.

———. "Spanish-English Bilingualism in San Antonio, Texas." Hernández-Chávez, Cohen, and Beltramo 77–98.

———. "The Speech of San Antonio, Texas." Williamson and Burke 570–82.

Scaglione, Aldo, ed. *The Emergence of National Languages.* Ravenna: Longo, 1984.

Scargill, M. H. *Modern Canadian Usage: Linguistic Change and Reconstruction.* Toronto: McClelland, 1974.

Schaffran, Janet, and Pat Kozak. "Inclusive Language." *More Than Words: Prayer and Ritual for Inclusive Communities.* Oak Park: Meyer-Stone, 1988. 4–7.

Schane, Sanford A., and Brigitte Bendixen. *Workbook in Generative Phonology.* Englewood Cliffs: Prentice, 1978.

Schele de Vere, M. *Americanisms: The English of the New World.* New York: Scribner, 1872.

Scott, Jerrie C. "The Influence of Spoken Language on the Writing of Black College Freshmen." Technical Report, 1981. ERIC ED 217 411.

Scripture, Edward Wheeler. "Analysis and Interpretation of Vowel Tracks." *Journal of the Acoustical Society of America* 6 (1933): 148.

———. *The Elements of Experimental Phonetics.* 1902. New York: AMS, 1973.

———. *Researches in Experimental Phonetics: The Study of Speech Curves.* Washington: Carnegie Inst., 1906.

Sealy, Pauline A., and Richard B. Sealock. "Place-Name Literature: United States and Canada." *Names* 20 (1972): 240–65.

Selvon, Samuel. *A Brighter Sun.* London: Longman, 1952.

———. *The Lonely Londoners.* London: Longman, 1972.

———. *Turn Again Tiger.* London: Heinemann, 1958.

Senior, Olive. *A–Z of Jamaican Heritage*. Kingston: Heinemann Caribbean, 1983.

———. *Summer Lightning and Other Stories*. London: Longman, 1986.

Shaughnessy, Mina P. *Errors and Expectations: A Guide for the Teacher of Basic Writing*. New York: Oxford UP, 1977.

Shuy, Roger W. "Differences in Vocabulary." Eschholz et al. 170–78.

———. *Discovering American Dialects*. Champaign: NCTE, 1967.

———. *The Northern–Midland Dialect Boundary in Illinois*. Pub. of the American Dialect Soc. 38. University: U of Alabama P, 1962.

———. "A Selective Bibliography on Social Dialects." *Linguistic Reporter* 10.3 (1968): 1–5.

Sills, David L., ed. *The International Encyclopedia of the Social Sciences*. 18 vols. New York: Macmillan, 1968.

Silva-Corvalán, Carmen. "Code-Shifting Patterns in Chicano Spanish." Elías-Olivares, *Spanish* 69–87.

Simon, John I. *Paradigms Lost: Reflections on Literacy and Its Decline*. New York: Crown, 1980.

Sitting in Limbo. Videocassette. With Fabian Dillon, Sylvie Clarke, and Debbie Grant. Writ. and prod. David Wilson and John N. Smith. Nat. Film Board of Canada, 1988.

Sledd, James, and Wilma R. Ebbitt, eds. *Dictionaries and That Dictionary*. Chicago: Scott, 1962.

Smith, Elsdon C. *New Dictionary of American Family Names*. New York: Harper, 1973.

Smith, Kenneth J., and Henry M. Truby. "Dialectal Variance Interferes with Reading Instruction." Paper presented at the Thirteenth Annual Convention of Intl. Reading Assn., 1968.

———. *Test of Phonic Skills and Phone Discrimination Tests*. Chicago: Harper, 1971.

Smith, Reed. *Gullah*. Columbia: Bureau of Pub., U of South Carolina, 1926.

Smitherman, Geneva, ed. *Black English and the Education of Black Children and Youth*. Detroit: Center for Black Studies, Wayne State U, 1981.

———. *Talkin and Testifyin: The Language of Black America*. Boston: Houghton, 1977.

Solé, Yolanda. "Language Attitudes towards Spanish among Mexican-American College Students." *Journal of LASSO* 2 (1977): 37–46.

Spolsky, Bernard, ed. *The Language Education of Minority Children*. Rowley: Newbury, 1972.

Spradley, James P. *Participant Observation*. New York: Holt, 1980.

Spradley, James P., and Brenda Mann. *The Cocktail Waitress: Woman's Work in a Man's World*. New York: Knopf, 1975.

Stalker, James. "Attitudes toward Language in the Eighteenth and Nineteenth Centuries." Greenbaum 41–47.

Standard College Dictionary. New York: Harcourt, 1966.

Sternglass, Marilyn. "Close Similarities in Dialect Features of Black and White College Students in Remedial Composition Classes." *TESOL Quarterly* 8 (1974): 271–83.

Stewart, George R. *American Place Names*. New York: Oxford UP, 1970.

———. *Names on the Land*. Boston: Houghton, 1967.

Stewart, William A. "Continuity and Change in American Negro Dialects." *Florida FL Reporter* 6 (1968): 3 +.

———. "Historical and Structural Bases for the Recognition of Negro Dialect." *Report of the Twentieth Annual Round Table Meeting on Linguistics and Language Studies*. Ed. James E. Alatis. Washington: Georgetown UP, 1969. 239–47.

———. "Sociolinguistic Factors in the History of American Negro Dialects." *Florida FL Reporter* 5 (1967): 11 +.

Stoddard, Albert. *Animal Tales Told in the Gullah Dialect.* 3 record albums with mimeographed transcripts ed. by Duncan Emrich. Library of Congress, 1949.

———. "Origin, Dialect, Beliefs, and Characteristics of the Negroes of the South Carolina and Georgia Coasts." *Georgia Historical Quarterly* 28 (1944): 186–95.

Stoney, Samuel G., and Gertrude M. Shelby. *Black Genesis*. New York: Macmillan, 1930.

The Story of English. 9 videocassettes. MacNeil-Lehrer-Gannett, 1986.

Story, G. M., W. J. Kirwin, and J. D. A. Widdowson, eds. *Dictionary of Newfoundland English*. Toronto: U of Toronto P, 1982.

Stronks, James B. "Chicago Store-front Churches: 1964." *Names* 12 (1964): 127–28.

———. "Names of Store-front Churches in Chicago." *Names* 10 (1962): 203–04.

———. "New Store-front Names in Chicago." *Names* 11 (1963): 136.

Sugar Cane Alley. Videocassette. Dir. Jean Denis Berenbaum. SUMAFA and Orca, 1984. In French [*Rue Cases-Negres* (1983)], with subtitles. 107 min.

Sumner, Isaiah Sanders. "Some Phases of Negro English." Master's thesis, U of Chicago, 1926.

Summey, George. *American Punctuation*. New York: Ronald, 1949.

———. *Modern Punctuation: Its Utilities and Conventions*. New York: Oxford UP, 1919.

Sunshine, Catherine A. *The Caribbean: Survival, Struggle, and Sovereignty*. Washington: EPICA, 1985.

Sweet, Henry. *Handbook of Phonetics*. Oxford UP, 1877.

Szucs, Loretto. *Chicago and Cook County Sources*. Salt Lake City: Ancestry, 1986.

Tannen, Deborah. "Talking New York: It's Not What You Say, It's the Way That You Say It." *New York* 30 Mar. 1981: 30–33.

Tarone, Elaine E. "Aspects of Intonation in Black English." *American Speech* 48 (1973): 29–36.

Tavoni, Mirko. "The 15th-Century Controversy on the Language Spoken by the Ancient Romans: An Inquiry into Italian Humanist Concepts of 'Latin,' 'Grammar,' and 'Vernacular.' " *Historiographia Linguistica* 9 (1982): 237–64.

Taylor-Delain, Marsha, P. David Pearson, and Richard Anderson. "Reading Comprehension and Creativity in Black Language Use: You Stand to Gain by Playing the Sounding Game!" *American Educational Research Journal* 22 (1985): 155–73.

Teschner, Richard, Garland Bills, and Jerry Craddock. *Spanish and English of United States Hispanos: A Critical, Annotated Linguistic Bibliography.* Arlington: Center for Applied Linguistics, 1975.

Thomas, Alan R., ed. *Methods in Dialectology.* Clevedon: Multilingual, 1988.

Thomas, Charles K. "Regional Types of American Pronunciation" and "Standard of Pronunciation." *Phonetics of American English.* New York: Ronald, 1947. 142–69 and 170–75.

———. "A Symposium on Phonetics and Standards of Pronunciation." *Quarterly Journal of Speech* 31.3(1945): 318–27.

Thompson, Roger M. "Mexican-American English: Social Correlates of Regional Pronunciation." *American Speech* 50 (1975): 18–24.

———. "Mexican-American Language Loyalty and the Validity of the 1970 Census." *International Journal of the Sociology of Language* 128 (1974): 7–18.

Thorndike-Barnhart High School Dictionary. 4th ed. Chicago: Scott, 1965.

Tovar, Inez. "The Changing Attitude of La Raza towards the Chicano Idiom." *Sociolinguistics in the Southwest.* Ed. Bates Hoffer and Jacob Ornstein. San Antonio: Trinity U, 1974. 63–74.

Travis, Mary. "Language in the Courtroom." Student paper. Winthrop College, 1985.

Truby, Henry M. "A Century of Idiolectites: Harbingers of Speaker Identification via Voiceprinting." Paper delivered at Intl. Linguistic Assn., New York, 1984.

———. "Language and Dolphins." *Actes du Xe Congrès International des Linguistes.* Bucharest: Editions de l'Académie de la République Socialiste de Roumanie, 1969. 533–40.

———. "The Perception and Common Misperception of Infant Pre-speech." *Proceedings of the Sixth International Congress of Phonetic Sciences.* Prague: Academia, 1967. 943–48.

———. "Phoneme, Allophoneme, Phone, and Allophone, Part 2." *Proceedings of the Eleventh International Congress of Linguists.* Bologna: Molino, 1972. 945–56.

———. "The Phoneme Illusion Invalidates Phonetic Transcription." *Proceedings of the Seventh International Congress of Phonetic Sciences, Montreal.* The Hague: Mouton, 1971. 159–60.

———. "Pleniphonetic Transcription in Phonetic Analysis." *Proceedings of the Ninth International Congress of Linguists.* The Hague: Mouton, 1964. 101–08.

———. "Prenatal and Neonatal Speech, 'Pre-speech,' and an Infantile-Speech Lexicon." *Word* 27 (1976): 57–101.

———. "Some Aspects of Acoustical Analysis of Newborn-Infant Vocalization." *Journal of Acoustical Society of America* 32 (1960): 1518(A).

———. "Sonocineradiography in Speechsound Analysis." *Papers in Linguistics and Phonetics to the Memory of Pierre Delattre.* The Hague: Mouton, 1972. 451–72.

————. "Sound-Spectrographic ('Soundprint') Analysis of Atlantic Bottlenose Dolphin Vocalization." Communication Research Inst., St. Thomas, VI, and Coconut Grove, 1965.

————. *Speechprint Spectrograms and Speech Cineradiograms*. Diss. U Lund, 1959. Expanded and reprinted. South Miami, 1993.

————. "Synchronized Cineradiography and Visual-Acoustic Analysis." *Proceedings of the Fourth International Congress of Phonetic Sciences, Helsinki*. The Hague: Mouton, 1961. 265–79.

————. "The Validity of Voiceprinting, Cryprinting, and Other Soundprinting." Miami: U of Miami Child Development Center, 1969.

————. "Voiceprint [Speechprint] Identification: Speechpattern Matching and Differentiation." *Identification News* (Apr. 1985): 3–15.

————. "Voice Recognition by Man, Animal, and Machine." *Proceedings of the 7th International Congress of Phonetic Sciences, Montreal*. The Hague: Mouton, 1971. 233–57.

————. "What the Speechprint Spectrogram Can and Cannot Do for Dialectology." Unpublished article, 1990.

————. *World Dolphin Foundation*. Key Biscayne: Marine Bioacoustic Research Lab., Mashta Island Point Lagoon. Privately published, 1971.

Truby, Henry M., James F. Bosma, and John Lind. *Newborn Infant Cry*. Bethesda: Natl. Inst. of Health; Stockholm: Karolinska's Children's Hosp., 1965.

Truby, Henry M., John Lind, and James F. Bosma. "Cry Sounds of the Newborn Infant." Wenner-Gren Norrtull's Research Lab Report 101, Stockholm, 1960. Truby, Bosma, and Lind 7–59.

Trudgill, Peter, ed. *Language in the British Isles*. Cambridge: Cambridge UP, 1984.

————. "New Dialect Formation and the Analysis of Colonial Dialects: The Case of Canadian Raising." Warkentyne, *Papers* 35–45.

————. *Sociolinguistics: An Introduction to Language and Society*. New York: Penguin, 1974.

Trudgill, Peter, and Jean Hannah. *International English: A Guide to Varieties of Standard English*. London: Arnold, 1982.

Turner, Lorenzo Dow. *Africanisms in the Gullah Dialect*. Chicago: U of Chicago P, 1949.

Twelve Thousand Words: A Supplement to Webster's Third New International Dictionary. Springfield: Merriam, 1986.

Underwood, Gary N. "How *You* Sound to an Arkansawyer." *American Speech* 49 (1974): 208–15.

United States Bureau of the Census. *A Compendium of the Ninth Census of the United States*. Comp. Francis A. Walker. Washington: GPO, 1872.

————. *Current Population Reports: Ancestry and Language in the U.S.* November 1979, Series P–23, No. 116. Washington: GPO, 1982.

————. *Report of the Population of the United States at the Eleventh Census: 1890, Part I*. Washington: GPO, 1895.

————. *The Statistics of the Population of the United States*. Washington: GPO, 1872.

Vallejo, Bernardo. "Linguistic and Socio-economic Correlations in the Spoken Language of Mexican-American Children." Bowen and Ornstein 165–82.

Vandermey, Randall. "Why Slang Is Winner of Language Wars." *Des Moines Register* 5 June 1989: C3.

Van Horne, Winston A., and Thomas Tonnesen, eds. *Ethnicity and Language*. Madison: U of Wisconsin System Inst. on Race and Ethnicity, 1987.

Vaughn-Cooke, Fay B. "Are Black and White Vernaculars Diverging?" *American Speech* 62 (1987): 12–32.

Veltman, Calvin. "Anglicization in the U.S.: Language Environment and Language Practice of American Adolescents." *International Journal of the Sociology of Language* 44 (1983): 99–114.

————. *Language Shift in the United States*. Berlin: Mouton 1983.

Viereck, Wolfgang, and Wolf-Dietrich Bald, eds. *English in Contact with Other Languages*. Budapest: Kiadó, 1986.

Viereck, Wolfgang, Edgar Schneider, and Manfred Görlach. *A Bibliography of Writings on Varieties of English, 1965–1983*. Amsterdam: Benjamins, 1984.

Wald, Benji. "English in Los Angeles: Searching for a Speech Community." *Style and Variables in English*. Ed. Timothy Shopen and Joseph Williams. Cambridge: Winthrop, 1981. 250–68.

————. "The Status of Chicano English as a Dialect of American English." Ornstein, *Form* 14–31.

Wallis, John. *Grammar of the English Language*. Trans. from Latin, J. A. Kemp. London: Longman, 1972.

Walmsley, Anne, ed. *The Sun's Eye*. Rev. ed. London: Longman Caribbean, 1989.

Warkentyne, H. J. "Attitudes and Language Behaviour." *Canadian Journal of Linguistics* 28 (1983): 71–76.

————. *Papers from the Fifth International Conference on Methods of Dialectology*. Victoria: Dept. of Linguistics, U of Victoria, 1985.

Warner, W. Lloyd, M. Meeker, and K. Eells. *Social Class in America*. New York: Harper, 1960.

Warriner, John E., et al. *Warriner's English Grammar and Composition: 11*. Rev. ed. with supplement. New York: Harcourt, 1958, 1969.

Watkins, Calvert. "Indo-European Roots." *The American Heritage Dictionary of the English Language*. Ed. William Morris. Boston: Houghton, 1969. 1505–50.

————, ed. *The American Heritage Dictionary of Indo-European Roots*. Boston: Houghton, 1985.

Watkins, Floyd C., and William B. Dillingham. *Practical English Handbook*. 8th ed. Boston: Houghton, 1988.

Webster, Noah. *Dissertations on the English Language*. 1789. Facsim. ed. Menston, Eng.: Scolar, 1967.

———. *A Grammatical Institute of the English Language.* 3 vols. 1783–85. Facsim. ed. Menston, Eng.: Scolar, 1968.

Webster's Collegiate Dictionary. 5th ed. Springfield: Merriam, 1948. *Webster's New Collegiate Dictionary.* 8th ed. Springfield: Merriam, 1976. *Webster's Ninth New Collegiate Dictionary.* Springfield: Merriam, 1983.

Webster's Dictionary. Paperback. N.p.: Ottenheimer, 1973.

Webster's Dictionary of English Usage. Springfield: Merriam, 1989.

Webster's New International Dictionary of the English Language. 2nd ed. Springfield: Merriam, 1934.

Webster's New Secondary School Dictionary. New York: American, 1961.

Webster's New World Dictionary of the American Language. College ed. New York: World, 1956. Student's ed. Cleveland: Collins, 1976. 2nd college ed. New York: Simon, 1980.

Webster's Third New International Dictionary of the English Language. Springfield: Merriam, 1961. 2 vols. Chicago: Encyclopaedia Britannica, 1966, 1986.

Weinreich, Uriel. *Languages in Contact: Findings and Problems.* The Hague: Mouton, 1953.

Weller, Georganne. "The Role of Language as a Cohesive Force in the Hispanic Community of Washington, D.C." Elías-Olivares, *Spanish* 215–34.

Wentworth, Harold. *American Dialect Dictionary.* New York: Crowell, 1944.

Whitehall, Harold. "The Orthography of John Bate of Sharon, Connecticut (1700–1784)." *American Speech* 22 (1947): 3–56.

Whiteman, Marcia Farr. "Dialect Influence in Writing." *Variation in Writing: Functional and Linguistic-Cultural Differences.* Ed. Whiteman. Hillsdale: Erlbaum, 1981. 153–66.

Whitley, M. Stanley. "*Hopefully*: A Shibboleth in the English Adverb System." *American Speech* 58 (1983): 126–49.

Whitney, Annie Weston. "Negro American Dialects." *Independent* 53 (1901): 1979–81, 2039–42.

Williams, Annette Powell. "Dynamics of a Black Audience." Kochman, *Rappin'* 101–06.

Williams, Eric. *From Columbus to Castro: The History of the Caribbean, 1492–1969.* London: Deutsch, 1970.

Williams, Frederick, et al. *Explorations of the Linguistic Attitudes of Teachers.* Rowley: Newbury, 1976.

Williams, John G. "A Study in Gullah English." *Charleston Sunday News* 10 Feb. 1895.

Williamson, Juanita V., and Virginia M. Burke, eds. *A Various Language: Perspectives on American Dialects.* New York: Holt, 1971.

Willis, Hulon. *Structure, Style, and Usage.* 3rd ed. New York: Holt, 1973.

Winer, Lise. "Caribbean English." *Oxford English: A Guide to the Language.* Ed. I. C. B. Dear. Oxford: Oxford UP, 1986. 275–77.

————. "Trini Talk: Learning an English Creole as a Second Language." *Diversity and Development in English-Related Creoles*. Ed. Ian F. Hancock. Ann Arbor: Karoma, 1986. 44–67.

Wise, Claude M. "Negro Dialect." *Quarterly Journal of Speech* 19 (1933): 522–28.

Witherspoon, Alexander M. *Common Errors in English and How to Avoid Them*. Philadelphia: Blakiston, 1943.

Wolfe, Thomas. "Only the Dead Know Brooklyn." *From Death to Morning: Fourteen Short Stories by Thomas Wolfe*. New York: Scribner's 1935. 91–97.

Wolfram, Walt. "Are Black and White Vernaculars Diverging?" *American Speech* 62 (1987): 40–48.

————. "Language Knowledge and Other Dialects." *American Speech* 57 (1982): 3–18.

————. "Language Variation in the United States." *Nature of Communication Disorders in Culturally and Linguistically Diverse Populations*. Ed. Orlando Taylor. San Diego: College-Hill, 1986. 75–115.

————. *The Study of Social Dialects in American English*. Englewood Cliffs: Prentice, 1974.

————. "Toward a Description of *A*- Prefixing in Appalachian English." *American Speech* 51 (1976): 45–56.

Wolfram, Walt, and Donna Christian. *Appalachian Speech*. Arlington: Center for Applied Linguistics, 1976.

Wolfram, Walt, and Ralph W. Fasold. *The Study of Social Dialects in American English*. Englewood Cliffs: Prentice, 1974.

Wolfram, Walt, and Robert Johnson. *Phonological Analysis: Focus on American English*. Washington: Center for Applied Linguistics, 1982.

Wolfson, Nessa. "Speech Events and Natural Speech: Some Implications for Sociolinguistic Methodology." *Language in Society* 5 (1976): 189–209.

Wood, Peter H. *Black Majority: Negroes in Colonial South Carolina from 1670 through the Stono Rebellion*. New York: Knopf, 1974.

Woods, Howard B. "A Socio-dialectology Survey of the English Spoken in Ottawa: A Study of Sociological and Stylistic Variation in Canadian English." Diss. U of British Columbia, 1979.

World Book Encyclopedia Dictionary. 2 vols. Chicago: Field Enterprises, 1966.

Wright, Roger. *Late Latin and Early Romance in Spain and Carolingian France*. Liverpool: Cairns, 1982.

Wykoff, George S., and Harry Shaw. *The Harper Handbook of College Composition*. New York: Harper, 1952.

Yellin, David. "The Black English Controversy: Implications from the Ann Arbor Case." *Journal of Reading* 24 (1980): 150–54.

Youmans, Gilbert. "Anymore on *Anymore*?: Evidence from a Missouri Dialect Survey." *American Speech* 61 (1986): 61–75.

Zelinsky, Wilbur. "North America's Vernacular Regions." *Annals of the Association of American Geographers* 70 (1980): 1–16.

Index